INDIANS OF THE GREATER SOUTHEAST

Published in cooperation with the Society for Historical Archaeology

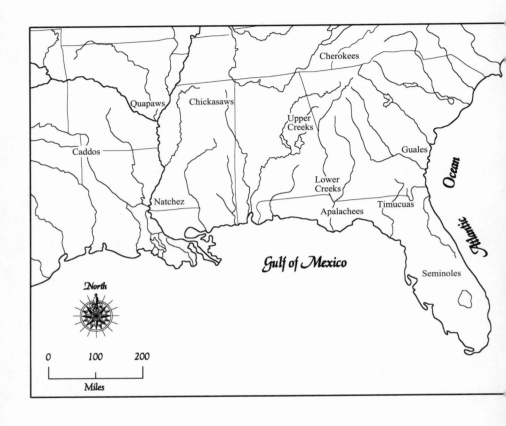

INDIANS OF THE GREATER SOUTHEAST

HISTORICAL ARCHAEOLOGY AND ETHNOHISTORY

EDITED BY

BONNIE G. McEWAN

University Press of Florida

Gainesville · Tallahassee · Tampa · Boca Raton
Pensacola · Orlando · Miami · Jacksonville · Ft. Myers

05 04 03 02 01 00 6 5 4 3 2 1

Library of Congress Cataloging-in-Publication Data
Indians of the greater Southeast: historical archaeology and ethnohistory /
edited by Bonnie G. McEwan
p. cm.
Includes bibliographical references and index.
ISBN 0-8130-1778-5 (c: alk. paper)
1. Indians of North America—Southern States—History. 2. Indians of
North America—Southern States—Antiquities. 3. Ethnohistory—Southern
States. 4. Archaeology and history—Southern States. 5. Southern States—
Antiquities. I. McEwan, Bonnie G. (Bonnie Gair), 1954–.
E78.S65 I52 2000
975'.00497—dc21 99-049534

The University Press of Florida is the scholarly publishing agency for
the State University System of Florida, comprising Florida A&M
University, Florida Atlantic University, Florida Gulf Coast University,
Florida International University, Florida State University, University of
Central Florida, University of Florida, University of North Florida,
University of South Florida, and University of West Florida.

University Press of Florida
15 Northwest 15th Street
Gainesville, FL 32611
http://www.upf.com

To William G. Haag,
for his enduring contributions to southeastern archaeology

BOOK

2000

...cGwan, B., ed.

ITAL

Indians of the Greater Southeast

Chaps. 9 & 10

Univ. of Florida Press; Gainesville

CONTENTS

FIGURES

TABLES

ACKNOWLEDGMENTS

This volume was made possible with the hard work and commitment of the contributing authors. During the past year some fell victim to natural disasters, while others changed jobs, relocated, had babies, and weathered family illnesses. Despite many legitimate reasons to withdraw from the project, they persevered, and I am grateful to them all. Gregory Waselkov and John Worth deserve special thanks for reviewing more than their fair share of manuscripts at the request of authors.

On behalf of the contributors, I thank the outside readers who commented on various chapters. Morris Arnold, Robert Carr, Charles Ewen, David Hally, John Hann, John House, David Kelley, Clark Spencer Larsen, Rochelle Marrinan, James Miller, Jeffrey Mitchem, John O'Hear, Timothy Perttula, John Scarry, and Frank Schnell all provided thoughtful and provocative reviews.

Ronald Michael, editor for the Society for Historical Archaeology, and Meredith Morris-Babb, editor in chief at the University Press of Florida, provided ongoing encouragement and logistical support. Judy Goffman served as our enthusiastic editor at the press. As always, I am very grateful for the institutional support given to me by James J. Miller, chief of the Florida Bureau of Archaeological Research, and George W. Percy, director of the Florida Division of Historical Resources. Without their blessing, this volume would not exist. Elyse Cornelison, Teri White, and Jean Wilson assisted with word processing and manuscript preparation. Elyse also developed many of the digital graphics.

My greatest debts are to my husband, Jeffrey M. Mitchem, and my mother, Martha W. McEwan. Jeff spent countless hours helping me finalize the manuscript, and Martha continues to impart wisdom and love to her children at every opportunity.

Thank you.

B.G.M.

INTRODUCTION

This volume grew out of a discussion at the 1997 midyear board meeting of the Society for Historical Archaeology (SHA) in St. Mary's City, Maryland. Christopher DeCorse commented on the paucity of contact period studies focused on Native Americans being presented at SHA's annual meeting and published in *Historical Archaeology*. His observation was both accurate and perplexing given the number of historical archaeologists working on sites with significant Indian components. This collection of essays on historic southeastern Indians is an initial step to correct this trend. It also marks the first copublication of the Society for Historical Archaeology and the University Press of Florida.

Few events of the past 500 years can claim equal significance to the maelstrom brought about by the European exploration and settlement of the Americas. This momentous enterprise irrevocably altered (and in some cases annihilated) indigenous cultures, and often changed their relationship to their homelands, which were frequently appropriated as European spoils of conflict. Yet, until recently, archaeological investigations of eastern North American native societies during the contact period have paled in comparison to prehistoric studies in the region. Almost fifteen years ago, William Fitzhugh noted: "Today, the archeologist interested in historic-period Indian cultures is in the same situation as the ethnologist studying the material culture of the eastern Indians. For both, life begins west of the Mississippi insofar as availability of documented collections is concerned. Despite a longer period of contact, more archeological sites, and documentary data, research in the eastern United States is just beginning to take advantage of this untapped resource" (1985:3).

The intervening years have witnessed a proliferation in archaeological and ethnohistorical studies focused on eastern Native American cultures owing, in large part, to the maturation of historical archaeology as a discipline. Documentary sources have provided archaeologists with the means to make quantum advances in their understanding of post-1500 native societies, and though some archaeologists have long been adept ethnohistorians (most notably Trigger 1976, 1985), the past few decades have seen a florescence in this trend. As this volume attests, archaeologists are becoming increasingly sophisticated in their application of documentary source materials to archaeological problems. Although not always explicitly discussed, most authors have drawn on ethnohistoric sources that have been evaluated against independent accounts, as well as other lines of archaeological, biocultural, and linguistic evidence.

The goal of this volume is to develop social histories of southeastern Indian cultures following European contact and to hypothesize about the relationship between native life and the material world during that time. Although the groups represented herein are among the most thoroughly researched, the availability of archaeological and documentary materials relevant to each is uneven and suggests many promising avenues for future research. The essays are presented in roughly chronological order; the initial chapters examine the responses of chiefdoms during the earliest episodes of sustained European contact, while the later ones document the long-term consequences of Euro-Indian relations as native groups underwent a broad range of social transformations. In most instances the authors have examined the social mechanisms that governed these relationships and how cultural patterns shaped the archaeological record. Many of the essays also explore the motivation and complicity of natives with regard to specific events, as well as their reasoned responses to the larger changing world. For those native groups living in contact with Spaniards, Catholicism was the most pervasive influence over social patterning, while native peoples whose primary interaction was with French and British colonists were generally more influenced by trade and other economic practices. In almost every instance, militaristic motivations played a significant role from both native and European perspectives since all were in need of allies in the conflicts over the natural and cultural resources of the Southeast. With few exceptions, the historic period brought about changes in political alliances, redistribution and exchange networks, and supporting ideologies of native societies, and many Indian leaders began to rely on Europeans to reinforce their status through political recognition and material tribute. Even those natives who clung steadfastly to their own beliefs were eventually drawn into the European orbit by one means or another.

For SHA's international readership, it may be useful to define the chronological constructs used throughout this volume. The temporal periods referred to as prehistoric, protohistoric, and historic are relative to each region and relate to the availability of documentary sources.

The prehistoric period in the territories that became part of the United States covers the greatest period of time and offers archaeologists a diachronic perspective of cultural evolution spanning millennia. It generally refers to all human activity predating A.D. 1500 and the arrival of Europeans. Since cultural traditions and esoteric knowledge were transmitted primarily by means of verbal communication throughout this period, our understanding of nonmaterial aspects of prehistoric life is extremely rudimentary.

The protohistoric period (also referred to as the early contact period) represents that transitional phase when native life was first affected by Europeans (post-1500). Euro-Indian interaction during this time was both direct and indirect through skirmishes, trade, pathogens, and other agents. Many of the essays address this critical phase and examine the initial reactions and strategies devised by aboriginal populations to cope with the stresses of their rapidly changing worlds. This is also the period when documentary records are first available. Most of these are European accounts based on glimpses of nonliterate native societies with whom the chroniclers had limited, if any, means of communication or understanding. Archaeological remains from this early contact phase are similarly problematic in that they are often difficult to isolate and interpret in a meaningful way. Thus the raw historical and archaeological data of the protohistoric period pose unique challenges to researchers.

As with the other temporal phases, the beginning of the historic period is also particular to each region, and sometimes differs within regions depending on variables such as coastal versus interior locations. It generally refers to that time when native peoples not only are written about, but also are writing about themselves and adding their perspective to the documentary record. For archaeologists, the historic period has great potential since, in addition to written evidence, a greater proportion of material remains have modern counterparts and interpretation can often be grounded in reality rather than conjecture.

Taken as a whole, the essays included herein provide the opportunity to examine cross-cultural diversity within a confined (albeit extensive) geographic region, and evaluate the contact experience as a series of case studies.

Differing trade policies, colonization strategies, and missionization efforts were met with a wide range of behaviors. Analysis of how and why individual tribes responded as they did under particular conditions is, in many instances, providing insights into nonmaterial and undocumented aspects of the historic period and, perhaps, precontact indigenous societies.

Bibliography

Fitzhugh, William W. (editor)
1985   *Cultures in Contact: The European Impact on Native Cultural Institutions in Eastern North America, A.D. 1000 to 1800.* Washington, D.C.: Smithsonian Institution.
Trigger, Bruce G.
1976   *Children of Aataentsic: A History of the Huron People to 1660.* Kingston: McGill-Queen's University Press.
1985   *Natives and Newcomers: Canada's "Heroic Age" Reconsidered.* Kingston: McGill-Queen's University Press.

EDITOR'S NOTE

The most contentious editorial issue related to this volume has been the use of tribal names in singular or plural form. While it is generally believed by ethnohistorians that it is inappropriate "to use the ethnological singular to indicate plural members of native tribes" (Axtell 1990:111), many archaeologists have not adopted this practice. Furthermore, at the time of this writing, neither the University Press of Florida nor the Society for Historical Archaeology had formal editorial policies on this matter. Since the contributors are acknowledged authorities on their respective tribal groups, and the way in which their phrases were constructed made blanket changes virtually impossible, I have left this aspect of each chapter as written as long as the authors were internally consistent. This was not done out of disrespect to native peoples but simply to allow each contributor latitude and editorial license. I thank George Sabo and Gregory Waselkov for their valued opinions on this subject.

Reference Cited

Axtell, James
1990   Humor in Ethnohistory. *Ethnohistory* 37(2): 109–25.

1

The Timucua Indians of
Northern Florida and Southern Georgia

Jerald T. Milanich

The European conquest of the Americas brought a new world to the Native Americans of the southeastern United States, one to which indigenous peoples sought to adjust as they coped with its challenges. Among the latter were disease-caused reductions in demographic levels, new ways of thinking, new status and roles, and new economic opportunities brought by Spanish, French, and British explorers, soldiers, colonists, missionary priests, and entrepreneurs.

One of the first native groups in La Florida, as the Southeast was named by Spaniards, to be in sustained contact with these new people from Europe were the Timucuan Indians. In the sixteenth century various Timucuan groups occupied the northern one-third of peninsular Florida and southern and southeastern Georgia as far north as the Altamaha River (fig. 1.1). This is a large territory, about 19,200 square miles, of which two-thirds is in Florida and one-third in Georgia.

It is estimated that as many as 200,000 Timucua lived in that region prior to contact with the Europeans, a population density of 10.4 people per square mile. That statistic is very much in line with density figures for similar native societies, such as the chiefdoms of the Bahamas and Hispaniola (Keegan 1992:162–63). The Timucua were never organized as a single political unit. Rather, at the time the first Europeans came to La Florida, the people we today refer to as the Timucua consisted of at least thirty-five simple chiefdoms.

As early as the 1520s the history of the Timucua began to be entwined with that of the European conquest of the Southeast. By the 1580s and 1590s and the initial founding of Franciscan missions among the Timucua-speak-

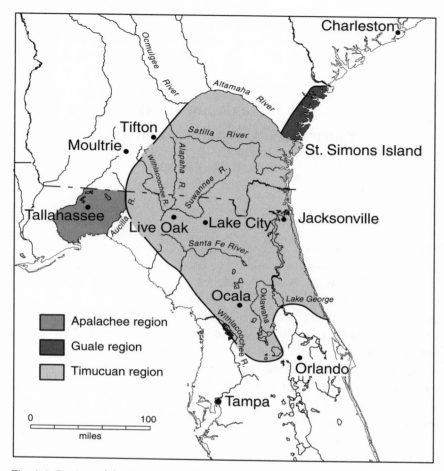

Fig. 1.1. Region of the Timucua Indians at the time of European contact. The exact southwestern boundary is uncertain.

ing people, a time prior to the first successful British colonies on the Atlantic seaboard, a significant number of the Timucuan chiefdoms had been impacted by European colonial endeavors.

During the initial expansion of the Franciscan mission system between 1595 and the 1620s, nearly all the Timucuan chiefdoms were incorporated into Spain's La Florida colony, as were the Guale Indians of the Georgia coast. In the 1630s other neighbors of the Timucua, the Apalachee Indians of eastern northwest Florida, similarly were colonized and organized into missions. As a consequence, in the second half of the seventeenth century all of these American Indians led lives quite different from those of their ancestors several generations earlier.

Our knowledge of the Timucua, none of whom survived past the mideighteenth century, comes from archaeological research and the interpretation of historical documents, the latter studied by both historians and anthropologists. Archaeological inquiry into the colonial period Timucua can be traced to John M. Goggin's (1949, 1952, 1953) pioneering work, which laid the groundwork for projects and interpretations of the 1960s and 1970s (for example, Deagan 1972, 1978; Loucks 1979; McMurray 1973; Milanich 1972, 1978; Symes and Stephens 1965). Linguistic research on the Timucua has a much longer history, one dating back into the nineteenth century and the work of Albert S. Gatschet and Raoul de la Grasserie. (A complete bibliography of nineteenth-century Timucuan linguistic studies can be found in Booker 1991.) Another notable figure in both linguistic and ethnohistorical Timucuan research is John R. Swanton (1916, 1922:320–87, 1929, 1946).

The 1980s and early 1990s saw a resurgence of interest in the Timucua in the form of interdisciplinary projects involving archaeologists, bioarchaeologists, historians, and others. In large part these projects were stimulated by (1) the excavation by the Florida Division of Historical Resources of Spanish missions in northwest Florida; (2) attempts to trace the 1539 route of the Hernando de Soto expedition through Timucuan territory; and (3) cultural resource management.

While only one or two archaeologists were investigating the Timucua in the 1950s, the team approach of this new generation of scholars, including graduate students, generated new data and reinterpretations of old (see, for example, Hoshower 1992; Johnson 1990, 1991; Saunders 1996; Weisman 1992; Worth 1992; see also the articles on the Timucuan missions in McEwan 1993 and Thomas 1990). There also were syntheses (Hann 1996; Milanich 1996; Worth 1995) and new linguistic studies (Granberry 1993).

As we might imagine, the synergistic effect of data collection and synthetic interpretation has pushed Timucuan studies forward at a rapid pace. Compared to what was known fifty years ago, our present understanding of the Timucua is light-years ahead. John Worth's (1998a, 1998b) impressive two-volume work on the Timucua offers insights into issues we could not even imagine a decade or two ago.

Who Were the Timucua and What Are Their Origins?

The Timucua Indians are defined by their language. All spoke dialects of the same language, one whose relationship with other American Indian languages is still being debated. Both Julian Granberry (1993) and Joseph Greenberg (1987:106–7, 336) have noted close linguistic ties to Chibchan-Paezan languages of South and Central America and cited the likelihood that the Timucua arrived in the Southeast from Venezuela. Other linguists agree that Timucua is unrelated to other Southeast Indian languages, though they do not accept the Chibchan-Paezan tie. (For a history of the classification of Timucua, see Goddard 1996.) Still others (such as Crawford 1979, 1988) cite linguistic ties to southeastern native languages.

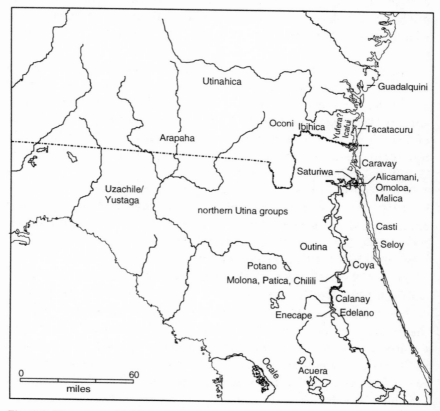

Fig. 1.2. Timucuan chiefdoms ca. 1565.

Table 1.1. Sixteenth-century dialects, archaeological cultures, and chiefdoms

Dialect	Culture	Chiefdom
Acuera	St. Johns	Acuera, Tucuru
Acuera(?)	Northern Safety Harbor	Ocale
Agua Dulce	St. Johns	Astina, Chilili, Coya, Edelano, Enecape, Molona, Omittagua, Onachaquara, Outina, Patica, Seloy
Icafui	Savannah(?)	Cascangue/Icafui, Ibihica(?)
Mocama	Savannah	Alimacani, Caravay, Casti, Guadalquini, Malica, Napa, Omoloa, Saturiwa
Oconi	Savannah(?)	Oconi
Potano	Alachua	Potano
Timucua	Suwannee Valley	Aguacaleyquen, Cholupaha, Napituca, Uriutina, Yustaga
Tucururu	Savannah(?)	Mocama-area chiefdoms, Tacatacuru
(?)	Lamar(?)	Arapaha
Yufera	Savannah(?)	Yufera

The archaeological data flatly contradict the linguistic conclusion that the origins of the Timucua lie outside the Southeast. As noted above, at the time the first Europeans came to La Florida, the Timucua consisted of at least a number of small chiefdoms. Although sharing a language, these chiefdoms were associated with different archaeological cultures with diverse histories. Figure 1.2 shows the Timucua chiefdoms, while table 1.1 lists them along with associated dialects of Timucua and associated archaeological cultures. (For more on the pre-Columbian cultures, see Milanich 1994.)

The various archaeological cultures associated with the pre-Columbian ancestors of the Timucua stretch back into antiquity hundreds and even thousands of years. In eastern Florida, including the St. Johns River drainage, we can trace the evolution of the St. Johns culture from the colonial period at least 5,000 years into the past to the time of the late Archaic period Mount Taylor culture. Similarly, we can show that the origins of the Suwannee Valley and Alachua cultures date to more than a millennium prior to the colonial period. In view of such data, any contention that colonists from South or Central America settled in the Southeast and introduced the

Timucuan language seems ludicrous. The overwhelming archaeological evidence strongly supports the claim that the ancestry of the Timucua lies in the Southeast.

Political and Social Organization

Our best evidence is that the Timucuan chiefdoms were simply organized, each consisting of two to ten villages and headed by a chief or *holata,* the individual Spaniards often called *cacique,* a title they brought to Florida from Caribbean Taino peoples. Within each chiefdom there was a main village whose *holata* received homage from the chiefs of the lesser villages. The higher-status chiefs may have been referred to as *utina* (*outina*) or *paracusi.* Timucuan clans were matrilineages ranked according to status; chiefs inherited their positions through the matrilineage of the highest-ranking clan. Most of the chiefs were men, but women served as chiefs, too. Some of the female chiefs may have inherited their positions when no suitable male was available; others came from towns that may have had a tradition of women chiefs.

Within each chiefdom there was a hierarchy of chiefly officials, including the *inija,* a member of the same lineage as the ranking chief and whose duties included speaking on behalf of the chief. Other chiefly officials responsible for specific duties may have been the individuals known as *anacotima,* second *anacotima,* and *afetema,* all of whom came from specific clans. These chiefly officials were among the village elders and other high-status individuals whom the Spaniards referred to as *principales.*

Within the council house located in each chiefdom's main village, the chief, chiefly officials, and other *principales* were seated according to their respective statuses, in turn tied to lineage and clan affiliations. The highest-ranking clan, that of the chiefs, was the White Deer clan. Other clans were Panther, Bear, Fish, Earth, Buzzard, and Quail.

In the early seventeenth century Father Francisco Alonso de Jesus described the role of chiefs among the Timucua: "They have their natural lords among them. . . . These govern their republics as head with the assistance of counselors, who are such by birth and inheritance. [The chief] determines and reaches decisions on everything that is appropriate for the village and the common good with their accord and counsels, except in the matters of favor. That the cacique alone is free and absolute master of these, and he acts accordingly; thus, he creates and places other particular lords, who obey and recognize the one who created and gave them the status and command that they hold" (quoted in Hann 1993:95–96).

At times, chiefdoms formed alliances or confederacies led by the chief of the most powerful chiefdom. We can document five such alliances in the sixteenth century. Alliances appear to have coalesced for military purposes and for other reasons. Within alliances chiefs were linked in part by a system of fictive kinship, though such ties may also have been linked to clan membership.

Utinas, holatas, and their assistants were civil/religious officials, guiding and governing their villagers. But in times of warfare a hierarchy of other officials apparently led, a pattern present among the later Creek peoples. The title awarded a Timucuan war chief may have been *uriutina* or *irriparacusi,* the prefix *uri* or *iri* meaning "war." Other chiefly officials associated with war may have held the titles *ibitano, toponole, bichara, amalachini,* and *itorimitono.*

Other important Timucua leaders or officials were the *isucu* (curer) and *yaba* or *jara* (shaman or native priest). Curers—native doctors—treated with various herbs, while the shamans performed a variety of rituals associated with gathering food, portending the future, finding lost items, and using magic to cure or to curse people. In general, Franciscan missionary friars viewed the rites and spells invoked by shamans as satanic and actively campaigned against them, working to substitute themselves and Catholicism for the native priests and native religious beliefs.

European Explorers and Early Spanish Missions

The first Timucua to be in contact with Europeans were Mocama dialect-speakers, perhaps the Guadalquini or a related group on St. Simons Island, Georgia. In 1525 and early 1526, scout ships that preceded the Lucas Vázquez de Ayllón expedition landed on the northern end of that island (Hoffman 1994a). Two years later, in 1528, the army of Pánfilo de Narváez marched northward from Tampa Bay (Hoffman 1994b) and entered the territory of the Yustaga (also called Uzachile), the Timucuan chiefdom— more likely an alliance of chiefdoms—between the Aucilla and Suwannee rivers in northern Florida. Beginning in 1623, eight missions were established in Yustaga towns (San Pedro y San Pablo de Potohiriba, a site on Lake Sampala, 8MD30; Santa Elena de Machaba; Santa Cruz de Cachipile; San Ildefonso de Chamile; San Matheo de Tolapatafi; San Miguel de Asile; San

Francisco de Chuaquin; and San Agustín de Urihica) (Hann 1990:470–76; Worth 1992:63–71). A ninth Timucuan mission probably should be included with this group: Santa María de los Angeles de Arapaje, which, by the early 1630s, was in south Georgia on the Alapaha River (Hann 1990:470–71; Worth 1992:70).

Eleven years after Narváez, Hernando de Soto's expedition, traveling north and west from lower Tampa Bay, also entered Yustaga territory. De Soto's army apparently first had entered Timucuan territory well to the south among the Ocale Indians, who lived near the Withlacoochee River in west-central Florida. By 1630, a single mission (San Luís de Eloquale) served the Ocale (Hann 1996:189), though by that time the Ocale may have been relocated east of their original location and much nearer the Acuera Indians, another Timucuan chiefdom (Worth 1998b:189). By that date a mission also served the Acuera (Santa Lucia de Acuera) (Hann 1996:178).

North of the Ocale and the Acuera were the Potano Indians. Narratives from the de Soto expedition accounts record the names of five separate villages in Potano territory, each a day's march apart along a major south-to-north trail (Itaraholata, Potano, Utinamocharra, Malapaz, and Cholupaha; Cholupaha may actually have been affiliated with a group other than the Potano). An alliance led by the Potano, the existence of which is not hinted at in any of the de Soto accounts, might have formed later in the sixteenth century in response to pressures brought by the European presence.

Beginning in 1606, four missions were established among the Potano (Santa Ana, San Buenaventura de Potano, San Miguel de Potano, and San Francisco de Potano, the Fox Pond site, 8AL272) (Hann 1990:24, 458–60). Two of the missions lasted only a few years; epidemics among the Potano apparently left the mission villages with small populations that were merged with other missions.

In 1539, when de Soto marched north out of Potano territory, his army entered the territory of the northern Utina, the name modern researchers have given to the alliance of Timucua chiefdoms centered in what today is Columbia, Hamilton, Suwannee, and, perhaps, northwestern Alachua counties. From the town of Cholupaha just south of the Santa Fe River, near the site of the later Santa Fé de Toloco mission (the Shealy site, 8AL190), de Soto's army marched westerly to Aguacaleyquen, whose chief headed the northern Utina alliance. The town of Aguacaleyquen probably was the later site of the seventeenth-century mission San Martín de Ayacuto, the Fig Springs site (8CO1) (Johnson 1990; Weisman 1992).

From Aguacaleyquen, de Soto's army traveled north to a small village near modern Lake City, Florida, before turning west and arriving at a town, the site of or near the later Santa Cruz de Tarihica mission (the Indian Pond site, 8CO229). Farther west, the army crossed the Suwannee River, entering the region of the Yustaga.

North of the Yustaga and northern Utina chiefdoms in south-central Georgia were a number of other Timucuan chiefdoms, though we know little about them. The Narváez and de Soto expeditions did not travel through the region, and only a few missions were established there, largely because of its relative remoteness from St. Augustine and the North Florida missions. One interior Georgia mission serving Timucua Indians was Santa Isabel de Utinahica at the confluence of the Ocmulgee and Oconee Rivers (Worth 1992:76; 1995:124). Another mission—Santiago de Oconi—served the Oconi, a Timucuan group in the Okeefenokee Swamp in southeastern Georgia (Worth 1992:183, 1995:50–51).

East of the Okeefenokee Swamp in Georgia were several other Timucuan chiefdoms: Cascangue, Icafui, Yufera, and Ibihica. The Cascangue and Icafui, closest to the Atlantic coast, may have been two villages within the same chiefdom or they were allied chiefdoms (Hann 1996:155, 173). Farther inland were the Yufera (Hann 1996:11), while the Ibihica chiefdom was still farther west, just east of the Okeefenokee Swamp between the St. Marys and Satilla Rivers (Worth 1998a:53, 1998b:191). San Lorenzo de Ibihica was founded after 1612 (Hann 1996:153–54), somewhere near the Charlton-Camden county line in the vicinity of Spanish Creek.

East of these mainland Timucuan chiefdoms were the Guadalquini on St. Simons Island, where San Buenaventura de Guadalquini (on the south end of the island) was established by 1609. To the south on Cumberland Island were the Mocama Indians. San Pedro de Mocama, one of the earliest Timucuan missions, was founded in 1587 in the town of Tacatacuru on the south end of the island at or near the Dungeness Wharf site. Farther south along the coast were more Timucuan groups, among whom missions also would be established. Santa María, on Amelia Island, was founded in 1606 at the town of Napa or Napica. Still another mission, San Juan del Puerto (founded in 1587), was on Fort George Island in the village of Alicamani just north of the mouth of the St. Johns River (Hann 1990:436; Worth 1995:198–99).

These coastal Timucuan chiefdoms formed an alliance in the sixteenth century, though its exact nature is uncertain.

Around St. Augustine were the Seloy Indians, another Timucua group who initially were served by mission Nombre de Dios, the first Franciscan mission in Spanish Florida. That same mission, as well as San Sebastián, located on the opposite end of St. Augustine, probably also served Indian laborers brought to that town to work for the Spaniards.

Inland from the northeast Florida coast and up (south) the St. Johns River were a number of other Timucua chiefdoms, many of which were in contact with the 1564–65 French colony of Fort Caroline and with the founders of St. Augustine in the later 1560s. Chief Saturiwa, whose main village was near the mouth of the St. Johns River, headed an alliance of villages on the lower portion of the river and adjacent coast that, the French were told, included thirty chiefs.

South of Saturiwa's alliance in the St. Johns River drainage was another Timucuan confederation of chiefdoms whose major chief was Outina. Outina's village, however, was west of the river in a region with good agricultural potential on the east-west trail that would become the mission period *camino real* leading from St. Augustine to the Franciscan missions in interior northern Florida (Johnson 1991). Outina's alliance, according to information given to the French in 1564, included forty chiefs. Perhaps the southernmost village in the alliance was Enecape, the Mount Royal archaeological site in Putnam County (8PU35) just north of Lake George. After about 1612–16, that site was the location of mission San Antonio de Enecape (Hann 1990:439–40, 1996:142).

Demography

Between 1595 and 1630 nearly all, if not all, of the Timucuan chiefdoms received Franciscan missions. But by 1595 not all the chiefdoms that are documented in earlier sixteenth-century accounts still existed. Epidemics resulting from direct and (relatively) sustained contact with French and then Spanish colonists, beginning in 1564, devastated the chiefdoms located near or in Fort Caroline, St. Augustine, and the St. Johns River valley west of St. Augustine. The chiefdoms of the Saturiwa alliance, for instance, were largely gone; the Mocama alliance was reconstituted with fewer members; and the Outina alliance chiefdoms had all but disappeared. Because of the demographic devastation in East Florida prior to 1595, only a handful of missions were needed to serve the chiefdoms of that region all the way to Lake George: Nombre de Dios in St. Augustine and San Juan del Puerto just north of the mouth of the St. Johns River. San Diego de Heleca, founded in 1624 where the *camino real* intersected the St. Johns River, probably was established for the sole purpose of providing people to operate a ferry across the river (Worth 1998b:165–66).

During the seventeenth and early eighteenth centuries, all the Timucua would suffer epidemic-caused depopulation. One epidemic is documented for 1595, the same year Franciscan mission efforts began in earnest. From 1613 to 1617, when the expansion of missions was under way into what the Spaniards called Timucua province—interior northern Florida between the St. Johns and Suwannee Rivers and extending into Georgia a few miles—epidemics were said to have killed half the mission villagers (Hann 1988: 175; Worth 1998b:10–11). In 1649–51 and 1654–55 other epidemics wiped out many more Timucua, leaving about 2,000–2,500 individuals. By 1700 that number had dropped to only several hundred.

As any anthropologist might imagine, demographic changes led not only to new political structures but to other changes as well. Many of the latter were settlement changes, attempts by the Spaniards to deal with the reality of declining native populations. Fewer Indians at the Timucuan missions meant fewer native laborers for the colony.

For instance, as populations dropped in the seventeenth century, Timucuan villages with few residents often were consolidated with other villages. At times people were moved from more populated villages to less populated ones. In general, such movements were north to south or southeast, from Georgia or Yustaga territory into the mission provinces of Timucua and Mocama (the latter from St. Augustine north to St. Simons Island, Georgia). I believe these movements, in part, are reflected in the appearance of new types of aboriginal ceramics at mission villages in Timucua and Mocama.

The ongoing demographic catastrophe in Timucua province in the seventeenth century also was in large part responsible for the changes that occurred following the Timucua Rebellion in 1656. John Worth (1992, 1998b:38–116) has shown that the rebellion, an attempt by the Timucua chiefs of interior northern Florida to free themselves from the demands of the Spanish military government, provided the governor of Spanish Florida, Diego de Rebolledo, with an excuse to reorganize totally the Timucuan mission system. Faced with inadequate labor to cultivate the fields adjacent to St. Augustine, operate ferries across rivers, and provide other services, the governor used the rebellion as an excuse to abandon some missions and relocate others, as well as to found new missions and shift populations—all attempts to distribute the remnant noncoastal Timucuan population along the *camino real.*

As a result, after the 1656 rebellion, the geography of the Timucuan missions in interior Florida was very different from that before the rebellion (figs. 1.3, 1.4). In that region the Timucua were relegated to small mission villages on the *camino real,* which, more than ever, served as a pipeline between St. Augustine and Apalachee province in northwest Florida, whose

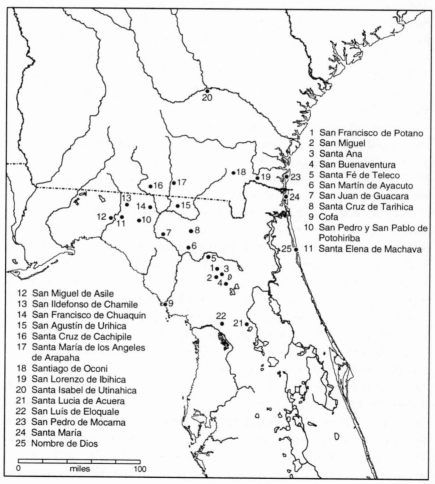

1 San Francisco de Potano
2 San Miguel
3 Santa Ana
4 San Buenaventura
5 Santa Fé de Teleco
6 San Martín de Ayacuto
7 San Juan de Guacara
8 Santa Cruz de Tarihica
9 Cofa
10 San Pedro y San Pablo de Potohiriba
11 Santa Elena de Machava

12 San Miguel de Asile
13 San Ildefonso de Chamile
14 San Francisco de Chuaquin
15 San Agustín de Urihica
16 Santa Cruz de Cachipile
17 Santa María de los Angeles de Arapaha
18 Santiago de Oconi
19 San Lorenzo de Ibihica
20 Santa Isabel de Utinahica
21 Santa Lucia de Acuera
22 San Luís de Eloquale
23 San Pedro de Mocama
24 Santa María
25 Nombre de Dios

Fig. 1.3. Missions among the Timucua Indians prior to 1656.

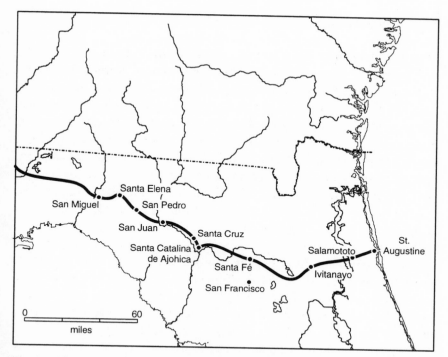

Fig. 1.4. Timucua missions on the *camino real* following the 1656 rebellion.

missions and agricultural fields constituted a large part of the colony's bread-basket.

Prior to the late 1980s, archaeologists, including myself, relied on key postrebellion documents to locate and identify the Timucuan missions (see, for example, Boyd 1938; Wenhold 1936). But those materials related only to the post-1656 rebellion missions. It was only in the 1980s that field surveys and excavations by Kenneth Johnson (1991) called into question our knowledge of Timucuan mission geography. John Worth's subsequent documentary research provided the explanation for what was observed archaeologically: the missions of Timucua had been geographically reorganized following 1656. Consequently, anyone working with collections or data from a Timucua province mission identified before the 1990s should consult more recent sources, which may offer new identifications for mission sites. For instance, the Fig Springs site (8CO1), once identified as Santa Catalina de Afuica, is now known to be San Martín de Ayacuto.

The Mission Timucua

After two decades of little progress, Franciscan efforts took hold in the 1590s. As John Worth (1998a) has shown, the friars, working in tandem with the colony's military government, systematically missionized each Timucuan chiefdom, working through existing native political structures while essentially assuming the roles once held by native priests. Timucuan chiefs traveled to St. Augustine to render obedience to the Spanish crown and accept baptism and gifts. Once a chief had agreed to become a Christian, missionary friars were sent to administer to his people. Typically, the first generation of converts was most difficult. But with children born and reared to adulthood at the Catholic missions, the Timucua became loyal, Christian members of the Spanish empire.

From the Spanish point of view, colonization of the Timucua Indians was a success, even though the La Florida colony would never produce the profits envisioned by its founders. For the Timucua, however, colonization could hardly be deemed positive. The establishment of Franciscan missions was intimately entwined with forced labor, directed culture change, resettlement, and, as we have seen, epidemic-caused depopulation.

The goal of the Franciscan missions was to save the souls of the Indians while shaping their minds and controlling their bodies, the latter in support of Spanish interests. Catholicism with its material culture replaced native beliefs and iconography. But it is important to realize that not all aspects of traditional Timucuan culture were supplanted. Friars concentrated on those features of Timucuan life that conflicted with Catholic teachings. Much was retained. Consequently, the lives of the mission Timucua were a curious blend of old and new.

Mission Villages

The architecture of the mission buildings with their churches, *conventos* (friaries), plazas, and other features are an example of the syncretism of new beliefs and old practices that typified the missions. But in the Timucua villages adjoining the mission compounds and in outlying, satellite villages, Spanish influence was hardly discernible. Let us take a quick look at the mission buildings, themselves material symbols of Christianity. Elements of architecture, painting, and statuary reinforced the tenets of Catholicism; to be Christian was to have a church or chapel in which to learn and worship, a sacred, physical place of sanctuary apart from everyday life. The importance of churches was well recognized by the Timucua, who had traditions of council houses, temples, and charnel houses, special buildings steeped in meaning and ritual.

Mission buildings almost always included a church, *convento*, and *cocina* (kitchen); there also were fences, plazas and atria, and bells and bell towers. Documents offer occasional tidbits of information about construction and the tools and hardware used, but much of our information comes from archaeological investigations. Those excavations suggest all the mission buildings were rectangular, with the church the largest, averaging about 60 by 35 feet, though there was considerable variation in size (Saunders 1990, 1993).

Churches were constructed by Timucua villagers working under the eyes of Franciscan friars. Consequently, most churches combined native techniques with Spanish ones: thatched roofs and support posts set in deep holes and (usually) wattle-and-daub walls assembled in part with iron tools and wrought iron hardware.

The earliest churches in chiefdoms whose chiefs desired friars may have been built by Indians using hardware and tools they were given in St. Augustine, again conforming to Spanish specifications. One example may be the small church at mission San Juan de Guacara at the Baptizing Spring site (8SU65) in southern Suwannee County, Florida (Loucks 1979), built in the early seventeenth century. The 27-by-33-feet clay-floored church, which contained few iron spikes, was walled on three sides, with the fourth open. A similar early church was excavated by Brent Weisman (1992) at the Fig Springs site in Columbia County, Florida. It may have been built about the time Father Baltasar López established a *visita* (church with a nonresident friar) there in the late sixteenth century. Again 27 by 33 feet, the same size as the San Juan church, the Fig Springs church contained an open nave and a wooden-floored sacristy and sanctuary, both enclosed by board walls. In the early seventeenth century, when Father Martín Prieto founded the *doctrina* of San Martín de Ayacuto in the same village, a larger, more substantial church was built. (*Doctrinas* were missions with resident friars.)

Churches fronted plazas or atria, the scene of religious processions, marriages, funerals, and baptisms. The atria also handled overflow crowds from the church nave. Fences or walls—some of wattle and daub—set off and enclosed areas within missions such as the church atria, gardens, and even the *conventos*.

Few religious artifacts are associated with churches; religious precincts were kept clean. Artifacts found most often are the wrought iron nails and spikes used in construction.

We know much less about mission *conventos* and *cocinas* than about churches. The information available from excavations suggests the former were as varied in construction techniques and sizes as churches (Saunders 1990, 1993). At San Juan de Guacara, the Baptizing Spring site, what apparently was the *convento* was a dirt-floored, almost square structure about 22 feet on a side, with a central hearth for cooking and heat. The *convento* of Santa Catalina on Amelia Island (associated with Guale Indians moved to what had been Timucua territory) was a two-room, wattle-and-daub building about 22 by 37 feet. It had roofed porches on two sides, one of which may have covered a storage facility. A shell-paved floor underlay one porch and extended around to a third side of the building. What seems to have been a separate *cocina* or kitchen was nearby. We still have much to learn about mission buildings and furnishings among the Timucua, though it is safe to say they bore little resemblance to the contemporary adobe missions of the southwestern United States or the later Franciscan missions of California.

Within the native quarters at the Timucua missions were houses for individual families and smaller storehouses—*garitas*—raised above ground to lessen their accessibility to animals. Mounds no longer were constructed. Excavations at three sites, San Juan de Guacara (Baptizing Spring), San Martín, and Richardson (8AL100) in southern Alachua County, all indicate the Timucua built their round houses using traditional materials: wooden posts and palm thatch. Iron hardware was rare or totally absent, in marked contrast to churches and *conventos* built to appeal more to Spanish tastes.

One Spanish account describes the Timucuan houses as pyramids; probably the wall posts were bent over and tied together above the center of the house, forming a pointed framework that was then thatched. The houses were relatively small, never more than 25 feet in diameter and usually smaller.

Each chiefdom's main village had a large, round council house. Because those villages were the ones in which missions were established, it is likely the Christian church and the native council house fronted the same village plaza. Individual council houses were the locus of village business, and it was there that villagers met to receive and exchange information. The houses also served as lodging for visitors, including Spaniards, and as the site of meetings between Indian leaders and Spanish officials.

Christians in Death

For most of the seventeenth century the Timucua lived as Christians and participated in Catholic rituals. When individuals died, they received Catholic burial rites and were interred in sanctified ground in the floor of a mission church or in a burial area nearby. The coming of the missions marked the end of the use of charnel houses and interment in lineage-maintained mounds, a pre-Columbian practice.

Excavations at the small open church at the Fig Springs site revealed burials outside the building in a *campo santo* (holy ground used for burial) (Hoshower 1992). Later, after San Martín de Ayacuto was founded at the same site, burial was in the floor of the nave of the much larger church erected to serve the new *doctrina* (Hoshower 1992; Saunders 1996). That pattern—interment around a small, temporary church followed by burial in the more permanent *doctrina* church—may have been most common.

Whether around or in a church, individuals were interred on their backs in shallow graves. Arms were folded on chests, at times with hands clasped, and bodies were placed in cloth shrouds secured with brass straight pins. On occasion, wooden coffins were used, possibly for the bodies of native leaders or members of their families.

Some people were buried holding or wearing items reflecting their Christian piety: crosses, religious medallions, and reliquaries. Some clutched rosaries of faceted, black glass beads. Other jewelry, most often glass beads, also found its way into graves.

Graves were aligned in the same direction as the long axis of the church with which they were associated. As more and more individuals were interred within a church's floor, what were once neat, well-ordered rows gave way to overlapping burials and a less organized pattern. It was not at all uncommon for older bones to be pushed aside to accommodate a new interment. In some instances, the remains of as many as ten people are within one 10-by-10-foot area of floor. Some graves contain more than one body.

New Ways of Living

Though the Timucua Indians retained important aspects of their old lives during the mission period, their cultures underwent changes as new beliefs and behaviors replaced or supplemented traditional ones. Missions offered new ways to think and to be. Christianity offered explanations for the new world in which the Timucua found themselves, a world in which native populations grew smaller and smaller in number and friends and relatives, stricken with diseases, died in large numbers.

In this new world Spanish friars, officials, and soldiers offered economic opportunities and material goods that seemed to outshine traditional ones. Through the missions the Timucua embraced a new faith, iron tools, the Spanish language, monogamy, and new foods. The process of culture change was directed in part by the Franciscan friars, who condemned selected old ways while insisting on new ones. Friars worked especially hard to eradicate those things they viewed as morally corrupt and at odds with Catholic beliefs.

Education of the mission Indians included teaching them to read and write Spanish. As early as 1595, Timucuan villagers at San Pedro de Mocama on Cumberland Island, Georgia, were speaking Spanish. Father Francisco Pareja of San Juan del Puerto devised a way to write the Timucua language and translated primers, devotional books, and even a confessional into the native language (Milanich and Sturtevant 1972). The Spaniards recognized that literacy was important for teaching Christian discipline and doctrine.

At the missions the Timucua were baptized, learned the catechism, and received Christian-Spanish names. The latter often included both an Indian clan or village name and a Christian name, proving identifications with traditional social ties and the new religion.

Mission Timucua sang the mass and offered morning and evening prayers. Religious festivals, holy days, and feast days of obligation—including Sundays; the feasts of Nativity (Christmas), Resurrection (Easter), and Pentecost; All Saints' Day; and the days of Epiphany, the Lord's Circumcision, the Lord's Ascension, Corpus Christi, the Purification of Our Lady, the Annunciation of Our Lady, the Assumption of Our Lady, the Nativity of Our Lady, and the Apostles St. Peter and St. Paul—each were marked with a mass. Fast days—all Fridays during Lent, the Saturday before Easter, and Christmas Eve—were observed as well.

The religious doctrine taught to the Indians was comprehensive. As historian Amy Bushnell (1994) has noted, in addition to the catechism, the Indians learned the Pater Noster, Ave Maria, and Salve Regina (prayers recited in Latin), and the Sign of the Cross and the Credo. They knew the Ten Commandments, the Seven Deadly Sins, the Fourteen Works of Mercy, and other doctrine. Some Catholic rites were even translated into the Timucuan language by Father Gregorio de Movilla. As a consequence, a wedding ceremony, for example, probably included words in Timucua, Spanish, and Latin.

The introduction of Christianity was accompanied by a host of other new items. Plants from Spain joined corn and other crops traditionally grown by the Timucua and were added to the villagers' diets. Remains of wheat, watermelons, peaches, figs, hazelnuts, oranges, and garbanzos all have been identified from mission archaeological sites (Ruhl 1990, 1993). Historical documents also record the presence in Spanish Florida of European greens, various herbs, peas, sugarcane, garlic, melons, barley, pomegranates, cucumbers, European grapes, cabbages, lettuce, and sweet potatoes. Wheat, whose flour was greatly preferred by Spaniards to ground corn flour, was cultivated in some abundance, though never with the success or in anywhere near the quantity of corn.

Not only did the Timucua cultivate crops to feed themselves and their families, but they were required to produce surpluses to sustain the colony's Spaniards, both the relatively few friars and soldiers stationed in the mission provinces and the much larger population of St. Augustine. Throughout the period of the missions, corn was the chief item of agricultural produce. It was produced by Indians and traded and sold by friars, Indian chiefs, government officials, and Spanish entrepreneurs. Corn became an item of exchange and perhaps the most important commodity within the colony. It also supported the missions themselves. Friars could trade mission-grown corn for credit that allowed them to purchase supplies for their missions.

The importance of corn in the seventeenth century led to the production of surpluses in the mission provinces, though in the second half of that century the declining Timucua population resulted in Apalachee province assuming the role of the major region of production. The surpluses were made possible by two factors: more acreage was planted, and iron tools—machetes, axes, and hoes—were used to facilitate clearing and weeding fields.

Very early in the mission period direct tributes in corn were collected by Spanish officials, but that practice gave way to the system of conscripted labor (*repartimiento*). In other words, rather than requiring mission villages to supply corn, the Spaniards forced the Indians to supply labor to grow corn in fields surrounding St. Augustine. But because Indian chiefs and friars learned there was profit in selling corn to feed St. Augustine, production in mission fields continued to be emphasized.

Corn destined for St. Augustine was harvested, shucked, and ground into meal or flour at the mission villages. Because it is more efficient to carry a pack with 80 pounds of meal rather than 80 pounds of corn-on-the-cob, it likely was meal or flour that was sent to St. Augustine, not ears of corn. Evidence for mass processing of corn is ubiquitous at every Timucuan mission village excavated to date. Hundreds, even thousands, of charred corncobs have been found. The best explanation is that the cobs, left after the kernels were removed and ground, were used as fuel for fires. The number of charred cobs found at even one mission site, such as Baptizing Spring, is many times the number of all the pre-Columbian cobs found to date in all of Florida and Georgia.

New foods requiring new methods of preparation may have resulted in new cooking and serving dishes. Fired clay ceramics made by native potters in the shape of Spanish plates, pitchers, and other tableware are common at missions. But it is more likely such ceramics were made for the use of the friars and soldiers stationed at the missions, who did not always have access to Spanish-made tableware. New animals also found their way to the missions. Chickens and pigs were raised for food and for export, and their remains have been identified at several mission sites.

Labor Drafts

Prior to contact with the Spaniards, it was the prerogative of the Timucuan chiefs to demand that their vassal villagers provide labor for various projects. Tribute labor was used to build mounds, produce corn and other products for the chiefs' storehouses, and for other purposes.

With the establishment of the missions, Spanish officials routinely used such tribute labor for themselves in support of the colony. Working through village chiefs—usually paying them in trinkets—the Spaniards set quotas for the number of adult males each mission village would provide. On the one hand, this was a continuation of a traditional system, with chiefs using their power to extract labor from their people. But mounds were no longer built, and the types of labors performed by the members of the labor drafts were different from those that preceded the mission period.

We now realize that the labor contribution of the mission Indians was huge, and, as noted above, it was necessary for the very existence of the colony. Indians grew and processed corn and were the burden bearers who transported it from the mission fields to St. Augustine. They also carried supplies from St. Augustine back to the missions.

Native men were conscripted to go to St. Augustine to provide labor for projects, or they remained there after transporting supplies, tending fields for the benefit of the residents of St. Augustine. Timucua laborers, some of whom spent as much as six months of the year in town, prepared, planted, and hoed fields and harvested crops, especially corn.

In St. Augustine, Indians also helped to build forts and other buildings, cut timber, and mine coquina on Anastasia Island southeast of town. Several hundred native people were involved in the construction of the stone Castillo de San Marcos in the 1670s. The fort was built to protect the town from possible raids by the British or their Carolinian colonists. Working as beasts of burden and living in and around St. Augustine added to health problems and increased the natives' susceptibility to the epidemic diseases that periodically swept though mission towns and St. Augustine itself.

In the region of the missions the Timucua and other mission Indians maintained the *camino real* by clearing brush, repairing creek crossings, and even building bridges. Where roads crossed rivers too deep to ford, villagers operated ferries. In the same region Timucua Indians also worked on Spanish ranches. Raising cattle, pigs, and chickens and cultivating corn and wheat on ranches were ways Spanish colonists in La Florida could try to turn a profit.

One of the earliest and most important ranches was in Timucua province in Potano Indian territory. By 1630, the ranch named La Chua and owned by La Florida's royal treasurer, Francisco Menéndez Márquez, was raising cattle on the north side of Paynes Prairie southeast of modern Gainesville, Florida. At that time the land on which the ranch was located no longer was controlled by the Potano, who had been hard hit by epidemics, but by a Timucuan chief, Lúcas Menéndez, head of the chiefdom whose main village harbored mission San Martín de Ayacuto. Though living fifty miles from the ranch, the chief apparently had usurped the land from the remnants of the Potano.

A second large ranch was near San Miguel de Asile, the westernmost Timucuan mission. Owned by Governor Benito Ruíz de Salazar Vallecilla, it began operation in 1645, growing corn and wheat and raising pigs (though its production was not great, and yields were insufficient to allow exportation of crops for sale). By 1652 the ranch was abandoned. In the latter half of the seventeenth century, it became easier for Spaniards to gain access to land in order to start ranches, and more were founded, scattered across northern Florida, including east of the St. Johns River.

Demise of the Timucua

Although depopulation would eventually have doomed the Timucua, their end was hastened by the establishment of English colonies in Virginia and the Carolinas. Beginning in the 1660s and increasing in the 1680s, raids on the Timucuan missions by native slavers, actively abetted by English-backed interests, pressured the missions. Some Indians fled; more were captured. The raids led to the resettlement of nonlocal Indians at missions in northern Florida as the Spaniards tried to maintain their needed labor force.

The end of the Timucua missions in the interior of La Florida came in 1702–5 when several large Carolinian and Indian raids destroyed them (as well as those of Apalachee). Survivors moved to new, refuge towns close to St. Augustine, where they continued to be served by Franciscan friars. A 1717 census lists ten such refuge villages, three of which were home to the approximately 250 Timucua Indians who survived. By 1726 that number had dropped to 157 Timucua, and two years later it was down to 70.

In 1752 there were only 29 Timucua living in a single refuge town just outside the walls of St. Augustine. A decade later in 1763, when Spain relinquished La Florida to the British, only a single Timucua Indian is listed among the native people shipped to the town of Guanabacoa in Cuba.

Bibliography

Booker, Karen M.
1991   Languages of the Aboriginal Southeast: An Annotated Bibliography. Native American Bibliography Series 15. Metuchen, N.J.: Scarecrow Press.
Boyd, Mark F.
1938   Map of the Road from Pensacola to St. Augustine, 1778. Florida Historical Quarterly 17:1–23.
Bushnell, Amy Turner
1994   Situado and Sabana: Spain's Support System for the Presidio and Mission Provinces of Florida. Anthropological Papers no. 74. American Museum of Natural History, New York.
Crawford, James M.
1979   Timucua and Yuchi: Two Language Isolates of the Southeast. In The Lan-

guages of Native America: Historical and Comparative Assessment, edited by L. Campbell and M. Mithun, 327–54. Austin: University of Texas Press.
1988   On the Relationship of Timucua to Muskhogean. In In Honor of Mary Haas: From the Haas Festival Conference on Native American Linguistics, edited by W. Shipley, 157–64. Berlin: Mouton de Gruyter.
Deagan, Kathleen A.
1972   Fig Springs: The Mid-Seventeenth Century in North-Central Florida. Historical Archaeology 6:23–46.
1978   Cultures in Transition: Fusion and Assimilation among the Eastern Timucua. In Tacachale, Essays on the Indians of Florida and Southeastern Georgia during the Historic Period, edited by J. T. Milanich and S. Proctor, 88–119. Gainesville: University Presses of Florida.
Goddard, Ives
1996   The Classification of Native Languages of North America. In Handbook of North American Indians, edited by William Sturtevant. Vol. 17, Languages, edited by Ives Goddard, 290–323. Washington, D.C.: Smithsonian Institution Press.
Goggin, John M.
1949   Cultural Traditions in Florida Prehistory. In The Florida Indian and His Neighbors, edited by J.W. Griffin, 13–44. Winter Park, Fla.: Rollins College Inter-American Center.
1952   Space and Time Perspective in Northern St. Johns Archeology, Florida. Yale University Publications in Anthropology 47. New Haven.
1953   An Introductory Outline of Timucua Archaeology. Southeastern Archaeological Conference Newsletter 3(3):4–17.
Granberry, Julian
1993   A Grammar and Dictionary of the Timucua Language. Tuscaloosa: University of Alabama Press.
Greenberg, Joseph H.
1987   Language in the Americas. Stanford: Stanford University Press.
Hann, John H.
1988   Apalachee: The Land between the Rivers. Gainesville: University Presses of Florida.
1990   Summary Guide to Spanish Florida Missions and Visitas with Churches in the Sixteenth and Seventeenth Centuries. The Americas 46:417–513.
1993   1630 Memorial of Fray Francisco Alonso de Jesus on Spanish Florida's Missions and Natives. The Americas 50:85–105.
1996   A History of the Timucua Indians and Missions. Gainesville: University Press of Florida.
Hoffman, Paul E.
1994a   Lucas Vázquez de Ayllón's Discovery and Colony. In The Forgotten Centuries: Indians and Europeans in the American South, 1521–1704, edited by C. Hudson and C. Tesser, 36–49. Athens: University of Georgia Press.
1994b   Narváez and Cabeza de Vaca in Florida. In The Forgotten Centuries: Indians and Europeans in the American South, 1521–1704, edited by C. Hudson and C. Tesser, 50–73. Athens: University of Georgia Press.

24   Jerald T. Milanich

Hoshower, Lisa M.
1992   Bioanthropological Analysis of a Seventeenth-Century Native American-
        Spanish Mission Population: Biocultural Impacts on the Northern Utina.
        Ph.D. diss., Department of Anthropology, University of Florida, Gainesville.
Johnson, Kenneth W.
1990   The Discovery of a Seventeenth-Century Spanish Mission in Ichetucknee State
        Park, 1986. *Florida Journal of Anthropology* 15:39–46.
1991   The Utina and the Potano Peoples of Northern Florida: Changing Settlement
        Systems in the Spanish Colonial Period. Ph.D. diss., Department of Anthropol-
        ogy, University of Florida, Gainesville.
Keegan, William F.
1992   *The People Who Discovered Columbus: The Prehistory of the Bahamas.*
        Gainesville: University Press of Florida.
Loucks, L. Jill
1979   Political and Economic Interactions between Spaniards and Indians: Archeo-
        logical and Ethnohistorical Perspectives of the Mission System in Florida.
        Ph.D. diss., Department of Anthropology, University of Florida, Gainesville.
McEwan, Bonnie G. (editor)
1993   *The Spanish Missions of La Florida.* Gainesville: University Press of Florida.
McMurray, Judith A.
1973   The Definition of the Ceramic Complex at San Juan del Puerto. Master's
        thesis, Department of Anthropology, University of Florida, Gainesville.
Milanich, Jerald T.
1972   Excavations at the Richardson Site, Alachua County, Florida: An Early-Sev-
        enteenth-Century Potano Indian Village (with Notes on Potano Culture
        Change). *Florida Bureau of Historic Sites and Properties Bulletin* 2:35–61.
        Tallahassee.
1978   The Western Timucua: Patterns of Acculturation and Change. In *Tacachale,
        Essays on the Indians of Florida and Southeastern Georgia during the Historic
        Period,* edited by J. T. Milanich and S. Proctor, 59–88. Gainesville: University
        Presses of Florida.
1994   *Archaeology of Precolumbian Florida.* Gainesville: University Press of Florida.
1996   *The Timucua.* Oxford: Blackwell.
Milanich, Jerald T., and William C. Sturtevant
1972   *Francisco Pareja's 1613 Confessionario: A Documentary Source for Timu-
        cuan Ethnography.* Tallahassee: Florida Department of State.
Ruhl, Donna L.
1990   Spanish Mission Paleoethnobotany and Culture Change: A Survey of the
        Archaeobotanical Data and Some Speculations on Aboriginal and Spanish
        Agrarian Interactions in La Florida. In *Columbian Consequences,* vol. 2,
        Archaeological and Historical Perspectives on the Spanish Borderlands East,
        edited by D. H. Thomas, 555–80. Washington, D.C.: Smithsonian Institution
        Press.
1993   Old Customs and Traditions in New Terrain: Sixteenth- and Seventeenth-
        Century Archaeobotanical Data from La Florida. In *Foraging and Farming in
        the Eastern Woodlands,* edited by C. M. Scarry, 255–83. Gainesville: Univer-
        sity Press of Florida.

Saunders, Rebecca
1990   Ideal and Innovation: Spanish Mission Architecture in the Southeast. In *Columbian Consequences,* vol. 2, *Archaeological and Historical Perspectives on the Spanish Borderlands East,* edited by D. H. Thomas, 527–42. Washington, D.C.: Smithsonian Institution Press.
1993   Architecture of the Missions Santa María and Santa Catalina de Amelia. In *The Spanish Missions of La Florida,* edited by B.G. McEwan, 35–61. Gainesville: University Press of Florida.
1996   Mission-Period Settlement Structure: A Test of the Model at San Martín de Timucua. *Historical Archaeology* 30(4):24–36.
Swanton, John R.
1916   Terms of Relationship in Timucua. In *Holmes Anniversary Volume: Anthropological Essays Presented to William Henry Holmes in Honor of his Seventieth Birthday,* 451–63. Washington, D.C.: J. W. Bryan Press.
1922   *Early History of the Creek Indians and Their Neighbors.* Smithsonian Institution, Bureau of American Ethnology Bulletin 73. Washington, D.C.
1929   The Tawasa Language. *American Anthropologist* 31:435–53.
1946   *The Indians of the Southeastern United States.* Smithsonian Institution, Bureau of American Ethnology Bulletin 137. Washington, D.C.
Symes, M. I., and M. E. Stephens
1965   A-272: The Fox Pond Site. *Florida Anthropologist* 18:65–72.
Thomas, David Hurst (editor)
1990   *Columbian Consequences,* vol. 2, *Archaeological and Historical Perspectives on the Spanish Borderlands East.* Washington, D.C.: Smithsonian Institution Press.
Weisman, Brent R.
1992   *Excavations on the Franciscan Frontier: Archaeology of the Fig Springs Mission.* Gainesville: University Press of Florida.
Wenhold, Lucy L.
1936   A 17th-Century Letter of Gabriel Díaz Vara Calderón, Bishop of Cuba, Describing the Indian Missions of Florida. *Smithsonian Miscellaneous Collections* 95(16). Washington, D.C.
Worth, John E.
1992   The Timucuan Missions of Spanish Florida and the Rebellion of 1656. Ph.D. diss., Department of Anthropology, University of Florida, Gainesville.
1995   *The Struggle for the Georgia Coast: An Eighteenth-Century Spanish Retrospective on Guale and Mocama.* Anthropological Papers no. 75. American Museum of Natural History, New York.
1998a   *The Timucuan Chiefdoms of Spanish Florida,* vol. 1, *Assimilation.* Gainesville: University Press of Florida.
1998b   *The Timucuan Chiefdoms of Spanish Florida,* vol. 2, *Resistance and Destruction.* Gainesville: University Press of Florida.

2

The Guale Indians of the Lower Atlantic Coast: Change and Continuity

Rebecca Saunders

This essay provides a brief introduction to the archaeology and ethnohistory of the Guale Indians. The burgeoning information on this subject, particularly in ethnohistory, necessitates that this presentation be somewhat selective; more comprehensive accounts of specific aspects of continuity and change in Guale lifeways can be found elsewhere. While much of this material is referenced throughout the text, it seems appropriate at the outset to make mention of the most recent and/or useful references. Excellent ethnohistorical research on the establishment, maintenance, and destruction of the Guale missions, much of it based on newly discovered and/or translated documents, can be found in Bushnell (1994) and Worth (1995). Jones's (1978) ethnohistorical overview of the Guale remains an outstanding resource. Larson's (1978) melding of the archaeological and ethnohistorical records is also exemplary. In discussing Spanish missionization throughout the United States, Weber's (1992) volume places the Guale experience in a broader context.

Archaeological overviews of the late prehistoric Georgia coast are available in a volume of *Early Georgia* dedicated to Irene period studies (Crook 1984; DePratter 1984; Larson 1984a, 1984b; Pearson 1984; Smith 1984), as well as in Crook (1986), Larson (1980), and Pearson (1977, 1979, 1980). Contact period and mission period Guale archaeological complexes are described in Larson (1978), and a recent summary of historic Guale archaeology has been provided by Thomas (1993).

This essay begins with a review of Guale lifeways during the contact period (circa A.D. 1500–1600), a time before long-term associations with Spanish and British colonial powers transfigured so much of Guale life.

Primary and secondary historical documents are incorporated with archaeological data from both late prehistoric and contact period sites to attempt a more rounded description of lifeways at this pivotal juncture. (Late prehistoric sites should provide a reasonably accurate picture of the Guale at contact, and their inclusion increases the database.) A discussion of the changes in those lifeways as a result of missionization, again using archaeological and ethnohistoric data, follows.

Archaeological and Ethnohistoric Information on the Contact Period Guale

Archaeological evidence indicates that from at least A.D. 1150 until the beginning of the Spanish mission period (A.D. 1565–1704), the precursors of the historically known Guale lived along the Georgia coast. They are known by archaeologists as the Savannah (A.D. 1150–1300) and Irene phase (A.D. 1300–circa 1600) peoples. (A more fine-tuned series of three Irene phase designations, based on Larson [1953, 1978], has been presented by Braley 1990.) "Archaeological, bioarchaeological, and historical evidence strongly suggests the human remains from [Guale] populations and the earlier prehistoric periods represent a diachronically continuous biological population" (Larsen et al. 1996:98–99). Within the Savannah and Irene phases, members of the cultures held in common the following: settlement patterns; social structure; mortuary practices; tool and craft production; decorative techniques; and, presumably, ideology. These techniques and ideas were in turn passed along, sometimes with modification, to the next generation—in other words, through the Savannah to the Irene and eventually the Guale. The Guale also shared many aspects of subsistence, social organization, and ideology with their contemporaneous neighbors. However, there were distinctive features, particularly in settlement systems and pottery decoration, that served (and still serve) to distinguish the "proto-Guale" from adjacent groups.

In this reconstruction of contact period Guale lifeways, archaeological information is drawn primarily from the Irene phase, though Savannah phase data are included when relevant to the discussion of continuity and change. Ethnohistoric evidence from the contact period gives more information on social structure and ideology than is available from archaeological evidence, but both databases suffer from biases that allow us to see the Guale only "through a glass darkly" (Axtell 1988). What is apparent from both datasets is that, despite population loss, relocation, and population amalgamation, the Guale were able to maintain a discrete social identity throughout the mission period.

Site and Social Hierarchies

Coastal Savannah and Irene phase occupations were confined to a narrow strip of maritime live oak forest on the barrier islands and adjacent mainland of the lower Atlantic coast (fig. 2.1). Irene sites were founded inland only along the Savannah River and the Altamaha River basins; elsewhere, the interior pine barrens constituted a western environmental barrier for Irene (and other) phase populations (Pearson 1979:55). The southern boundary of the Irene/Guale peoples appears to have been stable—at the Altamaha River—throughout prehistory and into the early mission period (Pearson 1977a:55). The northern boundary of the society, however, was more fluid. It is believed to have extended as far north as Edisto Island, South Carolina, in the Irene I phase (A.D. 1300–1450). In the Irene II phase (A.D. 1450–circa 1600), the northern boundary constricted, and Guale territory did not extend as far north as the Savannah River (Bushnell 1994:60; cf. Jones 1978:178). According to Anderson (1989:119–20, 1994:326), around A.D. 1450 the central and lower Savannah River basin was abandoned when it became a buffer zone between the rival chiefdoms of Ocute in central Georgia and Cofitachequi in South Carolina. This rivalry may have been caused, or exacerbated, by drought and consequent famine in the mid-fifteenth century (Anderson 1994:327; compare Braley [1990:99], who attributed the southern movement to the rise of Mississippian occupations along the Oconee River and the need for coastal populations to maintain direct lines of communication with them). These extreme environmental conditions may have precipitated the decline of the southeastern chiefdoms prior to the arrival of de Soto in 1539.

Like most other southeastern groups, Savannah and Irene phase peoples were organized into complex chiefdoms. These were regionally organized societies having at least two centralized, hierarchical decision-making levels interacting to coordinate activities among village communities (Anderson 1994:7). Jones (1978:200, 202–9) suggested a variation of this pattern for the contact period Guale, a dual chiefdom. He proposed that some Guale chiefdoms had two contemporaneous, coequal principal towns. These could be distinguished from secondary centers and lesser settlements by the fact

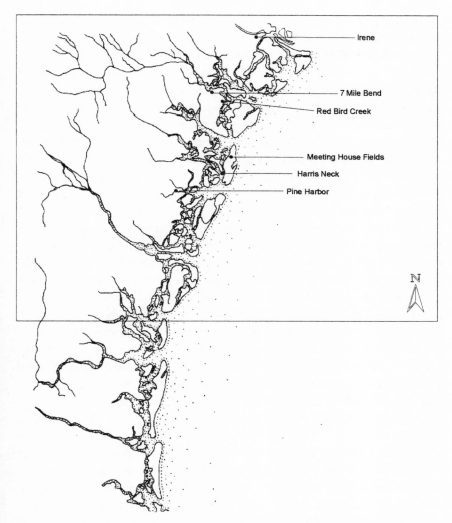

Fig. 2.1. Savannah and Irene phase sites mentioned in the text. Area shown is the Guale territory after 1450.

that principal leaders lived in them and that council meetings involving a variety of officials were held in them. There are possible archaeological manifestations of dual chiefdoms in "paired towns" in the interior Southeast. These proximate mound centers were once thought to have been occupied by allied towns within a small chiefdom (Williams and Shapiro 1990: 164). However, current archaeological models propose that power cycled between paired towns due to a number of environmental and sociopolitical factors (Anderson 1994; Williams and Shapiro 1990).

Regardless of their exact configuration, it is safe to say that Guale chiefdoms were neither as hierarchically organized nor as nucleated as their contemporaries in the interior. Indeed, Irene chiefdoms were not as complex as those of their forebears in the preceding Savannah phase. This is apparent from a comparison of the hierarchy of site types in the archaeological record. The best evidence for this hierarchy emerges from Pearson's (1977, 1980, 1984) settlement survey on Ossabaw Island. Pearson ranked Savannah and Irene phase sites on the basis of size, and, correlating those with environmental location, he established four size/function classes of sites. These ranged from the largest, multiple mound sites to the smallest, special purpose collection sites. He (Pearson 1979:91) noted that from the Savannah to the Irene phase there was "1. an increase in the total number of sites; 2. an increase in the total area of site occupation; 3. a shift from a 'nucleated' settlement structure in which a single site is totally dominant, to one in which a number of middle-sized sites develop and evidently become important in relation to the rest of the system; 4. an increase in, or possibly the appearance of, a large number of small probably temporary special activity sites." Pearson (1979:138–40) went on to suggest that this shift in settlement systems was a reflection of the breakdown of the Mississippian sociocultural system present in the Southeast prior to contact. He added that the nucleated Savannah system might reflect warfare, while the more dispersed Irene system was a response to the reliance on agriculture and the patchy distribution of suitable soils.

Ethnohistoric documents can be used to append social information to the structure of the intersite settlement pattern. Early and later documents indicate a matrilineal society (as was the case with most southeastern groups), in which power and privilege were conferred through the female line—not to females but to a mother's brother. In other words, a boy's uncle's social standing was more important to him than his father's. Thus, within a complex chiefdom, at the largest multiple mound (or council house—see below) site within a society, the paramount chief (*mico mayor*) resided with other important members of his lineage—his brothers and other male relatives related to him through his mother—and their families. Villages under his control, smaller mound sites, were likely administered by one of his brothers or nephews. These individuals (*caciques*), in turn, oversaw the smaller dispersed villages under their purview. (See Hann 1992; Jones 1978; and Larson 1978 for more information on political organization and native terminology.)

Tribute was paid to the elite; much of this was redistributed down the hierarchy. Elite men could be polygynous, keeping each wife in a separate house; there is some documentary mention of sororal polygyny (Larson 1978:126). Men, and perhaps elite women as well, possessed badges of office which both signified and conferred power, and their subjects treated them with deference and devotion. Spanish disregard for the rights of chiefs, particularly their entitlement to more than one wife and their exemption from labor, was to provoke the Guale into revolt against the Spanish in the sixteenth and seventeenth centuries. Nevertheless, chiefs had little coercive power. Decisions were made by consensus of all the principal men. According to Laudonnière (1975:14), "The men do nothing without assembling and counseling together thoroughly before arriving at a decision. They meet together every morning in the great public house where the king is and where he sits on a seat higher than all the others. There each, one after the other, comes and salutes him."

Paramount chiefdoms tend to be unstable for a number of reasons; power shifts frequently between inter- and intraregional centers (Anderson 1994: 7–52; Williams and Shapiro 1990). The changes in intersite hierarchies between the Savannah and Irene phases in Pearson's survey data, as well as in intrasite settlement patterning and burial practices at the Irene site (see below), may indicate an attempt by coastal populations to solve this problem.

The preeminent (paramount) Savannah/early Irene phase site was the Irene site (9CH1) near the mouth of the Savannah River (Anderson 1994: 174–86; Caldwell and McCann 1941; Crook 1986:38–42). This site contains the only platform mound identified in coastal Georgia. It was a political and ceremonial center occupied throughout the Savannah phase and into the Irene I phase, but was abandoned (along with the rest of the lower and central Savannah River basin) around A.D. 1450 (Anderson 1994:174). Savannah phase features at the site included the aforementioned platform mound, which had seven pentagonal construction levels. The first four construction phases were not mounds per se but surface structures with earth embankments. True platform mound stages with summit structures appeared by the fifth construction level. Most of the stages contained palisades, which may indicate defensive considerations. Other Savannah phase site features included a burial mound adjacent to the platform mound, a series of enclosures, and other, unidentified structures.

Irene phase peoples added a single, circular construction level to the platform mound, the surface of which was domed rather than flat. There was no evidence of a summit structure. Clearly the function of the mound changed at the time of the Irene phase occupation. Irene phase peoples also added a few interments to the burial mound but then abandoned both mounds. In place of the burial mound, a semisubterranean wattle-and-daub mortuary structure was constructed. A large council house ("the rotunda" in the original report) replaced the platform mound. It is clear from the ethnohistoric record (for example, in the Laudonnière account above) that council houses were used for meetings of the various elite in all Guale chiefdoms. The shift from the paramount platform mound to council houses in principal towns may correspond to the burgeoning of middle-level sites (for example, Pearson 1977, 1980) and, presumably, middle-level dignitaries. In other words, council houses may mark the emergence of the welter of native dignitaries with which the Spanish eventually had to interact: the *mico mayor, mico minor, inija, mandadores, aliagitas, tunaques, ibisache,* and *herederos* (Hann 1992:207–8; Jones 1978:200–201).

Villages and Daily Life

The bulk of the Guale population did not reside in a principal town. After clearing virtually the entire Irene site, Caldwell and McCann (1941:69) noted "the most impressive feature of the Irene site was the large proportion of presumably ceremonial buildings and enclosures [*sic*], and the relatively small number of possible habitations." Instead, as indicated by Pearson's (1977) Ossabaw Island data, as well as a host of other sites along the coast, the bulk of the Irene phase population resided in large (26,000 to 55,740 square meters) settlements generally lacking mounds; smaller, "community"-sized sites with small mounds; and special purpose, hunting or gathering sites. Larson's (1978:122) data from the Sapelo River area also suggest extensive habitation sites. The Pine Harbor site occupied over a mile of high ground along the Sapelo River and one of its tributaries. However, it is still unclear to what extent intrasite areas can be considered contemporaneous at that site (see below). In any event, the Irene phase population was probably not nucleated to any extent. The 1526 Ayllón expedition likened Guale settlements to Spanish rural farmsteads (Hoffman 1990:73; Oviedo 1959 IV:326, 327); most agree with Jones (1978:192) in describing the settlement pattern as one of "dispersed towns."

Residential sites display a distinctive intrasite settlement pattern. In contrast to, for instance, St. Johns phase sites to the south, which are characterized by extensive sheet middens, Savannah and Irene phase occupations contain discrete piles of shell midden. Pearson's (1984:4) map of the Red Bird Creek site suggests two clusters of these middens, with each cluster focused toward one of the two mounds present on the site. At the Meeting House Fields site, Middens E and H appear to have been the foci of a semicircular cluster of smaller middens (Saunders 2000a). At other sites, midden distribution seems more random (Larson 1978:122).

Presumably, these shell middens were adjacent to houses, though a one-to-one correlation between middens and houses has yet to be demonstrated. Nor has it been determined if these middens generally represent short- or long-term occupations. Indeed, it is unclear whether or not all, or even most, middens in a single site are contemporaneous. Radiocarbon dates and pottery analysis from Meeting House Fields indicated that the site occupation clustered into two discrete time periods, one late prehistoric and one post-contact (Saunders 2000a). If Meeting House Fields is typical, the apparent randomness of the intrasite settlement pattern might be resolved by determining which middens were contemporaneous. Radiocarbon dating a large proportion of middens at a site would provide some information; paddle matching of complicated stamped sherds and crossmending pottery and other artifacts between middens would be a stronger indication of contemporaneity. Once the issue of contemporaneity is resolved, more interpretation of the demonstrated variability in content between middens will be possible (see, for example, Dukes 1993; Pearson 1984; Saunders 2000a).

Though Jones (1978:199) predicted round houses, built along the same principles as council houses, the archaeological evidence for Irene phase housing consists of rectangular, wattle-and-daub structures. These have been found at Red Bird Creek, 7 Mile Bend (9BN7), Pine Harbor (Larson 1978:131), and the Irene site. Braley and others (1986:62–64) found the postholes of a partial late Irene phase wattle-and-daub house at Harris Neck (9MC41) associated with daub processing pits. The configuration of that structure, however, was obscure. Domestic structures were built using wall trenches (Red Bird Creek, 7 Mile Bend) or individually set posts (Irene, Harris Neck, Pine Harbor). Many of these structures had central fire pits.

One of the better preserved examples of Irene phase housing was reported from Red Bird Creek (early Irene phase; Pearson 1984). Complete dimensions of the habitation could not be determined; however, based on the location of the fire pit, presumably central, the structure measured 5.2 meters in width (Pearson 1984:8). As noted, posts were set into wall trenches. Major supports were of yellow pine; additional vertical structure was supplied by bundles of cane (*Arundinaria tecta*). Single strands of cane spaced at least 15 centimeters apart supplied the horizontal structure. Clay daub tempered with Spanish moss was applied to both sides of the wall structure in layers 0.6 to 5 centimeters thick on each side.

Elite residences do not appear to have been dramatically different architecturally from those of commoners. However, they may have been more elaborately decorated. René Laudonnière did not note the shape of Ouade's (Guale's) house but did describe a lavish interior: "His house was decorated with tapestries of various colored feathers up to the height of a pike. The place where the king slept was covered with fine workmanship and fringed in scarlet" (Laudonnière 1975:43).

We have very little information on the daily lives of the contact period Guale. There are few direct references to quotidian activities, sex roles, division of labor, or other aspects of social life in the early documents; archaeological evidence is lacking. Extrapolating from ethnographic references to southeastern societies as a whole, the principal economic unit was probably the lineage and the most important social unit the clan. Both men and women were compelled to marry outside of both the lineage and the clan (Hudson 1976). On the basis of physical anthropology at the Irene site, Hulse (1941:67–68) suggested that marriage residence was matrilocal, though Jones (1978:202) thought the evidence equivocal.

Two pairs of structural oppositions ruled the organization of labor: men as opposed to women and a cold season as opposed to a warm season (see also Adair 1930:448; Hudson 1976:259). According to Hudson (1976: 260), the division between the sexes was so complete that men and women were often seen as separate species; day-to-day activities kept men and women apart. Later European observers reported: "The little work that is done among the Indians is done by the poor Women, while the men are quite idle, or at most employed only in the Gentlemanly diversions of Hunting and Fishing" (Byrd 1929, quoted in Silver 1990:44). Laudonnière (1975:13) noted laconically, "The women do all the housework."

Subsistence and Health

The shell middens that characterize Irene phase sites are the most obvious indication of an estuarine and salt marsh subsistence focus (see also Crook 1986; DePratter and Howard 1980; Larson 1978, 1980; Pearson 1977, 1979, 1980). Oyster, usually accompanied by minor amounts of hard clam, ribbed mussel, and stout tagelus, dominate shell species. Analyses of fine-screened subsistence remains are available from Ossabaw Island (Pearson 1978, 1979), St. Catherines Island (Dukes 1993), Meeting House Fields (Russo 1991; Russo and Saunders n.d.; Saunders 2000a), Harris Neck (Braley et al. 1986), and Sapelo Island (Reitz 1982). At the Harris Neck site (9MC41), the contents of five late Irene phase (circa A.D. 1400) features were examined (Braley et al. 1986:133–72, 178–79). "Species identified from the site indicate a subsistence strategy focused on estuarine and salt marsh species, primarily oysters, fish of the drum family, sea catfishes, and diamond-back terrapins" (Braley et al. 1986:154). The small size of the fishes contributing the most biomass indicated that they were obtained through the use of nets or weirs in the estuaries. The occasional larger individuals could have been caught with hook and line or speared. Minor amounts of bird, snake, rabbit, and raccoon were consistently present.

Vertebrate fauna indicated that the site was occupied either year-round or reoccupied during all seasons (Braley et al. 1986:154). A growth ring study on *Mercenaria mercenaria* indicated exploitation in the spring, summer, fall, and early winter (Braley et al. 1986:172). Taken together, these data suggest year-round occupation at the site. Year-round site use was also indicated at Meeting House Fields (Russo 1991; Russo and Saunders n.d.; Saunders 2000a).

The archaeological information is fairly consistent with documentary evidence (including the De Bry engravings) of an estuarine fishing, hunting, and gathering tradition along the coast. The two databases diverge over the importance of agriculture along the coast and the degree of sedentism (see Saunders 2000b). Indeed, the ethnohistoric record is internally inconsistent as well. According to Laudonnière (1975:42), when Jean Ribault and his group of 150 men needed supplies at Charlesfort (among the Orista, see below) in 1562, the Orista could not supply everything the Frenchman needed, but referred Ribault to the Guale:

Being very sorry that they were not able to give any further aid, they advised the Frenchmen to go to the country of King Covecxis [possibly the coruler of a dual chiefdom with Oade; Jones 1978:203], a man of might and renown who lived in the southern part of this land, where there was an abundance in all seasons and a great supply of corn, flour [previously described as made of parched corn and as storable for long periods, Laudonnière 1975:13], and beans. They said that by his sole assistance they could live a very long time, but that before going to that land it would be wise to get permission from a king named Oade [Guale], a brother of Covecxis, who in corn, flour and beans was no less rich or generous and who would be glad to see them.

Thus, in places Laudonnière's account, along with Ribault's, indicated a food surplus in parts of Guale. However, speaking of the natives of the lower Atlantic coast in general, he indicated that "they do not sow any more than they feel is necessary for a period of six months, scarcely that" (Laudonnière 1975:15). Still generalizing, Laudonnière observed that the Indians left the coast during the winter. (Le Moyne contributed the precise dates of December 24 to March 15 for the Timucua [Alexander 1976:38]; Laudonnière [1975:121] stated January, February, and March with reference to the Timucuan Outina. Based on the experience of Fray Rogel in Orista, Barcía [1951:152] commented that Indians were scattered about the country for nine months out of the year.) However, elsewhere, Laudonnière's account suggests that maize and beans were available from storage during the winter months (see discussion in Jones 1978:189–94). Later (1569–70) Jesuit accounts from Guale and Orista depict a critical shortage of food and a transhumant lifestyle. The Jesuit correspondences have been the basis for models of Guale settlement and subsistence that depict seasonal subsistence shortages and population movements (Crook 1986).

Jones (1978) discussed the discrepancies between the French and Jesuit accounts. He concluded that the Jesuits exaggerated the poor subsistence base and transhumance of the Guale population to justify the failure of the Jesuit mission program. The Guale, Jones argued, had sufficient agricultural produce, along with other subsistence items, to maintain permanent residences. I have argued for a subsistence base adequate to sustain year-round settlements while conceding that French documents may exaggerate the productivity of the land to promote colonization (Saunders 2000b).

It may be, however, that the documents accurately reflected fluctuating environmental conditions at the time. In a recent article on drought during the colonial period in Virginia, Stahle and others (1998:565) presented tree ring data indicating "a prolonged drought from 1562 to 1571 that was most severe from 1565 to 1569." These data apply directly to the Jesuit experience in Virginia and might be applicable south through Guale territory. If so, then the drought began just as the French arrived, and reached its peak during the Jesuit occupation. In that case, both sides of the subsistence/settlement argument may contain some truth. What little good data are available from the archaeological record indicate late prehistoric coastal natives maintained an ample diet with sedentary subsistence practices. During climatic extremes such as those that coincided with the Jesuit accounts, the Guale may have drawn upon a repertoire of cultural responses that included survivals (seasonal transhumance) from earlier subsistence practices.

Little archaeological evidence of domesticates, maize in particular, has been uncovered in either coastal Savannah or Irene phase sites. Poor preservation of pollen in sandy coastal soils has frustrated attempts to identify corn pollen from Mississippi period sites along the coast; food preparation techniques, such as boiling as opposed to roasting, may prevent the preservation of kernels and cobs. Interesting data have emerged from stable isotope analyses, however. Stable carbon and nitrogen isotope analysis on the Savannah phase human skeletal remains from the Irene site indicated an increase in the reliance on maize agriculture and a decrease in the use of marine resources as compared to earlier periods. Coastal populations also have less negative $\delta^{13}C$ (increased maize consumption), but values on $\delta^{15}N$ (marine resources) were similar to those of the preceding period (Hutchinson et al. 1998; Larsen et al. 1992). Data on Irene phase burials from the Irene site, however, suggested a reversal. The $\delta^{13}C$ values were significantly more negative in burials from the Irene phase mortuary as compared with the Savannah phase mound, indicating less maize consumption. This is strongly correlated with other architectural and, presumably, sociopolitical changes at the site. However, coastal Irene phase sites do not show a similar decline. Data were limited, but the individuals from Irene phase contexts at Southend Mound I (9LI3) on St. Catherines Island, Georgia, had $\delta^{13}C$ values similar to those of the preceding St. Catherines (late Savannah) phase and also similar to those from the Irene Burial Mound (Hutchinson et al. 1998:table 2). These limited data do not seem to indicate the kind of agricultural intensification modeled by Pearson for coastal Irene populations. They also do not indicate social disruption at the level indicated by all of the different data at the Irene site.

For the Irene mound population in general, probably the elite of the society, Powell (1990:26) noted: "In particular, there is a low prevalence of porotic hyperostosis and cribra orbitalia" (Powell, unpubl), suggesting that severe chronic homolytic anemia was not a major health problem (Ortner and Putschar 1985; Steinbock 1976), despite the use of iron-poor foods—especially maize—in the Irene Mound diet and the intensive occupation of a restricted village area conducive to the continual exchange of endemic pathogens and contamination by fecal wastes (see also discussion in Larsen 1987, for alternative explanation). Hulse (1941:67) noted extreme tooth wear but few caries and "a number" of cases of osteomyelitis. (For a discussion on data suggesting that caries do not correlate with maize consumption, see Holland and O'Brien 1997.)

A final consideration in a discussion of contact period health concerns the evidence for epidemics. Researchers have speculated that the first epidemic on the Guale coast could have been introduced as early as 1526 by members of the Ayllón expedition. Documentary evidence for high mortality associated with epidemic diseases appears in Jesuit documents covering the period 1569–70 (Jones 1978). However, no archaeological evidence for epidemics has appeared for the period prior to 1600 on the Guale coast (Saunders 2000b).

Crafts and Cosmology

Our appreciation of the Guale and their predecessors as artisans is limited because only their inorganic artifacts have been preserved. Even direct references to Guale crafts are rare in the documents. However, documents do indicate a rich craft inventory for coastal natives in general; one that the Guale might be expected to share. Laudonnière (1975:20), for instance, mentioned the presents given by the "king" of a Timucuan group he and Ribault encountered: "At the leave-taking the king gave the captain a plume of egret feathers, dyed red, and a basket made from palm fiber, very artfully constructed, together with a great skin drawn upon and painted with pictures of various wild beasts, so vividly represented that they seemed almost alive."

Artifact inventories from Irene phase and contact period sites are usually limited to potsherds—many of which were used as hones for the variety of stone and shell tools—and subsistence remains. Relatively few artifacts reflecting the Southeastern Ceremonial Complex (SECC) are present on the coast, yet the motifs, representing the merging of art and iconography, craft and cosmology, leave the most detailed record of Irene phase social structure and superstructure. Cook and Pearson (1989:152) noted that at the Irene site "shell vessels, shell gorgets, chunkey stones, ceramic pipes, and if we consider Cult association in the broadest sense, the platform mound and mortuary buildings discovered at the site can be considered representative of Southeastern Ceremonial Complex symbolism." On the coast, SECC symbolism appears to have increased from a very low frequency in the Savannah phase to a low frequency in the Irene phase. The bulk of SECC items appeared in the contact period (Cook and Pearson 1989:154, 163). Mounds at the Pine Harbor site, for instance, contained "engraved shell gorgets with the coiled rattlesnake and cross, stone and copper ceremonial celts, clay pipes with cult symbols, incised pottery vessels with cult motifs, and conch shell bowls" (Larson 1978:127).

SECC symbolism appeared most frequently as motifs on pottery and pipes. Clay pipes bearing SECC symbolism are unique to the Guale area (Larson 1978:127). Cook and Pearson (1989:158) picture a number of pipes and note the most common motif as a "human head with a beaklike nose and a feather crest behind the head, possibly representative of an eagle or a falcon. Motifs such as barred ovals, the forked eye, and feathers appear as elements on these effigy pipes or by themselves." Midden M at Meeting House Fields yielded one and possibly two pipe fragments with SECC motifs (Saunders 2000a:73). Radiocarbon dates suggested that these were deposited in the contact period.

Cook and Pearson (1989:158–63) emphasize incised designs on pottery vessels as "our best sample of data for assessing aspects of chronology, cultural associations, and historical development of cult symbolism on the Georgia coast." No doubt if the semiotics of the individual symbols could be understood, along with the "grammar" of the combination of motifs, the vessels could be read as a text, providing keys to the cosmology, ideology, and power structure at that time. Elsewhere (Saunders 1992, 2000a), I have suggested that the filfot cross design stamped onto utilitarian vessels (and burial urns) on Irene and later Altamaha pottery was a symbol associated with southeastern cosmology. It was likely a variation of the "World Symbol," described by Hudson (1976:122) as the basic cosmological concept of the southeastern Indians. This symbol was virtually the only motif on Irene stamped wares. On the basis of a comparison of pottery attributes of the two components at Meeting House Fields, this motif, and most other stylistic attributes, persisted unchanged through the turbulent contact period. It is interesting, but at the moment inexplicable, that the motif becomes ubiquitous at the same time as the other documented social changes between the Savannah and Irene phases.

Summary

Using both archaeological and ethnohistoric information, we can develop a picture of the prehistoric and contact period Guale. Along with other southeastern groups, they were a hierarchically organized chiefdom with matrilineal descent. The elite received special treatment in life and in death, but power was limited. While the elite lived in ceremonial centers with mounds (and later, council houses), the bulk of the population was scattered along the marsh edge in sites typified, archaeologically at least, by discrete shell middens. The coastal environment provided a nutritious diet with an emphasis on estuarine resources and deer. Native plants, along with maize, also played a large role, though biased recovery in archaeological sites prevents a precise documentation of their contribution to the diet. This controversy may be resolved with more isotopic analysis of skeletal remains.

There appears to have been a fairly major reorganization of society, or at least of the elite, between what archaeologists have defined as the Savannah and Irene phases. This is reflected in changes in elite structures (platform mounds to council houses), burial practices, and maize consumption at the Irene site. In the coastal zone, maize consumption does not appear to have been affected, but intersite settlement patterning and the political structure became more dispersed. The timing of these reorganizations is consistent with similar changes throughout the Southeast and may ultimately be related to climate change. The Irene culture at contact was not as hierarchically organized as it was 250 years earlier, before the end of the Savannah phase. Nevertheless, there is demonstrable physical, social, and material continuity between the two phases (Caldwell and McCann 1941:69).

Mission Period Archaeology and Ethnohistory of the Guale

In Georgia, post-1600 mission period Guale manifestations have been divided into the Altamaha I and II phases by Caldwell (1971) and termed the Sutherland Bluff Complex by Larson (1978). In Florida, Guale occupations, which began at least as early as 1620 (see below), have been given the phase designation San Marcos. Space does not permit a recitation of the history of colonization and missionization of the Guale. In any event, excellent presentations are available in other sources, most recently Hann (1996) and Worth (1995). The story is taken up here after almost fifty years (1565–1600) of failed attempts at pacification of the Guale. After organized rebellions in 1576 and 1597, and devastating reprisals by the Spanish, Guale chiefs reluctantly accepted Spanish dominance in 1602. However, passive resistance to Spanish control continued throughout the mission period (Saunders 1998).

The following discussion concentrates on the Guale inside the mission system, both within original Guale territory and in Florida (after the contraction of Spanish territory to the boundaries of modern Florida in the 1680s). However, there were Guale in other situations. A number resided in St. Augustine as wives, concubines, and servants (Deagan 1983, 1990). The Tolomato, incendiaries in the aforementioned rebellions, were removed to a service town near St. Augustine in the 1620s. There they were "enserfed" to the presidio (Bushnell 1994:119). Even more Guale fled the area of effective Spanish control. As Jones (1978:208) noted, "The real history of the seventeenth-century Guale is actually not to be found on the island missions but rather in the interior pine forests to which they fled and regrouped."

Site Settlement and Social Hierarchies

The missionization of the Guale was begun after the Spanish had gained some forty years of experience in the pacification of the indigenous populations of the Caribbean and twenty to thirty years in parts of Latin America. In Guale, as elsewhere, pacification was accomplished by *reducción* (literally "reduction," though see Bushnell 1994:23), a process by which scattered populations were brought to settle in mission towns. (This process was not necessary in areas where aboriginal populations were already nucleated; see Deagan 1985:303; Hann 1988:28; Saunders 1990.) All were expected to live *bajo campana,* or "below the bell," no farther than half a league from the bell tower (Bushnell 1994:96). At present, however, archaeological surveys are inadequate, and we lack the necessary absolute or relative dating tools, to determine whether such a compact settlement system existed during the mission period.

It is clear, however, that compared to the site settlement patterns described above for the prehistoric and contact periods, mission period Guale settlement became increasingly centralized. Good data for this exists in the mission visitations periodically performed by the Spanish government. In the early 1680s, before the southward retreat, the province of Guale had six primary mission towns extending from the mouth of the Ogeechee River to the Altamaha River (Worth 1995:10). However, devastating population loss due to epidemic disease led to the amalgamation of one or more aboriginal towns into single mission villages both prior to and after this date (Worth 1995:15). With increasing population loss, these once-distinct mission settlements were also amalgamated (Worth 1995:10). For instance, Tupiqui was incorporated with Sapala and Satuache with Santa Catalina prior to 1675. All four groups were then amalgamated on Sapelo Island after the Chichimeco raid of 1680 (fig. 2.2). The intervillage hierarchical political system was destroyed (Milanich 1994:295). But chiefly lineages were retained, so that in the amalgamated missions there was "a curious collection of titular aboriginal leaders lacking actual roles as village headmen" (Worth 1995:10) in addition to the midlevel status positions that may have emerged in the Irene phase.

In spite of population aggregation and immigration of other groups such as the Yamassee, the territory covered by the Georgia missions steadily eroded. While many missions were originally established on the mainland, by the third quarter of the seventeenth century all had been removed to the barrier islands, on the (misguided) presumption that the islands were more defensible (see, for example, Worth 1995:fig. 1, appendix A). Then there was a series of convulsive moves to the south. In 1680 St. Catherines Island was abandoned after a second, devastating slave raid on Guale by the English-allied Chichimeco (Worth 1995:15–16, 30–31). The Santa Catalina Guale and Satuache settled on Sapelo Island alongside the Sapala and Tupiqui. The predations of the pirate Grammont on St. Augustine and Mocama missions in 1683 forced another southward movement. In 1684, the towns of Santa Catalina and Satuache were relocated to the Mission Santa Catalina on Amelia Island. As other groups prepared to relocate south, they were instead forced to the mainland by the appearance of more pirates (Worth 1995:40–41). The missions of Santo Domingo de Asajo and San Buenaventura de Guadalquini were burned. The Guale that remained were settled on Amelia Island, which had three aboriginal towns in 1685: Santa Catalina, San Felipe, and Santa Clara de Tupiqui. Governor James Moore's forces out of South Carolina attacked these settlements in 1702. The Guale made their last encampments around St. Augustine.

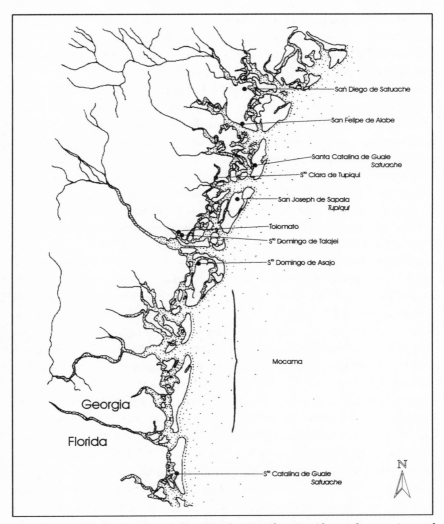

Fig. 2.2. Guale mission sites (after Worth 1995:fig. 2). Above the province of Mocama, the missions shown reflect the situation ca. 1675; Santa Catalina de Guale in Florida was established in 1684. Location of Tolomato is based on Worth (personal communication 1998).

Bushnell (1994:28) called the Florida mission "a fully functioning native town governed by an interlocking set of hereditary and elected native leaders ... accountable to the governor. ... While Christian Indians in the Southeast played an important part in supporting the Spanish friars, soldiers, and settlers, they did so with comparatively little change to their own material culture and political organization." Worth (1995:47) noted that "by the time the inhabitants of Guale and Mocama had been reduced to only a handful of refugee settlements, much of the traditional aboriginal hierarchy remained intact. ... Although the rapidity with which the settlement distribution of Guale and Mocama was transformed may have contributed to such continuity since many aboriginal leaders lived through the entire process, the maintenance of these chiefly lineages provides a remarkable example of the persistence of aboriginal culture in the face of the massive, and ultimately fatal, stresses of the European colonial era."

These arguments for continuity stress the endurance of forms, yet the content of Guale society had irrevocably changed. Many of the amalgamated mission *caciques* appear to have had no power whatsoever. Visitation documents indicate bickering between *caciques* in the same villages. Legitimate rulers appear to have had problems getting their subjects to obey and depended on Spanish support to retain control over their towns (see, for example, Worth 1995:72–73). *Caciques* played a part in supplying *repartimiento* labor to the crown, but many of their followers refused to comply. The passage of laws forbidding men to travel from village to village (Bushnell 1994:145) induces a vision of massive passive disaffection and dislocation (compare Worth 1995:30). Fugitivism was rampant.

Changes were not only political. The Spanish practice of isolating the young of the native elite for conversion—five were said to be living in the governor's house in St. Augustine in 1601 (Bushnell 1994:105)—resulted in "painful intergenerational conflicts" (Bushnell 1994:107). Analogizing the Florida situation to that of the Valley of Mexico, Bushnell (1994:107) suggested that "the retroactive monogamy imposed by Christian marriage turned many elite youths into bastards, ashamed of their mothers and angry with their fathers. Their new fathers, the padres, taught them to ridicule their pagan ancestors and heritage. Returning to their villages, the '*niños*' informed on their elders and went about in terrorist squads attacking pagan holy sites and images. ... They entered adult society drawing their importance from the new order and armed with the power to coerce." Closer to home, Fray Pareja (stationed at San Pedro de Mocama on Cumberland

Island, Georgia) noted in 1616 that "the younger generation which has been nourished on the milk of the gospel makes fun of and laughs at some old men and women who carelessly have recourse to these abuses (the aboriginal customs)" (Oré 1936:106).

Taken together, these data do not conjure a stable social and political situation. I submit that the sociopolitical system as described by the documents was in a transitional state and that many of the structures described were survivals rather than functioning units. Had the mission system survived, a very different sociopolitical structure would have necessarily evolved.

Villages and Daily Life

Certainly, just as settlement and sociopolitical patterns were changed, villages and village life were also altered. Some missions were founded in extant towns, but, after 1600, they were reestablished with security and transportation of goods as primary concerns. Nevertheless, some Guale mission period occupations can still be delimited by discrete middens. The Wamassee Head site (9LI13), presumably the native village site associated with Santa Catalina de Guale on St. Catherines Island, Georgia, contained a series of discrete shell middens (Brewer 1985:15). However, Larson (1978:132; Larson recorded Wamassee Head) noted a major shift in site characteristics from the late Irene (Pine Harbor) to the Sutherland Bluff complex (see also Braley et al. 1984:53–55). Instead of large, discrete shell middens, Sutherland Bluff sites had only scattered shell. Few systematic excavations have been undertaken in mission period Guale villages (as opposed to Spanish mission compounds), and fewer have been reported. The definition of intra-site structure and settlement types remains to be explicated for this phase. Yet at least for those Sutherland Bluff sites characterized by scattered shell, the implications for change in subsistence economy during this time are profound (see below).

Thomas (1993) summarized the archaeological information on aboriginal structures in Spanish contexts. If those uncovered by Larson (1953) were typical, rectangular configuration, wall trench structures continued to be made; individually set postholes disappeared. However, more interior partitions may have been built (Larson 1978:136), and the central fire pit apparently disappeared. Larson (1978:136) thought that larger, partitioned structures were attributable to native experiences in building churches and other Spanish structures. It is unclear why the central fire pit, probably used more for warmth than cooking, disappeared, unless it is a bleak indication of deforestation.

Settlement in the Spanish sphere obligated the neophyte population to labor for the Spanish. This labor took two forms. There was compulsory labor at the mission itself, organized as the *sabana* system, and labor for the presidio, organized in the *repartimiento* system. According to Bushnell (1994:111), the former was the native institution for public finance that was co-opted by the Spanish friars. Traditionally, *sabanas* were fields planted by commoners for the use of principal persons and to provide for reserves against famine or for warfare. Within the mission system, the harvest of an additional *sabana* was used to sustain the ministers, to help cover the costs of maintenance and repair for churches, and to buy ornaments and other things necessary for divine worship (Bushnell 1994:111). These fields were overseen by the resident friar, the *caciques,* and, in times of unrest, the military official assigned to the particular mission province (see Bushnell 1994:148–60). In addition to digging the *sabana,* men were required to act as "friars' boatmen, burdeners, guides, bodyguards, and couriers. They hunted and fished, returning with food for the convent kitchen as well as their families. They . . . went to the woods for charcoal or the timbers for buildings and fences. Women, for reasons of security, child care, and propriety, did most of the work in or near the town. With the help of the larger children, they collected the firewood, shelled and ground the maize, and gathered and processed the cassina, nuts, and oysters. They cleaned the church and its grounds. They planted and hoed the sabanas and gardens" (Bushnell 1994:112).

For the secular government, labor was organized in the *repartimiento* system, which replaced the *encomienda* system used in earlier colonization attempts in the Caribbean and Latin America. In the *repartimiento* system direct, long-term grants of native labor were eliminated and tribute was not paid to individuals. "Under the new and revised repartimiento administered by royal officials instead of private individuals, village authorities sent quotas of laborers in rotation to construct public works or perform other activities for the general welfare. They worked under regulated conditions and for a token *jornal* of one *real* a day" (Bushnell 1994:121, 122; see also McAlister 1984:211). This was paid in its equivalent in trade goods (Bushnell 1994: 122).

The number of laborers selected was based on a census provided by the friars. Those chosen were "escorted by soldiers, interpreters, and their own principales to St. Augustine or wherever else they were needed" (Bushnell 1994:122). Required labor included the cultivation of crops that supported the Spanish military and civilian population of St. Augustine and the construction of mission buildings, secular structures, and fortifications. The Guale were also required to keep a ferry service running between the barrier island missions and St. Augustine. The trip required one arduous ten- to twelve-league portage from San Pablo Creek to Tolomato. (Apparently there was a north-south road [Bushnell 1994:113–14]), but travel by canoe was preferred.)

Beyond the labor requirements, the daily lives of missionized Guale are difficult to reconstruct. No systematic recounting is known in the ethnohistoric records (Bushnell 1994:97, 102). According to Bushnell (1994:96), church instruction was most intense in the early conversions, where adults were expected to attend daily classes in Catholicism. She speculated that such demands, even at three days a week, left little opportunity to engage in either subsistence pursuits or social obligations. "Experience showed that when adult indoctrination was instituted on this demanding a scale without enlisting the cooperation of caciques and distributing gifts of food and clothing, attendance was ragged and half-converted people came and went" (Bushnell 1994:96). As adults matured in the system and children were born into it, the process was less intense and more participation in the *sabana* system was required.

Despite the attempts at rigorous indoctrination, labor demands and perceptions of unfair treatment by Spanish soldiers or other officials in matters of trade created resentment among the Guale. Many fled the system (Bushnell 1990, 1994; Saunders 1998). The Franciscans' devotion to discipline—whipping (Bushnell 1994:96) and pillorying (Weber 1992:113) were apparently common punishments for disobedience and often applied indiscriminately to commoners and chiefs alike—also created fugitives (Bushnell 1994:96; Saunders 1998; Weber 1992). In addition, many documents of the period allude to repeated assaults on the populations by epidemic disease (Larsen 1990:18–19). In addition, beginning as early as 1661 (Worth 1995:15), the Guale suffered attacks on the missions by other Native American groups, acting either independently or under the prompting of the English, and by pirates (see Worth 1995). It became clear to many Guale that neither the secular nor the sacred Spanish rulers could protect them. Individuals or whole families abandoned the missions to live with relatives in the unconverted interior and to gain access to English guns and other trade goods.

Subsistence and Health

While little information is presently available from Guale mission period villages, more or less direct evidence of individual and societal welfare is available from mission period cemeteries. However, the archaeological data available are inadequate to convey a total picture of the health of the Guale during the mission period. In particular, epidemics, by far the most devastating result of contact, generally do not involve the skeleton, and so direct evidence of epidemics is lacking (Ramenofsky and Galloway 1998:260). Other, more indirect, evidence of epidemics (the presence of mass burials, changes in demographic profiles, and so forth) may indicate increased mortality (see, for example, Larsen 1990), but the problem of equifinality arises in attempting to correlate such changes with disease.

Documents tell a different story. Correspondence of friars and secular officials indicates continued heavy population loss due to disease throughout the mission period. Indeed, populations in Guale fell so low that the Spanish allowed the Yamassee (a historic period aggregation of diverse interior and coastal peoples [Worth 1995:20]) to settle in unconverted towns under Spanish protection. By 1665 Yamassee villages provided more personnel for *repartimiento* labor than the Guale (Worth 1995:21). Curiously, without documentation it is not possible to distinguish Yamassee towns from those of the Guale. The mission period pottery of the two groups, at least in Florida, is identical at the type level. In any event, most Yamassee villages were abandoned in 1683, apparently in response to a raid on two Yamassee villages by the pirate Grammont (Worth 1995:37).

While the archaeological record of disease is elusive, bioanthropological analysis of mission period populations has confirmed narrative accounts of the labor demands on the Native Americans and shed new light on other aspects of lifeways at this time. Stable isotope analysis (Schoeninger et al. 1990) on bone from Guale mission period cemeteries indicated that the range of foods in the diet decreased, with more emphasis on maize and less on marine resources than in late prehistory. These data dovetail nicely with Larson's observations on quantity of shell at Sutherland Bluff complex sites. The decrease in nutritional quality led to an increase in caries, enamel hypoplasias, and iron-deficiency anemia. Data on bone strength, indicated by bone geometry, revealed that "relative to the Precontact Agricultural period, some males became more mobile (although on average they were less mobile) while females continued to decline in mobility" (Larsen et al. 1996: 110). This is consistent with the use of some male commoners as burden bearers. Circularity measurements on femora and humerii indicated less overall mobility but more mechanical demand on the humerus, perhaps due to subsistence activities or other labors demanded by the Spanish.

Despite disease and labor demands, some evidence indicates a population rebound in the late mission period Guale in Florida. Among the individuals interred at Santa Catalina de Guale on Amelia Island, survivorship may have increased over precontact agricultural populations. However, the same data could be interpreted as a reduction in fertility, which would indicate a population undergoing decline (Russell et al. 1990:49). Documentary evidence would suggest the latter. Larsen and others (1990:418) also noted a possible decrease in birthrate and an increase in mortality.

Crafts and Cosmology

Despite the odds, a number of researchers have been impressed with the coherency of Guale identifiers through time, particularly in pottery style. There was an abrupt change in certain attributes of Irene pottery around 1600 (Saunders 1992, 2000a). However, Altamaha and later San Marcos wares are recognizable as derivatives of Irene wares. Deagan (1990:307) noted that Guale pottery in St. Augustine demonstrated that "traditional Amerindian crafts persisted in a largely unaltered form through the entire colonial period." In my own research, I demonstrated that the relative frequency of different rim treatments and elaboration of Irene and Altamaha/San Marcos pottery types remained constant from the Irene phase to the end of the mission period (Saunders 1992, 2000a)—a result I find astonishing. The data support an extremely stable craft environment despite sociocultural upheaval in the mission period (and despite different sampling strategies at different sites). Indeed, two decorative techniques usually considered indicative of early Irene sites appeared at the Florida incarnation of Santa Catalina de Guale, where there was no local precedent.

However, two relatively dramatic changes were apparent in the ceramic assemblage at the 1684–1702 Florida Santa Catalina. Incised designs comprised 6.6 percent of the late Meeting House Fields (contact period) assemblage and 6.1 percent of the later (1602–84) proveniences at Santa Catalina de Guale in Georgia. When the Guale, along with the Satuache, were relocated to Florida, incising declined almost to the point of disappearance—to 1 percent in all site contexts. In addition, while the filfot cross, or a rectilinear equivalent, continued to be made at the Georgia mission in approximately the same quantities as at the Meeting House Fields site (the motif was recognized by the central dot on sherds in approximately 7 percent of the sherds at Meeting House Fields and 5 percent of the assemblages at the Georgia mission), in the Florida mission, only 2 percent of the sherds bore the World Symbol. These data indicate that whatever motives originally compelled the Guale to replicate their cosmological concepts on pottery had attenuated to a considerable degree. Nevertheless, the pottery continued to be recognizably Guale, suggesting the continuation of a social identity despite population loss, amalgamation, and relocation (Saunders 2001).

The Last of the Guale

These conditions continued after Moore's raid on the eastern mission system in 1702 (Arnade 1959). After the raid, which destroyed all the coastal missions, Native American populations were relocated around St. Augustine. The Spanish continued to record their presence by social group (see Hann 1996:296–325). There were a total of 189 Guale in two villages in 1711; 39 in a single village in 1718; and 187 in three villages in 1726. Just 34 adult individuals, and no children, were recorded in the single Guale village noted in 1728; and in three separate censuses in 1738 there were between 64 and 30 Guale recorded. There are no other data until 1752, when 12 men, 14 women, and no children, were recorded at the Guale village of Tolomato. In 1759, when the six settlements were consolidated into two, there were 10 Guale at Nombre de Dios and 6 at Tolomato. If any were still living in 1763, when the Spanish passed control of the colony to the English, the remaining Guale sailed for Cuba with the Spanish, leaving behind a tantalizing but incomplete record of themselves for us to decipher.

Bibliography

Adair, James
1930 [1775]   *The History of the American Indians.* New York: Promontory Press.
Alexander, Michael (editor)
1976   *Discovering the New World: Based on the Works of Theodore De Bry.* New York: Harper and Row.
Anderson, David G.
1989   The Mississippian in South Carolina. In *The Archaeology of South Carolina: Papers in Honor of Robert L. Stephenson,* edited by A. C. Goodyear III and G. T. Hanson, 101–32. Anthropological Studies no. 9. South Carolina Institute of Archaeology and Anthropology, University of South Carolina, Columbia.
1994   *The Savannah River Chiefdoms: Political Change in the Late Prehistoric Southeast.* Tuscaloosa: University of Alabama Press.
Arnade, Charles W.
1959   *The Siege of St. Augustine in 1702.* Gainesville: University of Florida Press.
Axtell, James
1988   Through Another Glass Darkly: Early Indian Views of Europeans. In *After Columbus: Essays in the Ethnohistory of Colonial North America,* 125–43. New York: Oxford University Press.
Barcía, Andrés Gonzáles
1951   *Barcía's Chronological History of the Continent of Florida.* Translated with an introduction by A. Kerrigan. Gainesville: University of Florida Press.
Braley, Chad O.
1990   The Lamar Ceramics of the Georgia Coast. In *Lamar Archaeology: Mississippian Chiefdoms in the Deep South,* edited by M. Williams and G. Shapiro, 94–103. Tuscaloosa: University of Alabama Press.
Braley, Chad O., Lisa D. O'Steen, and Irvy R. Quitmyer
1984   *Archaeological Investigations at 9McI41, Harris Neck National Wildlife Refuge, McIntosh County, Georgia.* Southeastern Archaeological Services, Athens, Ga.
1986   *Archaeological Investigations at 9McI41, Harris Neck National Wildlife Refuge, McIntosh County, Georgia.* Southeastern Archaeological Services, Athens, Ga.
Brewer, Mary A.
1985   Pottery from Wamassee Head. *Early Georgia* 13 (1–2):15–28.
Bushnell, Amy
1990   The Sacramental Imperative: Catholic Ritual and Indian Sedentism in the Provinces of Florida. In *Columbian Consequences,* vol. 2, *Archaeological and Historical Perspectives on the Spanish Borderlands East,* edited by D. H. Thomas, 475–90. Washington D.C.: Smithsonian Institution Press.
1994   *Situado and Sabana: Spain's Support System for the Presidio and Mission Provinces of Florida.* Anthropological Papers no. 74. American Museum of Natural History, New York.

52   Rebecca Saunders

Caldwell, J. R.
1971   Chronology of the Georgia Coast. *Southeastern Archaeological Conference Bulletin* 13:88–92.
Caldwell, J. R., and C. McCann
1941   *Irene Mound Site, Chatham County, Georgia.* Athens: University of Georgia Press.
Cook, Fred C., and Charles E. Pearson
1989   The Southeastern Ceremonial Complex on the Georgia Coast. In *The Southeastern Ceremonial Complex: Artifacts and Analysis,* edited by P. Galloway, 147–65. Lincoln: University of Nebraska Press.
Crook, Morgan R.
1984   Irene Manifestations on Sapelo Island. *Early Georgia* 12 (1–2):59–63.
1986   *Mississippi Period Archaeology of the Georgia Coastal Zone.* Laboratory of Archaeology Series Report no. 23. Georgia Archaeological Research Design Papers no. 1. University of Georgia, Athens.
Deagan, Kathleen
1983   *Spanish St. Augustine: The Archaeology of a Colonial Creole Community.* New York: Academic Press.
1985   Spanish-Indian Interaction in Sixteenth-Century Florida and the Caribbean. In *Cultures in Contact: The European Impact on Native Cultural Institutions in Eastern North America, a.d. 1000–1800,* edited by W. W. Fitzhugh, 281–318. Washington, D.C.: Smithsonian Institution Press.
1990   Accommodation and Resistance: The Process and Impact of Spanish Colonization in the Southeast. In *Columbian Consequences,* vol. 2, *Archaeological and Historical Perspectives on the Spanish Borderlands East,* edited by D. H. Thomas, 297–314. Washington, D.C.: Smithsonian Institution Press.
DePratter, Chester B.
1984   Irene Manifestations on the Northern Georgia Coast. *Early Georgia* 12 (1–2):44–58.
DePratter, Chester B., and J. D. Howard
1980   Indian Occupation and Geologic History of the Georgia Coast: A 5,000-Year Summary. In *Excursions in Southeastern Geology: The Archaeology-Geology of the Georgia Coast,* edited by J. D. Howard, C. B. DePratter, and R. W. Frey, 1–65. Geological Society of America, Guidebook 20. Georgia Department of Natural Resources, Atlanta.
Dukes, Joel A.
1993   Change in Vertebrate Use between the Irene Phase and the Seventeenth Century on St. Catherines Island, Georgia. Master's thesis, Department of Anthropology, University of Georgia, Athens.
Hann, John H.
1988   *Apalachee: The Land between the Rivers.* Gainesville: University Presses of Florida.
1992   Political Leadership among the Natives of Spanish Florida. *Florida Historical Quarterly* 71 (2):188–208.
1996   *A History of the Timucua Indians and Missions.* Gainesville: University Press of Florida.

Hoffman, Paul
1990   A New Andalucia and a Way to the Orient: The American Southeast during the Sixteenth Century. Baton Rouge: Louisiana State University Press.
Holland, Thomas D., and Michael J. O'Brien
1997   Parasites, Porotic Hyperostosis, and the Implications of Changing Perspectives. American Antiquity 62 (2):183–93.
Hudson, Charles
1976   The Southeastern Indians. Knoxville: University of Tennessee Press.
Hulse, Frederick S.
1941   Physical Anthropology. In Irene Mound Site, Chatham County, Georgia, by J. Caldwell and C. McCann, 57–68. Athens: University of Georgia Press.
Hutchinson, Dale L., Clark Spencer Larsen, Margaret J. Schoeninger, and Lynette Norr
1998   Regional Variation in the Pattern of Maize Adoption and Use in Florida and Georgia. American Antiquity 63 (3):397–416.
Jones, Grant D.
1978   The Ethnohistory of the Guale Coast through 1684. In The Anthropology of St. Catherines Island 1: Natural and Cultural History, by D. H. Thomas, G. D. Jones, and R. S. Durham, 178–209. Anthropological Papers, vol. 55, pt. 2. American Museum of Natural History, New York.
Larsen, Clark Spencer
1987   Bioarchaeological Interpretations of Subsistence Economy and Behavior from Human Skeletal Remains. In Advances in Archaeological Method and Theory, vol. 10, edited by M. B. Schiffer, 339–445. San Diego: Academic Press.
1990   Biological Interpretation and the Context for Contact. In The Archaeology of Mission Santa Catalina de Guale, vol. 2, Biocultural Interpretations of a Population in Transition, edited by C. S. Larsen, 11–25. Anthropological Papers no. 68. American Museum of Natural History, New York.
Larsen, Clark Spencer, Christopher B. Ruff, and Mark C. Griffin
1996   Implications of Changing Biomechanical and Nutritional Environments for Activity and Lifeway in the Eastern Spanish Borderlands. In Bioarchaeology of Native American Adaptation in the Spanish Borderlands, edited by B. J. Baker and L. Kealhofer, 95–125. Gainesville: University Press of Florida.
Larsen, Clark Spencer, Margaret J. Schoeninger, Dale L. Hutchinson, Katherine F. Russell, and Christopher B. Ruff
1990   Beyond Demographic Collapse: Biological Adaptation and Change in Native Populations of La Florida. In Columbian Consequences, vol. 2, Archaeological and Historical Perspectives on the Spanish Borderlands East, edited by D. H. Thomas, 409–28. Washington, D.C.: Smithsonian Institution Press.
Larsen, Clark Spencer, Margaret J. Schoeninger, Nikolaas J. van der Merwe, Katherine M. Moore, and Julia A. Lee-Thorpe
1992   Carbon and Nitrogen Stable Isotopic Signatures of Human Dietary Change in the Georgia Bight. American Journal of Physical Anthropology 89:197–214.
Larson, Lewis H.
1953   Coastal Mission Survey. Manuscript on file, Georgia Historical Commission, Atlanta.
1978   Historic Guale Indians of the Georgia Coast and the Impact of the Spanish Mission Effort. In Tacachale: Essays on the Indians of Florida and Southeast-

54   Rebecca Saunders

ern Georgia during the Historic Period, edited by J. T. Milanich and S. Proctor, 120–40. Gainesville: University Presses of Florida.

1980   Aboriginal Subsistence Technology on the Southeastern Coastal Plain during the Late Prehistoric Period. Gainesville: University Presses of Florida.

1984a   Introduction. Early Georgia 12 (1–2):41–43.

1984b   Irene Manifestations in the McIntosh County Tidewater Area. Early Georgia 12 (1–2):64–70.

Laudonnière, René

1975 [1586]   Three Voyages. Translated by C. Bennett. Gainesville: University of Florida Press.

McAlister, Lyle N.

1984   Spain and Portugal in the New World, 1492–1700. Minneapolis: University of Minnesota Press.

Milanich, Jerald T.

1994   Franciscan Missions and the Native Peoples in Spanish Florida. In The Forgotten Centuries: Indians and Europeans in the American South, 1521–1704, edited by C. Hudson and C. Tesser, 276–303. Athens: University of Georgia Press.

Oré, Luis Geronimo de

1936   The Martyrs of Florida (1513–1616). Translated and edited by M. Geiger. Franciscan Studies no. 18. New York: Joseph W. Wagner.

Ortner, D. J., and W. G. J. Putschar

1985   Identification of Pathological Conditions in Human Skeletal Remains. Smithsonian Contributions to Anthropology no. 28. Washington, D.C.

Oviedo y Valdés, Gonzalo Fernández de

1959   Historia General y Natural de las Indias (General and Natural History of the Indies). Madrid: Biblioteca de Autores Españoles.

Pearson, Charles E.

1977   Analysis of Late Prehistoric Settlement on Ossabaw Island, Georgia. Laboratory of Archaeology Series no. 12. University of Georgia, Athens.

1978   Analysis of Late Mississippian Settlement Patterns on Ossabaw Island, Georgia. In Mississippian Settlement Patterns, edited by B. D. Smith, 53–80. New York: Academic Press.

1979   Patterns of Mississippian Period Adaptation in Coastal Georgia. Ph.D. diss., Department of Anthropology, University of Georgia, Athens.

1980   Late Prehistoric Settlement Systems on Ossabaw Island, Georgia. In Excursions in Southeastern Geology: The Archaeology-Geology of the Georgia Coast, edited by J. D. Howard, C. B. DePratter, and R. W. Frey, 179–91. Guidebook 20. Department of Natural Resources, Atlanta.

1984   Red Bird Creek: Late Prehistoric Material Culture and Subsistence in Coastal Georgia. Early Georgia 12 (1–2):1–40.

Powell, Mary Lucas

1990   On the Eve of Conquest: Life and Death at Irene Mound, Georgia. In The Archaeology of Mission Santa Catalina de Guale, vol. 2, Biocultural Interpretations of a Population in Transition, edited by C. S. Larsen, 26–35. Anthropological Papers no. 68. American Museum of Natural History, New York.

Ramenofsky, Ann F., and Patricia Galloway
1998   Disease and the Soto Entrada. In *The Hernando de Soto Expedition: History, Historiography, and "Discovery" in the Southeast*, edited by P. Galloway, 259–79. Lincoln: University of Nebraska Press.

Reitz, Elizabeth J.
1982   Vertebrate Fauna from Four Coastal Mississippian Sites. *Journal of Ethnobiology* 2(1):39–61.

Russell, Katherine F., Inui Choi, and Clark S. Larsen
1990   The Paleodemography of Santa Catalina de Guale. In *The Archaeology of Mission Santa Catalina de Guale*, vol. 2, *Biocultural Interpretations of a Population in Transition*, edited by C. S. Larsen, 36–49. Anthropological Papers no. 68. American Museum of Natural History, New York.

Russo, Michael A.
1991   A Method for the Measurement of Season and Duration of Oyster Collection: Two Case Studies from the Prehistoric Southeast U.S. Coast. *Journal of Archaeological Science* 18:205–21.

Russo, Michael A., and Rebecca Saunders
n.d.   Season of Mollusk Consumption at Meeting House Fields. In *Meeting House Fields: Irene Phase Material Culture and Seasonality of St. Catherines Island*, by R. Saunders and M. Russo, 56–75. Manuscript on file, American Museum of Natural History, New York.

Saunders, Rebecca
1990   Ideal and Innovation: Spanish Mission Architecture in the Southeast. In *Columbian Consequences*, vol. 2, *Archaeological and Historical Perspectives on the Spanish Borderlands East*, edited by D. H. Thomas, 527–42. Washington, D.C.: Smithsonian Institution Press.
1992   Guale Indian Pottery: A Georgia Legacy in Northeast Florida. *Florida Anthropologist* 45(2):139–47.
1998   Forced Relocation, Power Relations, and Culture Contact in the Missions of La Florida. In *Studies in Culture Contact: Interaction, Culture Change, and Archaeology*, edited by J. G. Cusick, 402–29. Center for Archaeological Investigations, Occasional Paper no. 25. Southern Illinois University, Carbondale.
2000a   *Continuity and Change: Guale Indian Pottery, a.d. 1350–1702*. Tuscaloosa: University of Alabama Press.
2000b   Seasonality, Sedentism, Subsistence, and Disease in the Protohistoric: Archaeological vs. Ethnohistoric Data along the Lower Atlantic Coast. In *Protohistory and Archaeology: Advances in Interdisciplinary Research*, edited by C. B. Wesson and M. A. Rees, in press. Tuscaloosa: University of Alabama Press.
2001   Negotiated Tradition? Native American Pottery in *La Florida*. In *Practicing Traditions: An Archaeology of Historical Processes before and after Columbus*, edited by T. R. Pauketat. Gainesville: University Press of Florida, in press.

Schoeninger, M. J., N. J. van der Merwe, K. Moore, J. Lee-Thorpe, and C. S. Larsen
1990   Decrease in Diet Quality between the Prehistoric and Contact Periods on St. Catherines Island, Georgia. In *The Archaeology of Mission Santa Catalina de*

Guale, vol. 2, *Biocultural Interpretations of a Population in Transition*, edited by C. S. Larsen, 78–93. Anthropological Papers no. 68. American Museum of Natural History, New York.

Silver, Timothy
1990   *A New Face on the Countryside: Indians, Colonists, and Slaves in the South Atlantic Forests, 1500–1800*. Cambridge: Cambridge University Press.

Smith, Robin L.
1984   Irene Manifestations from the Altamaha River to the St. Marys River. *Early Georgia* 12(1–2):71–77.

Stahle, David W., Malcolm K. Cleaveland, Dennis B. Blanton, Matthew D. Therrell, and David A. Gay
1998   The Lost Colony and Jamestown Droughts. *Science* 280:564–67.

Steinbock, Robert T.
1976   *Paleopathological Diagnosis and Interpretation*. Springfield: C. C. Thomas.

Thomas, David Hurst
1993   *Historical Indian Period Archaeology of the Georgia Coastal Zone*. Georgia Archaeological Research Design Paper no. 8, Laboratory of Archaeology Series Report no. 31. University of Georgia, Athens.

Weber, David
1992   *The Spanish Frontier in North America*. New Haven: Yale University Press.

Williams, Mark, and Gary Shapiro
1990   Paired Towns. In *Lamar Archaeology: Mississippian Chiefdoms in the Deep South*, edited by M. Williams and G. Shapiro, 163–74. Tuscaloosa: University of Alabama Press.

Worth, John E.
1995   *The Struggle for the Georgia Coast: An Eighteenth-Century Spanish Retrospective on Guale and Mocama*. Anthropological Papers no. 75. American Museum of Natural History, New York.

3

The Apalachee Indians of Northwest Florida

Bonnie G. McEwan

The Apalachee Indians first encountered by Europeans are believed to be the lineal descendants of the late prehistoric peoples who inhabited the region. They occupied a territory in the Florida panhandle bounded by the Ochlockonee and Aucilla Rivers, approximately 30 miles east to west (fig. 3.1). The northern border of the province is believed to have corresponded roughly with the modern Florida-Georgia state line, while its southern boundary was formed by the Gulf of Mexico. Despite its limited areal extent, Apalachee province contained a number of microenvironments, including fertile hills and lowlands, lakes, estuaries, coastline, and woodlands that were conducive to intensive agriculture, hunting, fishing, and gathering.

The genesis of the historic period in Apalachee Province can be dated to 1519, when Alonso Álvarez de Pineda sailed along its southern coast. Within twenty years, Apalachee would become a greatly sought-after destination for two major Spanish *entradas* and ultimately the focus of an intensive missionization effort that would irrevocably change the cultural landscape of Florida.

There are few native groups within Spanish Florida whose initial and sustained interaction with Europeans has been so well documented or the subject of such intense archaeological interest as the Apalachees. However, despite this attention, the actual number of extensive archaeological investigations is quite limited. Much of this research has focused on the three paramount centers or capitals of Lake Jackson, Anhaica, and San Luis (fig. 3.2), which form a chronological and cultural continuum of at least six centuries, from A.D. 1100 to A.D. 1700 (Ewen and Hann 1998; Hann 1988a; Hann and McEwan 1998; Payne 1994a; Scarry 1996). The occupation of these capitals corresponds roughly with the late prehistoric, protohistoric,

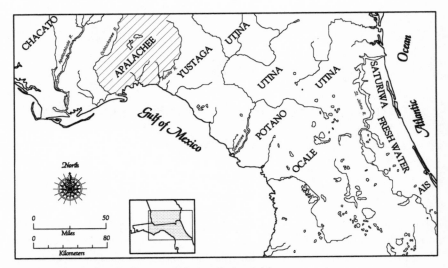

Fig. 3.1. Apalachee Indians and their tribal neighbors.

and historic (or mission) periods. They are also referred to as the following archaeological phases: Lake Jackson (A.D. 1100–1500), Velda (A.D. 1500–1633), and San Luis (A.D. 1633–1704) (Scarry 1996:195–212). The Apalachees of the historic period can be defined by the two later phases, which represent distinct episodes of contact: Spanish exploration and missionization.

Late Prehistoric Period

Located on the periphery of the Mississippian world, the late prehistoric Apalachees shared many traits with the other Mississippian societies of the interior Southeast including intensive maize agriculture, hierarchically structured sociopolitical organization, participation in an extensive exchange network, a fundamentally similar belief system, and a stratified settlement pattern (Brose and Percy 1978; Griffin 1985:63; Peebles and Kus 1977). It is believed that the Apalachees spoke a Muskogean language, probably a dialect of Hitchiti (Haas 1949; Kimball 1987, 1988). The Apalachees were politically distinct, had a different language, and had cult institutions and material culture that distinguished them from the Timucuans to the east (see Milanich, this volume; also Hann 1996a; Milanich 1996; Worth 1998a, 1998b).

The Mississippian capital of Apalachee province was located at Lake Jackson. A complex of seven earthen mounds, the site is believed to be the ceremonial center of an extensive network of highly dispersed outlying settlements (Bryne 1986; Marrinan and Bryne 1986; Smith and Scarry 1988), including single mound centers, farmsteads, and hamlets (Payne 1994a; Scarry 1990, 1996; Scarry and McEwan 1995). Following initial testing at Lake Jackson by Gordon Willey and Richard Woodbury during the summer of 1940 (Willey 1949), a number of researchers have conducted limited amounts of work at the site (see Payne 1994b for an overview of research at Lake Jackson). However, most of what we know about the late prehistoric Apalachee chiefdom has been derived from the fieldwork of John W. Griffin (1950), B. Calvin Jones (1982, 1991, 1994), and Claudine Payne (1994b), as well as subsequent analysis and interpretation by John F. Scarry (1985, 1990, 1996). Other Lake Jackson phase sites and features (see, for example, Fryman 1969; Jones 1990; Jones and Penman 1973; Marrinan

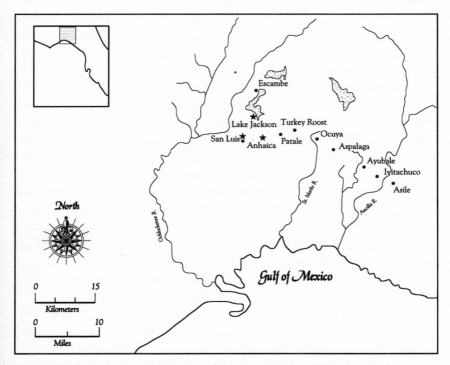

Fig. 3.2. Prehistoric, protohistoric, and mission period Apalachee capitals (★) and mission sites (•) located to date.

1993; Marrinan and Bryne 1986; Tesar 1980) have revealed provocative, albeit limited, data on burial practices, settlement, architecture, and ceramic traditions.

While both Griffin's and Payne's work at Lake Jackson focused primarily on the village area associated with the ceremonial center, Jones's excavations at Mound 3 resulted in the recovery of twenty-five burials associated with eight of twelve structural phases (Jones 1991:3). The orientation (heads to the northwest, northeast, southwest, and southeast) and positioning of individuals, ranging from fully extended to flexed, varied widely throughout the mound (Jones 1982:11, 36). Mortuary items associated with the interments included pottery vessels, copper and stone axes, copper inlaid bone hairpins, engraved shell gorgets, clay and steatite pipes, a galena necklace, shell beads and pendants, repoussé copper breastplates, and pearl beads (Jones 1982:12–13). The placement and regalia associated with many of the male burials indicates that they were likely high-status individuals who held positions of authority. Scarry (1996:200) suggested that specific artifact associations may signify two distinct social roles. He proposed that the highest-ranking individuals may be associated with symbolic items, while men who held lesser offices or roles may be those who were interred with weapons.

Two females and one child were also identified from Mound 3. It has been hypothesized that these individuals also held positions of authority sufficient to warrant burial with artifacts recognized as status markers and interment in the mound (Scarry 1996:200). However, it is also possible that the two women were spouses, servants, retainers, or others who chose or were selected to accompany the deceased into the afterlife (Hann 1993:99; Hudson 1976:328–29). There is no evidence that women ever attained chieftainships in Apalachee, at least during the post-1500 period for which we have documentation. And while the child may have been a member of a ruling lineage, the burial may represent a human sacrifice. During the mission period, at least some south Florida natives offered their children for sacrifice and burial with leaders in order to gain status (Villareal 1568; see also Hann 1991, 1998; John Hann, personal communication 1998).

There has been extensive speculation about the decline of the late prehistoric Apalachee chiefdom and the abandonment of the Lake Jackson mound center, citing both internal and external variables. John Scarry (1990:183) suggested that the cessation of mound construction, linked to the reallocation of labor, resulted from the replacement of one ruling faction by another.

Also, with the fall of major Mississippian centers such as Etowah in northwest Georgia, the Apalachee polity of the Lake Jackson phase lost critical
links to sources of prestige goods (Hally and Rudolph 1986:63–78; Payne
1994a:309; Scarry 1996:226–27). Shifting alliances in Apalachee province
are also indicated by the appearance of Lamar-tradition pottery characteristic of the Georgia Piedmont, reflecting a change in extraregional trade
networks (Scarry 1985:221–22, 1996:203–7) and, perhaps, migration from
the Chatahoochee Valley (Braley 1998; see also Worth, this volume).

Protohistoric Period

During the same year that Álvarez de Pineda explored Apalachees' coast
(1519), Hernán Cortés mounted his successful campaign against the Aztecs
(Díaz 1963; López de Gómara 1966[1552]) and Panama was founded, providing Spaniards with a Pacific base. From Panama, Pizarro launched his
attack against the Incas in 1531. Accompanied by a small force that included
Hernando de Soto, the Incas were conquered in less than two years. The
rapid fall of the two great native empires emboldened the Spaniards to
extend their domain throughout much of the Western Hemisphere.

To some extent, the Apalachees may have been victims of their own
success. They were apparently well known among other Florida natives as
a wealthy and fierce people. When the Pánfilo de Narváez expedition landed
near Tampa Bay in 1528 (Milanich and Hudson 1993:23), they were convinced by the natives of that area to travel to Apalachee. It has been suggested
that the natives of the Tampa Bay region encouraged the Spaniards to go
north not so much to accommodate the explorers' desire for riches, but to
rid themselves of the European intruders (Mitchem 1990a:52).

The account of Álvar Núñez Cabeza de Vaca, one of the four survivors of
the Narváez expedition, provides some insight into native perceptions of
Apalachee Province: "And he showed them a little bit of gold, and they said
there was none in that land, but only far from there, in the province that they
call Apalache, in which there was much gold in great quantity according to
what they gave [us] to understand by their signs. And everything whatsoever
that they showed to those Indians that it seemed to them [the Indians] that
the Christians held in value, they said there was much of that in Apalache"
(Hann 1996b:13).

The Narváez *entrada* reached Apalachee in June of 1528. The men spent
twenty-six days in the province, during which time they were repeatedly

attacked, prompting them to flee. The men and their horses made their way toward the coast and stayed at the village of Aute, which is believed to be near St. Marks. The most promising candidate for a site associated with the Narváez expedition is the St. Marks Wildlife Refuge Cemetery site, based on its distinctive assemblage of sixteenth-century remains including Nueva Cadiz beads and Clarksdale bells (Marrinan et al. 1990; Mitchem 1988). In Aute, Narváez and a number of his men became ill and eventually resorted to eating their horses for nourishment while continuing to suffer at the hands of Apalachee warriors. The surviving Spaniards fled Apalachee in makeshift boats constructed at Aute by sailing west along the Gulf coast, but most were lost at sea or en route to New Spain overland.

Although tales of gold proved to be apocryphal, wealth in the form of stored foodstuffs was first chronicled by Spaniards at this time. Armed with the information gleaned from the Narváez *entrada,* Hernando de Soto left Cuba for Spanish Florida on May 18, 1539 (Hoffman 1990:91). De Soto was better prepared than his predecessor, with more soldiers, meat "on the hoof" in the form of hogs, and plans to be reprovisioned en route.

There are four complete accounts of the de Soto *entrada,* written by Rodrigo Ranjel (sometimes rendered "Rangel"), Luis Hernández de Biedma, the "Gentleman of Elvas," and Garcilaso de la Vega. Each of these has been translated and analyzed in depth (Bourne 1904; Clayton et al. 1993; Ewen and Hann 1998; Galloway 1998; Milanich and Hudson 1993). The accounts of Rodrigo Ranjel, de Soto's secretary on the expedition, and the Gentleman of Elvas (whose identity has never been established) are believed to be the most accurate and useful sources, while that of Garcilaso de la Vega, which drew on the recollections of survivors decades after the expedition, is the least reliable.

These narratives provide a fascinating glimpse of the province during the five-month period in 1539–40 when de Soto and his army wintered in Apalachee. The province was described as having widely dispersed villages, only three of which were actually named by the de Soto chroniclers: Ochete, Ivitachuco, and Anhaica (also rendered Anhayca and Jinayca). The village of Anhaica was described as being the principal village, although it is believed that Apalachee at this time had eastern and western capitals. It was ruled by dual chiefs, a peace chief (Ivitachuco) and a war chief (Anhaica), who may have been related (Hann 1988a:100). During de Soto's encampment in Apalachee, it is likely that the war chief who resided at Anhaica enjoyed supremacy and thus his village was recognized by the chroniclers as the capital.

De Soto and his men remained under almost constant attack from warriors: "And they wintered there and remained until the fourth of March of the year one thousand and five hundred and forty, in which time many notable things happened with the Indians, who are the bravest of men. And from what will be said now the discerning reader will be able to conjecture their great spirits and daring. Two Indians challenged eight horsemen and they burned the settlement on two occasions and they killed many Christians with ambushes on some occasions. And although the Spaniards pursued them and burned them, they never showed any desire to come to peace" (Ranjel, quoted in Ewen and Hann 1998:152).

Despite their repeated efforts, the Apalachees failed to mount an effective campaign against the Spaniards. Although they were recognized by other natives as exceptionally fierce warriors, the Apalachees were no match for Spanish military stratagems, weapons, or cavalry. The very nature of native warfare, which depended primarily on hit-and-run raids and individual valor, put them at a severe tactical disadvantage against massive European-style assaults.

The presumed site of Anhaica was identified in 1987 by B. Calvin Jones in Tallahassee, Florida, near the state capitol. Mitigation was undertaken in advance of construction, which had already begun at the time the site was identified. In addition to the generally favorable hilltop location with nearby water, the site contained a unique material assemblage consisting predominantly of Fort Walton and Lamar ceramics, structural remains, and a variety of sixteenth-century Spanish ceramics, coins, beads, a crossbow quarrel, chain mail, and pig remains (Ewen and Hann 1998:106–7). Jones and Ewen identified three structures (Structure 1A and 1B, both of which were circular wattle-and-daub dwellings measuring 5 meters in diameter; and Structure 2, which had a prepared clay floor that extended 3.7 meters in diameter), a borrow pit, cistern, cooking pit, a child burial, and a human cremation (Ewen and Hann 1998:61–72). More than 90 percent of the artifact assemblage consisted of aboriginal pottery, 60 percent of which were Fort Walton types (Ewen and Hann 1998:76–77). Ewen identified Carrabelle Punctated var. Meginnis (36 percent of the assemblage) as a possible protohistoric marker for Apalachee; it is rare on precontact Lake Jackson phase sites and falls off again on San Luis phase sites (Ewen and Hann 1998:76–77).

The only other protohistoric site that has been intensively tested is the Velda site. Excavated by L. Ross Morrell, materials from the Velda site have been incorporated into the development of ceramic typologies (Scarry 1985), Apalachee cultural chronologies (Scarry 1996), regional settlement patterning (Smith and Scarry 1988), and architectural studies (Scarry and McEwan 1995), but a complete report including raw data from the Velda site has yet to be published. Investigations at the Velda site revealed evidence of two structures thought to be dwellings, a possible storage facility (*garita*), a central courtyard, and refuse areas. The remains of both structures consisted of two circular rows of posts. The interior posts of Structure 1 measured 5.75 meters in diameter, and the exterior row was 7.5 meters in diameter. Structure 2 was similar in size; the interior post row measured 5.5 meters in diameter and the exterior 7.0 meters (Scarry and McEwan 1995:485).

Scarry's analysis of ceramics from the Velda site revealed that Fort Walton types accounted for more than 70 percent of all pottery. Carrabelle Punctated *var. Meginnis* represented less than 1 percent of the total assemblage, and only 5.76 percent of all decorated pottery from this protohistoric village, which may date slightly later (circa 1600) than Anhaica (John F. Scarry, personal communication 1998). This finding suggests that Carrabelle Punctated may not be a consistent chronological marker; however, any conclusion must await additional study.

The archaeology of the protohistoric Apalachee Indians is distinguished by several characteristics. Although settlements remained dispersed to facilitate intensive maize production, the paramount center of the late prehistoric period had been replaced by dual capitals, governed by related rulers. Material assemblages continue to be dominated by Fort Walton ceramics, but they also contain a variable amount of transitional types indicative of shifting alliances and trade networks, and perhaps direct migration. Protohistoric sites in Apalachee have not yielded any materials representative of the complex iconography or extensive economic networks similar to those found in Mound 3 at Lake Jackson (Scarry 1996:203).

The Apalachees' intermittent contact with Spaniards is revealed through the presence of European materials at select sites such as the proposed location of Aute and the protohistoric capital of Anhaica. However, given the limited amount of time that the Narváez and de Soto *entradas* spent in the region, these sites could be characterized as pristine aboriginal villages containing a small but distinctive assortment of sixteenth-century European artifacts. Despite the fact that written records begin enhancing our understanding of the Apalachees during this time, the protohistoric period is one of the most poorly understood archaeological phases in the province and considerable work is needed to expand and refine the few insights we currently have.

The Mission Period

Although the Narváez and de Soto expeditions resulted in a significant loss of Apalachee life from skirmishes and imprisonment, the most lasting impact of these relatively brief encounters was the inadvertent introduction of European pathogens (Crosby 1972; Dobyns 1983; Milner 1980; Ramenofsky 1987; Smith 1987). Recurrent outbreaks of sickness, many fatal, undermined the confidence that the Apalachees had in their leaders, and chiefs sought to bolster their authority through Europeans.

The solicitation of missionaries was also prompted by the fact that their closest neighbors, the Timucuans, were already allied with the Spaniards. By 1607, Apalachee leaders sent word to the governor in St. Augustine requesting friars so that they might become Spanish subjects and adopt Christianity. As noted by one friar, "Some of the Indians obey their chiefs poorly, and the chiefs would like to gain control of their Indians with the aid and support of Your majesty" (Hann 1988a:12).

Apalachee leaders wanted to buttress their power through Spanish recognition and gifts. Spaniards had quickly learned to reinforce the status of cooperative native leaders in order to achieve control of the populations under their jurisdiction. As in precontact Apalachee society, leaders were distinguished by a number of factors, including their control of esoteric knowledge (which during the mission period included reading and writing), possession of exotic material goods, and distinctive residential architecture. The acceptance of Spanish sovereignty by Apalachee chiefs on behalf of their people also gave both the Apalachees and Spaniards crucial military allies.

The mission period in Apalachee province began in 1608, when Fray Martín Prieto visited the province in order to encourage peace with the neighboring Timucuans who were actively being missionized. Prieto estimated the population gathered at Ivitachuco to be 36,000 (Hann and McEwan 1998:27). It was also in the years immediately following Prieto's initial visit that other religious ventured into Apalachee and were generally well received.

The first two friars to settle in the province arrived in 1633. Although San Damián de Cupaica is the only mission for which a founding date is documented (1639), the principal villages of Ivitachuco and San Luis de Jinayca are also believed to have been among the earliest missions established. Francisco Martínez and Pedro Muñoz reported that within the first two years (by 1635), 5,000 of the estimated 34,000 population had been baptized (Hann and McEwan 1998:31). The Apalachees' desire for religious conversion appears to have been sincere, and the number of missions and converts continued to grow. By the 1670s, Apalachee province was described as being thoroughly Christianized (Hann 1994:340).

Although the Apalachee Indians were initially successful in their resistance to providing a labor tribute to Spanish officials, they yielded to this demand in exchange for pardons following the 1647 Apalachee uprising. Native men provided labor for construction projects in Apalachee and St. Augustine, they worked on Spanish farms and cattle ranches, they participated in extensive export activities, and some were trained in European military tactics and procedures. Apalachee women probably worked in the service of both their native community and as domestic laborers in Hispanic households at the provincial capital of San Luis. It is also likely that a number of Apalachee women married Spaniards residing at San Luis as a means of elevating their status and that of their children (McEwan 1993a, 1993b).

Of the eleven missions (along with twenty-four satellite settlements under their jurisdiction) established in Apalachee during the seventeenth century, nine were tested and tentatively identified by B. Calvin Jones in the 1960s and 1970s (Jones and Shapiro 1990): Ayubale (Scott Miller), Aspalaga, Ivitachuco, Escambe, San Luis, Ocuya, Asile, Turkey Roost, and Patale I (see fig. 3.2). The most persistent debate of the past decade has revolved around Jones's proposed model based on preliminary data from these nine sites. Specifically, he predicted the spatial arrangement of elements and architecture within Apalachee religious complexes (Jones and Shapiro 1990). The efficacy of this model has been challenged since it was based on limited testing rather than comprehensive excavations (Marrinan 1993; Saunders 1990, 1996). Indeed, investigations at all nine of the Apalachee mission sites, with the exception of San Luis and Patale, are preliminary and warrant additional study.

This examination of the mission period Apalachees will focus on San Luis. Although investigations at the Patale mission have been considerable and informative (Jones et al. 1991; Marrinan 1993), with the exception of the church, activity areas associated with the native population during this period have not yet been verified and reported. (See Marrinan 1993 for a summary of work published to date on Patale.)

Mission San Luis

The location of the site recognized today as San Luis was selected by Spaniards in 1656 for its strategic location on one of the area's highest hills, just over 200 feet above sea level. Seep springs provide a year-round source of water. The chief of San Luis de Jinayca (first referred to as San Luis de Talimali in 1675), along with a large native population, relocated to be near the Spaniards. From 1656 until the province was abandoned in 1704, San Luis was recognized as the provincial capital. Thus the town presents an unparalleled opportunity to study the physical and social development of a community that was occupied by both Apalachees and Spaniards from the time of its founding. San Luis was also demographically distinct from other Apalachee missions in that it was the only settlement with a cross section of Spanish residents, including soldiers, civilians (male and female), and clergy; European presence at other missions was generally restricted to a single friar. Therefore, it is the only mission where contact between a broad range of natives and Europeans was sustained over a period of almost fifty years or three generations.

The unique circumstances of San Luis make it an anomaly among Apalachee missions, and, as such, it may not provide a good model for other missions (Brose 1990). However, as an individual case study, it is an ideal candidate for examining culture change as a result of missionization in Apalachee province.

The archaeology of San Luis has been reported in numerous publications (Griffin 1951; Hann and McEwan 1998; McEwan 1991a, 1991b, 1992, 1993a; McEwan and Larsen 1996; McEwan and Poe 1994; Scarry and McEwan 1995; Shapiro 1987; Shapiro and Hann 1990; Shapiro and McEwan 1992). For the purpose of this essay, three presumably contemporaneous native areas will be considered: the Franciscan church, the Apalachee council house, and a chief's residence. These will be examined in order to evaluate sacred, secular, and domestic aspects of Apalachee life within a single community.

The Mission Church

The mission church at San Luis was identified in 1990, and work has periodically continued on this structure and associated features through 1997
(Lee 1995, 1997; McEwan and Larsen 1996; Shapiro and Vernon 1992).
Approximately 412 square meters have been excavated within and around
the perimeter of the 15.1-by-33.6-meter building. The long axis of the building is oriented east to west, with its entrance on the east end facing onto the
town's plaza.

Although the Franciscan church is generally considered a European context, the cemetery beneath its floor contained exclusively Native American
burials. In collaboration with bioarchaeologist Clark Spencer Larsen (University of North Carolina, Chapel Hill), a sample of the total burial population (estimated to be between 700 and 900 people) was excavated (Mc-
Ewan and Larsen 1996). At least 210 skeletal individuals were identified,
half of which were adults (Tung et al. 1998).

Not only did the Apalachees choose to be buried in the sanctified ground
beneath the floor of the church, but their interment was almost wholly
Christian in nature. Individuals were buried in an east-to-west alignment
parallel to the long axis of the church, with their heads in an easterly direction. The bodies were laid in a supine and extended position; most had their
hands clasped or folded on their chests in reference to the cross. Few pins
were recovered, suggesting that many individuals may have been wrapped
in a shroud without fasteners or interred without any covering.

As with prehistoric Apalachee burials, status is revealed through mortuary patterning within the cemetery. The most elite members of native society
are believed to be those individuals who were buried closest to the altar.
Gutiérrez (1991:61) documented that missionized Pueblo Indians could buy
their placement in mission churches; 19 pesos for burial close to the altar and
4 pesos for interment in the back of the church. While we have no recorded
evidence of such practices in Apalachee, interments near the sanctuary are
distinguished from the others by less postdepositional disturbance and
higher concentrations of grave goods. Coffin burials, which are rare in seventeenth-century Spanish Florida, are also clustered near the altar and are
indicative of more labor expenditure on these individuals.

There is also evidence that social position and political authority were
reinforced through burial orientation. While members of the congregation
were typically buried with their heads to the east, priests were usually in-

terred in the opposite direction, replicating their relationships in life. Excavations at San Luis have revealed three adult native burials near the altar whose heads are oriented to the west, opposite all the other interments. Two of these individuals were also buried in coffins. The unique orientation of these burials suggests that they were high-ranking Apalachees, and that they may have had a special relationship with the church. This would include such residents as Matheo Chuba and Juan Mendoza, both of whom were considered important native leaders at San Luis and who maintained close ties to the church. Mendoza was the *atequi,* or parish interpreter (Hann 1988a:107–8). It is also possible that one or more of these individuals were sacristans or members of the Third Order of Franciscans. Members of this lay order, whose patron saint was San Luis Rey de Francia, were often accorded special accommodation that could include preferential burial treatment.

One of these three individuals was an adult male (Burial 3), probably in his mid-thirties, who is believed to have died from a gunshot wound based on the close proximity of a .44-caliber lead shot near his lower vertebrae (Larsen et al. 1995). A significant quantity of lead shot and pellets was also recovered throughout the burial fill. Since there is no evidence that San Luis was ever attacked, this finding suggests that a number of other individuals were wounded or killed by gunfire. Unfortunately, extensive superimposition has made it impossible to associate clusters of shot or pellets with specific individuals other than Burial 3.

Grave goods associated with burials were primarily glass beads of various types, shapes, and colors (Mitchem 1990b, 1994, 1995, 1996). While some of these were undoubtedly from rosaries, such as faceted jet beads, many are believed to have been worn as necklaces or sewn onto clothing. There were also a number of beads manufactured from copper, shell, and stone. The quantity of quartz crystal beads and pendants found in the cemetery is particularly interesting since a number of these were also recovered from the chief's house at San Luis. Various native peoples have long believed that quartz crystal holds special powers to portend the future, bring luck in hunting, ensure rain, and aid in other matters (McEwan et al. 1997; Miller and Hamell 1986). The properties associated with quartz crystal by the Apalachees may have been altered during the mission period to incorporate Christian beliefs and symbols as evidenced by the recovery of an elaborate quartz crystal cross that is believed to have been made by a native artisan (McEwan et al. 1997). Four quartz pebbles were also found at the Patale mission cemetery in what is thought to be a shaman's bundle associated with a burial (Jones et al. 1991:85). Other funerary objects recovered from the cemetery at San Luis include pottery, lithics, an iron knife blade, copper sequins, jet *higas*, and brass crosses.

Since European Catholics typically included only a rosary, if anything, with interments, the inclusion of these assorted grave goods may have been one of the concessions that friars were willing to make to Native American converts. A similar behavior was noted by Alfonso Ortiz (1969:51–52) among the Tewa-speaking Pueblo Indians, where the priest and all non-Indians would leave the cemetery after performing Christian rituals. Natives were left to complete the burial, which typically included placing prized possessions with the deceased.

Mortuary patterning at San Luis reveals that the Apalachee Indians not only adhered to Christian burial traditions, including interment in the church cemetery and body treatment, but also incorporated many European status indicators, including proximity to the altar and coffin burial. The placement of women and children near the altar, some in coffins and some with elaborate grave offerings, suggests that there was no age or sex discrimination observed in the church cemetery (McEwan and Larsen 1996). This is significant since the age and sex of burials are often key to understanding the manner in which individuals participated in society (Larsen 1997; O'Shea 1984). Although the treatment of burials suggests a high degree of conformity to Christian doctrine, the inclusion of grave goods indicates one aspect of burial practices that remained distinctly Native American. The same basic pattern has been found at the Patale mission, the only other Apalachee mission period cemetery population from which there are extensive data (Jones et al. 1991; Marrinan 1993).

Council House

The Apalachee council house at San Luis was identified in 1985 by Gary Shapiro (Shapiro and McEwan 1992) and is the only historic period building of its kind found to date in Apalachee province. Council houses are well documented throughout much of the lower Southeast (Andrews and Andrews 1975; Bartram 1976; Fernández de Florencia 1678; Florencia 1695; Hann 1986a, 1988a; Laudonnière 1975; San Miguel 1902; Shapiro and Hann 1990; Van Doren 1955). These public structures were the physical and symbolic center of native communities where rituals were conducted and planting schedules, war preparations, civic disputes, and business matters were addressed. Council houses were also the site of social events such as dances. During the mission period, they were used for assembly when Spanish authorities conducted official visits, for posting ordinances, and possibly as jails. Council houses also served as lodges for Indians and Europeans alike, with facilities for cooking and sleeping.

The size and construction details of these structures varied greatly throughout geographic regions and tribal areas. However, there seems to have been a direct correlation between the size of a village and the size of its council house. The council house at San Luis was 36.4 meters in diameter and is estimated to have held between 2,000 and 3,000 people (Shapiro and Hann 1990; Shapiro and McEwan 1992). It was a conical building constructed of thatch with a large opening or skylight at the top. Jonathan Dickinson's account (Andrews and Andrews 1975) indicates that the roof opening in council houses could amount to one-third of the total building diameter. The interior contained two concentric rows of benches and a central hearth. It is believed that the door opened onto the southeastern edge of the central plaza at San Luis and, according to documentary accounts, elevated seats reserved for native leaders faced the door. It is noteworthy that the council house was constructed directly across the town plaza from the mission church, and both are believed to have been among the first structures built at the site.

The archaeological remains of the council house indicate no evidence of European influence in the design or construction of the building. The limited amount of hardware recovered archaeologically (primarily nail fragments) suggests that it was not used in the fabrication of the building but was likely salvaged from other locations, as iron was always a prized commodity and deemed valuable by both Apalachees and Spaniards.

A wide range (but small quantity) of European materials was recovered from the council house, including glass beads, bell fragments, a matchlock pan and cover, gunflints, lead shot, bottle fragments, and a diverse assortment of imported ceramics such as majolicas, coarse earthenwares, and Oriental porcelains. These items may have been gifted to native leaders who met daily in the council house or may have belonged to Europeans who stayed in the lodge. The vast majority of materials recovered, however, were native pottery and lithics which correspond to the functions traditionally associated with these structures including social and ceremonial activities.

Although virtually no vertebrate remains were recovered from the council house, plants identified from the building consisted primarily of indigenous maize, beans, squash, and sunflower (C. M. Scarry 1992:158). Yaupon holly (*Ilex vomitoria*), from which black drink is prepared, was recovered from the central hearth. The only Old World plants found in the assemblage were watermelon and wheat, but because Spaniards also used the council house as a lodge, it is unclear whether these were foods eaten by the Apalachees or Spaniards. There is, however, some documentation that Florida natives took an immediate liking to both watermelon and peaches (John Hann, personal communication 1998).

Chief's House

The chief's house was identified in 1992 as part of an investigation of the Apalachee settlement area at the capital mission. The structure is located on the southern edge of the central plaza at San Luis, adjacent to the Apalachee council house. Unlike typical residences of the prehistoric and protohistoric periods that measured between 6 and 8 meters in diameter (McEwan 1992; Scarry and McEwan 1995), this building was 20.5 meters in diameter. As with the council house, the chief's house was a circular thatch structure with a central hearth. There was a single row of benches lining the interior wall, under which a series of smudge pits was found.

In general, materials from the chief's house are very similar to those from the council house. Both assemblages reveal little disruption in ceramic traditions and a heavy reliance on stone tools and weapons. Although quantitatively small, European goods recovered from this residence included remains of firearms, which were among the most valued items given to native leaders. A wide variety of glass and quartz crystal beads and pendants were also recovered (Mitchem 1993), as were pig and cow remains (Reitz 1993a).

The impact of European domesticates on Apalachee diet is unclear. Isotope analysis of the skeletal remains of one of the elite individuals (Burial 3) revealed that he had a relatively low amount of maize in his diet, suggesting that most of his protein came from meat (Hutchinson et al. 1998; McEwan and Larsen 1996). Cowpea (black-eyed pea) was first found at the chief's house and subsequently identified from other areas of San Luis and at other Apalachee missions (C. M. Scarry 1993a). Le Page du Pratz referred to cowpeas as "Apalachean beans," causing speculation that they were traded to the interior Southeast through Apalachee province (Gremillion 1995:9). Wheat and garbanzo beans were the only other Old World plants identified from this structure and its associated features (C. M. Scarry 1993a).

There is every indication that basic native traits such as building design and construction, as well as activities including flint knapping, pottery production, and food and hide preparation, continued essentially unaltered throughout the mission period. However, archaeological evidence reveals that some specialized types of European goods and foods were available to native rulers.

Apalachee Settlement

As an expression of power and authority, Mississippian leaders' residences have been characterized as those that are the most labor intensive and situated on the highest mound (Payne 1994a:148–52). During the mission period, the proximity of native leaders to the Spanish community may have become a dominant factor and contrasts sharply with the settlement pattern of most Apalachees. Documentation indicates that Apalachee villages were considered very insecure as they were generally dispersed over 3 to 4 leagues (1 league = 2.6 miles) (Solana 1953[1702]).

At the time of this writing, only one possible commoner house has been found at San Luis. Several postmolds and a smudge pit have been identified in the Spanish village area amid European structural remains. It is believed that this building predates the Hispanic structures and may represent the displacement of native residents as the Spanish community at San Luis expanded. In a letter to the king, the Apalachee chiefs of Ivitachuco and San Luis stated that "the natives of San Luis are found withdrawn a league into the woods, for their places have been seized for the Spaniards" (Don Patricio and Don Andrés 1699, quoted in Boyd et al. 1951:25).

Discussion

The relationship between the Apalachees and Spaniards during the exploration and initial encounter phase was unequivocally hostile. However, by the time missionization of Apalachee province was undertaken almost a century later, native leadership was generally respected by Spanish authorities, who had long since learned to work through traditional hierarchies (Deagan 1985:299). Native rulers were given honorific titles by Spaniards, including "governor" to paramount rulers and "don" to members of chiefly lines (Hann and McEwan 1998:66). This recognition of native authority, however, did not protect them from abuses at the hands of Spaniards, who were known to inflict both verbal and physical insults on commoners and high-ranking Apalachees alike.

Initial European contact in Apalachee is indicated by beads, bells, and small quantities of other materials that were probably associated with temporary encampments or may have been given to native leaders. During the course of the mission period in Apalachee province (1633–1704), a full range of European materials became available to the native population, particularly Apalachee rulers. Imported beads, pottery, and cloth were common gifts, some of which may have had special symbolic significance to the native population (Miller and Hamell 1986). The most prized objects are believed to have been those that had technological and practical advantages (iron tools, firearms, and horses), but there is no evidence that native weapons or tools were ever effectively replaced by European counterparts.

Although the nature of prestige goods shifted during the historic period, it is believed that these items maintained their significance as powerful symbols of authority. Similarly, esoteric knowledge also changed, but it continued to legitimize native leaders as controllers of specialized information (Anderson 1994:44) and facilitated their interaction with Spaniards. For example, since literacy was an integral aspect of religious indoctrination and natives regarded it as somewhat magical, many rulers quickly became literate. There is evidence from a deed that the chief of Ivitachuco was literate as early as 1651 (Hann 1988a:27–28), and that several San Luis leaders were also able to read and write.

Native architectural and material remains from mission period contexts support documentary evidence that many Apalachee political and social traditions continued uninterrupted. And, despite Spanish opposition to activities such as the ball game and some dances (the length of dances was curbed, and some were eventually prohibited), these traditions never ceased.

There is no indication that the Apalachees' diet changed significantly from late prehistoric times through the historic period. Subsistence continued to be centered on intensive maize production supplemented by the collection of wild foods. And although there is evidence of limited availability of introduced plant foods to the native population (wheat, watermelon, cowpea, and garbanzo, among others), the preeminence of maize is evidenced archaeologically and by the almost two tons of maize seed needed to plant the community field associated with San Luis (Hann 1988a:145). The introduction of domestic animals may have had the greatest impact on local diet, but there is no indication that they ever supplanted traditional native foods.

However, Spanish settlement of Apalachee and the introduction of Old World plants and animals to the region (Reitz 1993b; C. M. Scarry 1993b), did create a different relationship between the Apalachees and their land. This new regimen was characterized by an intensification of agriculture, advanced technologies, and participation in a global economy. By the 1670s, Spaniards began engaging in a variety of agricultural enterprises in Apalachee using native labor, the success of which is apparent in the quantity and variety of agricultural goods exported from the province annually (Boniface 1971). Natives attempted to benefit from the vigorous Spanish economy by raising pigs and cattle for sale (for example, see the 1700 Leturiondo Memorial [Hann 1986b]). There were also unscrupulous native entrepreneurs, as evidenced by criminal proceedings against two Apalachee youths for making and attempting to pass counterfeit coins (Hann 1988b).

Both the archaeological and documentary record suggest that the Apalachees underwent the most profound changes in the religious and spiritual aspects of their lives. There is every reason to believe that adoption of Christian burial practices was a reflection of the Apalachees' sincere religious conversion. And while the incorporation of grave goods can be interpreted as the retention of precontact practices, it is likely that these goods are material indicators of a complex belief system that incorporated elements of both cultures.

Abandonment of Apalachee Province

During the historic period, the traditional enemies of the Apalachees were in many instances replaced by the enemies of the Spaniards. Between 1702 and 1704, the Apalachee missions were repeatedly attacked from the north by English raiders and their Creek allies. Those Apalachees who were not killed outright or enslaved during the raids migrated from their homeland. The vast majority of them traveled north to British territory and settled in the area around Augusta, Georgia. Some migrated westward to Mobile, and a small group fled with the Spaniards to St. Augustine. In 1711 most of the Apalachees who had relocated to St. Augustine (thirty-one) resided in a village outside a town known as San Luis de Talimali. By 1717 the name of the Apalachee village had changed to Our Lady of the Rosary of Abosaia

(Hann 1988a:287). Contrary to statements made elsewhere based on secondary sources (Hann 1988a:289; Hann and McEwan 1998:175), there were no Apalachees recorded on the 1763 list of evacuees who relocated to Cuba when Spain ceded Florida to England.

The most successful group of Apalachees were those who migrated west to Pensacola and then to Mobile, where they were invited by French authorities to settle. In 1704 Father Alexander Huvé commented that "you cannot believe the trouble the Apalachee are causing us. They are constantly asking for sacraments, and we cannot understand them anymore than we can make ourselves understood" (in Hann 1988a:306). The king of Spain was so impressed with several Apalachees who died heroic deaths in 1704 while professing their faith that he made a recommendation to the Vatican that they be considered for canonization.

Descendants of the Florida Apalachees currently reside in Louisiana. They continue to be practicing Catholics and have based their application for federal recognition on parish records.

Acknowledgments

Research in the chief's house and church complex at Mission San Luis was supported by the National Endowment for the Humanities (RO–22177–91 and RK–20111–94). Archaeological investigations in the council house were funded by a Historic Preservation Advisory Council Special Category Grant. Ongoing support of San Luis is provided by the state of Florida's Conservation and Recreation Lands (CARL) Trust Fund and the Florida legislature.

The diligence of my staff over the years has been essential to the productivity and success of our project. Jerry Lee, Jonathan Gray, and Heidi Broadfield have all been superb supervisors and assistants. Elyse Cornelison provided essential computer support, and Elyse, along with Teri White, assisted with the preparation of this manuscript.

I thank my colleagues whose work in Apalachee province has complemented my own. Charles R. Ewen, John H. Hann, Clark Spencer Larsen, Rochelle A. Marrinan, James J. Miller, Jeffrey M. Mitchem, and John F. Scarry all read and commented on the manuscript, and I incorporated many of their suggestions. However, any shortcomings or omissions are my own.

Bibliography

Anderson, David G.
1994   *The Savannah River Chiefdoms: Political Change in the Late Prehistoric Southeast.* Tuscaloosa: University of Alabama Press.

Andrews, Evangeline Walker, and Charles McLean Andrews (editors)
1975   *Jonathan Dickinson's Journal.* Stuart, Fla.: Valentine Books.

Bartram, William
1976   Observations on the Creek and Cherokee Indians, 1789, with prefatory and supplementary notes by E. G. Squier. *Transactions of the American Ethnological Society* 3(1):1–81. Originally published in 1853 by George P. Putnam. Milwood, N.Y.: Kraus Reprint Company.

Boniface, Brian G.
1971   A Historical Geography of Spanish Florida, circa 1700. Master's thesis, Department of History, University of Georgia, Athens.

Bourne, Edward G. (editor)
1904   *Narratives of the Career of Hernando de Soto in the Conquest of Florida.* New York: A. S. Barnes.

Boyd, Mark F., Hale G. Smith, and John W. Griffin
1951   *Here They Once Stood: The Tragic End of the Apalachee Missions.* Gainesville: University of Florida Press.

Braley, Chad O.
1998   *Yuchi Town (1Rv63) Revisited: Analysis of the 1958–1962 Excavations.* Report submitted to the Environmental Management Division, Fort Benning, Ga., by Southeastern Archaeological Services, Athens, Ga.

Brose, David S.
1990   Apalachee Impostors. Paper presented at the Forty-seventh Annual Meeting of the Southeastern Archaeological Conference, Mobile, Alabama.

Brose, David S., and George W. Percy
1978   Fort Walton Settlement Patterns. In *Mississippian Settlement Patterns,* edited by B. D. Smith, 81–114. New York: Academic Press.

Bryne, Stephen C.
1986   Apalachee Settlement Patterns. Master's thesis, Department of Anthropology, Florida State University, Tallahassee.

Clayton, Lawrence A., Vernon James Knight, Jr., and Edward C. Moore (editors)
1993   *The De Soto Chronicles: The Expedition of Hernando de Soto to North America in 1539–1543.* 2 vols. Tuscaloosa: University of Alabama Press.

Crosby, Alfred
1972   *The Columbian Exchange: Biological and Cultural Consequences of 1492.* Contributions in American Studies no. 2. Westport, Conn.: Greenwood Press.

Deagan, Kathleen
1985   Spanish-Indian Interaction in Sixteenth-Century Florida and Hispaniola. In *Cultures in Contact: The European Impact on Native Cultural Institutions in Eastern North America, a.d. 1000–1800,* edited by W. W. Fitzhugh, 281–318. Washington: Smithsonian Institution Press.

Díaz, Bernal
1963   *The Conquest of New Spain.* Translated with an introduction by J. M. Cohen. Harmondsworth, U.K.: Penguin.
Dobyns, Henry F.
1983   *Their Number Become Thinned.* Knoxville: University of Tennessee Press.
Ewen, Charles R., and John H. Hann
1998   *Hernando de Soto among the Apalachee: The Archaeology of the First Winter Encampment.* Gainesville: University Press of Florida.
Fernández de Florencia, Juan
1678   Letter to Governor Pablo Hita Salazar, San Luis de Talimali, August 30, 1678. Report Which the Principal Leaders Who Went to Make War on the Chiscas, Who Are Juan Mendoza, Matheo Chuba, Bernardo, the Cacique of Cupayca, and Bentura, the Inija of San Luis, Made in the Presence of Captain Juan Fernández de Florencia and Concerning How the War against the Chiscas Originated. In Hita Salazar, 1678, Archivo General de Indias, Santo Domingo, 226, Woodbury Lowery Collection, vol. 9. Transcribed and translated by J. H. Hann. Manuscript on file, Florida Bureau of Archaeological Research, Tallahassee.
Florencia, Joaquín de
1695   General Inspection That the Captain Joaquín de Florencia Made of the Provinces of Apalachee and Timucua, Interim Treasurer of the Presidio of St. Augustine of Florida, Judge Commissary and Inspector-General of Them by Title and Nomination of Don Laureano de Torres y Aiala, Knight of the Order of Santiago, Governor and Captain General of the Said Presidio, and Provinces by His Majesty 1694–1695. Archivo General de Indias, Escribanía of Cámara, legajo 157A, Cuaderno I, folios 44–205, Stetson Collection of the P. K. Yonge Library of Florida History, Gainesville. Transcribed and translated by J. H. Hann. Manuscript on file, Florida Bureau of Archaeological Research, Tallahassee.
Fryman, Frank
1969   Fieldnotes from the High Ridge Site (8Le117). Unpublished notes on file. Florida Bureau of Archaeological Research, Tallahassee.
Galloway, Patricia (editor)
1998   *The Hernando de Soto Expedition: History, Historiography, and "Discovery" in the Southeast.* Lincoln: University of Nebraska Press.
Gremillion, Kristen J.
1995   Comparative Paleoethnobotany of Three Native Southeastern Communities of the Historic Period. *Southeastern Archaeology* 14(1):1–16.
Griffin, James B.
1985   Changing Concepts of the Prehistoric Mississippian Cultures of the Eastern United States. In *Alabama and the Borderlands from Prehistory to Statehood,* edited by R. R. Badger and L. A. Clayton, 40–63. Tuscaloosa: University of Alabama Press.
Griffin, John W.
1950   Test Excavations at the Lake Jackson Site. *American Antiquity* 16(2):99–112.
1951   Excavations at the Site of San Luis. In *Here They Once Stood,* by Mark F.

Boyd, Hale G. Smith, and John W. Griffin, 139–60. Gainesville: University of Florida Press.

Gutiérrez, Ramón A.
1991   *When Jesus Came, the Corn Mothers Went Away: Marriage, Sexuality, and Power in New Mexico, 1500–1846.* Stanford, Calif.: Stanford University Press.

Haas, Mary
1949   The Position of Apalachee in the Muskogean Family. *International Journal of American Linguistics* 15(2):121–27.

Hally, David J., and James L. Rudolph
1986   *Mississippi Period Archaeology of the Georgia Piedmont.* Georgia Archaeological Research Design Papers no. 2. University of Georgia, Athens.

Hann, John H.
1986a   Translation of Governor Rebolledo's 1657 Visitation of Three Florida Provinces and Related Documents. *Florida Archaeology* 2:81–146.

1986b   Translation of Alonso de Leturiondo's Memorial to the King of Spain. *Florida Archaeology* 2:165–225.

1988a   *Apalachee: The Land between the Rivers.* Gainesville: University Presses of Florida.

1988b   Apalachee Counterfeiters in St. Augustine. *Florida Historical Quarterly* 67 (1):52–68.

1991   *Missions to the Calusa.* Gainesville: University Presses of Florida.

1993   1630 Memorial of Fray Francisco Alonso de Jesus on Spanish Florida's Missions and Natives. *The Americas* 50(1):85–105.

1994   The Apalachee of the Historic Era. In *The Forgotten Centuries: Indians and Europeans in the American South, 1521–1704,* edited by C. Hudson and C. Tesser, 327–54. Athens: University of Georgia Press.

1996a   *A History of the Timucua Indians and Missions.* Gainesville: University Press of Florida.

1996b   Translations of the Accounts of the Pánfilo de Narváez Expedition's Experiences in Florida. Manuscript on file, Florida Bureau of Archaeological Research, Tallahassee.

1998   Historic Era Aboriginal Peoples of South Florida. Manuscript in preparation. Florida Bureau of Archaeological Research, Tallahassee.

Hann, John H., and Bonnie G. McEwan
1998   *The Apalachee Indians and Mission San Luis.* Gainesville: University Press of Florida.

Hoffman, Paul E.
1990   *A New Andalucia and a Way to the Orient: The American Southeast During the Sixteenth Century.* Baton Rouge: Louisiana University Press.

Hudson, Charles
1976   *The Southeastern Indians.* Knoxville: University of Tennessee Press.

Hutchinson, Dale L., Clark Spencer Larsen, Margaret J. Schoeninger, and Lynette Norr
1998   Regional Variation in the Pattern of Maize Adoption and Use in Florida and Georgia. *American Antiquity* 63(3):397–416.

Jones, B. Calvin
1982   Southern Cult Manifestations at the Lake Jackson Site, Leon County, Florida: Salvage Excavation of Mound 3. *Midcontinental Journal of Archaeology* 7(1):3–44.
1990   A Late Mississippian Collector. *Soto States Anthropologist* 90(2):83–86.
1991   High Status Burials in Mound 3 at Florida's Lake Jackson Complex: Stability and Change in Fort Walton Culture. Paper presented at the Annual Meeting of the Southeastern Archaeological Conference, Jackson, Mississippi.
1994   The Lake Jackson Mound Complex (8LE1): Stability and Change in Fort Walton Culture. *Florida Anthropologist* 47(2):120–46.
Jones, B. Calvin, and John T. Penman
1973   *Winewood: An Inland Ft. Walton Site in Tallahassee, Florida.* Bureau of Historic Sites and Properties Bulletin no. 3. Division of Archives, History and Records Management, Tallahassee.
Jones, B. Calvin, and Gary N. Shapiro
1990   Nine Mission Sites in Apalachee. In *Columbian Consequences,* vol. 2, *Archaeological and Historical Perspectives on the Spanish Borderlands East,* edited by D. H. Thomas, 491–511. Washington, D.C.: Smithsonian Institution Press.
Jones, B. Calvin, John Hann, and John F. Scarry
1991   San Pedro y San Pablo de Patale: A Seventeenth-Century Spanish Mission in Leon County, Florida. *Florida Archaeology 5.* Florida Bureau of Archaeological Research, Tallahassee.
Kimball, Geoffrey
1987   A Grammatical Sketch of Apalachee. *International Journal of American Linguistics* 53(2):136–74.
1988   An Apalachee Vocabulary. *International Journal of American Linguistics* 54 (4):387–98.
Larsen, Clark Spencer
1997   *Bioarchaeology: Interpreting Behavior from the Human Skeleton.* Cambridge: Cambridge University Press.
Larsen, Clark Spencer, Hong Huynh, and Bonnie G. McEwan
1995   Death by Gunshot: Biocultural Implications of Trauma at Mission San Luis. *International Journal of Osteoarchaeology* 5:240.1–240.9.
Laudonnière, René
1975   *Three Voyages.* Translated by C. Bennett. Gainesville: University Presses of Florida.
Lee, Jerry W.
1995   1994–1995 Excavations in the Mission Church of San Luis. Manuscript on file, Florida Bureau of Archaeological Research, Tallahassee.
1997   1996–1997 Excavations in the Mission Church of San Luis. Manuscript on file, Florida Bureau of Archaeological Research, Tallahassee.
López de Gómara, Francisco
1966 [1552]   *Cortés: The Life of the Conqueror by His Secretary.* Translated and edited by L. B. Simpson. Reprint. Berkeley and Los Angeles: University of California Press.

Marrinan, Rochelle A.
1993   Archaeological Investigations at Mission Patale, 1984–1992. In *The Spanish Missions of La Florida*, edited by B. G. McEwan, 244–94. Gainesville: University Press of Florida.
Marrinan, Rochelle A., and Stephen C. Bryne
1986   Apalachee-Mission Archaeological Survey Final Report. Vol. 1. Manuscript on file, Department of Anthropology, Florida State University, Tallahassee.
Marrinan, Rochelle A., John F. Scarry, and Rhonda L. Majors
1990   Prelude to de Soto: The Expedition of Pánfilo de Narváez. In *Columbian Consequences*, vol. 2, *Archaeological and Historical Perspectives on the Spanish Borderlands East*, edited by D. H. Thomas, 71–82. Washington, D.C.: Smithsonian Institution Press.
McEwan, Bonnie G.
1991a   San Luis de Talimali: The Archaeology of Spanish-Indian Relations at a Florida Mission. *Historical Archaeology* 25(3):36–60.
1991b   The Archaeology of Women in the Spanish New World. In *Gender in Historical Archaeology*, edited by D. J. Seifert. *Historical Archaeology* 25(4):33–41.
1992   *Archaeology of the Apalachee Village at San Luis de Talimali*. Florida Archaeological Reports 28. Florida Bureau of Archaeological Research, Tallahassee.
1993a   Hispanic Life on the Seventeenth-Century Florida Frontier. In *The Spanish Missions of La Florida*, edited by B. G. McEwan, 295–321. Gainesville: University Press of Florida.
McEwan, Bonnie G. (editor)
1993b   *The Spanish Missions of La Florida*. Gainesville: University Press of Florida.
McEwan, Bonnie G., and Clark S. Larsen
1996   Archaeological and Biocultural Investigations in the Church Complex at San Luis. Final Report to the National Endowment for the Humanities, #RK–20111–94. Manuscript on file, Florida Bureau of Archaeological Research, Tallahassee.
McEwan, Bonnie G., and Charles B. Poe
1994   Excavations at Fort San Luis. *The Florida Anthropologist* 47(2):90–106.
McEwan, Bonnie G., Michael W. Davidson, and Jeffrey M. Mitchem
1997   A Quartz Crystal Cross from the Cemetery at Mission San Luis, Florida. *Journal of Archaeological Science* 24:529–36.
Milanich, Jerald T.
1996   *The Timucua*. Oxford: Blackwell.
Milanich, Jerald T., and Charles Hudson
1993   *Hernando de Soto and the Indians of Florida*. Gainesville: University Press of Florida.
Miller, Christopher L., and George P. Hamell
1986   A New Perspective on Indian-White Contact: Cultural Symbols and Colonial Trade. *Journal of American History* 73(2):311–28.
Milner, George R.
1980   Epidemic Disease in the Postcontact Southeast: A Reappraisal. *Midcontinental Journal of Archaeology* 5:39–56.

Mitchem, Jeffrey M.
1988   Archaeological and Ethnohistorical Evidence for the Location of Narváez's Aute. Paper presented at the Fifty-second Annual Meeting of the Florida Academy of Sciences, Tampa.
1990a   Initial Spanish-Indian Contact in West Peninsular Florida: The Archaeological Evidence. In *Columbian Consequences*, vol. 2, *Archaeological and Historical Perspectives on the Spanish Borderlands East*, edited by D. H. Thomas, 49–60. Washington, D.C.: Smithsonian Institution Press.
1990b   Analysis of Beads and Pendants from San Luis de Talimali (8LE4): The Cemetery and Church. Manuscript on file, Florida Bureau of Archaeological Research, Tallahassee.
1993   Apalachee Village Beads and Pendants, San Luis de Talimali, 1992 Field Season. Manuscript on file, Florida Bureau of Archaeological Research, Tallahassee.
1994   Analysis of Personal Adornment Items from the Cemetery at Mission San Luis (8LE4): 1993 Excavations. Manuscript on file, Florida Bureau of Archaeological Research, Tallahassee.
1995   Analysis of Personal Adornment Items from the Cemetery at Mission San Luis (8LE4): 1994 Excavations. Manuscript on file, Florida Bureau of Archaeological Research, Tallahassee.
1996   Personal Adornment Items from the Cemetery at Mission San Luis (8LE4): 1995 Excavations, with Addenda from the 1994 Excavations. Manuscript on file, Florida Bureau of Archaeological Research, Tallahassee.
Neuerburg, Norman
1995   *Saints of the California Missions*. Santa Barbara, Calif.: Bellerophon Books.
Ortiz, Alfonso
1969   *The Tewa World: Space, Time, Being, and Becoming in a Pueblo Society.* Chicago: University of Chicago Press.
O'Shea, John
1984   *Mortuary Variability: An Archaeological Investigation.* Orlando: Academic Press.
Payne, Claudine
1994a   Mississippian Capitals: An Archaeological Investigation of Precolumbian Political Structure. Ph.D. diss., Department of Anthropology, University of Florida, Gainesville.
1994b   Fifty Years of Archaeological Research at the Lake Jackson Site. *Florida Anthropologist* 47(2):107–19.
Peebles, Christopher S., and Susan M. Kus
1977   Some Archaeological Correlates of Ranked Societies. *American Antiquity* 42:421–48.
Ramenofsky, Ann F.
1987   *Vectors of Death: The Archaeology of European Contact.* Albuquerque: University of New Mexico Press.
Reitz, Elizabeth J.
1993a   Vertebrate Remains from the Apalachee Village at San Luis de Talimali. Manuscript on file, Florida Bureau of Archaeological Research, Tallahassee.
1993b   Evidence for Animal Use at the Missions of Spanish Florida. In *The Spanish*

Missions of La Florida, edited by B. G. McEwan, 376–98. Gainesville: University Press of Florida.

San Miguel, Fray Andrés de

1902   Account of the Difficulties That the People of a Ship Called "The Lady of Mercy" Endured and Concerning Some Things That Occurred in That Fleet. In *Dos Antiguas Relaciones de la Florida,* compiled by Genaro Garcia, 155–226. Tip. y Lit. de J. Aguilar Vera y Comp., Mexico. Transcribed and translated by J. H. Hann. Manuscript on file, Bureau of Archaeological Research, Tallahassee.

Saunders, Rebecca

1990   Ideal and Innovation: Spanish Mission Architecture in the Southeast. In *Columbian Consequences,* vol. 2, *Archaeological and Historical Perspectives on the Spanish Borderlands East,* edited by D. H. Thomas, 527–42. Washington, D.C.: Smithsonian Institution Press.

1996   Mission Period Settlement Structure: A Test of the Model at San Martín de Timucua. *Historical Archaeology* 30(4):24–36.

Scarry, C. Margaret

1992   Plant Remains from the San Luis Council House and Church Complex. Archaeology at San Luis: Part One, Appendix VI. *Florida Archaeology* 6. Florida Bureau of Archaeological Research, Tallahassee.

1993a   Identification, Analysis, and Report on Botanical Remains from the Apalachee Village at San Luis. Manuscript on file, Florida Bureau of Archaeological Research, Tallahassee.

1993b   Plant Production and Procurement in Apalachee Province. In *The Spanish Missions of La Florida,* edited by B. G. McEwan, 357–75. Gainesville: University Press of Florida.

Scarry, John F.

1985   A Proposed Revision of the Fort Walton Ceramic Typology: A Type-Variety System. *Florida Anthropologist* 38(3):199–233.

1990   The Rise, Transformation, and Fall of Apalachee: A Case Study of Political Change in a Chiefly Society. In *Lamar Archaeology: Mississippian Chiefdoms in the Deep South,* edited by M. Williams and G. Shapiro, 175–86. Tuscaloosa: University of Alabama Press.

1996   Stability and Change in the Apalachee Chiefdom. In *Political Structure and Change in the Prehistoric Southeastern United States,* edited by J. F. Scarry, 192–227. Gainesville: University Press of Florida.

Scarry, John F., and Bonnie G. McEwan

1995   Domestic Architecture in Apalachee Province: Apalachee and Spanish Residential Styles in the Late Prehistoric and Early Historic Period Southeast. *American Antiquity* 60(3):482–95.

Shapiro, Gary

1987   Archaeology at San Luis: Broad-Scale Testing, 1984–1985. *Florida Archaeology* 3. Florida Bureau of Archaeological Research, Tallahassee.

Shapiro, Gary N., and John H. Hann

1990   The Documentary Image of the Council Houses of Spanish Florida Tested by Excavations at the Mission of San Luis de Talimali. In *Columbian Consequences,* vol. 2, *Archaeological and Historical Perspectives on the Spanish*

Borderlands East, edited by D. H. Thomas, 511–26. Washington, D.C.: Smithsonian Institution Press.

Shapiro, Gary, and Bonnie G. McEwan
1992   Archaeology at San Luis: Part One, The Apalachee Council House. *Florida Archaeology* 6. Florida Bureau of Archaeological Research, Tallahassee.

Shapiro, Gary, and Richard Vernon
1992   Archaeology at San Luis: Part Two, The Church Complex. *Florida Archaeology* 6. Florida Bureau of Archaeological Research, Tallahassee.

Smith, Marion F., Jr., and John F. Scarry
1988   Apalachee Settlement Distribution: The View from the Florida Master Site File. *Florida Anthropologist* 41:351–64.

Smith, Marvin T.
1987   *Archaeology of Aboriginal Culture Change in the Interior Southeast: Depopulation during the Early Historic Period.* Gainesville: University Presses of Florida.

Solana, Manuel
1953 [1703]   Manuel Solana to Governor Zuñiga, San Luis, October 22, 1702. Translated by M. F. Boyd. *Americas* 9(4):468–70.

Tesar, Louis D.
1980   *The Leon County Bicentennial Survey Report: An Archaeological Survey of Selected Portions of Leon County, Florida.* Miscellaneous Project Report Series no. 49. Florida Bureau of Historic Sites and Properties, Tallahassee.

Tung, Tiffiny A., Clark S. Larsen, and Bonnie G. McEwan
1998   The Bioarchaeology of San Luis de Talimali. Paper presented at the Southeastern Archaeological Conference, Greenville, South Carolina.

Van Doren, Mark (editor)
1955   *Travels of William Bartram.* New York: Dover Press.

Villareal, Francisco
1568   Letter, Brother Francisco de Villareal to Father Juan Rogel, Tequesta, January 23, 1568, in *Zubillaga, Monumenta Antiquae Floridae* 1946, 235–40. Translation by J. H. Hann in A. M. Parks, *Where the River Found the Bay,* 1985(2):31–36.Report prepared under contract for the City of Miami by the Florida Division, Archives, History and Records Management, Tallahassee.

Willey, Gordon R.
1949   *Archaeology of the Florida Gulf Coast.* Smithsonian Miscellaneous Collections no. 113. Washington, D.C.: Smithsonian Institution.

Worth, John
1998a   *The Timucuan Chiefdoms of Spanish Florida,* vol. 1, *Assimilation.* Gainesville: University Press of Florida.
1998b   *The Timucuan Chiefdoms of Spanish Florida,* vol. 2, *Resistance and Destruction.* Gainesville: University Press of Florida.

4

The Chickasaws

JAY K. JOHNSON

The Chickasaws emerge from prehistory at the dawn of the written record of the interior Southeast. De Soto and his men, fresh from a near defeat at the battle of Mavilla, spent the winter of 1540–41 at Chicasa, a Chickasaw village in what is now northeast Mississippi. Their stay was an uneasy one and ended when the Chickasaws set fire to the village in a predawn attack. The Spaniards retreated to the west across northern Mississippi. Like most interior tribes, the Chickasaws spent the next century and a half dealing with the Europeans indirectly. There is little mention of them in historic documents until the founding of the English and French colonies at Charles Town and Biloxi at the end of the seventeenth century.

The Chickasaws were quick to take advantage of their strategic location on the frontier of the colonial South during the Indian slave-trading period of the early eighteenth century. Because of their early access to the new tools of warfare and hunting, the Chickasaws were able to raid for slaves to the west and north with remarkable success. As more and more of their neighbors established trade relations with the Europeans, the initial advantage of their extreme western location was transformed into a liability, especially when trade shifted from slaves to skins.

However, the Chickasaws assumed a new role in the politics of the region, a role that built on their reputation as fierce warriors which they had established during the slave trade. Both the English and the French recognized the importance of the Chickasaws in their strategic position between the French colonies in Louisiana and Illinois and dealt with them accordingly. Therefore, our understanding of the colonial era is not complete without having a clear picture of how the Chickasaws figured in the international conflicts that raged throughout the South during that period.

Recent research using both historic documents and archaeological data has suggested that the Chickasaws were much more subtle in their relations with the Europeans than previously thought. Factions within the tribe dealt with the French and then the English and sometimes with both. And we are beginning to be able to identify these factions in the archaeological record.

By the mid-eighteenth century the Chickasaws were much reduced in number and influence. They played a peripheral role in the American Revolution, siding with the British. The first Indian agent from Washington did not arrive to live among them until 1801. By that time the Chickasaws had abandoned the cluster of villages they had lived in for most of the eighteenth century and spread across northern Mississippi in response to a final shift in subsistence from trading deerskins to running free-range cattle. The Chickasaws' removal to Oklahoma was set in motion in 1836 with the Treaty of Pontotoc and implemented the next year.

The Chickasaws have long been one of the best known of the southern Indians, both in terms of archaeology and ethnohistory. They are described in detail in an early and widely available account (Adair 1986 [1775]), and because of their strategic place in the political geography of the colonial South, early French (Rowland and Sanders 1927, 1929, 1932; Rowland et al. 1984a, 1984b) and British (McDowell 1955, 1958, 1970) documents discuss their situation at length. John Swanton (1922, 1928) used historic documents and a limited amount of ethnographic fieldwork to produce his descriptions of the Chickasaws, and Arrell Gibson (1971) relied almost exclusively on Swanton for the early chapters of his book on the Chickasaws. During the late 1930s, Moreau Chambers, Jesse Jennings, and Albert Spaulding conducted excavations in anticipation of the construction of the Natchez Trace Parkway near present-day Tupelo in northeast Mississippi. Jennings's (1941, 1944) reports on this work set the foundation for Chickasaw archaeology. Not only were his reports unusually detailed for this period of American archaeology, but he also made extensive use of the rich historic resources then available.

As a result of salvage archaeology in advance of the rapid expansion of Tupelo during the last decade, four eighteenth-century Chickasaw sites have recently been excavated (Blake 1992; Breitburg 1997; Johnson 1997a; Johnson et al. 1994b; O'Hear and Ryba 1998; Wild 1997; Yearous 1991). Furthermore, the recent discovery of four letters written by an Englishman from Charles Town during a 1708 visit to the Chickasaw villages (Nairne

1988) has added many more details to our picture of Chickasaw social organization as well as their economic and political situation at the beginning of the colonial era. Finally, archaeological research on terminal prehistoric and protohistoric sites to the south of Tupelo (Johnson 1991, 1996; Johnson and Sparks 1986; Johnson et al. 1991; Sparks 1987) has begun to yield information about the origins of the Chickasaws.

This is, then, an opportune time to review what we know about the Chickasaws. Beginning with material that dates to the end of the fifteenth century, and concluding with the Chickasaws' removal from Mississippi in 1837, this chapter traces major developments in the evolution of the Chickasaws from deer hunting and corn agriculture, to slave trade and deerskin trade, to subsistence farming and cattle. It is satisfying to me, as an archaeologist, to be able to document how much archaeology has contributed to our evolving understanding of the documentary data.

First Contact

Hernando de Soto and his men crossed the Tombigbee River in December of 1540 and entered Chickasaw territory. The Spaniards were in search of a village to commandeer so that they could spend the winter indoors, eating from the Indians' supply of corn. They soon discovered Chicasa, the "principal town" of the Chickasaws. One of the accounts places the size of the village at twenty huts and suggests that it may have been palisaded (Clayton 1993a:100, 104); another indicates that there were 200 huts but makes no mention of a palisade (Clayton 1993b:366). All agree that Chicasa was located on a rolling upland savanna interspersed with clumps of hardwoods. Many small villages were located in the region surrounding the winter camp. These facts are recounted in varying detail in the four accounts of the expedition (now issued in a new translation and brought together in two volumes; Clayton et al. 1993a, 1993b).

The Spaniards spent nearly four months at Chicasa until a Chickasaw attack during the early morning hours burned the village and nearly overcame the expedition. After regrouping, de Soto retreated to the west, across what is now north Mississippi, to continue his search for gold. Considering the length of their stay and the intensity of the interaction between the Spaniards and the Chickasaws, there is surprisingly little information about the latter. In particular, the glimpses we get of the nature of Chickasaw leadership are ambiguous (DePratter 1983) and can be interpreted as indicating that the Chickasaws were either a chiefdom (Hudson et al. 1990) or a tribe (Johnson 1997b).

Fortunately, there is a body of archaeological data that can be brought to bear on the question. The only physiographic zone in northeast Mississippi that matches the setting for Chicasa as described in the chronicles is the Black Prairie. A long narrow deposit of chalk and marl begins in Tennessee, enters Mississippi from the north, and forms an arc, passing into Alabama about a third of the way down the boundary between the two states. This substratum resulted in a physiographic zone marked by upland prairies crossed by fairly broad stream bottoms draining east into the Tombigbee River.

A master's thesis (Sparks 1987) and several survey reports (Johnson and Curry 1984; Johnson et al. 1984) provided a first look at upland prairie settlement in Clay County, Mississippi (Johnson and Sparks 1986). The resulting settlement model formed the basis for a research project directed specifically at exploring the late prehistoric settlement of the prairie and, if fortunate, locating the de Soto winter camp. Although the location of Chicasa remains elusive (there is a curious paucity of sixteenth-century European artifacts from northeast Mississippi considering the amount of time the Spanish were in the region), this project did derive a good picture of the prairie settlement pattern, which has direct implications for the origins of the Chickasaws (Johnson 1991, 1996; Johnson and Lehmann 1996; Johnson et al. 1994a).

The typical upland site in the prairie portion of Clay County is a rather small scatter of mostly plain, live shell–tempered sherds located on thin soils on bluffs overlooking small, second- and third-order stream bottoms. We were fortunate enough to find and test the Waide site (22Cl764), an upland site which had not been destroyed by erosion or cultivation. A dense midden deposit yielded what appears to be a single component ceramic assemblage as well as an array of animal bones. The sherds are distinguished by a minority of incised and punctated types along with Alabama River Applique, a rim treatment which is distinct from the notched fillet characteristic of later Chickasaw sites. All the sherds were tempered with live shell. Notched fillets and Alabama River Applique were also found in small numbers in the upland prairie surface collections. None of these sites yielded sherds that could be assigned to an earlier period. This, and a pair of late fifteenth-century radiocarbon dates from the Waide site, led us to conclude that the shift in settlement from the river terrace locations characteristic of the Mississippian period to the upland locations typical for the historic Chickasaws occurred abruptly and relatively late in the prehistory of the region.

Not everyone agrees with this interpretation. Homes Hogue and Evan Peacock (1995), Peacock (1995), and Janet Rafferty (1996) obtained earlier dates from sites in the Black Prairie to the south of Clay County and documented what appears to have been a different settlement pattern elsewhere in the Black Prairie. They point out that many of the small upland site assemblages containing plain, live shell–tempered sherds could just as well be Mississippian period hamlets. Since the eighteenth-century Chickasaws used fossil shell to temper their ceramics, the live shell distinction is critical. In fact, a careful look at the upland settlement in Lee County, Mississippi, the documented focus of the eighteenth-century Chickasaws, suggests that the prairie uplands were not much used until late in the prehistory of the region (Johnson 1996). That is, the large majority of the shell-tempered sherds from an extensive survey of the county (Stubbs 1983) are tempered with fossil shell. Moreover, diagnostic Chickasaw types and the potential proto-Chickasaw type, Alabama River Applique, are not found on any of the many large Mississippian period sites excavated in preparation for the construction of the Tennessee-Tombigbee Waterway. In fact, the Yarborough site (22Cl814), located in the bottoms of one of the major tributaries of the Tombigbee River as it crosses the Black Prairie in Clay County (Solis and Walling 1982), is the only nonupland site in northeast Mississippi to have yielded any prehistoric or protohistoric Chickasaw pottery types.

So even if the shift to upland settlement was gradual, occurring over several centuries late in the Mississippian period, by about A.D. 1450 the major river terraces and bottomland of the Tombigbee had been abandoned and the population had relocated to the uplands of the Black Prairie. This is where the de Soto *entrada* found the Chickasaws in 1540, bringing us back to the question of Chickasaw social organization. Not only had the ancestors of the Chickasaws abandoned the river terraces, they quit building platform mounds. The settlement pattern was likewise simplified, with no appreciable difference between sites in terms of size. That is, the two- or three-tiered settlement hierarchy of the Mississippian period had been replaced with one that is much less suggestive of centralized control. If the Chickasaws at the time of first contact were not completely a tribe, they were certainly something less than the full-fledged chiefdoms of the Mississippian period. And the archaeological data clearly indicate that this reorientation of settlement and social organization preceded the entrance of Europeans into the Southeast.

Following the de Soto expedition, the Chickasaws appear to have remained in the Black Prairie. They continued to include fragments of mussel shell in their pottery but began to decorate their pots with a narrow fillet of clay just below the rim on the exterior of the vessel. This fillet was often notched and is diagnostic of historic Chickasaw ceramics. Pottery with this notched fillet has been found in the portion of the Black Prairie to the north of West Point and south of Tupelo. It is characteristically made on paste that includes live shell temper and is not found with trade goods. This suggests the protohistoric Chickasaws moved north from Chicasa during the sixteenth century (fig. 4.1).

Janet Rafferty's (1996) seriation of surface collections from several Lee County sites led her to conclude that the Chickasaws started adding fossil shell to their ceramics during the second half of the seventeenth century. Atkinson's (1987) study of ceramics and trade goods allowed him to map the concentration of Chickasaw settlement in the Tupelo region during the seventeenth and eighteenth centuries (see fig. 4.1). According to Stubbs (1992) and Morgan (1996), this settlement shift was a defensive strategy in response to the unrest brought on by the early colonial period.

Second Contact

Following the de Soto debacle, Europeans were slow to reenter the interior Southeast. The next recorded encounter with the Chickasaws occurred in 1682, when La Salle's expedition met a small group of Chickasaws who were several days from their village on the bluffs of the Mississippi River near present-day Memphis (Stubbs 1982b). This brief contact with the French had little impact on either party.

The next Europeans to contact the Chickasaws were English explorers out of Charles Town whose primary goal was opening trade relations with the Indians of the interior. Henry Woodward may have contacted the Chickasaws as early as 1685 (Moore 1988:71; Nairne 1988:50). This initial contact established a trade route that was to become a significant element in the relationship between the Chickasaws and the Europeans. It was also to be important in the balance of power between the Chickasaws and their neighbors.

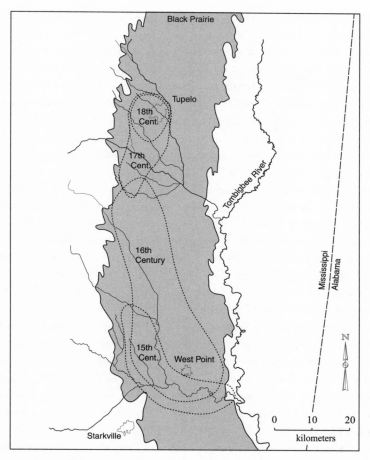

Fig. 4.1. Chickasaw settlement in the Black Prairie (seventeenth- and eighteenth-century distribution following Atkinson 1987).

The primary emphasis of the early trade with Charles Town was slaves. The Chickasaws and other Indians in the Southeast captured one another to trade to the Europeans for guns, ammunition, horses, and other less critical items. In fact, when Henri de Tonti led a French treaty mission from Mobile to the Chickasaws in 1702, he encountered a Chickasaw party raiding for slaves in Choctaw territory. The Chickasaws were accompanied by an Englishman, and English slave traders sat in on a council in the Chickasaw villages that Tonti attended. Tonti's letters indicate that the Chickasaws were located in the Black Prairie to the south of modern-day Tupelo, Mississippi (Galloway 1982).

The Tonti and La Salle documents contain tantalizing hints about the turn-of-the-century Chickasaws that corroborate information found in a much fuller English account. In 1708 Thomas Nairne journeyed from Charles Town to the Chickasaw villages in order to evaluate the Chickasaws as potential allies and trading partners. Four letters written during this journey were recently discovered and published (Nairne 1988). Because Nairne had a good deal of previous experience in dealing with Indians of the Southeast (Moore 1985, 1988) and because he was explicitly interested in documenting Chickasaw customs and social organization as a guide for traders and policy makers in Charles Town, these letters contain a remarkable amount of data. It would be possible to rewrite Swanton's (1928) reconstruction of Chickasaw culture using the Nairne letters alone.

Fortunately, the first half of the eighteenth century is also well covered by official colonial documents. The French policy toward the Chickasaws wavered from alliance and trade, through open hostility with major military campaigns in 1736 and 1740, to war by proxy using the Choctaw as their agents. Starting with the beginning of the Louisiana colony in 1699, the Chickasaws figure prominently in the correspondence between the colonial governors and their superiors in Paris, particularly when making excuses for failed attacks on the Chickasaw villages. A large body of the French documents relating to Mississippi have been collected, translated, and published in five volumes (Rowland and Sanders 1927, 1929, 1932; Rowland et al. 1984a, 1984b).

The Chickasaws were no less important to English interests in the Southeast, but published English documents are less comprehensive, consisting for the most part of communications from traders which happened to become part of the official records of Charles Town. Three volumes of records specifically relating to the Indian trade have been transcribed and published (McDowell 1955, 1958, 1970), and the records of the Grand Council covering the years 1721–72 (Born 1955) are available on microfilm from the Library of Congress. The colonial records for Georgia have been published in thirty volumes covering the period from 1732, shortly after the founding of the colony, to 1782. The first volume was published in 1904, and the last came out in 1985. Allen Chander and Kenneth Coleman were the principal editors. Because they were more populous and closer to the British settlements, the Creeks and the Cherokees receive a good deal more attention than the Chickasaws.

Taken together, and allowing for the biases inherent in the different accounts, these documents provide a rich resource for studying the Chickasaws. The Chickasaw villages continued to be located in the Black Prairie (Galloway 1982; Nairne 1988) but shifted north from their apparent fifteenth-century location. They had congregated in several villages on the uplands near the junction of Kings Creek and Town Creek in central Lee County, Mississippi. By the beginning of the eighteenth century, the Chickasaws were clearly a tribe. Although there were chiefs and the position was passed down to a sister's son (Nairne 1988:39), the chief's power was limited and major decisions were made in council (Nairne 1988:39).

Nairne (1988:38–39) attributed the diminished authority of the peace chiefs to the economic impact of the slave trade, which provided access to trade goods and prestige outside the traditional social structure. Although the slave trade also made the war chiefs' position more important in economic terms, their power was limited to matters of war and they had no authority otherwise (Nairne 1988:44).

Firearms and horses were a major focus of the slave trade, and the Chickasaws' access to these items early in the colonial period, along with their situation at the western terminus of the upper Creek trade path, led to "success in the warr against their Bow and Arrow Neighbours, for they chancing to proure a Trade with us, soon made themselves terrible to those who wanted that advantage, so they have now the reputation of the most military people of any about the great river" (Nairne 1988:38).

A map of the trade routes into the interior of the early colonial Southeast (fig. 4.2) clearly illustrates the Chickasaws' advantage during this period. They had access to guns and ammunition well before the Indians to the west and north. The Chickasaws are known to have raided far and wide during the early years of the eighteenth century and may, in fact, have contributed to the depopulation of the Mississippi alluvial valley in northwest Mississippi, an area that was densely populated during the Mississippian period and the site of several apparent chiefdoms when de Soto passed through the region (Hudson et al. 1990). According to an early French observer, their "warlike disposition had prompted them to invade several nations, whom they have indeed destroyed, but not without diminishing their own numbers by those expeditions" (Le Page du Pratz 1975:310).

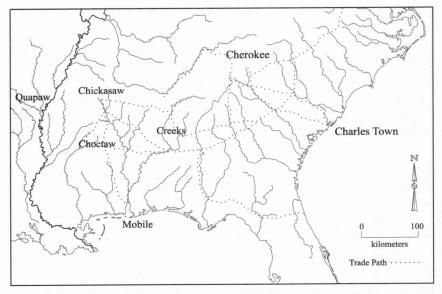

Fig. 4.2. Map of the southeastern United States showing selected Indian groups and early eighteenth-century trade routes (after Crane 1929: frontispiece).

Their early technological advantage in war may also explain the dispro-portionate amount of land the Chickasaws claimed. Although they were always one of the smallest of the major Indian groups in the Southeast, the Chickasaw territory was not much smaller than that of the more populous Choctaws, Cherokees, and Creeks (table 4.1). The size of the territories was computed by digitizing the treaty cessions directly from photocopies of the Royce (1899) treaty maps. Territory that was claimed by more than one tribe (portions of west-central Tennessee and northwest Alabama were ceded by both the Chickasaws and Cherokees) was figured into the territory of both groups. Population estimates follow Wood (1989:66–72, table 1). The 1685 estimates show the Chickasaws to have had more than three and a half times as much treaty land per capita as the Choctaws and 27 percent more land per capita than the Creeks. Cherokee and Choctaw figures are similar. The disparity between land claimed and population size became even more pro-nounced for the Chickasaws during the course of the eighteenth century as their population declined. By 1790, on the eve of the treaty negotiations, the Chickasaw population had rebounded somewhat, but they still claimed

Table 4.1. Treaty territory and population estimates for major southeastern tribes

	Chickasaw	Choctaw	Creek	Cherokee
Treaty territory (sq. mi.)	37,060	40,920	62,130	45,850
Population				
1685	7,000	28,000	15,000	32,000
1700	5,000	21,000	9,000	16,000
1715	4,000	16,000	10,000	11,000
1730	3,100	9,200	11,000	10,500
1745	2,300	12,200	12,000	9,000
1760	1,600	13,300	13,000	7,200
1775	2,300	14,000	14,000	8,500
1790	3,100	14,700	15,000	7,500

Sources: Territory computed from Royce (1899); population figures from Wood (1989).

nearly twice as much land per capita as the Cherokees and more than four times as much as the Choctaws.

Following the end of the Yamassee War in 1717, deerskins replaced slaves as the primary commodity traded out of the Southeast through Charles Town and other ports (Braund 1993; Crane 1929). However, the war had disrupted the network of British alliances with the interior tribes, and the French were quick to recognize the advantage.

The Charles Town council journals for the decade following the war indicate a primary concern with negotiations aimed at establishing peace with the remnant of the Yamassee and reestablishing relationships with the Creeks and Cherokees. In fact, at one point, English trade with the Chickasaws was prohibited. In September of 1726, Tobias Fitch was among the Upper Creek in Alabama negotiating a treaty between the Creeks, Cherokees, and English. He wrote back to say:

May it please your Honour
Here is arrived severall Traders from the Settlements bound to the Chickasaws with a considerable Quantity of Goods & I have by them an account of severall more a comming up here bound to the same places.
Those that are arrived I have stopped their proceeding any further till orders from your Honour for the following reason.
It has been made appear that the Chickesaw killed on Samuel Fox near Savanno Town his horse and Cloathes being found in the said

Indians possession & that one of the Chickesaws did at the [hocanass?] declare the same to white men those & this very Fellow that discovered it was killed by the Chickesaw King this is what happend three years past.

Likewise an Account brought here by the stinking Lingo Indians [?] who have lately been at this Chickesaw Town that there is Now a white mans Scalp set up in the Square which is a man that Chambers thought had been run to the French when he was last there but the Chickesaws had killed him all which they boast of the white People are afraid to prevent it. (South Carolina Council Journals 1725–26)

In a letter posted from Tookeybatchcys and dated September 25, 1726, Fitch responded to a proposal to include the Chickasaws in the three-way treaty negotiations:

As to Including the Chickesaw in the peace I do assure your honour it cannot be done for I never saw no people [Upper Creeks] more Incenst that there are against the Chickesaws as you will find by their discourse & as to their meeting in Charles Towne I shall [observe?] to them if any occasion, but it my Opinion that there will be no peace. (South Carolina Council Journals 1725–26)

On October 7, 1726, the lower house of the council at Charles Town sent a letter to the upper house spelling out their position on the Chickasaw trade.

Your honour is likewise desired to give direction to Capt Fitch to Suffer the Traders to the Chickesaws to trade amongst the Creeke Indians with the same privilidges as the Creek Traders and that they be under the same restrictions as they are Except Paying for their Licences to the Publick Treasuree. (South Carolina Council Journals 1725–26)

Meanwhile, the French view of the Chickasaws was different. Governor Bienville, in a memoir written in 1726, summarized the various Indian tribes and their relationships with the colony.

Finally the last Indian nation is that of the Chickasaws consisting of eight hundred men. They occupy six or seven villages. It is a very fine country thirty-five leagues to the north of the Choctaws. These people breathe nothing but war and are unquestionably the bravest of the continent. However the war that I have had made on them by the Choctaws has obliged them to come and ask me for peace several times. I granted it to them before departing from Louisiana. They are very good hunters. They carry on every year a commerce in deerskins for which the English of Carolina trade with them, but the latter since they were betrayed in 1715 have always been on their guard and would not be reluctant to give up the match provided we had something with which to attract the Chickasaws to our side. I know that they will prefer us to the English when they are certain they will find what they need in our warehouses. (Rowland and Sanders 1932:538)

In a memoir to a council convened to consider a Chickasaw peace offer in 1724, Bienville specified the advantages and disadvantages of ending the conflict. In the process he spelled out the French colonial strategy.

And finally this war was in keeping with our interests and our security in that it kept apart these two nations [Choctaws and Chickasaws] who, displeased with an alliance with us because of the fact that it has been impossible for us up to the present time to furnish them with the things they need, which sooner or later would have become prejudicial to us, whereas by keeping them always at war as we have done we have preserved for ourselves the friendship of the most populous of the two. (Rowland and Sanders 1932:457)

He goes on to conclude that there are now sufficient trade goods to satisfy both the Chickasaws and the Choctaws and peace should be made. The council agreed on December 2, 1724 (Rowland and Sanders 1932:459). However, the French inability to supply sufficiently the deerskin trade (Rowland and Sanders 1929:537) and the Chickasaws' refusal to turn over the Natchez refugees who had fled to the Chickasaw villages following the Natchez Rebellion in 1729 put an end to the possibility of a formal alliance between the Chickasaws and the French.

Following these attempts at diplomatic relations, the French settled on a policy of aggression, which was solidified by an attack on the Chickasaw villages of Ogoula Tchetoka and Ackia by French-led forces from Illinois and Louisiana in 1736. Meanwhile, the Englishmen out of South Carolina and later Georgia expanded their trading sphere to include the Chickasaws. The picture that emerges is one in which the corporate English traders maintained a trade relationship with the Chickasaws that the bureaucratic French could not match. As a consequence, the English were able to force the French into conflict with the Chickasaws, thereby creating a battle zone between the French colonies in Louisiana and Illinois (Crane 1929; Gibson 1971; Phelps 1957; Usner 1992). This traditional view of politics and trade on the western frontier is just one aspect of the historic accounts that can be refined using the archaeological record.

A primary goal of the excavations directed by Jennings in the late 1930s was the discovery of the village of Ackia. Four Chickasaw sites were excavated, and several more in the vicinity of Tupelo were recorded. Jennings summarized his results in an *American Antiquity* article (Jennings 1944) and presented them in much more detail in a monograph-length report (Jennings 1941). Although he failed to identify the site of the battle of Ackia, his description of Chickasaw material culture, particularly the ceramics, provides a base from which all subsequent analyses must begin (Atkinson 1987; Stubbs 1982a).

In particular, James Atkinson (1985a, 1985b, 1987) made good use of Jennings's reports, National Park Service collections, and more recent, primarily small-scale surveys to explore various aspects of Chickasaw culture. In fact, a recently discovered French map—the result of a reconnaissance following the battle of Ackia—contributed to Atkinson's (1985b) identification of specific Chickasaw village sites, including Ackia. It appears that one of the sites that Spaulding dug was Ackia, but he and Jennings failed to recognize it. Perhaps more significant, this research clearly identified the locations of the two major groups of Chickasaw villages during the early eighteenth century: the Large Prairie and the Small Prairie.

The Large Prairie villages, including Ougoula Tchetoka, were situated along the ridge that separates the upper Kings Creek drainage from Town Creek to the north. An examination of the distribution of sites in this area (fig. 4.3) shows a nearly continuous occupation along this ridge, beginning at the town of Belden in the west and running southeast for approximately three miles. One of Jennings and Spaulding's excavated sites (22Le505 [MLe 90]) is located on this ridge, and a second (22Le524[MLe 14]) is just across Kings Creek to the south. Jennings (1941:178–80) was the first to note the significance of the exclusive occurrence of Fatherland Incised, a characteristic Natchez pottery type, in the collections from these sites. The Large Prairie villages served as a refuge for the Natchez after they abandoned their homeland in southwest Mississippi, fleeing the French in 1730.

The Small Prairie villages are situated about two miles to the southeast of the Large Prairie, in the southern portion of present-day Tupelo, near the junction of Town and Kings creeks.

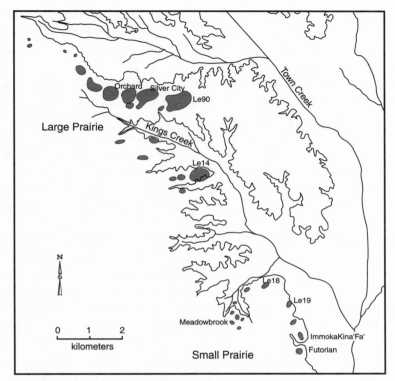

Fig. 4.3. Large Prairie and Small Prairie Chickasaw site locations.

One of the collections that Atkinson analyzed was salvaged by Park Service personnel during the construction of a furniture factory in what was the Small Prairie (Elmore 1955). The Futorian site (22Le566) was divided into a north component and a south component during excavation, and these divisions appear to have chronological significance (Johnson et al. 1994a). The North Refuse contained various incised ceramics made of paste with live shell temper, lithic artifacts are made mostly from heat treated Tuscaloosa gravel, and European trade goods are absent. The South Refuse contained ceramics tempered with fossil shell, some of which were decorated with a narrow ridge of clay located just below the rim. Both are ceramic markers for the eighteenth-century Chickasaws. A few thumbnail scrapers were found, and the gray (probably Fort Payne) chert, which predominates on eighteenth-century sites, is also present. A single glass bead documents what was to become a central factor in Chickasaw life. The North Refuse is estimated to date to between 1600 and 1680, with the South Refuse dating to the late seventeenth or very early eighteenth century. Both components yielded bison bones, but they were much more common in the earlier portion of the site (Johnson et al. 1994a).

Most of the Small Prairie sites were destroyed by residential and commercial development during the 1950s and 1960s. Local collectors recall that almost every house lot that was cleared in the Lee Acres subdivision contained Chickasaw burials rich in European trade goods. Large private collections were gathered, and in 1981 John Stubbs directed a project designed to record these collections. Unfortunately, he met with limited success in gaining access to this material, and there are still many unstudied collections in Tupelo. However, Stubbs conducted a systematic survey of a substantial portion of the region surrounding Tupelo. The result is a much clearer picture of Chickasaw settlement (Johnson et al. 1989; Stubbs 1983) and material culture (Stubbs 1982a). Like the late prehistoric and protohistoric prairie sites to the south in Clay County (Johnson 1991), eighteenth-century Chickasaw sites are situated on the upland ridges in places where thin soils would have supported prairie grasses before widespread agricultural practices modified the landscape. Both Janet Rafferty (1995) and David Morgan (1996) studied Stubbs's collections and developed pottery seriations that document a shift from live shell temper to fossil shell temper that is accompanied by other changes in decoration and appendages. The ceramic changes are corroborated by differences in lithic artifacts and trade goods.

Urban expansion into the Large Prairie lagged behind the destruction of the Small Prairie but began in earnest during the mid-1980s and has nearly been completed. Aside from the sites dug by Jennings and Spaulding, only two others have been salvaged from this area. David Dye conducted a weeklong test of the Orchard site (22Le519) in advance of a housing development. However, because no federal money was involved, the only legal protection for the site rested on the state burial law. When no burials were found, the research ended. Even so, several large pit features were excavated, and a good deal of material was recovered, some of which has been analyzed on a volunteer basis, including plant (Blake 1992), faunal (Breitburg 1997), and lithic (Johnson 1997a) material.

More recently, a portion of the Silver City site (22Le520) was excavated to make room for a Tennessee Valley Authority service center (Wild 1997). In spite of the site name, no burials were found during the project and relatively few trade goods were recovered. Silver City is located just to the east of the Orchard site along the same ridge upon which most of the Large Prairie sites are situated. Artifactual data suggest that the two sites are roughly contemporaneous, dating to relatively early in the eighteenth century. However, the presence of a few Fatherland Incised sherds in the Orchard site collections suggests that it was occupied at least until the time of the Natchez Rebellion and subsequent retreat to the Large Prairie in 1730. The Large Prairie was the location of several villages in 1736 at the time of the first major French attack (Atkinson 1985b). In fact, the Chickasaw occupation along the Large Prairie ridge is nearly continuous, and village designation is difficult.

The most recent of the Chickasaw village excavations was conducted by John O'Hear at a Small Prairie location that is now the site of an extension of the North Mississippi Medical Center. Fieldwork was conducted during the summer of 1996, and first drafts of various portions of the final report give some measure of the contribution this project will make to our understanding of the Chickasaws (O'Hear and Ryba 1998). The site (22Le907) is named ImmokaKina'Fa,' and the salvaged portion appears to date to the late seventeenth and early eighteenth centuries. The project is also significant because, after thorough but noninvasive study, the human remains that were recovered were reinterred on site by the descendants of the Chickasaws.

Several interesting patterns in the early eighteenth-century Chickasaw occupation of northeast Mississippi are beginning to emerge as a result of these recent research projects. We are now in a position to develop a fine-grained chronology. Chickasaw villages typically contain what Jennings called midden pits. These large shallow depressions were dug into the silty clay overlying the chalk substratum of the Black Prairie to a depth of 2 or 3 feet. They are usually 10 to 12 feet in diameter. The purpose for which these pits were dug is open to speculation. They may have been borrow pits from which clay for plastering the walls of the houses was mined, or reservoirs to hold water for stock or household use, or both. At any rate, the pits were ultimately filled with trash and are a rich source of artifacts on sites that are typically badly disturbed by cultivation and terracing. O'Hear and his coworkers were able to seriate the pits at ImmokaKina'Fa,' detecting many of the trends noted by earlier workers. These data, in combination with temporal data available from sites like Futorian and Orchard, should ultimately allow a chronology measured in terms of decades. The implications of this kind of chronological control for understanding the dynamic changes in Chickasaw culture that occurred during the colonial period are obvious.

As usual, ceramics are the primary focus of these chronological studies, and they have served to refine patterns observed by Jennings and his successors. For example, the shift from live shell temper to fossil shell temper appears to have occurred late in the seventeenth century, along with several changes in vessel decoration (O'Hear and Ryba 1998; Rafferty 1995; Morgan 1996). European trade items are also useful, especially glass beads. However, most beads have a temporal span that is too broad for the kind of chronological control being attempted, and assemblage level analysis is generally more informative, particularly the relative proportion of the collection made up of glass or metal artifacts (O'Hear and Ryba 1998).

Assemblage level analysis of the faunal material is another potential source of chronological data. The occurrence of bison in a physiographic zone like the Black Prairie is not surprising, but they seem to have come in earlier than previously thought. Rather than being a historic response to an abandoned field econiche created by aboriginal depopulation (Rostlund 1960), they seem to occur first in late prehistoric times on the prairie and remain through the early eighteenth century (Johnson et al. 1994a). There is no evidence for a decline in Chickasaw population until the beginning of intensive trade and warfare initiated by the founding of permanent French and English colonies in the Southeast. All of the early eighteenth-century Chickasaw sites in the Tupelo area contain positive or probable bison bone. Bear is also much more common on Chickasaw sites than on earlier ones. And, of course, domesticated animals like horse, pig, and cow show up in increasing numbers as the historic period progresses (Breitburg 1997; O'Hear and Ryba 1998).

Perhaps because of the rapid changes in subsistence, technology, and economics that occurred during the early colonial period, lithic artifacts are unusually useful in dating Chickasaw sites. There was a dramatic reorganization of the tool production technology that appears to have occurred at the very end of the seventeenth century. The chert that was available on the gravel bars in the Tombigbee River not too far distant was replaced by a light gray tabular Fort Payne chert, which had to have been imported a minimum of 50 miles from bedrock deposits in the Tennessee River drainage to the northeast. Moreover, a sizable portion of this new raw material was transformed into amorphous cores used to produce flake tools, most of which were used without modification. Other flakes were used in producing small, distinctive bifaces and equally diagnostic unifacial scrapers. Atkinson (1987) was the first to recognize the distinctive nature of this assemblage and its resemblance to similar tool kits associated with late prehistoric occupations in the Mississippi River Valley to the west. Detailed analysis of the lithic artifacts from the Orchard site (Johnson 1997a) and the ImmokaKina'Fa' site (O'Hear and Ryba 1998) have begun to explore the implications of these artifacts for interpreting Chickasaw economics.

Beyond the shift to an entirely different raw material, the early eighteenth-century lithic assemblages from the Chickasaw sites are remarkable in that they include several artifact forms that are more common in raw material source areas. For example, amorphous cores, a common lithic artifact on early eighteenth-century Chickasaw sites, spend raw material in order to expedite tool production and are therefore usually rare outside of a source area. Likewise, early stages of biface manufacture are usually confined to source areas where production failures can easily be replaced. Early eighteenth-century Chickasaw sites contain the full range of biface production rejects. This suggests that the Chickasaws were taking advantage of the new mobility provided by horses to transport and stockpile Fort Payne chert in the Tupelo area villages, virtually eliminating the need to conserve raw material or preform tools in the source area (Johnson 1997a).

But why the shift to Fort Payne chert in the first place? It might be explained by the sudden and coincident occurrence of thumbnail scrapers. These tools were made on a specialized flake which would have been difficult to manufacture from the relatively small gravels that occur in the Tombigbee Drainage. And this leads to the more interesting question of the introduction of a relatively elaborate tool kit just at the twilight of stone tool production in the Southeast. The timing of the first appearance and the distribution of these artifacts across the Southeast suggests they were a response to the deerskin trade. Wear pattern analysis of a small sample of scrapers from ImmokaKina'Fa' (O'Hear and Ryba 1998) supports this argument since the majority of the artifacts examined were used in hide scraping. However, these tools are much more common at the Large Prairie sites than at sites in the Small Prairie, and it is this phenomenon that allows us to move beyond technology and gain insights into the Chickasaws' social organization and trade alliances.

Like most of the historic southeastern Indians, the Chickasaws were organized into clans and moieties, but local village groups were also important and sometimes village membership was a primary consideration. "The interests of a man or woman centered more in the local group than in the larger divisions" (Swanton 1928:203). The geographic division of the Chickasaw villages into the Large Prairie and Small Prairie may have reflected a more fundamental partition. As noted earlier, it was the Large Prairie villages that took in the Natchez refugees, and Natchez ceramics are found only in the Large Prairie. It is certainly no coincidence that the war chief lived in the village of Ougoula Tchetoka, one of the Large Prairie villages. Imayatabe le Borgne, the peace chief, so emphatically opposed the Natchez presence among the Chickasaws that he threatened to relocate Ackia and two other Small Prairie villages to live among the Choctaws (Galloway 1996). At the time when the Large Prairie villages had cut all ties with the French, the principal leader of the Small Prairie villages was attempting to maintain some sort of relationship with them. Both village groups continued to trade with the British. In fact, the French (Rowland and Sanders 1927:305) claim that there were English traders behind the palisades at the battle of Ackia. The British contend otherwise (Chander 1910:278).

Archaeology suggests that alliance with both the French and the English paid off for the Small Prairie villages. Not only did large amounts of trade goods come out of these sites during the looting that accompanied the Lee Acres development, the differences between the Large and Small Prairie sites in terms of the lithic assemblages are informative. Thumbnail scrapers are a common feature of the early eighteenth-century Southeast along the western and northern boundaries, at the extreme limit of the French and English trade routes (Johnson 1997a). This probably reflects the relative availability of metal tools that could substitute for stone in hide processing. Viewed from this perspective, the relative scarcity of stone scrapers in the Small Prairie collections may be the result of the fact that these villages had better access to trade goods because they dealt with both the English and the French.

Mid-Eighteenth Century

Prior to the discovery of the Nairne letters, the primary historic source on the Chickasaws was James Adair's *History of the American Indians* (1986 [1775]). Adair was an English trader out of Charles Town who lived among the Chickasaws from 1744 to 1750 and again from 1761 to 1768. In fact, the major portion of Adair's work was written during his second stay with the Chickasaws (Williams 1930). The first 230 pages of his book are devoted to "Observations, and Arguments, in Proof of the American Indians' Being

Descended from the Jews." Although the work displays many biases rather openly, Adair appears to have made his case for locating one of the lost tribes of Israel in a fairly objective manner. That is, most of what he reports is corroborated by other observers. In fact, Charles Hudson (1977) argued that, because of this focus, Adair recorded a good deal more data on religious and social customs than any other eighteenth-century writer. Adair is not nearly as objective about the French, the missionaries, the colonial government in Charles Town, or the Choctaw. And he regularly refers to the Chickasaws as his gallant friends or in similar terms. Still, there is a tremendous amount of information about the Indians of the Southeast, especially the Chickasaws.

The other major midcentury source is the record of Bernard Romans's visit to the Chickasaws in the winter of 1771 and 1772. Romans was a surveyor for the British colonial government in Pensacola, and some of his maps of what was then considered West Florida were published in 1775, along with a book-length description of the native inhabitants, landscape, and vegetation. This was the same year that Adair's *History* came out. Their accounts of the Chickasaws could not be farther apart. Romans (1961:40) asserted that the Chickasaws were "the most fierce, cruel, insolent, and haughty people, among the southern nations."

Both sources compress time, describing a sort of ethnographic present; it is not always clear whether a ceremony or custom was practiced in former times or was observed by Adair or Romans. Still, these works give us some sense of the changes that had resulted from the Chickasaws' intensive contact with Europeans for more than half a century. Each commented on the small number of Chickasaws who remained to hold out against their more populous neighbors, and Adair indicated that they were just a fraction of their former size. Although the deerskin trade continued, "most of them are of late grown fond of the ornaments of life, of raising live stock, and using a greater industry than formerly, to increase wealth" (Adair 1986:390 [1775]). In spite of this shift in subsistence, the Chickasaws continued to live in several small villages closely congregated on the prairie for defensive purposes (Adair 1986:378[1775]; Romans 1961:40).

The French colonial records (Rowland and Sanders 1927, 1929, 1932; Rowland et al. 1984a, 1984b) continue through 1763, and the Charles Town trade records cut off at 1765 (McDowell 1955, 1958, 1970). Many of the British documents relating to Mississippi from the colonial administrators in Pensacola and Mobile dating between 1763 and 1766 have been published in an edited volume (Rowland 1911). All of these documents contain valuable information about the Chickasaws. All sources agree that the Chickasaws had lost their earlier advantages, first as the westernmost tribe to have access to the new technology of warfare and later as the key players in an unofficial British policy of containment. Population estimates show a remarkable reduction in size by midcentury (Wood 1989). A Chickasaw petition to Charles Town in 1753 describes their situation.

> That we have for many Years past been surrounded by our Enemies, in particular, the Chactaws who are very numerous, and so well acquainted with our Situation, that it's scarcely possible for us much longer to defend ourselves in this Place without some Assistance from your Excellency and Honours. All our Hunting Ground is always full of Enemies so that we are not able to kill Deer half sufficient to purchase Necessaries for our Families, no Ammunition, and Guns to preserve our Wives and Children from becoming Slaves to our Enemies. The Paths that the English Traders come to us is often covered with our Enemies, whereby their Goods is often lost, as also the Lives of the white Men, and we by endeavoring to guard them, and their Goods into this Nation is often cut off. (McDowell 1958:458)

The Meadowbrook site (22Le912), located on the western edge of the Small Prairie, is the only excavated Chickasaw site that dates to the mid-eighteenth century. Although a partial house pattern and several scattered post molds were discovered, the ridge upon which the site is located had been terraced and badly eroded as the result of years of cultivation (Yearous 1991). Consequently, the majority of the recovered artifacts came from the thirteen burial pits that were deep enough to escape destruction. However, most of the burials had been vandalized. A total of 5,995 artifacts of European origin were found at Meadowbrook, the majority of which are glass beads. Taken together, the beads, buttons, and gun spalls suggest a date no earlier than 1729 and no later than 1760. The average of the bead dates is 1750, indicating a likely midcentury date for the burials. The scarcity of stone tools and lack of thumbnail scrapers supports this assignment.

More than half (fourteen) of the twenty-three individuals from the Meadowbrook burials were bundles; only three were clearly primary interments. This runs counter to the traditional picture of Chickasaw burial practices where the body is buried immediately upon death (Adair 1986:190[1775]; Cushman 1962:404; Nairne 1988:48; Romans 1961:47). This apparent discrepancy between archaeology and ethnohistory led to a review of the documents and the realization that the Chickasaws buried in the flesh except when the individual died away from home (Adair 1986:189[1775]). The large proportion of bundle burials at Meadowbrook may reflect the tenuous situation of the Chickasaws by 1750, when war parties and attacks on hunting expeditions resulted in an unusual number of deaths by violence, at some distance from the village. (Johnson et al. 1994b)

Commissaries, Agents, and Missionaries

The end of the Seven Years War in 1763 marked a shift in the balance of power in the Southeast, with the British gaining control over part of the French holdings east of the Mississippi, including the Chickasaw territory. British Indian policy provided for resident agents to be assigned to each of the tribes. These commissaries were charged with supervising trade policies established in a series of congresses involving tribal leaders and colonial officials. The arrangement was fairly short lived, ending with the conclusion of the American Revolution. During those hostilities, the Chickasaws sided with their old allies, the British. At one point they attacked and laid siege to an American fort south of the mouth of the Ohio River. The Chickasaw territory was claimed for a short time by Spain, which licensed trade into the interior to British agents Panton and Leslie, John Turnbull, and James Joyce. American Indian agents were assigned to the tribes of the old Southwest around the turn of the century; a Chickasaw agency was established in 1801 near present-day Houlka to the southwest of the major settlements in the Tupelo area. Monroe mission, funded by the Presbyterian Church, was founded in 1820 near the Natchez Trace several miles north of the agency.

The old intertribal schism between the pro-British and pro-French factions was first translated into pro-British and pro-Spanish then pro-American and pro-Spanish. A third faction consisting of mixed blood descendants of British traders complicated internal politics. The sons of James Logan Colbert were prominent tribal leaders and played an important role in the treaties that led, ultimately, to the Chickasaws' removal in 1837.

Gibson's (1971:58–184) chapters on this period are a good deal more satisfactory than his discussion of the first half of the eighteenth century, perhaps because abundant, traditional historic sources are available. Still, there is a curious neglect of readily available archaeological data as well as some critical historic accounts, such as H. B. Cushman's *History of the*

Choctaw, Chickasaw, and Natchez Indians (1962). First published in 1899, Cushman's book drew upon the author's personal experiences growing up at Mayhew mission in Choctaw territory, as well as a good deal of memory ethnography gathered in Oklahoma from Indians born in Mississippi (Debo 1962). Once again, it is necessary to guard against the kind of time compression that occurs under such circumstances. Many of the customs described by Cushman were certainly not practiced during his lifetime. Still, his book provides valuable information on early nineteenth-century Chickasaw life.

Perhaps the single most important document in terms of locating the Chickasaw settlements at the turn of the century is Dr. Rush Nutt's diary of a visit to the Chickasaw territory in 1805. Jennings (1947) annotated and published a transcript of those portions of the diary that deal with the Chickasaws. At the time of Nutt's visit, the Chickasaws had all but abandoned the congregated villages of the eighteenth century, having "settled out for the benefit of their stock" (Jennings 1947:42). Only eight years before his visit "the whole nation was contained (or nearly so) in these old towns, but by the advice of the agent & other officers of government, they have settled out, made comfortable cabins, enclosed their fields by a worm fence, & enjoy the benefits of their labour, & stock, and are measurably clothed by their own industry" (Jennings 1947:43). Specific population centers were located by compass bearing and distance from the federal agent's headquarters near Houlka, and it is clear that the Chickasaws had settled throughout most of north Mississippi.

Recent research in the National Archives uncovered a wealth of data relating to the establishment and maintenance of the Chickasaw agency and resulted in a history and abstract of documents, both of which are in manuscript form (Atkinson 1997, 1998). What emerges is a much clearer picture of the relationship between the Chickasaws and the various Indian agents assigned to them as well as a view of some of the evolving relationships within the tribe.

By the turn of the century, the Chickasaws had undergone another shift in subsistence. The deerskin trade was no longer viable, and most lived by keeping cattle, subsistence farming, or, after 1805, government allotment. This transformation was the result of a number of factors, including nearly 100 years of intensive hunting, increased interaction with Europeans, and a government policy of enculturation. "The Indians are falling off from their former customs & habits very fast. . . . They are done with the hunt. The men have laid down their gun & tomahawk and taken up the implements of husbandry" (Jennings 1947:49). By Cushman's (1962:394) time, log houses had replaced traditional wattle and daub.

The records suggest that although the villages of the eighteenth century no longer existed, village identity persisted, with families from the same village relocating near one another. Still, this change in settlement strategy must have had an impact on Chickasaw social organization, one that would be interesting to measure archaeologically. However, because the Chickasaws of this period had adopted so many of the European customs and artifacts, they become essentially invisible in the archaeological record. Atkinson's (1985a) surface collection of material from the site of the Chickasaw agency (22Cs521), known to have been occupied from 1801 to 1825, includes a good sample of European ceramics from that period, a fair number of Choctaw sherds, a few possible Creek sherds, but no identifiable Chickasaw material. The Choctaw artifacts are explained by reference to Nutt's account of Choctaws living in the vicinity of the agency at the time of his visit in 1805. Atkinson (1985a:60) speculates that the Chickasaws had stopped producing ceramics by the beginning of the nineteenth century.

In fact, the only clearly Chickasaw material dating to this period has been recovered from burials. The first of the early nineteenth-century Chickasaw burials to be reported was described by Calvin Brown (1926:349–53) in his pioneering *Archeology of Mississippi*. This burial was found three miles southwest of the town of New Albany, which is located in north Mississippi about twenty miles northwest of the eighteenth-century Chickasaw villages around Tupelo. Brown (1926:349–50) provided the following list of grave goods:

2 big dinner plates of chinaware; 3 saucers;
6 china cups or bowls; 2 metal spoons;
2 metal knives; 22 feet of trade beads;
1 Jefferson medal of silver
1 pair of silver bracelets, 2.75 inches wide;
1 pair of silver bracelets, 2 inches wide;
10 silver brooches or buckles, 1.79 to 3.94 inches in diameter
Quantities of silver pendants, rings, and other ornaments
1 cane borer and 4 bored cores

All but the china were donated to the Mississippi Geological Survey in 1923 and were eventually accessioned into the Museum of Anthropology collection at the University of Mississippi. These artifacts were returned to the Chickasaw Nation in 1998.

Jefferson Peace Medals were minted in 1801 and distributed to prominent Indian leaders shortly thereafter. The other indicators of chronology are, of course, the glass beads. The "22 feet of trade beads" amounted to 1,305 glass beads, which have been classified according to method of manufacture, shape, and color (table 4.2), following conventions established by Good (1972), Brain (1979), and Smith and Good (1982). Not only do these publications provide excellent discussions of bead typology, they all have color photographs, a necessity in classifying beads. Many of the beads that accompanied the peace medal correspond exactly to beads in the collections described by Good (1972) and Brain (1979), both of which include eighteenth-century material; Good's contains early nineteenth-century artifacts as well.

Although beads are a common artifact on Chickasaw sites from the Tupelo area, only three collections have been described in comparable detail. ImmokaKina'Fa' (O'Hear and Ryba 1998) and Silver City (Wild 1997) both date to the beginning of the eighteenth century, while Meadowbrook (Yearous 1991) appears to be somewhat later. When the beads from these three sites are grouped by method of manufacture and compared to the Jefferson Peace Medal collection, some patterns become evident (table 4.3). Drawn beads with rounded ends appear to have been more common early in the eighteenth century, while untumbled drawn beads predominate in the Meadowbrook collection, which is thought to date to the midcentury. The peace medal securely dates the New Albany burial to sometime after 1801, and there is a dramatic difference in the beads. Wound beads, most of which are small and round or oblong, are the most common bead form, followed closely by drawn beads with hexagonal cross sections and ground facets on the corners. The latter are common at Creek sites only after the Red Stick Rebellion of 1812 (Marvin Smith, personal communication 1998).

Similar beads can be identified in the illustrations of trade items recovered from six Chickasaw burials in the village area of the Bynum Mounds site (22Cs503 [MCs 16]), which was excavated by National Park Service archaeologists in preparation for the construction of the Natchez Trace (Cotter and Corbett 1951:pl. 6). Without restudying the beads, a more detailed comparison is not possible except that, in a portion of a report by Arthur Woodward quoted in the Bynum monograph (Cotter and Corbett 1951:15), it is noted that "the small, dark red faceted bead is the one which I believe was sold by

Table 4.2. Beads from Jefferson Peace Medal burial located near New Albany, Mississippi

Attributes	Count
Drawn beads	
Round cross section	
Simple construction	
Untumbled	
Type 1 Opaque dark blue iridescent patina, 9–10 mm long, 3 mm diameter	6
Brain type IA3 (1650–1833, mean 1726)	
Type 2 Opaque dark burgundy, 5–10 mm long, 3–4 mm diameter	8
Like Good 121 except not tumbled; "untumbled specimens were found at Wichita sites, 1740–1820"	
Tumbled	
Type 3 Opaque white, 14 mm long, 8 mm diameter	1
Brain IIA1 (1600–1836, mean 1739)	
Good 96 (1670–1830)	
Type 4 Translucent amber, 5 mm long, 6 mm diameter	1
Type 5 Translucent burgundy, 2–3 mm long, 3 mm diameter	17
Type 6 Opaque light blue, 2 mm long, 3 mm diameter	4
Brain IIA4 (1699–1890, mean 1748)	
Type 7 Opaque dark burgundy, 2 mm long, 4 mm diameter	1
Brain IIA5 (1600–1890, mean 1745)	
Compound construction	
Untumbled	
Type 8 Opaque white with outer layer of clear glass, 3–5 mm long, 3–4 mm diameter	31
Brain IIIA2 (1650–1835, mean 1748)	
Good 118	
Tumbled	
Type 9 Opaque white with outer layer of clear glass, 3–4 mm long, 2–3 mm diameter	125
Brain IVA1 (1600–1890, mean 1754)	
Good 117 (1660–1833)	
Type 10 Transparent light green with outer layer of opaque brick red, 2–4 mm long, 3–5 mm diameter; resemble Cornaline d'Aleppo except a final layer of clear glass is not evident	94
Brain IVA2 (1600–1836, mean 1727)	
Hexagonal cross section	
Simple construction	
Faceted	
Type 11 Clear, short, 5–6 mm long, 5–6 mm diameter	382
Good 21	

(continued)

Table 4.2—*continued*

Type 12	Clear, long, 12–16 mm long, 5 mm diameter	7
Type 13	Translucent burgundy, 4–7 mm long, 5–6 diameter Good 17 (1760–1838)	11
Type 14	Transparent dark blue, 7 mm long, 6 mm diameter Good 10 (1760–1836)	1
Type 15	Transparent light blue, 3–4 mm long, 5–6 mm diameter Good 12	2
Type 16	Transparent green, 4 mm long, 4 mm diameter Good 16 (1760–1838)	1

Wound beads
Oval/barrel shaped

Type 17	Opaque white, look like shell beads, 6 mm long, 3–5 mm diameter Brain WID1 (1700–1833, mean 1789) Good 38 (1767–1820)	7
Type 18	Opaque dark burgundy, 6–8 mm long, 3–5 mm diameter Brain WID4 (1719–1833) Good 38 (1767–1820)	10
Type 19	Opaque red, fragmentary, 5 mm diameter	1
Type 20	Translucent burgundy, weathered with a good deal of pitting on surface and silver patina, 7–9 mm long, 4–5 mm diameter	27

Round/donut shaped

Type 21	Translucent burgundy, weathered same as type 20, 4–5 mm long, 4–5 mm diameter	525
Type 22	Translucent burgundy, same as type 21 but larger, 7 mm long, 8 mm diameter	1
Type 23	Translucent burgundy, same as type 21 but larger still, 10 mm long, 11 mm diameter	1
Type 24	Translucent dark blue, 5 mm long, 7–8 mm diameter	20
Type 25	Translucent dark blue, 10 mm long, 12 mm diameter Good 46 (1720–50)	1
Type 26	Translucent green, 7 mm long, 9 mm diameter	1
Type 27	Translucent amber, 6–7 mm long, 6 mm diameter Brain WIA3 (1700–1830, mean 1764)	2
Type 28	Translucent milky with amber cast, 3–5 mm long, 4–5 mm diameter	6
Type 29	Translucent clear, white weathering, 4–5 mm long, 8 mm diameter	8
Type 30	Transparent clear, silver patina, 8–9 mm long, 10–11 mm diameter Brain WIE1	6

Molded

Type 31	Transparent clear, "raspberry" pattern Brain WIIB2 (1550–1836, mean 1730)	1

Table 4.3. Glass trade beads from Chickasaw sites in northeast Mississippi (percentage breakdown)

	Immoka-Kina'Fa (N=707)	Silver City (N=46)	Meadow-brook (N=5,612)	Peace Medal (N=1,305)
Drawn Beads				
Round cross section				
Simple construction				
Untumbled	4.67	6.52	76.27	1.07
Tumbled	93.07	71.74	7.73	1.84
Compound construction				
Untumbled	0.71	8.70	11.05	2.38
Tumbled	5.37	4.35	4.79	16.78
Hexagonal cross section				
Simple construction				
Faceted	0.14	0.00	0.00	30.96
Wound Beads	0.71	8.70	0.16	46.97

Sources: ImmokaKina'Fa' (O'Hear and Ryba 1998), Silver City (Wild 1997), Meadowbrook (Yearous 1991).

the traders during the first three decades at least [of the nineteenth century] as 'mock garnet.' The other faceted beads are of the first half of the nineteenth century. At an earlier period, early eighteenth and seventeenth centuries, the faceted beads were molded, and later, in the early twentieth they were machine molded or pressed."

In fact, the historic period burials contained many European artifacts, including a silver alloy hat band or coronet, gun parts, spoons, cups, pendants, and brooches. Most were judged by Woodward to belong to the period between 1820 and 1830. The remarkable absence of native-made Chickasaw artifacts outside the burials was noted by the excavators and attributed to acculturation (Cotter and Corbett 1951:35).

Perhaps the most remarkable Chickasaw burial from this time period was discovered during the grading done in preparation for a subdivision in south Tupelo in 1956. This burial was located just to the south of the Tupelo hospital, to the east of the Lee Acres subdivision, and just to the north and on the same ridge as the ImmokaKina'Fa' site recently excavated by O'Hear and his coworkers. Although the grave goods are no longer available for study, a detailed inventory and photographic record were preserved and a report of this find is in preparation (Atkinson and Bushman 1998). The burial contained a wealth of artifacts, including gold-plated uniform buttons, an epaulette, and a Washington Peace Medal. It is this last item, in conjunction with a good deal of historical research, that has allowed Atkinson to identify the burial as that of Piomingo, the principal military leader of the Chickasaws during most of the last half of the eighteenth century. Piomingo died in about 1798 after having received a Washington Peace Medal in 1792. It is interesting to note that the burial contained no glass beads.

Conclusions

Chickasaw archaeology and history offer many opportunities to study intercultural relations and politics of the Southeast during the colonial era. We can follow the Chickasaw transition from a typical Mississippian subsistence pattern to one based on upland prairie settlement. The impact of the colonial trade, first in slaves and then in deerskins, is clear in both the archaeological and documentary records. The final transformation of the Chickasaws into subsistence farmers with an emphasis on free-range cattle is evident in the dispersal from the nucleated villages in the Tupelo area which occurred in the 1790s.

The rich documentary and archaeological records allow questions about acculturation, adaptation, and technology to be addressed in a way that goes beyond culture history. Unfortunately, because most of the eighteenth-century Chickasaw settlements were concentrated in a single location in the Black Prairie, and that location coincides almost exactly with one of the largest cities in northern Mississippi, much of the archaeological record of this critical century in Chickasaw development has been destroyed. There is still, as Atkinson's recent visits to the National Archives have illustrated, a great deal of untapped archival data. In addition, the large collections of material excavated by Jennings and Spaulding more than half a century ago are stored in the Southeastern Archeological Center of the National Park Service in Tallahassee. At least some of the artifacts collected by Chambers remain at the Mississippi Department of Archives and History in Jackson. Further study of these collections would add a good deal to our understanding of the early eighteenth-century Chickasaws.

One of the reasons that we can trace the evolution of the Chickasaws with such confidence is that the three major tribal groups that survived into the eighteenth century in Mississippi—the Chickasaws, Choctaws, and Natchez—can be easily distinguished on the basis of ceramics, settlement pattern, and social organization. There appears to be a rather strong correspondence between material culture and ethnic identity. However, it is likely that this is an illusion, created by the happenstance that the eighteenth-century survivors are well separated geographically. Once you attempt to identify the smaller groups mentioned in the historic records, namely, the Alibamus or Chachumas in northeastern Mississippi (Atkinson 1979), or try to correlate the protohistoric polities of the Yazoo Basin with the rich archaeological record there (Brain 1988), the difficulty in identifying ethnic groups on the basis of ceramics or any other aspect of the archaeological record becomes obvious. The only reason it is so easy for archaeologists working with historic tribes in Mississippi is that we are dealing with isolated remnants of a complex spatial and temporal continuum in which polity and material culture blended in such a way that ethnic boundaries are difficult to detect. In addition, each of the three major survivors reached the eighteenth century by a different route. What is exciting is our improving ability to trace those routes and to understand the consequent events using both archaeology and history.

Acknowledgments

Several people commented on earlier drafts of this essay. Principal among them were Jim Atkinson, Pat Galloway, John O'Hear, and Greg Waselkov. I was not always wise enough to take their advice, but the final product is surely improved where I did. I thank them and the several coauthors who have worked with me on Chickasaw material from Mississippi.

Bibliography

Adair, James
1986 [1775]   *History of the American Indians*. Reprint of 1930 edition, edited by
        S. C. Williams. New York: Promontory Press.
Atkinson, James R.
1979   A Historic Contact Indian Settlement in Oktibbeha County, Mississippi. *Journal of Alabama Archaeology* 25:61–82.
1985a   A Surface Collection from the Chickasaw Agency Site, 22-Cs-521, on the Natchez Trace in Chickasaw County, Mississippi. *Mississippi Archaeology* 20:46–63.

1985b   The Ackia and Ogoula Tchetoka Chickasaw Village Locations in 1736 during the French-Chickasaw War. *Mississippi Archaeology* 20:53–72.
1987   Historic Chickasaw Cultural Material: A More Comprehensive Identification. *Mississippi Archaeology* 22:32–62.
1998   History of the Chickasaw Indian Agency East of the Mississippi River. Manuscript.

Atkinson, James R. (compiler and editor)
1997   *Records of the Old Southwest in the National Archives: Abstracts of Records of the Chickasaw Indian Agency and Related Documents, 1794–1840.* Cobb Institute of Archaeology, Mississippi State University, Starkville.

Atkinson, James R., and Joyce E. Bushman
1998   Death of a Chickasaw Leader: The Probable Grave of Piomingo. Manuscript in preparation.

Blake, Leonard W.
1992   Corn from the Orchard Site. *Mississippi Archaeology* 27:60–71.

Born, Lester K.
1955   *British Manuscripts Project: A Checklist of the Microfilms Prepared in England and Wales for the American Council of Learned Societies, 1941–1945.* Washington, D.C.: Library of Congress.

Brain, Jeffrey P.
1979   *Tunica Treasure.* Papers of the Peabody Museum of Archaeology and Ethnology, Harvard University 71. Cambridge, Mass.
1988   *Tunica Archaeology.* Papers of the Peabody Museum of Archaeology and Ethnology, Harvard University 78. Cambridge, Mass.

Braund, Kathryn E. H.
1993   *Deerskins and Duffels: The Creek Indian Trade with Anglo-America, 1685–1815.* Lincoln: University of Nebraska Press.

Breitburg, Emanuel
1997   Faunal Remains from Site 22Le520, Lee County, Mississippi (with commentary on site 22Le519). Appendix B in Archaeological Investigations of the Fifteen-Acre Tract for the Proposed Construction of the Tennessee Valley Authority Customer Service Center, City of Tupelo, Lee County, Mississippi, by Michael J. Wild. Master's thesis, Department of Sociology and Anthropology, University of Mississippi, Oxford.

Brown, Calvin
1926   *Archeology of Mississippi.* Mississippi Geological Survey, Oxford.

Chander, Allen D.
1910   *The Colonial Records of the State of Georgia.* Vol. 21. Atlanta: Chas. P. Byrd (state printer).

Clayton, Lawrence A., Vernon James Knight, Jr., and Edward C. Moore (editors)
1993a   *The De Soto Chronicles: The Expedition of Hernando de Soto to North America in 1539–1543.* Vol. 1. Tuscaloosa: University of Alabama Press.
1993b   *The De Soto Chronicles: The Expedition of Hernando de Soto to North America in 1539–1543.* Vol. 2. Tuscaloosa: University of Alabama Press.

Cotter, John L., and John M. Corbett
1951   *Archeology of the Bynum Mounds.* Archeological Research Series no. 1. National Park Service, U.S. Department of the Interior, Washington, D.C.

Crane, Verner W.
1929   *The Southern Frontier, 1670–1732.* Ann Arbor: University of Michigan Press.

Cushman, Henry B.
1962   *History of the Choctaw, Chickasaw, and Natchez Indians.* Edited by A. Debo. Stillwater, Okla.: Redlands Press.

Debo, Angie
1962   Foreword. In *History of the Choctaw, Chickasaw, and Natchez Indians* by H. B. Cushman, edited by A. Debo, 7–10. Stillwater, Okla.: Redlands Press.

DePratter, Chester B.
1983   Late Prehistoric and Early Historic Chiefdoms in the Southeastern United States. Ph.D. diss., University of Georgia, Athens. University Microfilms, Ann Arbor.

Elmore, Francis
1955   *Preliminary Report on Archaeological Investigations at Futorian Furniture Factory.* Report on file, Natchez Trace Parkway, Tupelo.

Galloway, Patricia K.
1982   Henri de Tonti du Village des Chacta, 1702: The Beginning of the French Alliance. In *La Salle and His Legacy: Frenchmen and Indians in the Lower Mississippi Valley,* edited by P. K. Galloway, 146–75. Jackson: University Press of Mississippi.
1996   Ogoula Tchetoka, Ackia, and Bienville's First Chickasaw War: Whose Strategy and Tactics? *Journal of Chickasaw History* 2:3–10.

Gibson, Arrell M.
1971   *The Chickasaws.* Lincoln: University of Nebraska Press.

Good, Mary Elizabeth
1972   *Guebert Site: An 18th-Century, Historic Kaskaskia Indian Village in Randolph County, Illinois.* Central States Archaeological Societies Memoir 2. Wood River, Illinois.

Hogue, S. Homes, and Evan Peacock
1995   Environmental and Osteological Analysis at the South Farm Site (22OK534), a Mississippian Farmstead in Oktibbeha County, Mississippi. *Southeastern Archaeology* 14:31–45.

Hudson, Charles M.
1977   James Adair as Anthropologist. *Ethnohistory* 24:311–28.

Hudson, Charles M., Marvin T. Smith, and Chester B. DePratter
1990   The Hernando de Soto Expedition: From Mabila to the Mississippi River. In *Towns and Temples along the Mississippi,* edited by D. H. Dye and C. A. Cox, 181–207. Tuscaloosa: University of Alabama Press.

Jennings, Jesse D.
1941   Chickasaw and Earlier Indian Cultures of Northeast Mississippi. *Journal of Mississippi History* 3:115–226.
1944   The Archaeological Survey of the Natchez Trace. *American Antiquity* 9:408–14.
1947   Nutt's Trip to the Chickasaw Country. *Journal of Mississippi History* 9:35–61.

Johnson, Jay K.
1991   Aboriginal Settlement and First Contact in Northeast Mississippi. *National Geographic Research and Exploration* 7:492–94.

1996   The Nature and Timing of the Late Prehistoric Settlement of the Black Prairie in Northeast Mississippi: A Reply to Hogue, Peacock, and Rafferty. *Southeastern Archaeology* 15:244–49.

1997a   Stone Tools, Politics, and the Eighteenth-Century Chickasaw in Northeast Mississippi. *American Antiquity* 62:215–30.

1997b   Chiefdom to Tribe in Northeast Mississippi: A Culture in Transition. In *Historiography of the Hernando de Soto Expedition*, edited by P. K. Galloway, 295–312. Lincoln: University of Nebraska Press.

Johnson, Jay K., and H. Kim Curry

1984   *Final Report, Cultural Resources Survey in the Chuquatonchee Creek Watershed, Chickasaw, Clay, Monroe, and Pontotoc Counties, Mississippi*. Report submitted to Soil Conservation Service, Jackson, Miss., by Center for Archaeological Research, University of Mississippi, Oxford. Contract no. 53–4423–3–439.

Johnson, Jay K., and Geoffrey R. Lehmann

1996   Sociopolitical Devolution in Northeast Mississippi and the Timing of the de Soto Entrada. In *Bioarchaeology of Native American Adaptation in the Spanish Borderlands*, edited by B. J. Baker and L. Kealhofer, 38–55. Gainesville: University Press of Florida.

Johnson, Jay K., and John T. Sparks

1986   Protohistoric Settlement Patterns in Northeastern Mississippi. In *The Protohistoric Period in the Mid-South: Proceedings of the 1983 Mid-South Archaeological Conference*, edited by D. H. Dye and R. C. Brister, 64–82. Mississippi Department of Archives and History Archaeological Report 18. Jackson.

Johnson, Jay K., Patricia K. Galloway, and W. Belokon

1989   Historic Chickasaw Settlement Patterns in Lee County, Mississippi: A First Approximation. *Mississippi Archaeology* 24:45–52.

Johnson, Jay K., Jenny D. Yearous, and Nancy Ross-Stallings

1994b   Ethnohistory, Archaeology, and Chickasaw Burial Mode during the Eighteenth Century. *Ethnohistory* 41:431–46.

Johnson, Jay K., H. Kim Curry, James R. Atkinson, and John T. Sparks

1984   *Final Report, Cultural Resources Survey in the Line Creek Watershed, Chickasaw, Clay, and Webster Counties, Mississippi*. Report submitted to the Soil Conservation Service, Jackson, Miss., by Center for Archaeological Research, University of Mississippi, Oxford. Contract no. 53–4423–2–314.

Johnson, Jay K., Susan L. Scott, James R. Atkinson, and Andrea B. Shea

1994a   Late Prehistoric/Protohistoric Settlement and Subsistence on the Black Prairie: Buffalo Hunting in Mississippi. *North American Archaeologist* 15:167–79.

Johnson, Jay K., Geoffrey R. Lehmann, James R. Atkinson, Susan L. Scott, and Andrea B. Shea

1991   *Protohistoric Chickasaw Settlement Patterns and the de Soto Route in Northeast Mississippi*. Final report submitted to the National Endowment for the Humanities and the National Geographic Society.

Le Page Du Pratz, Antoine S.

1975   *The History of Louisiana*. (1774 London edition edited by J. G. Tregle, Jr.) Baton Rouge: Louisiana State University Press.

McDowell, William L., Jr. (editor)
1955   Journals of the Commissioners of the Indian Trade, September 20, 1710–
        August 29, 1718. South Carolina Archives Department, Columbia.
1958   Documents Relating to Indian Affairs, May 21, 1750–August 7, 1754. South
        Carolina Archives Department , Columbia.
1970   *Documents Relating to Indian Affairs, 1754–1765*. Columbia: University of
        South Carolina Press.
Moore, Alexander
1985   Thomas Nairne's 1708 Western Expedition: An Episode in the Anglo-French
        Competition for Empire. In *Proceedings of the Tenth Annual Meeting of the
        French Colonial Historical Society,* edited by P. M. Boucher, 47–58. Washing-
        ton D.C.: University Press of America.
1988   Introduction. In *Nairne's Muskhogean Journals, the 1708 Expedition to the
        Mississippi River,* edited by A. Moore, 3–31. Jackson: University Press of
        Mississippi.
Morgan, David W.
1996   Historic Period Chickasaw Indians: Chronology and Settlement Pattern. *Mis-
        sissippi Archaeology* 31:1–39.
Nairne, Thomas
1988   *Nairne's Muskhogean Journals, the 1708 Expedition to the Mississippi River,*
        edited by A. Moore. Jackson: University Press of Mississippi.
O'Hear, John, and Elizabeth A. Ryba (editors)
1998   Excavations at the ImmokaKina'Fa' Site (22Le907), Lee County, Mississippi.
        Manuscript in preparation.
Peacock, Evan
1995   Test Excavations at an Upland Mississippian Site in Oktibbeha County, Mis-
        sissippi. *Mississippi Archaeology* 30:1–20.
Phelps, Dawson A.
1957   The Chickasaw, the English, and the French, 1699–1744. *Tennessee Historical
        Quarterly* 16:117–53.
Rafferty, Janet
1995   A Seriation of Chickasaw Pottery from Northeast Mississippi. *Journal of
        Alabama Archaeology* 4:180–207.
1996   Settlement Patterning as an Independent Variable: Understanding Similarities
        in Woodland and Mississippian Settlement Patterns. *Southeastern Archaeol-
        ogy* 15:230–43.
Romans, Bernard
1961   *A Concise Natural History of East and West Florida* (facsimile reprint of 1775
        edition). New Orleans: Pelican Publishing.
Rostlund, Erhard
1960   The Geographic Range of the Historic Bison in the Southeast. *Annals of the
        Association of American Geographers* 50:395–407.
Rowland, Dunbar (editor)
1911   *Mississippi Provincial Archives, English Dominion.* Vol. 1, 1763–1766. Mis-
        sissippi Department of Archives and History, Jackson.

120   Jay K. Johnson

Rowland, Dunbar, and A. G. Sanders (editors)
1927   *Mississippi Provincial Archives, French Dominion.* Vol. 1, *1729–1740.* Mississippi Department of Archives and History, Jackson.
1929   *Mississippi Provincial Archives, French Dominion.* Vol. 2, *1701–1729.* Mississippi Department of Archives and History, Jackson.
1932   *Mississippi Provincial Archives, French Dominion.* Vol. 3, *1704–1743.* Mississippi Department of Archives and History, Jackson.
Rowland, Dunbar, A. G. Sanders, and Patricia K. Galloway (editors)
1984a   *Mississippi Provincial Archives, French Dominion.* Vol. 4, *1729–1748.* Baton Rouge: Louisiana State University Press.
1984b   *Mississippi Provincial Archives, French Dominion.* Vol. 5, *1749–1763.* Baton Rouge: Louisiana State University Press.
Royce, Charles C.
1899   *Indian Land Cessions in the United States.* Eighteenth Annual Report of the Smithsonian Institution, Bureau of American Ethnology, 1896–97. Washington, D.C.
Smith, Marvin T., and Mary Elizabeth Good
1982   *Early Sixteenth-Century Glass Beads in the Spanish Colonial Trade.* Greenwood, Miss.: Cottonlandia Museum Publications.
Solis, Carlos, and Richard Walling
1982   *Archaeological Investigations at the Yarborough Site (22C1814).* University of Alabama Office of Archaeological Research Report of Investigations 30. Moundville.
South Carolina Council Journals
1725–26   Legislative Journals, February 1725–May 1726. American Council of Learned Societies, British Manuscripts Project, Public Record Office 25/1, C.O. 5/429, South Carolina. Library of Congress call no. microfilm 041 (D).
Sparks, John T.
1987   *Prehistoric Settlement Patterns in Clay County, Mississippi.* Archaeological Report 20. Mississippi Department of Archives and History, Jackson.
Stubbs, John D., Jr.
1982a   A Preliminary Classification for Chickasaw Pottery. *Mississippi Archaeology* 17:50–57.
1982b   The Chickasaw Contact with the La Salle Expedition. In *La Salle and His Legacy: Frenchmen and Indians in the Lower Mississippi Valley,* edited by P. K. Galloway, 41–48. Jackson: University Press of Mississippi.
1983   A Report Presenting the Results of Archaeological Survey in Lee County, Mississippi, June 1981 to June 1983. Manuscript on file, Mississippi Department of Archives and History, Jackson.
1992   Chickasaw Settlement Patterns in the Eighteenth and Nineteenth Centuries. Paper presented at the Thirteenth Mid-South Archaeological Conference, Tuscaloosa, Alabama.
Swanton, John R.
1922   *Early History of the Creek Indians and Their Neighbors.* Smithsonian Institution, Bureau of American Ethnology Bulletin 73. Washington, D.C.

1928 Social and Religious Beliefs and Usages of the Chickasaw Indians. Forty-fourth Annual Report of the Smithsonian Institution, Bureau of American Ethnology, 169–273. Washington, D.C.

Usner, Daniel H.

1992 *Indians, Settlers, and Slaves in a Frontier Exchange Economy: The Lower Mississippi Valley before 1783.* Chapel Hill: University of North Carolina Press.

Wild, Michael J.

1997 Archaeological Investigations of the Fifteen-Acre Tract for the Proposed Construction of the Tennessee Valley Authority Customer Service Center, City of Tupelo, Lee County, Mississippi. Master's thesis, Department of Sociology and Anthropology, University of Mississippi, Oxford.

Williams, Samuel Cole

1930 Introduction. In *History of the American Indians,* edited by S. C. Williams, vii–xxx. 1986 reprint. New York: Promontory Press.

Wood, Peter H.

1989 The Changing Population of the Colonial South: An Overview by Race and Region, 1685–1790. In *Powhatan's Mantle: Indians in the Colonial Southeast,* edited by P. H. Wood, G. A. Waselkov, and M. Thomas Hatley, 35–103. Lincoln: University of Nebraska Press.

Yearous, Jenny D.

1991 Meadowbrook: An Eighteenth-Century Chickasaw Village. Master's thesis, Department of Sociology and Anthropology, University of Mississippi, Oxford.

5

The Caddos of the Trans-Mississippi South

ANN M. EARLY

With their friends they keep unchangeable peace.

When agents for France and Spain began to compete for the lands, resources, and allegiances of native peoples in the woodlands west of the Mississippi River Valley at the turn of the eighteenth century, they both sought to secure alliances with the Caddos, settled agriculturalists with well-ordered communities who commanded the respect of neighboring tribes in both the woodlands and the plains. The near ancestors of these people had experienced an earlier encounter with Europeans when the de Soto expedition marched through the region in an abortive attempt to reach Mexico (Bruseth 1992; Kenmotsu et al. 1993; Schambach 1989; Young and Hoffman 1993). Demographic and cultural changes, unobserved by Europeans, had probably affected Caddo societies, however, even before missionaries and traders first described their lifeways in the late seventeenth century (Perttula 1992). Our view of early historic Caddo culture, which is the subject of this essay, therefore is clouded not only by the idiosyncrasies of European recorders and historical accident but also by the reality of a people already responding to the biological and cultural instruments of European colonization.

Any inventory of the communities and larger population aggregates that comprised the Caddos is only an approximation. Lists compiled by various diarists are incomplete and inconsistent in transcribing community names. Europeans, as was the case elsewhere in the Southeast, were also encountering people on a trajectory of rapid and fluid change. This encompassed population movements, both in avoidance of threat and attraction toward trade partners and allies, consolidation after population decline brought about by warfare and disease, and changes in some elements of lifeways in response to the introduction of key European imports such as the horse. Firsthand accounts contain ephemeral references to some groups, such as the Cahinnio, who were encountered only briefly along the Ouachita River and then disappear from colonial era records. Their identity and affiliation can be only vaguely glimpsed through the documents.

Historic Caddo Groups

By the early eighteenth century, several geographic clusters of communities emerge that constitute the most commonly enumerated Caddo groups (Swanton 1942) (fig. 5.1). The largest cluster was situated in the mixed woodland and savanna environment of the Neches and Angelina drainages in east Texas. Although nearly thirty groups have been mentioned, eleven communities or polities, including the Nadaco, the Hainai, the Nacono, and the Nacogdoche, form the core of this Hasinai Caddo population (Griffith 1954:47; Perttula 1992:220; Story 1978:51). A second cluster of communities was distributed along the Great Bend area of the Red River, a rich alluvial valley habitat supporting a mosaic of bottomland hardwood forest, prairie enclaves, and a maze of backswamps, capillary drainages, and abandoned river channels. Here were found the Kadohadacho, Upper Nasoni, Upper Natchitoches, and Nanatsoho villages (Smith 1998:175)—referred to collectively as the Kadohadacho cluster. The Great Bend communities remained more remote from direct colonial era affairs and encounters than the east Texas and Louisiana Caddos by ecological and cultural accident: the Red River downstream was virtually impassible because the channel was blocked by a vast tangle of uprooted trees and other vegetation, and overland travel eastward to Arkansas Post and southwest to the Rio Grande was long and inconvenient. Unfortunately the Great Bend communities were also more exposed to predation by Osage bands from the north.

Downstream on the Red River and east of the Neches and Angelina villages was another population cluster that included the lower Natchitoches and Doustioni villages. Additional communities—the Yatasi and Petit Caddos between the Great Bend and Natchitoches regions, the Adai (Adaes) and the Ais between the Natchitoches and the Neches-Angeline groups—retained their identity through much of the eighteenth century and are also considered Caddos.

These population blocks, particularly the Hasinai and Great Bend groups, have been characterized as confederacies (see Swanton 1942:7) that

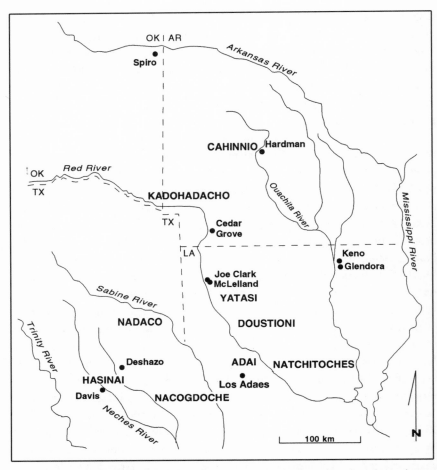

Fig. 5.1. Map showing historic Caddo locations and selected archaeological sites mentioned in the text.

incorporated internal ranking of communities, perhaps embodying rankings among kin groups residing in them. Among the Hasinai, the Hainai came to be recognized as the principal community. Along the Great Bend, the Nasoni may have been the paramount community at first contact, although the Kadohadacho became the dominant group later in the eighteenth century, probably through the influence and longevity of a series of charismatic leaders (Bolton 1908; Smith 1995, 1998; Swanton 1942:5). There have also been occasional references to the aggregate of all these communities as a single southern Caddo confederacy, but this is more a modern phenomenon than a formal relationship existing in the early historic period (Bolton 1987:25). Over time, the Hasinai (and Nadaco [Anadarko]), Natchitoche, and Kadohadacho names came to embody the major divisions of the Caddos as the populations became reduced and consolidated, and they remain as recognizable components of the modern Caddo tribe (see, for example, Carter 1995; Newkumet and Meredith 1988; Smith 1995, 1998; Story 1978).

While early observations of Hasinai and Great Bend communities indicate that some form of formal confederacies existed, the antiquity of this relationship is open to question. Depopulation from disease and increased conflict with tribes moving east and south across the southern Plains in the late seventeenth century alone created a new cultural geography to which the confederacies might have been a recent and short-lived response (Hickerson 1996; Perttula 1992:220–21). The paramount leadership position of *xinesi,* in which ultimate secular and sacred authority were vested, and the elaborate protocols of collective obligations and deference associated with the position, decline by the mid-eighteenth century. Community autonomy and local kin-based and secularized leadership appear to become the norm, although much about the workings of Caddo societies in this century was never recorded or can be glimpsed only very indirectly through records of occasional encounters between European and Indian. The colonial practice of imposing political and trade relations through the designation of community leaders chosen by European criteria has undoubtedly further obscured the actual structure and workings of the native social system.

Some evidence indicates that considerable diversity existed among Caddo population groups. Dialect differences were present and remembered even in recent times, and references have been made to mutually unintelligible dialects, although the scant linguistic research has not confirmed this (Lesser 1979:270; Lesser and Weltfish 1932:13). Eyewitness accounts of material culture and social roles suggest regional differences. House styles and community organizational plans varied sufficiently between some settlements (or population nodes) that several early travelers took note (see Joutel and Casañas, both cited in Swanton 1942:148–49). Attitudes toward, and treatment of, sacred fires that were central to the calendar of community rituals differed between Hasinai and Natchitoches population groups (Chabot 1932:36), and seemingly conflicting descriptions exist of roles and treatment of shamans (Chabot 1932:28) and governing and nongoverning elites (Wyckoff and Baugh 1980). These may signal not just the weaknesses of the ethnohistoric record and internal changes resulting from population loss and external pressures, but also preexisting variability among Caddo populations that have deeper historical roots.

Prehistoric Antecedents

Archaeological studies indicate that the Caddo lifeway emerges across a broad expanse of the Trans-Mississippi South shortly before A.D. 1000. Although the causal factors and mechanisms involved in this emergence remain obscure and contested, the ancestral population from which the Caddos emerge is generally accepted to have been local Woodland era societies now variously referred to most often as Early Ceramic (Bruseth 1998: 51; Story 1990:293) or Fourche Maline (see, for example, Jeter et al. 1989; Sabo et al. 1988; Schambach 1982, 1998; Story 1990). Among the characteristics attributed to the prehistoric Caddo tradition are the cultivation of maize, cucurbits, beans, and other domesticated plants that anchored a subsistence base which also included many wild plant and animal resources; the dispersal of the population in small residential settlements; the construction of mounds and civic-ceremonial centers that served as the foci of mortuary and ritual activities; an elaboration of material culture that included use of bows and arrows, manufacture of a diverse and technically accomplished, regionally distinctive ceramic assemblage; the creation and acquisition through extraregional trade of objects that served as ritual paraphernalia, tokens of rank and personal wealth, and mortuary offerings; and social changes witnessed by the elaborate and differential mortuary treatment afforded some members of society. On general and specific levels, the Caddo archaeological tradition compares closely with contemporary cultural phenomena elsewhere in the Southeast and indicates that some fundamental principles of social order, cosmology, and adaptation were shared, to varying degrees, through a series of processes that included direct contact.

These transformations are revealed, with varying degrees of clarity because the archaeological record is very uneven, over about 200,000 square kilometers (Perttula 1992:7, fig. 1). Ironically, the two early Caddo sites best known outside the small community of Caddo specialists—the Davis site (see Davidson 1997; Ford 1997; Newell and Krieger 1949; Story 1997, 1998) and the Spiro site (Brown 1996)—are situated virtually at opposite margins of this broad area, and although rich in information about some aspects of prehistoric Caddo development, they cannot be taken out of hand as models for development in the vast landscape between them. In fact, one challenge has been raised (by Schambach 1993) to the inclusion of Spiro and neighboring sites in the Arkansas Valley of northwest Arkansas and northeast Oklahoma in the prehistoric Caddo area.

Current understanding of the approximately 700-year Caddo archaeological tradition indicates that populations within separate river valley segments developed locally distinctive material assemblages that can be considered variations on the common Caddo theme. This is most visible in carefully nuanced local differences in shape and decoration of ceramics. While there are widely shared similarities in the kinds of vessels made and in the repertoire of decorative techniques and motifs appropriate for individual vessel classes, variations in shape and design combinations are evident within drainage segments and likely represent maps of distinct sociopolitical groups. Differences among other elements of material culture remain to be elucidated. One challenge to regional archaeologists is remaining sensitive to this diversity while investigating prehistoric Caddo societies and using the ethnohistoric literature on historic Caddo groups.

The Ethnohistoric Record

The means and motives of encounters between Caddo communities and Europeans (and Texans and Americans in the nineteenth century) varied, and followed the already well-known objectives of different colonial powers. The Spaniards sought the Caddos as souls to be missionized, political allies against French incursions from the Mississippi Valley, and political and military supporters against a variety of potentially dangerous Southern Plains tribes that included the Osage, the Apaches, and a loose assemblage of other groups referred to as the Norteños, comprising the Wichitas, Kichais, Tonkawas, and others (see Hickerson 1996 for recent studies of Caddo colonial history; La Vere 1993; Sabo 1987; Smith 1995, 1996). Repeated attempts were made to establish missions and presidios among the east Texas Caddos in the late seventeenth and early eighteenth centuries, all of which ended in failure for a variety of reasons. Conforming with Spanish expectations would have required substantial changes in settlement organization—and perhaps in traditional food-producing patterns—as well as relinquishing native religious practices. Spanish authorities also expected the Caddos to reject the lure of well-provisioned French traders and rely exclusively on an essentially unreliable and depauperate array of material goods transported the longer distance from south of the Rio Grande.

French interests were focused on trade, not only of skins, bear oil, salt, and other local resources, but also of items to be procured on the plains: bison skins, Apache slaves, and cattle and horses that could be taken from other groups or secured from feral herds. Shortly after the French were established in the Lower Mississippi Valley in 1700, they began developing economic and political ties with native groups west of the Mississippi through a network of trading posts and by the movement of individual traders into native communities. The most directly affected Caddo groups were those residing along the Red River, but the Hasinai and their neighbors, including the small population of Spanish clerics and soldiers who inhabited the isolated colonial outposts, also benefited from this source of goods. French trade aspirations ultimately extended beyond native communities to larger Spanish settlements south and west of the Caddos.

The Caddos found relationships with French traders and officials more congenial than with the Spanish authorities, even after the legal transfer of Louisiana to Spain in 1763. French traders brought guns and a wide array of other material goods. Economic activities were imbedded in a social context of reciprocal exchange and interpersonal relations that were apparently compatible with native systems of kin relations and authority structure (La Vere 1993). Possessing a steady supply of trade goods, courted by both France and Spain, and maintaining much of their territorial and political integrity, the Caddos had an influential role in political and economic affairs among European and Indian societies in the Trans-Mississippi South through much of the eighteenth century.

Our understanding of Caddo society is contingent on the different colonial objectives of France and Spain. Diaries and reports of Spanish missionaries and expedition leaders provide most of the firsthand accounts of early historic Caddo culture. Since these encounters took place almost exclusively among the east Texas settlements, the accessible ethnohistoric record is almost entirely derived from Hasinai Caddo society (Bolton 1987; Griffith 1954; Swanton 1942). In contrast, while the French documents are a rich source of information on periodic and significant formalized episodes of encounters between French explorers, trading officials, bureaucrats, and the Caddos (Sabo 1987), those traders who had the closest and most enduring relationships with Caddo communities left few written descriptions behind.

Although it has been common practice to extend Hasinai cultural practices to all Caddo groups, future search for information, especially about Red River valley populations, will doubtless bring into focus regional differences that we cannot elucidate today. The brief summary of early historic Caddo culture that follows draws heavily on these more accessible Spanish sources.

The core domestic unit of Caddo society was an extended family that resided in a permanent farmstead adjoining garden plots, woodlots, and a permanent water source. The most commonly described dwelling was circular, conical or dome-shaped, and constructed of poles, wattle, and thatch. Within the building, sleeping platforms and partitions served as personal spaces for various family members, and high shelves and lofts supplied storage space for food and other belongings. Ancillary buildings included aboveground food storage bins, roofed summer work platforms, and birthing huts. Other architectural styles of domestic structures may have also existed: photographs of a mid-nineteenth-century farmstead of Caddo refugees in central Oklahoma show oval or rectangular buildings with horizontal ridgepoles and overhanging, thatched, and bark-covered roofs (Swanton 1942:pl. 14).

Each farmstead was situated apart from its neighbors, presumably by stretches of undeveloped forest or prairie, and a single community often extended for several miles along a stream valley. In some instances, clusters of houses formed a hamlet or local neighborhood within the larger community (Chabot 1932; Swanton 1942).

In addition to written descriptions of community plans, we have an anonymous drawing made in 1691 by a member of the Domingo Teran de los Rios expedition that visited a Great Bend Caddo community, probably either the Upper Nasoni or the Kadohadacho village (Swanton 1942:pl. 1). This sketch is compatible with information on Hasinai communities and provides supplementary information about two of the key focal points within the larger community (fig. 5.2).

Close to the geographic center of each community was the homestead of the *caddi*, or community leader. Special buildings for community-wide events and for meetings of the council of elders and other authorities sometimes stood near or within the *caddi*'s compound. A second focal point for important events and ritual activities was the temple complex. The Teran map shows the temple situated on a low mound that was located at the far edge of the community. Some instances of mound use for temple platforms may have continued well into the eighteenth century (Swanton 1942:154,

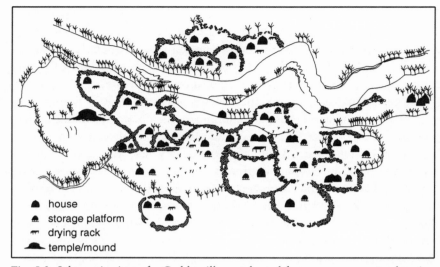

Fig. 5.2. Schematic view of a Caddo village, adapted from an anonymous drawing done at a village along the Great Bend of the Red River during the 1691 Teran de los Rios expedition.

citing De Mezieres), but mounds are not commonly described in the contemporary accounts. The Hasinai appear to have given up this custom before historic contact.

The temple complex was also where the *xinesi,* the paramount religious authority, apparently resided. This location at the margin of a community, or perhaps better characterized as at the boundary between neighboring communities, was probably important on both political and cosmological levels. Adjoining communities evidently shared the use of a single temple complex for some purposes and would have been subject to the overarching authority of the *xinesi,* who with his assistants maintained the sacred temple fire, communicated with important supernatural beings, and supervised the ritual calendar. In some instances, additional important ritual buildings and structures used for meetings of community councils were situated near the temple complex (Chabot 1932:24–25; Hatcher 1927:216; Wyckoff and Baugh 1980).

Historic Caddo social organization was clearly based on principles of hierarchy. In the public realm, several categories of leaders, almost always men, filled a nested set of roles that organized social, ritual, political, and economic activities in spheres of influence that moved from family and clan to community and ultimately to confederacy level. The upper levels of the hierarchy were the positions of *xinesi, caddi* (*caddices,* plural), and *canahas,* which were hereditary within an "otherwise matrilineal kinship system" (Sabo 1998:159). Europeans reported that succession was ideally through a male line, and an expectable assumption at the time was that this public power passed through a patriline (Wyckoff and Baugh 1980:239). With an imperfect understanding of Caddo language and kinship terminology, however, outsiders may have misunderstood male authority passing through a matriline.

Drawing on kinship data collected primarily in the nineteenth and early twentieth centuries, George Sabo (1998) showed that Caddo kinship was consistent with principles of Crow kinship terminology. Going farther to examine elements of cosmology, myth, and rituals witnessed in the early historic period, he proposed that the overarching organizational principles of Caddo society that were manifested in both the human and supernatural realms were hierarchical relationships based on principles of seniority and relative strength. Social actions, ritual performances, economic activities, and material constructions are imbedded within these principles and make many aspects of Caddo culture in the early historic period more comprehensible (Sabo 1998).

Extensive descriptions of the roles, responsibilities, and material correlates of Hasinai leaders derived from early historic accounts are available (see Bolton 1987; Griffith 1954; Swanton 1942; Wyckoff and Baugh 1980). Briefly, the *xinesi* exercised paramount authority over religious affairs on behalf of several communities and was the principal point of contact between the Caddos and a hierarchical assemblage of beings and entities in the supernatural realm. There are indications that in some instances a hierarchically ordered group of *xinesi* presided over some population blocks. A *caddi,* or headman, and the *canahas,* a group of elders, exercised authority within each community, with the former often supervising both local rituals and political affairs. In recognition of these authority positions, community members followed a protocol of deference and obligation that included supplying the *xinesi* with food and other provisions, constructing special elevated seats in some residences that were to be used only by visiting elites, and yielding to authorities who organized community-wide activities that ranged from house building and planting everyone's cornfields to key events in the annual ritual calendar.

Beneath this group of leaders were several subordinate and more specialized positions. In the realm of community affairs, the *tanmas* enforced decisions made by the *caddi* and acted variously as town criers, monitors of public behavior, and supervisors of public activities. *Chayas* served as pages or assistants to the *canahas*. It is unclear whether recruitment to these community positions was based on personal qualities, kinship relationships, or both. In the intersection of Caddos with supernatural forces, *connas*, or shamans, apparently fulfilled a number of roles for both individuals and the larger community that included curing sickness, divination, and assisting with ritual activities.

One special social category, that of *amayxoya* or warrior, seems to have been based on personal valor in warfare and was an honorific title given to any eligible man. Communities elected a war chief from these ranks, who is reported to have had a public role in greeting strangers, but whose other duties or privileges are uncertain (Wyckoff and Baugh 1980:235). Since raids against old enemies or new antagonists—fueled by the increased material value of horses, captives, and other loot, by heightened tensions caused by population movements and colonial pressures, and probably by internal stresses accompanying population loss—were likely increasing at the time, the importance and prestige of the *amayxoya* may have been ascendant through the historic period.

The Caddos were bound together as communities, and as inhabitants of a cosmos that they shared with an ordered array of supernatural beings, through an annual ritual calendar with four important events. These events dealt primarily with the successful production of food resources and included a late winter forecasting ceremony at the beginning of the year, a spring planting ceremony, a first fruits celebration in summer, and a concluding after-harvest ceremony. Many activities, some conducted only by elite individuals and others including members of the community at large, comprised each of these celebrations; some of the activities were familiar elsewhere in the Southeast, such as drinking a laurel tea, smoking tobacco, and making offerings to the sacred temple fire. Ritual actors were often segregated by sex and age grade, but both men and women in the community appear to have had important, albeit complementary, roles in the program of carefully choreographed events that made up each ceremony. Descriptions of these ceremonies have appeared in several places (for example, Griffith 1954; Swanton 1942), but attempts to explore the meanings imbedded in these and other rituals such as formal greeting or calumet ceremonies have only recently begun (Newkumet and Meredith 1988; Sabo 1987, 1992). Further exploration of the rituals witnessed early in the contact period, and those that survived—or developed—through the episodes of culture change down to the present, is likely to provide both a better understanding of the historic Caddos and models for guiding archaeological research into the initial contact populations and their ancestors.

The Archaeology of the Historic Caddos

Although many Caddo communities remained in their ancestral valleys through most of the eighteenth century and documents give clues to the migration patterns of others, virtually no named historic sites have been located or studied by archaeologists. The lack of sites is particularly unfortunate because this may be one of the few areas in the Southeast where the trajectories of a native group's history from its prehistoric antecedents into the colonial period might be revealed through archaeology. There are many reasons why these investigations have not been pursued. Erosion, alluviation, and stream channel migration have doubtless buried or destroyed many recent sites, as has modern development. Lack of research programs directed to searching for and testing potential sites is also a factor, as is the problem of discerning likely ethnic identity of poorly documented sites. Traditional native-made goods and European replacements were shared among many tribal and ethnic (and multiethnic) communities at the same time that communities were coalescing around some short-term associations of many remnant groups.

In the Hasinai area of east Texas there has been only one extensive investigation of a historic Caddo site, the Deshazo site, which was located about 13 kilometers west of Nacogdoches on a tributary of the Angelina River. Before the site was flooded by Lake Nacogdoches in the mid-1970s, large sections were stripped to reveal nine circular structures and an array of other features and midden deposits that were portions of an early historic community. Few European trade goods were found during this investigation, but graves dug nearby in the 1930s yielded several hundred glass beads and an array of other non-native artifacts and are believed to be associated with the community. The scarcity of trade items, particularly gun parts, and an absence of bison and horse bones lend support to archaeomagnetic dates of 1710+/-34 and 1715+/-31 (Good 1982:78). They suggest that the site was occupied largely before a French trading post established at Natchitoches in 1714, and the east Texas Spanish missions resettled after 1716, both brought a supply of trade goods into the area (Story 1982, 1995).

Near the Deshazo site, about 20 percent of the much smaller and slightly more recent Mayhew site was also stripped (about 270 square meters) in 1975. No structures were found, but the site was identified as a single Hasinai farmstead (Kenmotsu 1992). Neither of these sites has been identified with a historically named Caddo village.

At least sixty-two sites in northeastern Texas are believed to have historic native, probably Caddo, components, but the information comes mainly from surface collections, secondhand reports of pot digger discoveries, and other unsystematic and unpublished sources (Story 1990:table 85 and fig. 56). Among these sites are several that may be components of the Great Bend communities served by Jean-Baptiste Bénard de La Harpe's 1719 trading post, but the location of the post and identification of the villages remain inconclusive (Gilmore 1986; Miroir et al. 1973; Wedel 1978; Williams 1964).

Downstream along the Great Bend in southwest Arkansas where at least two Kadohadacho villages were situated in the eighteenth century (Flores 1984), efforts to find historic Caddo sites have also been largely unsuccessful. The Cedar Grove site, identified as a late Caddo farmstead, is the only extensively excavated candidate. Traces of a single circular structure, a midden scatter, and a small cemetery were found. Two broken bone discs from the fill of one burial might be items of European manufacture or inspiration, but no other trade goods were found (Kay 1984:194, fig. 13-18). Using several lines of evidence, researchers concluded that the farmstead was occupied in the very early eighteenth century (Trubowitz 1984) before the establishment of the Red River French trading posts.

Farther south along the Red River near modern Shreveport, two more small neighboring farmsteads were recently stripped. The McLelland and Joe Clark sites both had circular houses, midden scatters, refuse pits, and small cemeteries. The only possible European trade goods found were two pieces of brass in the midden within one structure at McLelland (Kelley 1997:96), but artifact comparisons with Cedar Grove and other Red River sites indicate that these farmsteads were also occupied very early in the eighteenth century. Kelley (1997:ii) suggested that the site may be part of the village of the Nakasa, one of the enigmatic groups named or misnamed in early historic records who also may have been the Yatasi, the Natache (Swanton 1942:13), or some other component of the Red River Caddo population cluster.

In the Natchitoches vicinity along the Red River valley, a few sites disturbed by modern developments over the last fifty years yielded burials and other deposits that seem to belong to settlements of the historic Natchitoches and allied communities that merged into a single group in the eighteenth century. The small collection of artifacts and observations reveals little about these settlements beyond the association of European trade goods and a few aboriginal pottery types such as Natchitoches Engraved (Gregory and Webb 1965; Walker 1935; Webb 1945), although the burial of two horses accompanied by pottery vessels indicates the rapid incorporation of this key element of Caddo-European trade into the indigenous ritual sphere (Walker 1935). Since these discoveries, no search for additional historic period native settlements in the Natchitoches area has yielded substantive information about colonial era Caddo lifeways. However, Jeffrey Girard's recent attempt to locate residential sites associated with the historic cemeteries indicates that the dispersed residential community plan was maintained along the Red and Cane rivers through much of the eighteenth century (Girard 1997). (The Cane River is a recently abandoned channel of the Red.)

In the northeast corner of the Caddo area, a long-term search for post-contact Caddo settlements in the Ouachita River basin in Arkansas has failed to disclose any site with trade goods that might belong to a historic Cahinnio village. The closest candidate is the Hardman site, where extensive excavation revealed circular structures, family grave plots, and midden scatters that were part of a community of Caddo saltmakers (Early 1993). A single red seed bead found in grave fill was the only possible early European artifact. Several lines of evidence including ceramic comparisons suggest that the site was abandoned shortly before A.D. 1700.

Downstream from Hardman near the confluence of the Ouachita River and Bayou Bartholomew in northern Louisiana, C. B. Moore's discovery of elaborate Caddo ceramics and trade goods at the Keno and Glendora sites led to an assumption that this locality was occupied by historic Caddo groups. Recent reanalysis of the evidence now demonstrates that Moore's illustrations of fancy Caddo pots are misleading, and that these artifacts were trade goods in local non-Caddo communities (Kidder 1990, 1993, 1998), probably brought to the area through the Ouachita Valley salt trade (Early 1993:234).

Colonial era European settlements among Caddo groups have also received attention from archaeologists. The most substantial research has been undertaken at the colonial presidio Nuestra Señora del Pilar de Los Adaes, the easternmost outpost of Spanish authority founded in 1721 near the Adai community, less than 20 miles from the infant French post at Fort St. Jean Baptiste, now Natchitoches, along the Red River. A mission, San Miguel de Cuellar de Los Adaes, was established nearby but was destined to languish like the other east Texas missions, unable to convert the local Caddos or to resettle them under mission control in the vicinity. Presidio Los Adaes became the capital of the province of Texas in 1729, but until its abandonment in 1772 it remained a small, relatively ineffective symbol of Spain's claim to east Texas. More important was its role as an economic node and point of intersection for native, French, and Spanish interaction that was often carried out in defiance of official government authority.

Archaeological investigations over many years have revealed portions of the presidio buildings and information useful for examining the nature of relationships among native, Spanish, and French populations (Avery 1996; Gregory 1973, 1983). Although Los Adaes existed in practice as a multiethnic community, the archaeological investigations speak more clearly to the nature of European acculturation rather than to the direct effects of the European presence on the local Caddo communities, which remain unstudied.

About 50 miles west of Los Adaes, along the path to the Rio Grande, Spanish authorities established Mission Nuestra Señora Dolores de los Ais to minister to the Ais Caddo community. Although ultimately as unsuccessful as its sister missions in converting the local Indians, Dolores de los Ais existed, with a brief abandonment between 1719 and 1721, from 1716 to 1773 and was thus contemporary with the Los Adaes settlement to the east. Archaeological and documentary research has been conducted toward locating and examining the mission site (Corbin 1977, 1989, 1996; Corbin et al. 1980), but this work also reveals more about the non-Caddo inhabitants of the mission than about the Caddos themselves.

In sum, most of what we know about the historic Caddo people comes from documents written by Europeans and from remembered traditions revealed by modern Caddo descendants of a once diverse collection of many ancestral groups. Some important archaeological studies of native communities inhabited in the earliest years of sustained contact with the French and Spanish colonial enterprises have been produced. The potential for learning more about the impact that the contest between France and Spain for influence over the Caddo and their neighbors had on Europeans and Caddos alike, however, has hardly been approached. We know a substantial amount about what Europeans saw and thought about the native people whose allegiance they courted, but much remains to be done to appreciate the effects of contact on the Caddos themselves, and to tell the fuller story of their adaptation to their changing world.

Bibliography

Avery, George
1996   Eighteenth Century Spanish, French, and Caddoan Interaction as Seen from Los Adaes. *Journal of Northeast Texas Archaeology* 7:27–68.
Bolton, Herbert E.
1908   The Native Tribes about the East Texas Missions. *Quarterly of the Texas State Historical Association* 11:249–76.
1987   *The Hasinais: Southern Caddoans as Seen by the Earliest Europeans.* Edited by R. Magnaghi. Norman: University of Oklahoma Press.
Brown, James A.
1996   *The Spiro Ceremonial Center: The Archaeology of Arkansas Valley Caddoan Culture in Eastern Oklahoma.* Memoirs of the Museum of Anthropology no. 29. University of Michigan, Ann Arbor.
Bruseth, James E.
1992   Artifacts of the de Soto Expedition: The Evidence from Texas. *Bulletin of the Texas Archeological Society* 63:67–97.
1998   The Development of Caddoan Polities along the Middle Red River Valley of Eastern Texas and Oklahoma. In *The Native History of the Caddo: Their Place in Southeastern Archeology and Ethnohistory,* edited by T. K. Perttula and J. E. Bruseth, 47–68. Texas Archeological Research Laboratory Studies in Archeology 30. Austin.
Carter, Cecile E.
1995   *Caddo Indians: Where We Come From.* Norman: University of Oklahoma Press.
Chabot, Frederick C.
1932   *Excerpts from the Memorias for the History of the Province of Texas.* Memorias by Padre Fray Juan Agustin de Morfi. San Antonio: Naylor Printing.
Corbin, James E.
1977   *Archeological Research at 41SA25, Mission Dolores de los Ais.* Department of Sociology and Anthropology, Stephen F. Austin State University, Nacogdoches.
1989   Spanish-Indian Interaction on the Eastern Frontier of Texas. In *Columbian Consequences,* vol. 1, *Archaeological and Historical Perspectives on the Spanish Borderlands West,* edited by D. H. Thomas, 269–77. Washington, D.C.: Smithsonian Institution Press.
1996   Spanish-Caddoan Interaction in Eastern Texas. *Journal of Northeast Texas Archaeology* 7:20–26.
Corbin, James E., T. C. Alex, and A. Kalina
1980   *Mission Dolores de los Ais.* Papers in Anthropology no. 2. Stephen F. Austin State University, Nacogdoches.

Davidson, Billy
1997   Appendix 2: Preliminary Study of the Faunal Remains from the George C. Davis Site, 1968–1970 Excavations. *Bulletin of the Texas Archeological Society* 68:108–11.

Early, Ann M. (editor)
1993   *Caddoan Saltmakers in the Ouachita Valley: The Hardman Site.* Research Series 43. Arkansas Archeological Survey, Fayetteville.

Flores, Dan L. (editor)
1984   *Jefferson and Southwestern Exploration: The Freeman and Custis Accounts of the Red River Expedition of 1806.* Norman: University of Oklahoma Press.

Ford, Richard I.
1997   Appendix 1: Preliminary Report on the Plant Remains from the George C. Davis Site, Cherokee County, Texas, 1968–1970 Excavations. *Bulletin of the Texas Archeological Society* 68:104–7.

Gilmore, Kathleen
1986   *French-Indian Interaction at an 18th-Century Frontier Post: The Roseborough Lake Site, Bowie County, Texas.* Contributions in Archaeology no. 3. Institute of Applied Science, North Texas State University, Denton.

Girard, Jeffrey S.
1997   Historic Caddoan Occupation in the Natchitoches Area: Recent Attempts to Locate Residential Sites. *Caddoan Archeology* 8(3):19–31.

Good, Carolyn E.
1982   Analysis of Structures, Burials, and Other Cultural Features. In *The Deshazo Site, Nacogdoches County, Texas,* vol. 1, edited by D. A. Story, 51–112. Texas Antiquities Permit Series no. 7. Texas Antiquities Committee, Austin.

Gregory, Hiram F.
1973   Eighteenth Century Caddoan Archaeology: A Study in Models and Interpretation. Ph.D. diss., Department of Anthropology, Southern Methodist University, Dallas.

1983   Los Adaes, the Archaeology of an Ethnic Enclave. In *Historical Archaeology of the Eastern United States,* edited by R. W. Neuman, 53–57. Geoscience and Man, vol. 23. Baton Rouge: Louisiana State University.

Gregory, Hiram F., Jr., and Clarence H. Webb
1965   European Trade Beads from Six Sites in Natchitoches Parish, Louisiana. *Florida Anthropologist* 18(3):15–44.

Griffith, William Joyce
1954   *The Hasinai Indians of East Texas as Seen by Europeans, 1687–1772.* Philological and Documentary Studies 3. Middle American Research Institute, Tulane University, New Orleans.

Hatcher, Mattie A. (editor)
1927   Descriptions of the Tejas or Asinai Indians, 1691–1722. *Southwestern Historical Quarterly* 30:206–18.

Hickerson, Daniel A.
1996   The Development and Decline of the Hasinai Confederacy. Ph.D. diss., Department of Anthropology, University of Georgia, Athens.

Jeter, Marvin D., Jerome C. Rose, G. Ishmael Williams, Jr., and Anna M. Harmon
1989   *Archeology and Bioarcheology of the Lower Mississippi Valley and Trans-*

Mississippi South in Arkansas and Louisiana. Research Series 37. Arkansas Archeological Survey, Fayetteville.

Kay, Marvin
1984   Late Caddo Subtractive Technology in the Red River Basin. In *Cedar Grove: An Interdisciplinary Investigation of a Late Caddo Farmstead in the Red River Valley*, edited by N. L. Trubowitz, 174–206. Research Series 23. Arkansas Archeological Survey, Fayetteville.

Kelley, David B. (editor)
1997   *Two Caddoan Farmsteads in the Red River Valley: The Archeology of the McLelland and Joe Clark Sites*. Research Series 51. Arkansas Archeological Survey, Fayetteville.

Kenmotsu, Nancy A.
1992   The Mayhew Site: A Possible Hasinai Farmstead, Nacogdoches County, Texas. *Bulletin of the Texas Archeological Society* 63:135–73.

Kenmotsu, Nancy A., James E. Bruseth, and James E. Corbin
1993   Moscoso and the Route in Texas: A Reconstruction. In *The Expedition of Hernando de Soto West of the Mississippi, 1541–1543: Proceedings of the de Soto Symposia 1988 and 1990*, edited by G. A. Young and M. P. Hoffman, 106–31. Fayetteville: University of Arkansas Press.

Kidder, Tristram R.
1990   The Ouachita Indians of Louisiana: An Ethnohistorical and Archeological Investigation. *Louisiana Archaeology* 12:179–202.

1993   The Glendora Phase: Protohistoric-Early Historic Culture Dynamics on the Lower Ouachita River. In *Archaeology of Eastern North America: Papers in Honor of Stephen Williams*, edited by J. B. Stoltman, 231–60. Archaeological Reports no. 25. Mississippi Department of Archives and History, Jackson.

1998   Rethinking Caddoan–Lower Mississippi Valley Interaction. In *The Native History of the Caddo: Their Place in Southeastern Archeology and Ethnohistory*, edited by T. K. Perttula and J. E. Bruseth, 129–43. Texas Archeological Research Laboratory Studies in Archeology 30. Austin.

La Vere, David L.
1993   Strangers for Family: Gifts, Reciprocity, and Kinship in Caddoan-Euroamerican Relations, 1685–1835. Ph.D. diss., Department of Anthropology, Texas A&M University, College Station.

Lesser, Alexander
1979   Caddoan Kinship Systems. *Nebraska History* 60(2):260–71.

Lesser, Alexander, and Gene Weltfish
1932   Composition of the Caddoan Linguistic Stock. *Smithsonian Miscellaneous Collections* 87(6):1–15. Washington, D.C.

Miroir, M. P., R. King Harris, Jay C. Blaine, Janson McVay, Donald C. Book, Floyd Cigainero, Roger McVay, Joe B. Raffaelli, Jr., and Paul E. Schoen
1973   Benard de la Harpe and the Nassonite Post. *Texas Archeological Society Bulletin* 44:113–68.

Newell, H. Perry, and Alex D. Krieger
1949   *The George C. Davis Site, Cherokee County, Texas*. Society for American Archaeology Memoir no. 5. Menasha, Wisconsin.

Newkumet, Vynola B., and Howard L. Meredith
1988   *Hasinai: A Traditional History of the Caddo Confederacy.* College Station: Texas A&M University Press.

Perttula, Timothy K.
1992   *The Caddo Nation.* Austin: University of Texas Press.

Sabo, George III
1987   Reordering Their World: A Caddoan Ethnohistory. In *Visions and Revisions: Ethnohistoric Perspectives on Southern Cultures,* edited by G. Sabo III and W. M. Schneider, 25–47. Athens: University of Georgia Press.

1992   Rituals of Encounter: Interpreting Native American Views of European Encounters. *Arkansas Historical Quarterly* 51:54–68.

1998   The Structure of Caddo Leadership in the Colonial Era. In *The Native History of the Caddo: Their Place in Southeastern Archeology and Ethnohistory,* edited by T. K. Perttula and J. E. Bruseth, 159–74. Texas Archeological Research Laboratory Studies in Archeology 30. Austin.

Sabo, George III, Ann M. Early, Jerome C. Rose, Barbara A. Burnett, Louis Vogele, and James P. Harcourt
1988   *Human Adaptation in the Ozark-Ouachita Mountains.* Research Series 31. Arkansas Archeological Survey, Fayetteville.

Schambach, Frank F.
1982   An Outline of Fourche Maline Culture in Southwest Arkansas. In *Arkansas Archeology in Review,* edited by N. L. Trubowitz and M. D. Jeter, 132–97. Research Series 15. Arkansas Archeological Survey, Fayetteville.

1989   The End of the Trail: The Route of Hernando de Soto's Army through Southwest Arkansas and East Texas. *The Arkansas Archeologist* 27/28:9–33.

1993   Some New Interpretations of Spiroan Culture History. In *Archaeology of Eastern North America: Papers in Honor of Stephen Williams,* edited by J. B. Stoltman, 187–230. Archaeological Report no. 25. Mississippi Department of Archives and History, Jackson.

1998   *Pre-Caddoan Cultures in the Trans-Mississippi South.* Research Series 53. Arkansas Archeological Survey, Fayetteville. Reprint of 1970 Ph.D. diss., Department of Anthropology, Harvard University, Cambridge.

Smith, F. Todd
1995   *The Caddo Indians: Tribes at the Convergence of Empires 1542–1854.* College Station: Texas A&M University Press.

1996   *The Caddos, the Wichitas, and the United States, 1846–1901.* College Station: Texas A&M University Press.

1998   The Political History of the Caddo Indians, 1686–1874. In *The Native History of the Caddo: Their Place in Southeastern Archeology and Ethnohistory,* edited by T. K. Perttula and J. E. Bruseth, 175–81. Texas Archeological Research Laboratory Studies in Archeology 30. Austin.

Story, Dee Ann
1978   Some Comments on Anthropological Studies concerning the Caddo. In *Texas Archaeology: Essays Honoring R. King Harris,* edited by K. House, 46–68. Dallas: Southern Methodist University Press.

1990   Cultural History of the Native Americans. In *The Archeology and Bioarcheology of the Gulf Coastal Plain,* vol. 1, by D. A. Story, J. A. Guy, B. A. Burnett,

M. D. Freeman, J. C. Rose, D. G. Steele, B. W. Olive, and K. J. Reinhard, 163–366. Research Series 38. Arkansas Archeological Survey, Fayetteville.

1997   1968–1970 Archeological Investigations at the George C. Davis Site, Cherokee County, Texas. *Bulletin of the Texas Archeological Society* 68:1–104, 111–13.

1998   The George C. Davis Site: Glimpses into Early Caddoan Symbolism and Ideology. In *The Native History of the Caddo: Their Place in Southeastern Archeology and Ethnohistory*, edited by T. K. Perttula and J. E. Bruseth, 9–43. Texas Archeological Research Laboratory Studies in Archeology 30. Austin.

Story, Dee Ann (editor)

1982   *The Deshazo Site, Nacogdoches County, Texas.* Vol. 1. Texas Antiquities Permit Series no. 7. Texas Antiquities Committee, Austin.

1995   *The Deshazo Site, Nacogdoches County, Texas.* Vol. 2. Texas Archeological Research Laboratory Studies in Archeology 21. Austin.

Swanton, John R.

1942   *Source Material on the History and Ethnology of the Caddo Indians.* Smithsonian Institution, Bureau of American Ethnology Bulletin 132. Washington, D.C.

Trubowitz, Neal L. (editor)

1984   *Cedar Grove: An Interdisciplinary Investigation of a Late Caddo Farmstead in the Red River Valley.* Research Series 23. Arkansas Archeological Survey, Fayetteville.

Walker, Winslow M.

1935   A Caddo Burial Site at Natchitoches, Louisiana. *Smithsonian Miscellaneous Collections* 94(14). Washington, D.C.

Webb, Clarence H.

1945   A Second Historic Caddo Site at Natchitoches, Louisiana. *Bulletin of the Texas Archaeological and Paleontological Society* 16:52–83.

Wedel, Mildred M.

1978   *La Harpe's 1719 Post on Red River and Nearby Caddo Settlements.* Texas Memorial Museum Bulletin 30. Austin.

Williams, Stephen

1964   The Aboriginal Location of the Kadohadacho and Related Tribes. In *Explorations in Cultural Anthropology*, edited by W. H. Goodenough, 545–70. New York: McGraw Hill.

Wyckoff, Don G., and Timothy G. Baugh

1980   Early Historic Hasinai Elites: A Model for the Material Culture of Governing Elites. *Mid-Continental Journal of Archaeology* 5(2):225–88.

Young, Gloria A., and Michael P. Hoffman (editors)

1993   *The Expedition of Hernando de Soto West of the Mississippi, 1541–1543: Proceedings of the de Soto Symposia 1988 and 1990.* Fayetteville: University of Arkansas Press.

6

The Natchez of Southwest Mississippi

Karl G. Lorenz

As to what you say of your being the son of the Sun, if you will cause
him to dry up the great river [the Mississippi], I will believe you: As
to the rest, it is not my custom to visit any one, but rather all, of
whom I have ever heard, have come to visit me, to serve and obey
me, and pay me tribute, either voluntarily or by force: If you desire
to see me, come where I am, if for peace, I will receive you with
special good will; if for war, I will await you in my town; but neither
for you, nor for any other man, will I set back one foot.

Account by a Gentleman from Elvas, quoted in Bourne 1904:154–55

The story of the Natchez Indians has intrigued people for centuries. Some are
fascinated by the unusual exogamous marriage practice of the Natchez elite,
who married only commoners. Many look to the Natchez as being one of the
best-documented examples of early historic period lifeways of southeastern
native cultures. Still others are intrigued by the practice of human sacrifice
of the chiefly retinue upon the death of an elite member of the Sun descent
group, a practice reminiscent of elite burial practices at the great Mississippian mound center of Cahokia (Fowler 1977). For others, the use of platform mounds for temples and chiefly residences supports the argument that
the Natchez were a surviving remnant of late prehistoric Mississippian chiefdom societies (Steponaitis 1978).

Regardless of the perspective one takes, the story involves the waxing and
waning power of a Native American people complicated by the interference
of Europeans who were colonizing North America. Some of their more
powerful chiefs, like the *cacique* from Quigualtam, were able to wield a great
deal of power as attested to by his audacious statement (quoted above) made
to Hernando de Soto in the wake of the Spanish path of pillage and plunder.

In contrast, during the later historic period, other Natchez chiefs struggled to keep all of their supporters within the French fold.

Both archaeology and ethnohistory provide information about the Natchez and their ancestors who inhabited the Natchez Bluffs of southwestern Mississippi. Archaeology provides a continuous record of occupation of people in the Natchez Bluffs region from the late prehistoric period through the historic period (A.D. 1200–1730), while the protohistoric (A.D. 1550–1680) and historic period (A.D. 1680–1730) occupations, characterized by European contact, are enriched by historic accounts from the sixteenth-century Spanish and the seventeenth- and eighteenth-century French exploration of the lower Mississippi River Valley.

Background

Within the Natchez Bluffs region, the Natchez spoke a Muskhogean-related language (Haas 1956; Swanton 1911) and occupied the inland tributaries east of the Mississippi River. During the late prehistoric and protohistoric periods, their territory extended over 200 kilometers from the Homochitto River to the south to the Big Black River near present-day Vicksburg in the north (fig. 6.1). During the historic period, their territory decreased in size to cover only about 65 kilometers from the banks of St. Catherine's Creek in the south to Fairchild's Creek and the South Fork of Coles Creek in the north (Brown 1985:2–3). Settlements have been recorded within the loess bluffs physiographic region, which is characterized by high rounded hills with stream valleys that provide suitable expanses of level, well-drained soils for supporting a horticultural subsistence base. Rainfall averages over 150 centimeters per year, with runoff draining into the many small intermittent creeks comprising the heavily dissected uplands. In addition to the loess hills uplands, the bottomland swamps of the Mississippi alluvial plain were exploited by the Natchez for their fauna and flora. Overall, the upland and bottomland regions consisted of coniferous and deciduous forests containing deer, bear, mountain lion, bobcat, fox, rabbit, skunk, opossum, squirrels, ducks, geese, numerous species of freshwater fishes, and alligator (Brain 1978:335; Cleland 1965:96; Neitzel 1965:9–10).

The earliest recorded account of the Natchez begins with their ancestors from what many scholars (Brain 1978; Brown 1982; Galloway 1995; Swanton 1911) believe to be the province of Quigualtam, a powerful Indian nation described in the early Spanish accounts of the conquistador Her-

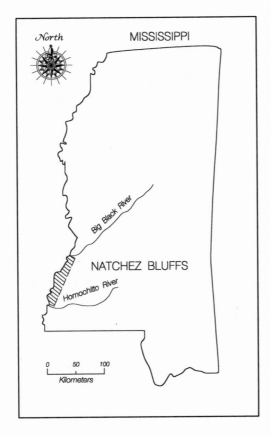

Fig. 6.1. Natchez occupation area (after Brown 1985).

nando de Soto. Warriors from Quigualtam were briefly engaged in a hostile encounter with de Soto and his Spanish conquistadors in 1542. De Soto challenged and often captured and held hostage every southeastern chief that he encountered, but when he received the response from the chief of the province of Quigualtam, de Soto was sufficiently intimidated to carefully avoid any direct confrontation with this apparently powerful Indian nation. In fact, as they were leaving the province of this great Natchez ancestor, de Soto's men were chased and bombarded with volleys of arrows by warriors from Quigualtam, barely escaping with their lives (Clayton et al. 1993:154–58).

Over 140 years elapsed between de Soto's *entrada* into the southeastern interior of the United States and the next time the Natchez are mentioned in the historic record. Despite tremendous upheaval leading to the disintegration of many southeastern Indian cultures as a result of European-intro-duced diseases, late seventeenth- and early eighteenth-century French accounts still found the Natchez to be one of the most formidable tribes in all of the Mississippi Valley. French chroniclers reported that the authority of the Natchez principal chief, the Great Sun, was as absolute as that of a king. He ruled with despotic power and could determine which of his subjects would live or die if any one of them displeased him (Swanton 1911).

The tribe's existence, however, was cut short in 1731 when 700 French soldiers were responsible for the tribe's dispersal among a number of English-allied southeastern tribes, including the Chickasaw of Mississippi and the Creek of Alabama (Albrecht 1946). How is it that such a powerful, long-lived Indian nation that repelled de Soto and his conquistadors and survived the cataclysmic effects of European diseases should succumb so easily and completely to such a relatively small French force? With careful study of the sixteenth-century Spanish historic documents and seventeenth- and eighteenth-century accounts by French colonists, soldiers, and missionaries, and a review of what is known of the archaeology of these once proud and powerful people, this chapter seeks to shed new light on this problem, which has vexed anthropologists for the last century.

Natchez Ancestors

Late Prehistoric Period

Archaeological evidence shows that the Natchez and their ancestors were firmly rooted in the Natchez Bluffs region of southwestern Mississippi from A.D. 1200 onward and belonged to the Plaquemine archaeological culture, a southerly variant of the Mississippian cultural tradition. With the exception of ceramic technology, material culture from Plaquemine sites mirrors that from Mississippian sites, with platform mound architecture, maize farming, and a settlement distribution pattern characterized by variation in site sizes ranked by successive degrees of importance within chiefly societies. The ceramics, however, are distinctly different as they lack shell tempering; instead a clay-grit tempering agent is added to the paste.

Archaeologists believe that both the Mississippian and Plaquemine cultural traditions included a number of autonomous petty and paramount chiefs who had political control over their own chiefdoms, which encompassed localized regions in river valleys. They also believe that each chiefdom administered the political affairs of its support population living in dispersed farmsteads and hamlets (for a review, see Steponaitis 1986). Detailed analysis of site duration and mound use in northern Georgia indicates that Mississippian chiefdoms were spaced at least 40 kilometers apart and lasted no more than 100 years (Hally 1996).

Archaeological and ethnohistoric case studies of chiefdoms from around the world show that there were several competing forces that affected the stability and instability of the operation of chiefdoms. These forces contributed to a transformational process inherent in all regional chiefdoms that Anderson (1994:9) referred to as "cycling," wherein decision-making levels within a regional chiefdom fluctuate between one (simple chiefdom) and two (complex chiefdom) levels above the community household level. In her ethnohistorical study of sixteenth-century Panamanian chiefdoms, Helms (1979:28) pointed out that even though a chief has the genealogical right to rule, he still faces "challenges to his power from high-status competitors."

If Hally's archaeological patterns from northern Georgia and Anderson's process of chiefly cycling reflect a larger southeastern sociopolitical pattern, then the late prehistoric Plaquemine tradition in the Natchez Bluffs region (A.D. 1200 to 1500) would be expected to conform to it. Beyond test excavations, the Natchez region has received relatively little archaeological excavation, with the exception of the Fatherland site, the Grand Village of the Natchez. Limited test excavations have been conducted at some of the larger mound centers, which include Anna (Cotter 1951; Beasley 1998; Brown 1997), Emerald (Cotter 1951; Steponaitis 1974), Gordon (Cotter 1952), and Foster (Steponaitis 1974). Thus more can be said about changes in settlement patterning using survey data. Because excavation data are limited for the mound sites, less can be inferred about mound site functions across time and space.

In their explanation for settlement pattern shifts from one platform mound center to another in the Natchez Bluffs region from the late prehistoric to the protohistoric period, Brain (1978) and Brown (1973) made the observation that chiefdoms from the later phases often arose as a result of fission and migration from older, existing chiefdoms. This is demonstrated by the fact that each late prehistoric phase in the Natchez Bluffs is dominated by the central mound center whose name is given to each phase (Brain 1978). Thus the Anna phase (A.D. 1200–1350) is characterized by the Anna site as the dominant mound center with eight platform mounds, but at least four other smaller mound centers located within Hally's 40-kilometer area of a chiefdom are occupied during the same phase. In the succeeding Foster phase (A.D. 1350–1500), the Foster and Emerald sites appear to share importance as the largest occupied mound centers. In addition, the Foster and Emerald mounds were contemporaneous with three smaller mound sites, including the Anna site, now less intensively occupied than in the previous phase. In the protohistoric Emerald phase (A.D. 1500–1680), the Emerald Mound site dominates the landscape along with four subsidiary centers, including the Foster site now subordinate along with the Fatherland site, known in the later historic period by the French as the Grand Village of the Natchez. Thus it is clear that in the Natchez Bluffs a series of power shifts was occurring from A.D. 1200 all the way into the historic period, with the waxing and waning power of key mound centers controlled by powerful chiefs. A monograph updating everything known about the archaeology of the Natchez Bluffs region since the work of Brain (1978), Brown (1973, 1985), and Steponaitis (1974) is currently in preparation by these researchers (Brain et al. n.d.) but not available for incorporation into this essay.

Protohistoric Period

Most Mississippian polities were at their cultural peak from A.D. 1000 to 1550, but after this time the political power of the chiefs decreased as a result of internal forces. This development is reflected in the archaeological record by a marked decline in long-distance exchange of valuable commodities of copper and marine shell (Milner 1990; Steponaitis 1991). During the protohistoric period (A.D. 1550–1680), numerous mound centers were abandoned across the Southeast. In most regions of the Southeast the more complex chiefdom societies were replaced by smaller, less powerful tribal entities that did not build mounds.

During this period, many Native American populations throughout the Southeast were decimated by European-introduced infectious diseases for which they had no natural immunity. Epidemics of smallpox, measles, influenza, and typhus wiped out whole culture groups, and demographers estimate that a very high percentage of the original pre-European contact Native American population in North America was lost to disease over this 150-year period (Dobyns 1983; Milner 1980; Ramenofsky 1987). French accounts from the eighteenth century record a Natchez legend of a past time when the sacred fire, kept burning in their temples at all times as a link to their supernatural deity of the Sun, was extinguished. Such a calamity led to

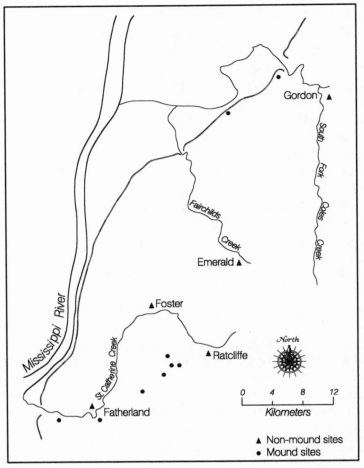

Fig. 6.2. Protohistoric Emerald phase site distribution in the Natchez
Bluffs (after Brown 1985).

a great mortality of all of their people. Nine Great Sun chiefs are said to have
died in succession within a four-year period (Swanton 1911:172). This ancient legend of the sacred fire being extinguished could very well be a meta-
phorical reference to the time when European diseases were wiping out
whole villages across the Southeast, leaving no survivors to bury the victims.

This Mississippian cultural decline does not appear to have occurred in
quite the same way in the Natchez Bluffs region of Mississippi after A.D.
1550. The archaeological settlement record for the protohistoric period

(A.D. 1550–1680) in the Natchez Bluffs region indicates quite clearly that the largest number of settlements with platform mound architecture was occupied during this period in the Emerald phase (fig. 6.2), attesting to the political power of Quigualtam, the polity ancestral to the Natchez. Moreover, the province of Quigualtam can be firmly placed geographically within the immediate area around the Emerald Mound site, containing the second largest prehistoric mound in North America, rising to a height of over 37 feet (12 meters) (Brown 1982; Cotter 1951). The presence of the ceramic type Fatherland Incised, a clay-grit tempered bowl or bottle decorated on the exterior with incised nested scrolls, provides a marker for the protohistoric and the succeeding historic periods. No evidence has yet been recovered

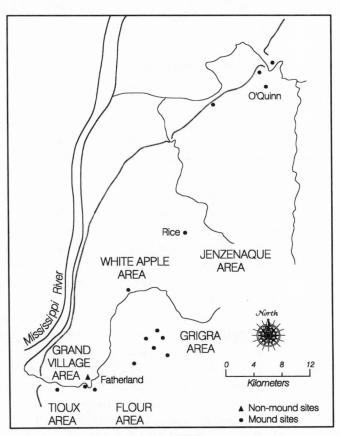

Fig. 6.3. Historic Natchez phase site distribution in the Natchez Bluffs (after Brown 1985).

from the dominant Emerald Mound site to suggest that it was occupied during the historic period (Steponaitis 1974).

The record goes on to show, however, that the number of mound centers and their associated populated village areas drops from five in use during the protohistoric period to only one during the historic period of the Natchez. This reduction attests to the fact that even the mighty Natchez did not fully escape the debilitating effects of European contact. In addition, a political power shift is evident during this transitional time, as the Emerald Mound center gave way to the rise in power of the Fatherland site (Grand Village of the Natchez) (fig. 6.3). Not only is this principal Natchez village the home of the Great Sun and his brother, the Great War Chief, Tattooed Serpent, but it is the village from which nearly all of the French observations of the Natchez were conducted.

French Historic Record of the Natchez

Overview

Despite a scaling down in size and prominence from the sixteenth to the eighteenth century, Natchez culture survived the effects of European contact, and even their oral tradition recounting these perilous times survived well into the historic period. Anyone interested in the details of everyday life among the Natchez should certainly consult Swanton's (1911) monograph, but for the purposes of this essay, I would like to highlight two areas of Natchez culture that have been steeped in controversy and have led to conflicting interpretations. These include the operation of the Natchez descent system and the nature of the Great Sun's political authority among his people. While the first issue can be examined using only the historic documents, the second issue can be explored using both historic accounts and archaeological patterns from across the Natchez regional settlement system.

The French historic record of the Natchez from 1682 to 1731 includes letters and journals written by missionaries (de Montigny, St. Cosme, Gravier, de la Vente in Shea 1861 and Gosselin 1906; Charlevoix in French 1851; du Ru in Butler 1934; Le Petit in Thwaites 1959), soldiers (Bienville in Rowland and Sanders 1929; Dumont de Montigny 1753; Iberville in McWilliams 1981; La Salle and Tonti in Cox 1905, French 1853, Margry 1887; Penicaut in McWilliams 1953; Richebourg in French 1851), and colonists (Le Page du Pratz 1758). The published primary accounts from the missionaries are based on rarely more than a few weeks' stay among the

Natchez and provide only passing glimpses, while accounts from some of the soldiers and the colonist Le Page du Pratz represent a more intensive exposure to Natchez lifeways, suggesting that these chroniclers had some ability to converse in the Natchez language. The accounts of Penicaut (1699–1721), Dumont de Montigny (1723–29), and Le Page du Pratz (1720–28) present the greatest volume of information on Natchez material culture, social and religious customs, and political organization. Swanton (1911) is the best secondary source on the Natchez, providing an extensive accounting of most of the above French historic sources in his 365-page monograph devoted to all Indian tribes of the lower Mississippi Valley.

According to French chroniclers, the Natchez Great Sun was said to have ruled over a chiefdom made up of anywhere from six (Le Page du Pratz 1758) to nine (Penicaut in McWilliams 1953) village districts located along tributary streams of the Mississippi River in southwestern Mississippi near the present-day town of Natchez. Eighteenth-century French estimates of population size range from 4,000 to 6,000 people, with an able fighting force of 1,500 warriors. It was at the one surviving mound center, known archaeologically as the Fatherland site, where the paramount chief, the Great Sun, and his brother, Tattooed Serpent, resided (Swanton 1911:39–44).

According to the eighteenth-century French historic accounts, the Great Sun had supreme jurisdiction over civil affairs and the Tattooed Serpent oversaw political affairs of peace and war of the entire tribal nation. The Great Sun had the authority to give feasts, receive tribute, punish wrongdoers, and serve as the mediator with the supernatural. His brother, Tattooed Serpent, could hold councils to form alliances with outside groups or incite his people to go to war (Le Page du Pratz 1758; Dumont de Montigny 1753).

Power was also wielded in the economic domain, with numerous examples from ethnohistoric accounts of Natchez Sun chiefs exhibiting great access to wealth, communal support of their own maize fields, and exclusive access to choice food items served at communal feasts. The Natchez Great Sun was the community's central accumulator of foodstuffs and goods in the form of tribute paid to him by the common people. Ethnohistoric accounts relate that the Great Sun, however, redistributed very little of his collected tribute back to the common people, and what little did go back was in the form of large communal feasts sponsored by the Great Sun, using the tribute obtained from the very people attending the feasts (Swanton 1911:110–18). In sum, the Natchez Great Sun and Tattooed Serpent possessed more wealth than commoners and had special rights and privileges that marked them as elite.

Natchez Descent System

One unique phenomenon that set the Sun elite apart from the rest of the commoner population was their proscription against marrying one another. Instead, according to Swanton's (1911) interpretation of French chroniclers, members of the Natchez nobility could only marry commoners. Here is where several researchers (Brain 1971; Fisher 1964; Hart 1943; Josselin de Jong 1928; Knight 1990; MacLeod 1924; Mason 1964; Quimby 1946; Tooker 1963; White et al. 1971) over the last seventy-five years have tried to modify Swanton's interpretation of this marriage custom in such a way that it could be understood within the broader context of marriage practices of southeastern Indians. A short summary of their arguments is necessary to orient the reader to this controversial topic. (Unfortunately, archaeology sheds no light on the debate.) For those intrigued by these issues, a close reading of all of the authors in this debate is recommended.

John Swanton (1911:107–8) interpreted the Natchez social system as follows: There were two major social groupings—nobles and commoners—with the nobility divided into the three "classes" of Suns, Nobles, and Honored People. The nobility could only marry among the commoners, who were referred to by the Natchez Suns as "Stinkards." Being a matrilineal society, the ruling Sun Lineage was perpetuated through female Suns, and degenerated through male Suns, so that offspring descended through male nobility would inherit one status level below their father. One participant in this debate (Hart 1943) recognized, however, that at some point the commoner class would become depleted and no spouses would be available for marriage to the nobility.

Most of the later researchers agree with Swanton's interpretation of noble exogamy (Josselin de Jong, Hart, Quimby, Fisher, Brain, Knight, and White, Murdock and Scaglion) but offer their own explanations for just how such a system could have operated without exhausting the available pool of commoner spouses. In general, three different explanations have been offered for the successful functioning of the Natchez descent system. Some have argued for a kind of asymmetrical descent whereby only male offspring degenerated in noble rank from male nobility, while female offspring of male nobles reckoned descent from their commoner mothers in true matrilineal fashion (Fisher 1964; Hart 1943; White et al. 1971). Given this unusual descent system, White and others (1971:375–76) also argue that the lack of any mention of Honored women in the French accounts suggests that the Honored category was a rank of men among the commoner class. Only a few men would have inherited this rank from their Noble fathers, while the majority would have achieved this status by way of performing acts of military valor or ritual sacrifice of a close relative upon the death of a member of the ruling Sun family.

Second, it has been argued that assimilation of outside Tunican-speaking groups into the Natchez descent system was a short-term solution to replenishing the pool of available commoner spouses (Brain 1971; Quimby 1946). Proponents of this argument contend that the unusual exogamous marriage system noted by eighteenth-century French observers was a relatively recent manifestation of a formerly endogamous nobility. Changes in the original system served to incorporate into the Natchez social system foreign peoples dispossessed of their lands and lifeways by the effects of European contact. Some of those involved in this debate (White et al. 1971:372) refute this possible explanation by noting that such assimilation of outside groups could reduce the rate of Stinkard depletion but not stop the growing numbers of Nobles and Honoreds descended from Suns.

Finally, others have suggested that the Natchez "classes" described by Swanton were nothing more than exogamous ranked clans or moieties with patterns of descent common to such other southeastern tribes as the Chickasaw, Creek, Caddo, Timucua, and Apalachee (Josselin de Jong 1928; Knight 1990). Shared features between the aristocratic social systems of the historic period Natchez and the Timucua of peninsular Florida included: "an exogamous nobility, a matrilineal royal family, agnatic inheritance as a mechanism for preserving noble status among children of chiefs, and an eventual fall off to commoner status among chiefly collaterals" (Knight 1990:13–14). Therefore, the exogamy of Suns should be interpreted as a common aspect of moiety exogamy whereby a member of the noble moiety must marry among the commoner moiety.

Others reject Swanton's interpretation of exogamy of the entire nobility and make the argument that a closer reading of the primary French sources indicates that only Suns were exogamous (MacLeod 1924; Mason 1964; Tooker 1963). According to this interpretation, members of the Sun royal matrilineage would be recognized within three degrees of consanguineal relationship to the royal matriline of ruling Suns (sibling, first cousin, second cousin) (Le Page du Pratz 1758:II:334–35; Penicaut, in Swanton 1911:159). Additionally, Natchez nobility and commoner alike would be prohibited from marrying within three degrees of relationship to one another. Therefore, Suns could not marry Suns because they would be breaking an incest taboo that applied to all Natchez. Instead, Suns could marry anyone who was more than three collateral generations removed from the ruling Sun matriline, such as Nobles (third, fourth, and fifth cousins of the ruling Sun matriline), Honored People, or Stinkards.

These latter researchers agree that some form of asymmetrical descent was operating. Noble and Honored were merely titles given to offspring descended through male Suns or to people promoted to a higher rank by way of achieved successes, through acts of military valor or performance of ritual sacrifice. Perhaps Sun-Stinkards marriage was preferred because of a need to adhere to two Natchez customs. The first custom states that the spouse of a Sun had to be put to death when the Sun died to accompany him or her to the afterlife, while the other custom dictated that a Sun could never be put to death. Stinkard spouses of Suns could live a life of royalty during their lives, and then at the death of their Sun spouse, accompany him or her into the afterlife. People of Honored or Noble rank apparently did not gain enough advantages by marrying a Sun to justify having his or her life cut short when the Sun spouse died (Tooker 1963:368). A careful review of some key passages from the primary sources may help to clarify these conflicting arguments over whether the Natchez possessed an exogamous nobility.

With respect to whether the entire Natchez nobility (that is, Suns, Nobles, and Honored People) was exogamous and thus required to marry only commoner Stinkards, the chronicler Penicaut says, "In the same manner, a noble girl, that is to say, a daughter of a woman of chief nobility (*fille d'une femme de chef noble*) [that is, of the Sun matrilineage], when she wishes to marry, is only able to marry a commoner" (Margry 1887:5:450–51). This passage makes it clear that Suns must marry Stinkards, but the French phrase noted above was mistranslated by Swanton to mean the daughter of a wife of a male Sun. Therefore, in addition to Sun exogamy, Swanton argued for the exogamy of the Noble rank. If indeed this daughter of a male Sun was one rank below that of her father, she would be of Noble rank and therefore only able to marry a commoner.

In another passage, however, Dumont de Montigny refers to a female Sun's husband, "whom she is able to choose if she wishes from among the Stinkards and who is rather her slave than her master" (Swanton 1911:104). Le Page Du Pratz (1758:2:397) comments that because Suns are obligated to put their spouses to death when they die and no Sun can ever be put to death, they are obligated to marry beneath their station. Any rank below that of Sun would qualify as marrying beneath a Sun's station. Therefore, from the preceding two passages, it would appear that Suns cannot marry Suns, since they must follow the Natchez customs of avoiding incest and murder of Suns. Penicaut is the only account that specifically states that Suns must marry Stinkards; yet no mention of Noble exogamy is offered in his account. The other two independent accounts leave open the possibility that Sun-Stinkard marriage was preferred rather than required.

The majority of researchers already mentioned in this debate argue that the Natchez descent system was based on castes or classes, but even this contention is inconsistent with the ethnohistoric sources. A castelike social organization would imply the fixed nature of status or rank in one's lifetime, with no opportunity to change rank from commoner to member of the nobility (Haviland 1999:326). This is clearly not the case, for one chronicler mentions the fact that Stinkard men could rise to Honored status, and in turn men of Honored status could rise in rank to Nobles by military accomplishment (Le Page du Pratz 1758:2:395). Calling the Natchez descent categories *classes* is also misleading. This term usually implies large stratified economically based social groups whose membership in any given class cross-cuts kinship and is not based on age or sex (Keesing 1981:312), but in the Natchez case, status is clearly tied to genealogical degrees of relationship to the ruling matrilineage.

If indeed there was no requirement for noble-commoner marriage, and instead exogamy was defined by the Natchez marriage prohibition within three degrees of relatedness, then each status rank would have been exogamous and the argument for clan-based descent might not be appropriate here. Clans are defined as descent groups whose membership is so large as to be composed of multiple lineages that cannot actually trace the genealogical links to their common ancestor (Haviland 1999:300). In fact, arguments for a clan-based system by Josselin de Jong (1928) and Knight (1990) rely heavily on Swanton's mistranslation of Noble exogamy. Without such supporting evidence, a clan-based descent is still possible, but a lineage-based system where members are able to trace their genealogical links to the founding ancestor becomes the more plausible explanation. It would seem, then, that Suns could not marry Suns, Nobles could not marry Nobles, and even Stinkards within three degrees of consanguineal relationship to one another could not marry each other, or else this would violate the three-degrees-of-relatedness incest taboo. Moreover, if indeed each status category was exogamous within three degrees of relatedness, this would not place an undue burden on the Stinkard commoner rank to supply spouses to Suns and Nobles since Stinkards would not be the only eligible spouses for Suns and Nobles.

With regard to whether the descent system was asymmetrical, Penicaut makes it clear that when the Great Sun (paramount chief) marries a Stinkard, the children, be they boys or girls, are Nobles. Le Page du Pratz (1758:2:395) supports this statement when he says that the children of male Suns are Nobles and the male children of these Nobles were only Honored People. Dumont de Montigny (1753:178–79) repeats this when he refers to the children of male Suns as Nobles, their children as Honored People, and their children's children as Stinkards. Regarding Honored People, Dumont de Montigny clarifies his last statement and says that birth gives this rank to all the grandsons of the Great Sun. Thus three independent accounts of the French support the claim that both male and female children inherited Noble status from their Sun fathers, thus calling into question the argument for asymmetrical descent.

It would also appear that the rank of Honored Person was indeed an honorific title conferred on men (but not women) at birth. Both men and women, however, could achieve this title by sacrificing their infant upon the death of a Sun (Dumont de Montigny 1753:181). It is instructive to note that in each of the above cases the chroniclers use terms such as *children* and *boys and girls* to denote which offspring of male Suns will inherit Noble status. However, when specifically mentioning Honored status, each chronicler emphasizes the male offspring as the heir to the title, using terms like *grandsons* and *male children*. White and his coauthors (1971:375) remark that this is a clear indicator of the agnatic asymmetrical descent of the offspring of male nobility. They do not, however, explain why only Noble males have this asymmetrical descent system for their offspring and why the same kind of system was not operating for the children of male Suns. As the reader can see, the chroniclers are quite clear when they mean children of both sexes as opposed to instances when specific mention is made of male offspring of Nobles inheriting the title of Honored, which does not appear to have been a descent category.

In support of Honored status being an honorific title bestowed on male children of Noble men, Penicaut mentions only Suns, Nobles, and Stinkards as comprising the entire social system. He comments that noble status is lost by the seventh generation as it is passed through the collateral matriline of Suns. White and others (1971:375–76) argue that because there is no mention of Honored women, the daughters of Noble males must inherit their Stinkard mother's commoner status. As I have argued, however, if descent was not asymmetrical, but instead the Honored status was a title bestowed only on the male offspring of Nobles or achieved by commoner men or women, then according to Penicaut's three-category descent system, the next inherited rank below Nobles should be that of commoners, or Stinkards. This interpretation is logically consistent with a system of matrilineal descent whereby the ruling lineage was perpetuated through the female line. Why should female offspring of Sun males belong to a different status rank than their brothers and not benefit from their own father's aristocratic status when their father's sister's daughters (their first cousins) are perpetuating the line of royal succession? If females were allowed to achieve Honored status by sacrificing their infants at the funeral of a Sun, it seems that women could possess the same Honored title as men. Therefore, both men and women could possess the noble status ranks of Suns and Nobles, and the honorific title of Honored, thus negating the need for asymmetrical descent to explain the Natchez marriage system.

In summary, after reviewing all the arguments in the debate and all the significant accounts from Penicaut, Dumont de Montigny, and Le Page du Pratz, we can propose a workable system that requires neither asymmetrical descent nor the mandatory exogamy of the nobility (be they lineages, clans, or moieties) to marry only among the commoners. It would appear that the Natchez were not organized into a class- or caste-based social system either. Inheritance of rank or status was clearly based on genealogical descent from the ruling Sun matriline, whereby the Sun rank or status level was defined by three degrees of matrilateral separation from the ruling matriline headed by the eldest Sun female (called White Woman). The fourth, fifth, and sixth degrees of removal along the female line of descent would have inherited the rank of Noble, with the seventh generation inheriting the commoner Stinkard status. On the male line of descent from male Suns on the direct line of rulership (Great Sun and Tattooed Serpent), each generation of boys and girls would have inherited one lower rank than their fathers. In one generation status degenerated to Noble, in the next generation the children of male Nobles degenerated to Stinkard status, with the exception of the boys inheriting the honorific title of Honored to set them into an equivalent level of prestige or respect with those commoners recognized for their military accomplishments or religious sacrifice. Because Sun rank or status was based on three degrees of genealogical separation from the ruling matriline, the same genealogical distance defined whom one could and could not marry. Exogamy between each ranked descent group of the nobility (that is, Suns and Nobles) would be the inevitable result.

Natchez Sociopolitical Organization

If indeed the French sources were accurate as to the absolute political decision-making authority of the Natchez Great Sun chief, one should expect the Natchez to have had a fairly consistent foreign policy toward Europeans. But this expectation does not jibe with historic accounts of the Natchez exhibiting unpredictable, hot and cold relations with the French. Moreover, French comments regarding the absolute authority of the Great Sun are not supported by a closer reading of the details of historic events that unfolded in the early eighteenth century between the Natchez and the French. Could there be another, more plausible explanation that accounts for these apparent inconsistencies in the French accounts? Rather than taking the French statements at face value, one can gain a clearer picture of Natchez power relationships within their chiefdom by carefully reviewing the events recorded in the French historic documents.

Anthropologists reviewing European ethnohistoric accounts of descriptions of Native American lifeways are often faced with the problem of a kind of colonial bias built into the European perception of native peoples. The French bias of the presumed absolute authority of the Natchez Great Sun is one example of what ethnohistorian Patricia Galloway refers to as "observational blind spots," which can color an account and reduce its credibility (Galloway 1986:119). These biases are referred to as blind spots because the European observers just did not see or fully understand certain aspects of Native American lifeways. The French eighteenth-century observers had no comparable example in their own culture of how a Natchez chief governed, and so they interpreted aspects of Natchez politics through their own European filter. Owing to the highly deferential behavior of the Natchez toward their Great Sun, the French falsely concluded that he was a king like their own Sun King, Louis XIV, with equivalent powers. Indeed, conflicting historic accounts by the French make it appear that the Great Sun reigned more than he governed, and that his political authority was more limited and perhaps more fragile than he or the French believed it to be (Hudson 1976:210). However, while some French accounts testify to the despotic authority of the Great Sun over his people, other accounts note how war chiefs from outlying Natchez villages operated independently of and in opposition to the wishes of the Great Sun.

Another blind spot that colored French accounts of Natchez political authority was the French confusion between the concept of the "nation" of the Natchez and the "village" called Natchez. This blind spot springs from European ignorance of native people's self-declared tribal names, a common mistake made during the period of first contact with Native Americans of North America. To give one well-known example: when Christopher Columbus first encountered the Taino tribe in the Caribbean, he referred to them as Indians because he thought he had reached India. In another example, the word *Eskimo* is not a self-declared name for the Arctic-dwelling native people, but rather a derogatory term initially used by Algonkin tribes. It means "raw meat eaters," a reference to one of the Inuit's (the self-declared name for Canadian Arctic Eskimo meaning "people") cultural practices involving the consumption of frozen, raw polar bear meat (Spencer et al. 1977:58). The mistake made by the French regarding the name of the Natchez tribe follows the same pattern of European ignorance.

The earliest published reference to the Natchez people from the French explorer La Salle in 1682 mentions a brief stay by the French in the village of the people who call themselves Nahy or Natché (Swanton 1911:187). The next reference to the Natchez in 1699 does not mention them by the popular name with which anthropologists are familiar. In his travels along the Mississippi River, the French explorer and founder of New Orleans, Iberville, came to rely a great deal on native informants for information about other neighboring tribes. It was in this context that an informant from a tribe near the Natchez referred to a people known as the Thecloel, who inhabited nine villages, one of which was named Naches (McWilliams 1981:73). Here is good supporting evidence for the argument that the tribal name Natchez was mistakenly imposed by the French on the Thecloel tribe. The tribal name Thecloel literally means "people of Thé," the name of their original ancestor who descended from the sun.

Therefore, it was the village called Natchez with which the French were politically allied and interacted frequently. Any political alliances forged by the French with either the Great Sun or Tattooed Serpent held only for those Natchez villages allied with the Grand Village. This lack of French understanding of the semiautonomous nature of the Natchez village districts helps to explain why the French were often so confused by the friendliness of the Great Sun while their own settlers were being ambushed by Natchez raiders.

Another good example of this misuse of the terms *nation* and *village* comes from Iberville's 1699 account, where he comments that a calumet (peace pipe) ceremony with a local chief and seven others resulted in a French alliance with four nations east of the Mississippi, one of which included the Natchez. But at least four of the names mentioned by Iberville in fact belonged to villages or parts of tribes, so in these cases the French had not made an alliance with whole unified tribal nations (McWilliams 1981:47–48). Instead, this encounter demonstrated the degree to which villages could function autonomously when deciding affairs of peace and war.

The misuse of the term *nation* for *village* led the French to miss some important features of the Natchez political structure. Although the concept of opposing Natchez political factions was well documented by the French, they still saw the Great Sun as having ultimate authority over all nine Natchez villages and thus as responsible for any hostilities against the French. It was well known that the eighteenth-century Natchez consisted of two opposing political factions (Albrecht 1944, 1946; Brain 1982; Brown 1978, 1982, 1985, 1991; Neitzel 1965; Swanton 1911); the one led by the Grand Village and its allies in Flour and Tioux villages was pro-French, while the other faction led by the White Apple village and its allies in Jenzenaque and Grigra villages was pro-English. What these accounts fail to emphasize is that the Great Sun of the Grand Village did not have absolute authority over all of the villages making up the Thecloel or Natchez tribe. Instead, the absolute authority wielded by the principal Suns of the Grand Village was in most cases limited to their own village domain, centered on the village called Natchez.

Much of this confusion can be clarified in the context of the colonial expansion of the French and English in the southeastern interior of North America, and the manner in which this expansion affected the two opposing Natchez political factions already in existence prior to European contact. From the time of La Salle in 1682, the French started establishing trading outposts all along the Mississippi River Valley, while the English traders were moving southwestward toward the Mississippi River from the Carolina English colony. By 1700, English traders were among the Quapaw in Arkansas and the Chickasaw, who were located in present-day northern Mississippi (Swanton 1911:192). In fact, a British map from the early eighteenth century (Anonymous 1715) noting the location of tribes within Mississippi has the Chickasaw territory extending 150–200 miles from the Big Black River valley in west-central Mississippi across to modern-day Tupelo, Mississippi, in the northeastern corner of the state. In support of such a large territorial range, accounts from La Salle's expedition along the Mississippi River note that a Chickasaw party was encountered just south of present-day Memphis, Tennessee, and even joined the expedition downriver until they chose to leave La Salle's party when they arrived at the Natchez villages, presumably their allies (Stubbs 1982:46). According to later eighteenth-century French descriptions, the pro-English Natchez villages were located to the north and east of the Grand Village and would have been about 100 miles south of Chickasaw territory. This geographic location would place them nearer to the Chickasaw than the French-allied Natchez and in the direction of the presumed English contact. In contrast, the Grand Village and its allies of Flour and Tioux were located nearest to the Mississippi River and thus were more likely to engage in trade with the French.

Independent confirmation of the two observational blind spots of French chroniclers can be best documented with the original French observers' accounts of major altercations between the Natchez and the French. These observers called the first three of these altercations the First (1716), Second (1722), and Third (1723) Natchez Wars. They referred to the final altercation that ultimately led to the Natchez demise as the Natchez Rebellion of 1729. A brief historical review of the first and last of these altercations demonstrates a consistent pattern of hostility against the French by the Natchez faction allied with the English.

The First Natchez War involved the murders of four French traders by raiders led by the Natchez war chief of White Apple village (also called White Earth). In attempting to resolve this initial conflict, the French commander, Bienville, sought to call a meeting of Natchez chiefs. In the accounts of de Richebourg, a captain under Bienville, we get a glimpse of Natchez factional politics in action (Swanton 1911:201–3). The chiefs called to meet with Bienville pleaded innocent to any involvement in the councils held to invite the English into their villages and went on to implicate three rebellious war chiefs from the villages of Hickories (also called Jenzenaque), White Apple, and Grigra, part of the pro-English Natchez faction. These rebellious chiefs were said by Tattooed Serpent to have "assumed so much authority in *their nation* [emphasis mine] that they were more feared and obeyed" than he and his brother the Great Sun (Swanton 1911:202). In an independent account from the French chronicler Penicaut, it seems that the Natchez village of White Apple often entertained English traders, suggesting a possible economic motive for the murders of the four Frenchmen.

In another account involving Natchez hostility against the French during the Second Natchez War, Tattooed Sepent makes a very clear distinction between his pro-French "nation" and the other Natchez nations hostile to the French. He goes on to say that his own Grand Village and the village of Flour did not commit such crimes against the French, and "besides all of *his* [emphasis mine] people were friends of the French and carriers for them; that it was then useless to come and declare war against them; that *his nation* [emphasis mine] was entirely unwilling to have war with the French" (Swanton 1911:210).

Tattooed Serpent's use of the term *nation* in the above quotations from the First and Second Natchez Wars refers not to the entire tribe but rather to a village of the Natchez. In sum, the preceding accounts provide us with a clear admission by a chiefly authority of the Grand Village that a power struggle was currently under way and that these pro-English villages seemed to be gaining increasing popular support, so much so that the Grand Village feared their increasing authority.

The tenuous control of the Grand Village over the people of its entire chiefdom was brought into further jeopardy upon the death of Tattooed Serpent in 1725. He had always been friendly to the French and had always been the peacemaker with the French after each Natchez hostility; the loss of this French ally was to strengthen the power of the pro-English Natchez faction. The political power of the Grand Village was further weakened in 1728 by the death of the Great Sun, another ally of the French (Albrecht 1946:341; Swanton 1911:220–21). Such a shift in Natchez political power set the stage for the final period of Natchez-French hostility, known as the Natchez Rebellion of 1729.

According to the French chroniclers, this revolt was provoked by the outrageous demands of a tyrannical commandant of the French Fort Rosalie. In his own selfish interest, this commandant, named de Chopart, sought to commandeer a piece of land belonging to the chief of the White Apple village as a location for his own plantation (Giraud 1987:397; Swanton 1911:222). It comes as no surprise that this chief, a member of the pro-English Natchez faction, was reluctant to give up his ancestral claim to this land to one of his hated enemies, who had sought to exterminate his village several times in the past. Furthermore, the political power of the French-allied Natchez was weakened after the deaths of the two principal Suns of the Grand Village and the appointment of a new Great Sun who was both young and inexperienced. Certainly, the Sun chief of the English-allied White Apple village now had more political clout as a senior ranking Sun among all of the Natchez villages than his young newly appointed rival in the Grand Village. Natchez hostility against the French culminated in a massacre, on November 29, 1729, of more than 200 men, women, and children residing in the French settlements in the Natchez vicinity, including Fort Rosalie, and both plantations of St. Catherine and White Earth (Giraud 1987:398–400).

It was not until January of 1731 that the French were able to catch up with the Natchez, who had erected a fort on the western side of the Mississippi River. Before they could capture everyone within the fort, somewhere between 75 and 250 Natchez warriors (sources give conflicting estimates) escaped and went to live among the pro-English Chickasaw Indians. Only the newly appointed Great Sun and about 100 of his loyal followers were captured and subsequently enslaved on French plantations in the West Indies (Albrecht 1946:347–49; Swanton 1911:247). Upon his capture, the Great Sun pleaded his innocence in the Natchez revolt by telling the French commander that he was "too young to speak, and that it was the ancients who had formed this criminal project" (Swanton 1911:247). There is a strong likelihood that the "ancients" consisted of a council dominated by senior pro-English-faction war chiefs and principal warriors who had been engaged in over fifteen years of persistent hostility against the French. Here we have a clearer picture of how Natchez politics operated. The young Great Sun of 1731 confessed that he had very little political power to put a stop to the designs of this pro-English faction, thus leading to a shift in Natchez political power from the Grand Village to the village of White Apple and its allies in the villages of Jenzenaque and Grigra.

The Great Sun was the eldest male in the direct ancestral line to the original Sun ancestors (Dumont de Montigny 1753:1:178). However, his younger brothers possessed the same bloodline and exercised some degree of authority as chiefs in their own villages beyond the Grand Village (McWilliams 1953:88). Hence the Great Sun was first among his equals, causing conflict with competing political authorities. It would appear that membership in the royal Sun lineage accorded the chiefs of each "nation" greater authority among their own people than those in the other Natchez "nations."

Archaeology of the Historic Period Natchez

Although the detailed accounting of events from French chroniclers from the early eighteenth century paints a picture of a struggle for political supremacy among competing Natchez villages, it is the archaeology that best reflects the competition for European trade goods between the pro-English and pro-French Natchez village factions. If the Natchez Grand Village was indeed the central village of the Great Sun, who had absolute political and economic control over his people, then the archaeology of this settlement should reflect such chiefly power and control.

Two excavation reports from the Fatherland site (Neitzel 1965, 1983), the Grand Village of the Natchez, record that historic European artifacts were found with elite burials in the Natchez temple. Yet the archaeologist Robert S. Neitzel who excavated the settlement of the Natchez Great Sun described the quantity of European trade goods as meager. In fact, the trade goods associated with all of the twenty-seven individuals buried at Fatherland, including that of Burial 15, presumed to be the Great Sun who died in 1728, would not even equal the contents of a few scattered graves from the smaller, weaker, historic Tunica tribe neighboring the Natchez (Neitzel 1983:84, 107). The trade goods from elite mound contexts included such articles as glass beads, catlinite (a soft red stone mined in the Upper Midwest) pipes, gunflints, iron gun parts, brass and silver bells, and brass finger rings (Neitzel 1965:50–51). The total number of glass beads recovered from excavation of all twenty-seven burials exceeded 1,600 (see table 6.1).

In contrast, two other historic period sites in the Natchez Bluffs region recently investigated by archaeologists were found to be Natchez cemetery sites presumably associated with nearby nonelite, nonmound settlements (Brown 1985). Known as the Rice and O'Quinn sites, these two cemetery sites for the most part contained very similar types of European trade goods as those found at the Fatherland site excavations. The Rice and O'Quinn sites are known through private collections, and thus artifact totals should be regarded as minimal estimates since some private collections from the sites were not available for examination by archaeologists and a number of burial artifacts in other collections had already been sold before they were examined by archaeologists (Brown 1985:57–73, 81–93). It is important to note that only the Rice burial site has burial provenience information. Therefore, examinations of burial pattern types (extended vs. flexed vs. secondary bundle) and artifact associations cannot be made for the O'Quinn site. Despite this limitation, the sample of fifty-four whole aboriginal ceramic vessels from the O'Quinn site represents the largest whole vessel sample from a single site in the entire Natchez Bluffs region—even larger than the collections from Rice (n = 38) or Fatherland (n = 41)(Brown 1985:57). In addition,

Table 6.1. Fatherland Site burial data

Grave lot numbers	1	2	3	4	5	6	7	8	9	10	11	12	13	14	15	16	17	18	19	20	21-25	26	Total
Burial types																							
Extended				1				1		1				1		1	1	1		1		1	9
Assoc. skulls					1							1		1					1				4
(Extended#)					#6							#15		#15					#16				
Box bundles							2						1								5		8
Isolated skulls	1	1	1			1			1		1												6
Ceramics																							
Addis Plain																							
var. *St. Catherine*	1							1							1			1	1				5
var. *Unspecified*						5																	5
Chicot Red																							
var. *Grand Village*																			1				1
Coles Creek Incised																							
var. *Hardy*								1															1
Fatherland Incised																							
var. *Fatherland*	1	1	2	1		4		1	3	2				1		2		1	2				21
var. *Snyders Bluff*				1					1														2
Leland Incised																							
var. *Unspecified*														2									2
Maddox Engraved																							
var. *Emerald*																		1					1
Mazique Incised																							
var. *Manchac*															1								1
Plaquemine Brush																							
var. *Plaquemine*						2																	2
Total ceramics	2	1	2	2	0	11	0	3	4	2	0	0	0	3	2	2	0	3	4	0	0	0	41

(continued)

Table 6.1—*continued*

Grave lot numbers	1	2	3	4	5	6	7	8	9	10	11	12	13	14	15	16	17	18	19	20	21–25	26	Total
European trade goods																							
Glass beads	60	0	120	300	0	60	0	326	74	0	91	60	0	60	91	60	60	0	180	70	0	0	1,612
Iron ax heads					1										1								2
Wire ear coils							4								7								11
Copper arm bracelets							13																13
Copper gorgets					1																		1
Brass religious medals				2																			2
Brass sleigh bells			18											20			2						40
Brass finger rings							2													7			9
Brass thimble				1																			1
Silver spoons																1							1
Silver sleigh bells									1								2						3
Faience crockery vessels															2								2
Iron cooking pots															2								2
Flintlock pistol															1								1
Stone discoidals					2										3								5
Kaolin pipes															1								1

Source: Compiled from Neitzel 1965:40–44, 50–51.

a number of the same ceramic types and varieties were found with elite burials at Fatherland and with the presumably commoner burials at Rice and O'Quinn.

Brown (1971) and Galloway (1995) each noted, however, that Natchez elite burial practices as described by the French comprised three interment stages. The first stage consisted of exposing the corpse on a scaffold or burial in pits in the temple floor. The second stage involved exhumation of the corpse, defleshing and placing the remains in chests or baskets on temple shelves. The third and final phase related to the French by the Natchez temple guardian, but never actually witnessed by any French observer, consisted of the removal of the disarticulated remains from the temple and final burial in an undisclosed location. Galloway (1995:292–94) concluded from this that any primary, in-flesh interments represent an incomplete burial process and the ultimate fate of the remains of Natchez chiefs is unknown.

However, upon examination of the burial patterns recovered from the excavations at Fatherland by Chambers in 1930 and by Neitzel in 1962, at least two burial stages are clearly evident. The first burial stage of primary interment is reflected by the nine extended adult burials containing numerous grave goods of both aboriginal and European manufacture. While the second stage involving the placement of human remains on shelves in baskets or chests would be difficult to recover archaeologically, in at least two instances, disarticulated bones were found buried in wooden chests in the floor of the mortuary temple of Mound C. Thus it would appear that in at least two instances, the third stage never took place, and perhaps the final resting place for the chiefs was not outside the temple, as the French were told, but in the temple floor in wooden chests.

Additional research by James Brown (1981) on the archaeological identifiers of rank in burial treatment is especially instructive to the Natchez case. Brown identified three key factors that help us discriminate between differences in social status and rank: (1) differential age/sex profiles, (2) the effort-expenditure of energy and wealth, and (3) the presence/absence of symbols of authority found with each burial type. According to Brown, deviation from a normal age/sex ratio of those interred suggests restrictive recruitment of particular age/sex categories into particular ranks. Moreover, the greater the social rank, the greater the expenditure of energy and wealth should be found in burial treatment. Finally, symbols of authority should be restricted to those members vested with authority over the entire group (Brown 1981:29–30). When these three factors are applied to presumably "elite" burials in the Mound C temple floor at the Fatherland site (table 6.1) as compared with the supposed "commoner" burials at the outlying Natchez cemetery site at Rice (table 6.2), some striking similarities between the two sites become evident.

With regard to the deviation from normal age/sex ratios of those interred, both sites had around 30 percent of their burials represented by primary extended adult interments (nine of twenty-seven burials at Fatherland and three of eleven burials at Rice). Although poor bone preservation did not allow for determination of sex, the male gender was inferred by Neitzel (1965) in the presence of certain artifact classes (that is, iron axes, brass bells, wire ear coils, and iron coil arm bracelets) that were mentioned by eighteenth-century French chroniclers as having been used or worn by men (Swanton 1911:55, 127). The Fatherland site appears to have similar representation of isolated skull burials (six of twenty-seven, or 22 percent) as the Rice site (two of eleven, or 18 percent). In four instances at Fatherland, these skulls are in very close association (within 24 inches) with extended adult interments (#5 adult skull, #12 child's teeth, #14 child's teeth, and #19 adult skull) and may represent war trophies or infants sacrificed in honor of the deceased individuals. Fatherland also has the only evidence (among Natchez sites excavated to date) for secondary bundle burials of skulls and long bones buried in wooden chests. Remains of two chests were recovered, with two skulls and long bones in one chest and six skulls and long bones in the other chest. In the chest of six skulls and long bones, no artifacts were found in association, but the other chest contained brass finger rings on the phalanges and iron and copper arm bracelets on one of the humeri (Neitzel 1965:42). Thus the greatest difference between the Fatherland and Rice burial treatments resides in the exclusive privilege of the royal Sun matrilineage being interred in the temple as primary extended or secondary bundle burials in wooden chests. Penicaut noted that only the first three families of Suns were interred in the temple, thus lending support to the elite status of those twenty-seven individuals buried in the floor of Mound C. In contrast, the burials at the outlying cemetery site of Rice are not associated with a mortuary temple mound, yet the artifact assemblages differ very little between the two burial sites.

The expenditure of wealth on particular burials at Rice is equivalent to that connected with the Fatherland temple mound burials with regard to some artifact classes and even exceeds Fatherland in the abundance of European glass trade beads. Although the Fatherland site alone yielded the

Table 6.2. Rice Site burial data

Grave lot numbers	1	2	3	4	5	6	7	8	9	10	11	Total
Burial types												
Extended	1	1			1							3
Indeterminate			1	1		1	1	1	1	1	1	8
Ceramics												
Addis Plain												
var. Addis	1	2	1	1			1					6
var. Ratcliffe					1							1
var. St. Catherine			1									1
var. Unspecified			1		1				2	1		5
Coleman Incised												
var. Unspecified	1											1
Coles Creek Inc.												
var. Unspecified	1											1
Fatherland Incised												
var. Fatherland	3	2	1		1		1	1	1			10
var. Snyders Bluff						1						1
var. Stanton							1					1
var. Unspecified			1	1						1	2	5
Maddox Engraved												
var. Emerald		1										1
var. Unspecified		1										1
Mazique Incised												
var. Manchac	1							1				2
Mississippi Plain												
var. Unspecified	1											1
Natchitoches Engraved												
var. Unspecified	1											1
Total ceramics	7	9	3	1	4	2	3	2	3	2	2	38
European trade goods												
Glass beads[a]	5,767	70	383			12				665	1,120	8,017
Iron ax heads					1							1
Copper bells	[b]					1						1+
Brass finger rings	1											1
Bone discoidals		1		1								2

Source: Brown 1985:225, table 29.
[a] All glass beads have been identified as standard early eighteenth century (Brown 1985:93).
[b] Several copper bells for grave lot number 1 were noted in private collections but were not always available for quantification.

exclusive presence of some artifact types like gun parts, faience crockery, and silver spoons, the cemetery site of Rice contained a far richer abundance of European glass trade beads than was found at Fatherland. The number of burials recorded at the Rice site (eleven) was less than half the number at Fatherland (twenty-seven), yet the combined glass bead count at Rice totaled over 8,000—five times the number recovered at Fatherland. Comparing the average number of glass beads per burial, one finds that the Rice site exceeds Fatherland by a factor of ten, resulting in an average bead count at Rice of over 1,336 beads per burial (where beads were present) compared to only 134 beads per burial at Fatherland. One extended adult interment at Rice (Burial 1) was buried with nearly 5,800 glass beads; in comparison, the highest bead count from a single extended adult burial (Burial 4) at Fatherland totaled only 326 beads. Burial 1 at Rice was not the exception to the rule, however, as three other burials each exceeded the highest bead count of Burial 4 at Fatherland. Thus the amount of European trade wealth in beads amassed by those affiliated with the Rice cemetery far outweighed the efforts of the elite at Fatherland. Regarding burials interred with both ceramic vessels and glass beads, 55 percent of Rice burials fell into this category, as compared with only 31 percent of the Fatherland burials.

The energy expenditure in pottery production for interment purposes seems to have been virtually the same for Fatherland and Rice. Forty-one ceramic bowls, bottles, and jars represented ten ceramic varieties from Fatherland burials, as opposed to thirty-eight vessels of similar shapes represented by thirteen ceramic varieties at Rice. Six ceramic varieties were found at both sites (Addis Plain *var. Addis* and *var. St. Catherine,* Fatherland Incised *var. Fatherland* and *var. Snyder's Bluff* [red slipped], Mazique Incised *var. Manchac,* and Maddox Engraved *var. Emerald*), suggesting a fair degree of cultural continuity. An examination of the average number of ceramic vessels interred in each burial yielded very similar results for both Fatherland and Rice: 3.1 vessels per burial at Fatherland compared to 3.5 vessels per burial at Rice. Where ceramic vessels were found with burials, the common pattern at both sites was to have at least one bowl or jar and one bottle per burial, perhaps representing the food and beverage needed to sustain the deceased in the afterlife.

All things considered, it would appear that even though the Fatherland elite burials were restricted to the temple mound, the amount of wealth expenditure was actually greater at the outlying Rice site.

The final factor noted by Brown (1981) that has yet to be examined is the distribution of symbols of authority at each burial site. Such symbols of authority might include paraphernalia used in overseeing the affairs of peace and war, namely, the peace pipe and war club. While not found in burial contexts at either Rice or Fatherland, a sandstone effigy pipe and three catlinite peace pipe fragments were found in the midden of two small outlying nonmound Natchez sites. Because catlinite pipes were used by chiefs of historic period tribes throughout North America in the calumet peace pipe ceremony to cement alliances or call an end to hostilities (Brown 1985), it would appear that affairs of peace and war were not the sole domain of the Great Sun and Tattooed Serpent from the Grand Village of Natchez. Another symbol of authority, however, was found at both Fatherland and Rice: the iron ax or hatchet. The Fatherland site has only two temple mound burials interred with iron axes, which Le Page du Pratz observed were symbols of military authority that replaced the indigenous wooden war club (Swanton 1911:127). In contrast, Burial 5 at Rice site has an iron ax head, while Burial 1 has nearly 5,800 European glass trade beads.

Neitzel (1965) argued convincingly for Burial 15, a primary extended adult interment associated with numerous grave goods, being the best candidate for the remains of the Great Sun of the Grand Village, who died in 1728. If this is indeed the case, Burial 1 or Burial 5 at Rice have some similar burial patterns, suggesting the possibility that these individuals were members of the Natchez elite as well. Perhaps they were rebellious Sun war chiefs described in the French historic sources who hailed from the outlying English-allied Natchez village of Jenzenaque. Judging from the similar burial treatment as Burial 15 at Fatherland (primary extended, with similar pottery types, and iron hatchet), these two individuals at Rice may have commanded equivalent degrees of authority among their own local followers as the Sun chiefs of the paramount center of the Grand Village.

In summary, a detailed comparison of European artifact distribution patterns between Fatherland and outlying, nonmound historic period sites from a fifty-year period (1680–1730) makes it clear that European trade goods were accessible to almost every member of Natchez society. Ironically, it would seem that the outlying settlements, presumed by archaeologists to fall within the geographic areas of those villages allied with the English, had much better access to European glass trade beads than the presumed paramount center of the Grand Village. Moreover, symbols of chiefly authority are found at both the Grand Village of the Natchez and in the outlying English-allied village and cemetery areas, calling into question the absolute degrees of authority vested in the Great Sun and Tattooed Serpent residing in the paramount center. Herein lies archaeological evidence to support the French ethnohistoric sources presented earlier concerning the ability of the pro-English Natchez faction to declare war and make peace with the French without the approval of the Great Sun or the Tattooed Serpent of the Grand Village. Thus, while burial treatment of Natchez elite and commoner may indeed have followed different prescribed patterns as noted by the French, the striking similarities in burial treatments at Fatherland and Rice make it evident that Rice was not just a commoner cemetery, but one that clearly reflects elite Natchez chiefly burial patterns.

Conclusion

A review of the workings of the descent system makes it clear that the historic period Natchez were organized into ranked status levels based on the genealogical distance to the ruling Sun matrilineage. While marriage and kinship rules appear to have been strictly followed, so that nobility of the same rank could not marry one another, there appears to have been a great deal of political autonomy among members of the Sun matrilineage. The historic accounts of the Natchez wars with the French all help to reveal the French observational blind spots regarding Natchez political organization. These accounts point to the rebellious nature of the English-allied Natchez villages and the lack of authority of the Great Sun of the Grand Village in these villages' political and economic affairs. The political authority of the Great Sun appears to have extended only to the villages of Flour and Tioux, which seemed to be allied with the "nation" or village of Natchez. It would follow that the villages of White Apple, Jenzenaque, and Grigra were also separate semiautonomous "nations," who were free to declare war and make peace with whomever they wished. Each "nation" seemed to possess a great war chief with influential powers over its own local population.

The striking similarities between burial patterns of individuals at the Fatherland and Rice sites help to further support the idea that members of the Sun lineage were accorded very similar burial treatment, regardless of whether they resided in the Grand Village paramount center or in any one of the outlying villages. Symbols of authority, such as the catlinite peace pipes and iron axes, also suggest that the outlying villages were relatively autonomous, making political decisions to go to war with the French and economic decisions to trade with the English without the consent of the

Great Sun of the Grand Village. In a related vein, the fact that the Rice burials were richer in glass trade beads overall than the Fatherland burials is suggestive of the outlying English-allied Natchez villages' superior ability to gain greater access to European trade goods than those villages allied with the French.

Thus with the aid of both historic documents and archaeology of the Natchez Bluffs region, we can now see how the Natchez went through periods of waxing and waning political power. Their power appears to have peaked during the time of de Soto in the protohistoric period. However, the European presence in the late seventeenth and early eighteenth centuries served to intensify the factionalism inherent in Natchez politics and to undermine the paramount chief's political and economic authority. European intervention tore the Natchez nation in two, with one faction supporting French interests while the other faction tried to undermine the French at every opportunity, leading to a great deal of confusion among the French. The cleavage of political authority among the Natchez led the French to mistrust them and weakened the power of the Natchez Great Sun of the Grand Village. Such an unstable political situation was more than the Natchez chiefdom could endure, ultimately resulting in their dispersal as an autonomous tribe at the hands of their supposed European allies.

Bibliography

Albrecht, Andrew C.
1944   The Location of the Historic Natchez Villages. *Journal of Mississippi History* 6(2):67–88.
1946   Indian-French Relations at Natchez. *American Anthropologist* 48(3):321–54.
Anderson, David G.
1994   *The Savannah River Chiefdoms: Political Change in the Late Prehistoric Southeast.* Tuscaloosa: University of Alabama Press.
Anonymous
1715   *The Distribution of Indian Tribes in the Southeast about the Year 1715: Redrawn from a Blueprint of the Original among the British Archives.* Map on file, Mississippi Department of Archives and History, Jackson.
Beasley, Virgil R.
1998   Feasting and Mound Construction at the Mound 4, Block 1 locale, the Anna Site (22AD500), Adams County, Mississippi. Master's thesis, Department of Anthropology, University of Alabama, Tuscaloosa.
Bourne, Edward Gaylord (translator)
1904   *Narratives of the Career of Hernando de Soto in the Conquest of Florida.* 2 vols. New York: Allerton.

174   Karl G. Lorenz

Brain, Jeffrey P.
1971   The Natchez "Paradox." *Ethnology* 10(2):215–22.
1978   Late Prehistoric Settlement Patterning in the Yazoo Basin and Natchez Bluffs Regions of the Lower Mississippi Valley. In *Mississippian Settlement Patterns,* edited by B. D. Smith, 331–68. New York: Academic Press.
1982   La Salle at the Natchez: An Archaeological and Historical Perspective. In *La Salle and His Legacy: Frenchmen and Indians in the Lower Mississippi Valley,* edited by P. Galloway, 49–59. Jackson: University Press of Mississippi.
Brain, Jeffrey P., Ian W. Brown, and Vincas P. Steponaitis
n.d.   Archaeology of the Natchez Bluffs. Manuscript on file, Peabody Museum of Archaeology and Ethnology, Harvard University, Cambridge.
Brown, Ian W.
1973   Settlement Patterns in the Bluff Area of the Lower Mississippi Valley. Honors thesis, Department of Anthropology, Harvard University, Cambridge.
1978   The Natchez Indians: Archaeological Contributions to Settlement Locations. Revised manuscript version of a paper presented at the seventeenth French Regime Symposium, Natchez.
1982   An Archaeological Study of Culture Contact and Change in the Natchez Bluffs Region. In *La Salle and His Legacy: Frenchmen and Indians in the Lower Mississippi Valley,* edited by P. Galloway, 176–93. Jackson: University Press of Mississippi.
1985   *Natchez Indian Archaeology: Culture Change and Stability in the Lower Mississippi Valley.* Archaeological Report 15. Mississippi Department of Archives and History, Jackson.
1989   The Calumet Ceremony in the Southeast and Its Archaeological Manifestations. *American Antiquity* 54(2):311–31.
1991   Historic Indians of the Lower Mississippi Valley: An Archaeologist's View. In *Towns and Temples along the Mississippi,* edited by D. Dye and C. Cox, 227–38. Tuscaloosa: University of Alabama Press.
1997   *Excavations at the Anna Site (22Ad500), Adams County, Mississippi: A Preliminary Report.* Edited by I. Brown. Report on file, Gulf Coast Survey, University of Alabama, Tuscaloosa.
Brown, James A.
1971   The Dimensions of Status in the Burials at Spiro. In *Approaches to the Social Dimensions of Mortuary Practices,* edited by J. A. Brown, 92–112. Society for American Archaeology Memoir 25. Washington, D.C.
1981   The Search for Rank in Prehistoric Burials. In *The Archaeology of Death,* edited by R. Chapman, I. Kinnes, and K. Randsborg, 25–37. Cambridge: Cambridge University Press.
1990   Archaeology Confronts History at the Natchez Temple. *Southeastern Archaeology* 9(1):10.
Butler, Ruth Lapham (editor)
1934   *The Journal of Paul Du Ru, February 1 to May 8, 1700.* Chicago: Caxton Club.
Clayton, Lawrence A., Vernon James Knight, Jr., and Edward C. Moore (editors)
1993   *The De Soto Chronicles: The Expedition of Hernando de Soto to North America in 1539–1543.* 2 vols. Tuscaloosa: University of Alabama Press.

Cleland, Charles E., Jr.
1965   Analysis of the Faunal Remains of the Fatherland Site. In *Archaeology of the Fatherland Site: The Grand Village of the Natchez*, by R. S. Neitzel. Anthropological Papers of the American Museum of Natural History, vol. 51, pt. 1:96–101. New York.
Cotter, John L.
1951   Stratigraphic and Area Tests at the Emerald and Anna Mound Sites. *American Antiquity* 17(1):18–32.
1952   The Gordon Site in Southern Mississippi. *American Antiquity* 18(2):110–26.
Cox, Isaac J. (editor)
1905   *The Journeys of Rene Robert Cavalier Sieur de LaSalle*. New York: Allerton.
Dobyns, H. F.
1983   *Their Number Become Thinned: Native American Population Dynamics in Eastern North America*. Knoxville: University of Tennessee Press.
Dumont de Montigny, Louis Francois Benjamin
1753   *Memoires Historiques sur la Louisiane*. 2 vols. Paris: Le Mascrier.
Fisher, J. L.
1964   Solutions for the Natchez Paradox. *Ethnology* 3:53–65.
Fowler, Melvin L.
1977   The Cahokia Site. In *Explorations into Cahokia Archaeology*, 2d rev. ed., edited by M. Fowler, 1–30. Illinois Archaeological Survey, Bulletin 7. Urbana.
French, Benjamin F. (editor)
1851   *Historical Collections of Louisiana*. Vol. 3. New York: D. Appleton.
1853   *Historical Collections of Louisiana*. Vol. 5. New York: Lamport, Blakeman, and Law.
Galloway, Patricia
1986   The Direct Historical Approach and Early Historical Documents: The Ethnohistorian's View. In *The Protohistoric Period in the Mid-South: 1500–1700*, edited by D. Dye and R. Brister, 14–23. Archaeological Report no. 18. Mississippi Department of Archives and History, Jackson.
1995   *Choctaw Genesis, 1500–1700*. Lincoln: University of Nebraska Press.
Giraud, Marcel
1987   *A History of French Louisiana*. Vol. 1, *The Reign of Louis XIV, 1698–1715*. Baton Rouge: Louisiana State University Press.
Gosselin, L'Abbé Amedée
1906   Les Sauvages du Mississippi (1698–1708): D'Après la Correspondance des Missionaires des Missions Étrangères de Quebec. *Congrès International des Americanistes*, fifteenth session, 31–51.
Haas, Mary R.
1956   Natchez and the Muskogean Languages. *Language* 3:61–72.
Hally, David J.
1996   Platform-Mound Construction and the Instability of Mississippian Chiefdoms. In *Political Structure and Change in the Prehistoric Southeastern United States*, edited by J. F. Scarry, 92–127. Gainesville: University Press of Florida.

176   Karl G. Lorenz

Hart, C. M. W.
1943   A Reconsideration of the Natchez Social Structure. *American Anthropologist* 45:374–86.
Haviland, William A.
1999   *Cultural Anthropology.* 9th ed. Fort Worth, Tex.: Harcourt Brace.
Helms, Mary
1979   *Ancient Panama: Chiefs in Search of Power.* Austin: University of Texas Press.
Hudson, Charles
1976   *The Southeastern Indians.* Knoxville: University of Tennessee Press.
Josselin de Jong, J. P. B.
1928   The Natchez Social Class System. *Proceedings of the International Congress of Americanists* 23:553–62.
Keesing, Roger M.
1981   *Cultural Anthropology: A Contemporary Perspective.* 2d ed. Fort Worth, Tex.: Holt, Rinehart, and Winston.
Knight, Vernon J., Jr.
1990   Social Organization and the Evolution of Hierarchy in Southeastern Chiefdoms. *Journal of Anthropological Research* 46(1):1–23.
Le Page du Pratz, Antoine S.
1758   *Histoire de la Louisiane.* 3 vols. Paris.
MacLeod, William Christie
1924   Natchez Political Evolution. *American Anthropologist* 26:201–29.
Margry, Pierre (editor)
1887   *Découvertes et Établissements des Français dans L'Ouest et dans le Sud de L'Amérique Septenrionale, 1614–1754.* Vol. 5. Paris.
Mason, Carol
1964   Natchez Social Structure. *Ethnohistory* 11:120–33.
McWilliams, Richard G. (translator and editor)
1953   *Fleur de Lys and Calumet: Being the Penicaut Narrative of French Adventure in Louisiana.* Baton Rouge: Louisiana State University Press.
1981   *Iberville's Gulf Jounals.* Tuscaloosa: University of Alabama Press.
Milner, George R.
1980   Epidemic Disease in the Postcontact Southeast: A Reappraisal. *Midcontinental Journal of Archaeology* 5:39–56.
1990   The Late Prehistoric Cahokia Cultural System of the Mississippi River Valley: Foundations, Florescence, and Fragmentation. *Journal of World Prehistory* 4(1):1–43.
Neitzel, Robert S.
1965   *Archaeology of the Fatherland Site: The Grand Village of the Natchez.* Anthropological Papers of the American Museum of Natural History, vol. 51, pt. 1. New York.
1983   *The Grand Village of the Natchez Revisited: Excavations at the Fatherland Site, Adams County, Mississippi, 1972.* Archaeological Report no. 12. Mississippi Department of Archives and History, Jackson.
Quimby, George I.
1946   Natchez Social Structure as an Instrument of Assimilation. *American Anthropologist* 48:134–37.

Ramenofsky, A.
1987   *Vectors of Death: The Archaeology of European Contact.* Albuquerque: University of New Mexico Press.
Rowland, Dunbar, and Albert G. Sanders (editors and translators)
1929   *Mississippi Provincial Archives, French Dominion.* Vol. 2, *1701–1729.* Mississippi Department of Archives and History, Jackson.
Shea, John G. (translator and editor)
1861   *Early Voyages Up and Down the Mississippi.* Albany, Ga.: Munsell.
Spencer, Robert F., Jesse D. Jennings, Elden Johnson, Arden King, Theodore Stern, Kenneth Stewart, and William Wallace
1977   *The Native Americans: Ethnology and Backgrounds of the North American Indians.* 2d ed. New York: Harper and Row.
Steponaitis, Vincas
1974   The Late Prehistory of the Natchez Region: Excavations at the Emerald and Foster Sites, Adams County, Mississippi. Honors thesis, Department of Anthropology, Harvard University, Cambridge.
1978   Location Theory and Complex Chiefdoms: A Mississippian Example. In *Mississippian Settlement Patterns,* edited by B. D. Smith, 417–54. New York: Academic Press.
1986   Prehistoric Archaeology in the Southeastern United States, 1970–1985. *Annual Review of Anthropology* 15:363–404.
1991   Contrasting Patterns of Mississippian Development. In *Chiefdoms: Power, Economy, and Ideology,* edited by T. Earle, 193–228. Cambridge: Cambridge University Press.
Stubbs, John D., Jr.
1982   The Chickasaw Contact with the La Salle Expedition in 1682. In *La Salle and His Legacy: Frenchmen and Indians in the Lower Mississippi Valley,* edited by P. Galloway, 41–48. Jackson: University Press of Mississippi.
Swanton, John R.
1911   *Indian Tribes of the Lower Mississippi Valley and Adjacent Coast of the Gulf of Mexico.* Smithsonian Institution, Bureau of American Ethnology Bulletin 43. Washington D.C.
Thwaites, Reuben G. (editor)
1959   *The Jesuit Relations and Allied Documents.* Vols. 66–68. New York: Pageant.
Tooker, Elizabeth
1963   Natchez Social Organization: Fact or Anthropological Folklore? *Ethnohistory* 10:358–72.
White, Douglas R., George P. Murdock, and Richard Scaglion
1971   Natchez Class and Rank Reconsidered. *Ethnology* 10:369–88.

7

The Quapaw Indians of Arkansas, 1673–1803

GEORGE SABO III

When we arrived within half a league of the Akamsea, we saw two canoes coming to meet us. He who commanded stood upright, holding in his hand the calumet, with which he made various signs, according to the custom of the country. He joined us, singing very agreeably, and gave us tobacco to smoke; after that, he offered us sagamité, and bread made of Indian corn, of which we ate a little. He then preceded us, after making a sign to follow him slowly. A place had been prepared for us under the scaffolding of the chief of the warriors; it was clean, and carpeted with fine rush mats. Upon these we were made to sit, having around us the elders, who were nearest to us; after them, the warriors; and, finally, all the common people in a crowd.

Kellogg 1917:254

With these words attributed to the Jesuit missionary Jacques Marquette, the Arkansas or Quapaw Indians entered into the history recorded by Europeans to chronicle their exploration and settlement of the Mississippi Valley. But as this passage shows, the event also marked the reception of French travelers into a Native American community with its own systems of belief and behavior and its own mode of history. Indeed, the elements of this reception reveal much about the structure and dynamics of the Quapaw community that Marquette encountered in 1673. It is obvious, for example, that this community had a social structure composed of discrete categories of individuals, including "commanders" or leaders, elders, warriors, "common people," and outsiders. Equally obvious is the use of space and position during special events to signal statuses and roles attached to those categories. Requiring a bit more interpretation are the food sharing and tobacco smoking. Even so, we remain well within the boundaries of Southeastern ethnology to suggest that food sharing was a sociogenic act extending a metaphor of kinship to the feast participants. Similarly, tobacco smoking was a ritual to sanctify the event, based on the belief that the fragrant, dissipating smoke facilitated communication with creative powers whose sanction gave legitimacy to the newly formed relationships.

In sum, the purpose of the Quapaw reception of Marquette and his companions was to transform the visitors' status from that of outsiders to recognized members of a single, multiethnic community. Interactions between the Quapaws and the French—henceforth based on a structure of mutual obligations among kin—could proceed toward shared goals. To put this in less abstract terms: When Marquette arrived on the scene the Quapaws badly wanted access to European trade goods, including firearms and munitions, to counter rival nations who already had them. They employed the means within their culture that seemed most likely to ensure success—the ritual creation of kinship bonds and their ancillary obligations of cooperation and support. Thus the first steps were taken along the path leading to an intercultural framework or "middle ground" of shared meanings and ways of acting that enabled Indians and Europeans to work together in pursuit of common goals (White 1991:50–51).

This essay examines Quapaw responses to Europeans during the seventeenth and eighteenth centuries in order to identify features of the indigenous cultural system that became part of the middle ground. To address this topic in proper detail would require far more space than is available here. (See Arnold 2000 for a more extensive treatment of this topic.) I concentrate on cultural phenomena revealed in selected events that mark important moments in the history of Quapaw interactions with French and Spanish colonists.

Quapaws in the Late Seventeenth Century

The Lower Mississippi Valley contains extensive tracts of fertile soils distributed along numerous tributaries, sloughs, and abandoned channels. Periodic inundation recharges soil nutrients, but the unpredictable frequency and severity of flooding pose hazards to settlement and agricultural activities. Local variations in temperature and precipitation add to these risks. Nonetheless, the biological productivity of the region supported extensive late prehistoric communities (Jeter et al. 1989; Morse and Morse 1983).

When Hernando de Soto led his army of Spanish conquistadors across the Mississippi River in 1541, they encountered extensive and densely populated agricultural communities in what is now east-central Arkansas. Clashes with the Spaniards, European diseases, and the ecological impacts of severe and protracted drought conditions (Stahle et al. 1985) led to massive depopulation during subsequent decades. When Marquette and his companion Louis Jolliet in 1673 and Robert Cavalier, Sieur de La Salle, and Henri de Tonti in 1682 descended the Mississippi River on their famous voyages of discovery, the only communities they visited in this region were four Quapaw villages located near the confluence of the Arkansas and Mississippi Rivers. The village of Kappa was on the west side of the Mississippi several miles above the Arkansas. Tongigua was farther downstream on the east side. Two other villages, Tourima and Osotuoy, were located several miles up the Arkansas River (see fig. 7.1).

Quapaw villagers lived in bark-covered longhouses, each occupied by several families. The Jesuit missionary Jacques Gravier observed forty such houses at Kappa in 1700 (Thwaites 1896–1901 65:119). They were arranged around a central open plaza where ceremonies and public events took place. A meeting house with a capacity for several hundred people stood near the plaza, along with an open-sided arbor containing an elevated platform where community leaders sat during public ceremonies. Unlike other Mississippi Valley tribes, the Quapaws apparently had no mortuary structures for keeping the remains of their deceased leaders, nor did they maintain "sacred fires" (Swanton 1911:166). The total population in 1682 numbered somewhere between 6,000 and 15,000 persons, with the lower number probably being the more accurate one (Baird 1980:37).

The Quapaws, along with the Omaha, Osage, Ponca, and Kansa, are speakers of the Dhegiha Siouan family of languages or dialects (Hollow and Parks 1980:69). The Quapaws were the only Dhegiha speakers in the Lower Mississippi Valley in the seventeenth century. Their closest neighbors included the Osages and Illinois to the north, the Shawnees and Chickasaws to the east (across the Mississippi), the Taensas and Tunicas to the south, and the Caddos to the west.

Quapaw social organization is poorly documented for the colonial era. Their attempt in 1727 to employ the calumet ceremony to confer the status of "father" on the Jesuit missionary Paul du Poisson suggests the existence of patrilineal descent groups (Thwaites 1896–1901 67:255–57). Later information confirms that these descent groups, in common with Omaha and Osage clans, were divided into two moieties, called the Earth People and the Sky People (Dorsey 1897:229–30). Among Dhegiha speakers (especially the

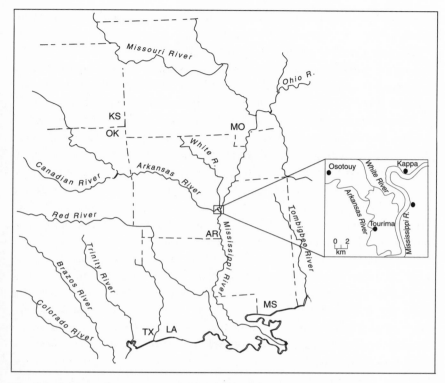

Fig. 7.1. Quapaw locations ca. 1700 (after Baird 1980).

Omahas and Osages), each clan possessed a unique relationship with a spirit being or power through which rights to perform specific rituals were secured. Earth People clans performed rituals that sustained the physical and material well-being of the community, while Sky People clans performed complementary rituals involving spiritual affairs (Barnes 1984:68–103). The moieties were symbolically represented by two sacred pipes; these were cared for by one of the Earth People clans but filled and lit for ceremonial use by one of the Sky People clans. Moiety division also regulated marriage via a rule of exogamy, the two intermarrying sides reflecting the same interdependency represented in the use of sacred pipes and in the complementary distribution of ritual duties. These interdependent relationships provided the basis for a distinctive Dhegiha theme: "the idea that the unity of the tribe as a whole is prior to the particular ways it is divided up" (Barnes 1984:59–60). It would be most surprising if this Dhegiha pattern of egalitarian interdependency and complementary opposition did not also obtain for seventeenth-century Quapaw social organization.

Quapaw villages functioned as independent political units, each with its own leader and council of elders. Leaders had limited authority, as reflected in statements Quapaw "chiefs" made to French and Spanish officials claiming an inability to compel members of their communities, particularly warriors, to heed their commands (Delanglez 1964:263). When necessary, community decisions could be made on the basis of a consensus reached through public debate. Village leaders sometimes acted in unison when circumstances affected the tribe as a whole. French explorer Bénard de la Harpe identified the leader of the Kappa village as a "great chief" in 1721, but there is no evidence that this individual was able to exert greater authority than any other leader (Smith 1951:350). The designation may reflect an earlier, more hierarchical form of political organization.

The Quapaws were sedentary agriculturalists who also engaged in seasonal hunting, fishing, and gathering activities. Corn was the dietary staple, which Marquette observed in growth stages indicating that it was sown three times per year (Kellogg 1917:255). According to French explorer Henri Joutel, vast fields—some extending 4 or 5 square miles—yielded abundant crops that also included beans, pumpkins, melons, sunflowers, peaches, plums, and other produce (Margry 1876–86 3:462). Persimmons, berries, grapes, and a variety of nuts were collected. Buffalo, common in Arkansas during the early part of the colonial era, were actively pursued (Le Page du Pratz 1774:173). A variety of forest and forest-edge species was also hunted, including bear, deer, small mammals, and birds. Fish were speared from dugout canoes, and waterfowl were taken with the aid of live decoys (Bossu 1982:44).

Quapaws shared their world with spirit beings and forces represented by the sun, moon, and thunder (Bossu 1771:106–7). Tonti spoke of the Quapaws "adoring all sorts of animals" (Kellogg 1917:298). Bienville (Rowland and Sanders 1927–84 3:532) commented on the Quapaw belief in a "supreme being who is a spirit." Father Paul du Poisson, struck by Quapaw reaction to a picture he displayed of Saint Régis, provides information on the identity of this spirit: "*Ouakantaqué*, they exclaim, *it is the Great Spirit!*" (Thwaites 1896–1901 67:323). In the Dhegiha thought world, Wakonda was an invisible and mysterious life force that created the conditions necessary for the perpetuation of all living things by joining together primordial male and female forces represented by the sun and the moon (Fletcher and

La Flesche 1911:134–35). This ontology provided a key metaphor that transcended other aspects of the cultural system. For example, the relationship of the Earth People and Sky People moieties was perceived as analogous to the relationship between females and males, respectively. In the tribal circle, the Sky People clans were arranged on the north side, which symbolically represented the "left" and "above" designations associated with the category "male"; the Earth People clans, arranged on the south side of the circle, symbolically represented the "right" and "below" designation associated with the "female." A cultural theme based on these relationships is that the unified community is greater than the sum of its parts (descent groups, moieties, left side, right side, et cetera), each of which depends upon a counterpart unit to realize its function or potential (Barnes 1984:50–67).

Ceremonies celebrating these interdependencies were held at various times of the year. Spring planting and summer Green Corn ceremonies observed at the beginning of the nineteenth century were undoubtedly also practiced during the colonial era (Ashe 1808:305–80; Nuttall 1980:106). Europeans witnessed, and occasionally took part in, a variety of occasional events. The French traveler and writer Jean-Bernard Bossu observed that a wide variety of circumstances prompted ceremonial dances, including religion, medicine, joy, ritual, war, peace, marriage, death, play, hunting, and lewdness. Preparations for warfare were particularly extensive and involved feasts, war councils, dances, and demonstrative acts such as cutting a war symbol consisting of two crossed arrows painted red into a tree at the edge of enemy territory (Bossu 1962:61–63). Curing rituals were conducted by shamans and priests; anthropologist James Owen Dorsey described curing societies that existed in the nineteenth century (Dorsey 1894:393–94).

Thomas Nuttall, who visited the Quapaws in 1819, also reported that each family had a guardian spirit (such as snake, buffalo, owl, raven, or eagle) which bestowed various benefits (Nuttall 1980:98). A family's practical activities would temporarily cease upon the death of an animal representing the guardian spirit's species, suggesting that many utilitarian activities were perceived as socialized interactions with what we might regard as the natural world (another reflection of the interdependency theme).

An animal regarded as sacred by one family was not necessarily taboo to others, as the following anecdote related by Bossu suggests. (Bossu's fanciful tales must always be read with caution, however.) A Tunica hunter was traveling with Bossu's party en route to Arkansas from the Red River. At one point during the journey, the hunter grabbed Bossu's gun and shot a large rattlesnake through the head as it slithered ominously across the Mississippi River. Later, upon hearing about the Tunica's dexterous aim, some Quapaws honored him with the title "Chevalier of the Rattlesnake" and "tattooed around his body the figure of a serpent with its head falling on a place which ladies will permit me to let them guess" (Bossu 1982:36).

A final element of Quapaw religious belief that appears to have been of considerable importance during the colonial era concerns the relationship between members of the living community and their deceased ancestors. French missionary Pierre Charlevoix described mourning rituals he observed in 1721, when the community was suffering the ravages of European diseases: "I saw a woman weeping over her son's grave, and pouring a great quantity of sagamity upon it. Another had lighted a fire beside a neighboring tomb, probably in order to warm the deceased person" (Charlevoix 1923: 231). Commandant Orieta in 1775 wrote to Governor Unzaga that the Quapaws told anyone visiting Arkansas Post that "they want to die on the land where they were born as their ancestors did." Furthermore, in their tribal councils Quapaw leaders urged community members not to forsake their "homeland, the land of their birth, in which so much of the blood of their ancestors is buried" (José Orieta to Luis de Unzaga y Amezaga, December 25, 1775, AGI PC, *leg.* 189B:29). From this, it appears that Quapaws defined their homeland as the territory demarcated by spiritual connections with ancestral souls symbolically represented at burial sites.

Two kinds of external relationships were noted in early colonial accounts. Warfare with neighboring tribes was frequently mentioned by colonial officials. Consisting typically of raids involving small numbers of warriors, these skirmishes probably maintained geographic space between adjacent populations. By the late seventeenth century, however, English traders from Carolina were supplying firearms and munitions to the Chickasaws, Creeks, and Natchez in return for their participation in the deerskin and slave trades (Usner 1992:16). Slave raiding soon began to alter geopolitical relations in the region. Among other effects, the level of hostilities between Quapaws and Chickasaws, who lived along opposite sides of the Mississippi River, increased.

A second means of dealing with outsiders involved the calumet ceremony, which was used to create and sanctify alliances and other forms of friendly relations. This ceremony actually consisted of a series of performances— feasts, gift exchanges, pole-striking rituals (in which warriors proclaimed deeds performed in service to their communities while striking a ceremonial post with their weapons), and dances—which in aggregate extended fictive kinship ties to esteemed outsiders. Quapaw rituals performed to create these ties can be interpreted as attempts to impose the theme of interdependency and complementary opposition on their interactions with European allies (Sabo 1991, 1995).

While the Quapaws shared many cultural characteristics with other tribes in the Lower Mississippi Valley, several features distinguished them from their neighbors. These include linguistic affiliation, use of longhouse dwellings, lack of ancestor temples and sacred fires, and a patrilineal kinship system. Such anomalies bear on the question of Quapaw origins, which has puzzled scholars for more than a century. There is not space here to review the matter in detail, but many archaeologists, ethnologists, and linguists have argued that seventeenth-century Quapaws were recent immigrants to the region (see, for example, Dorsey 1885, 1897; Fletcher and La Flesche 1911; Hoffman 1986, 1990, 1991, 1993a, 1993b, 1994, 1995; Jeter 1986; McGee 1894; Rankin n.d.). This hypothesis is based not only on their cultural distinctiveness in the Lower Mississippi Valley but also on discrepancies between seventeenth-century French descriptions of the Quapaw and sixteenth-century descriptions of the populous, hierarchically organized chiefdoms that Hernando de Soto encountered in the region. The immigration hypothesis is also consistent with Quapaw oral traditions, according to which they forced Tunicas out of the region after splitting from their linguistic relatives during a migration from the Ohio Valley (Bizzell 1981).

Material similarities between protohistoric (A.D. 1500–1700) "Quapaw phase" sites and late prehistoric manifestations in the region have led other scholars to argue that Quapaws descended from indigenous Mississippian cultures (Morse 1991; Morse and Morse 1983). Linguistic analysis of Lower Mississippi Valley place names reported in the de Soto chronicles, however, yields no evidence of sixteenth-century Siouan speakers in the Arkansas region, although several communities visited by the Spaniards may well represent Tunica speakers (Rankin 1993). Some archaeologists have thus argued that the material similarities between prehistoric and protohistoric sites in the region could reflect immigration of a Siouan-speaking population that adopted the material technology of the indigenous groups they displaced (Henning 1993). Differences in the bioarchaeological characteristics of late prehistoric and protohistoric populations in the region lend some support to this hypothesis (Murray 1989).

In his numerous publications cited above, Hoffman calls this discrepancy between the archaeological and historical evidence of Quapaw origins the Quapaw Paradox. It is worth noting that arguments on both sides of this debate employ essentially the same archaeological data; most of these data were assembled prior to the 1970s and present numerous problems to modern researchers (Jeter et al. 1989:57–70; Jeter et al. 1990:32–96). When Phillips (1970:943–44) defined the Quapaw phase, he regarded as conclusive Ford's (1961) identification of the Menard site (now the Menard-Hodges site) as the Quapaw village of Osotuoy near which Henri de Tonti established a trading house in 1686. While Menard-Hodges certainly remains our best candidate for the historic site of Osotuoy, archaeologists today wish for better contextual evidence concerning the association of French trade goods and aboriginal materials at the site. Alternative cultural affiliations have also been suggested for many sites formerly subsumed under the Quapaw phase designation, some of which are now considered Tunican (Hoffman 1986, 1990, 1994, 1995; Jeter 1986). Both circumstances leave us uncertain about the material characteristics of historic Quapaws. Consequently, a preference has developed for use of the term *Menard complex* (instead of *Quapaw phase*) to refer to these sites.

Since Menard complex sites remain viable candidates for protohistoric antecedents of historic Quapaws, it is worth summarizing their material characteristics here. (See Hoffman 1986; Jeter et al. 1989:221–33; and House 1991, 1997 for more specific details.) The ceramic complex is characterized by a predominance of Mississippi Plain, *var. Nady* pottery. The most common decorated ceramics are Wallace Incised, *var. Wallace*. Red slipped (Old Town Red) and painted (Carson Red on Buff, Avenue Polychrome, Nodena Red and White) ceramics are also common. Vessel forms include "helmet" bowls, rim effigy bowls, globular bottles with various neck shapes, "teapots," and Conway style headpots. Natchezan, Caddoan, and Tunican ceramics are present as minority components of these assemblages. Common stone tools include Nodena points, Madison points, and thumbnail endscrapers. Sites are generally small and compact, some with evidence of fortification and containing platform mounds, plazas, and conical burial mounds. What little evidence there is for subsistence points to a mixed economy based on corn agriculture, hunting, and fishing. Mortuary patterns exhibit considerable variation. Based on his recent work at the Noble Lake site, House (1997) has defined two chronologically successive phases, which he calls "horizons," for the Menard complex: an A.D. 1500–1600 Poor horizon, followed by an A.D. 1600–1700 Douglas horizon.

The most pressing need at the moment is to find a historic Quapaw site that can be related via documentary evidence to a known community, from which aboriginal materials can be obtained from unambiguous archaeological contexts. The implications of the middle ground scenario sketched in this essay suggest, however, that historic Quapaw sites may not be easily distinguished from contemporaneous European sites. If Quapaws and Europeans did coalesce into a multiethnic community, material differences between the two groups may not be discernable (with the likely exception of differences in residential architecture). Surveys conducted in the Wallace Bottoms area, adjacent to Menard-Hodges, during the summer of 1998 resulted in the discovery of at least one candidate site (in addition to Menard-Hodges itself), but confirmation awaits further investigation.

Quapaw Interactions with French and Spanish Colonists

It is surely no exaggeration to claim Quapaw interactions with French and Spanish colonists were dominated by the quest for access to trade goods, especially firearms and munitions. As mentioned earlier, rival nations in the Mississippi Valley had already acquired such goods via English traders from Carolina. The uneven distribution of firearms from English sources seriously affected the region's volatile geopolitical relationships. The Quapaws (who themselves might have only recently been involved in a forceful displacement of the Tunicas) complained in 1673 that the armed Indians Marquette and his companions had recently met (this was undoubtedly a reference to the Chickasaws) "were their enemies, who barred their way to the sea, and prevented them from becoming acquainted with the Europeans, and from carrying on any trade with them" (Kellogg 1917:255). Their eagerness for the material rewards of European alliance set the stage for other aspects of Quapaw interaction with the French and Spanish.

Two circumstances attracted Europeans to the Arkansas region following Marquette's and La Salle's explorations. First, neither the French nor the Spanish, at any time during their dominion over the Louisiana Territory, had enough of a population base or military force to defend their claim to the region against the ever-present threat of English encroachment from Carolina. The only way to maintain effective control was to enlist the support of populous and strategically located Indian tribes. While the Quapaws were never a very populous nation (and they grew less so over time), they were well positioned to prevent the Chickasaws from disrupting Mississippi River travel between the trading entrepôts at Kaskaskia and New Orleans (Arnold 1991; González López-Briones 1983). Second, the Arkansas region was evidently a veritable Garden of Eden in the seventeenth and eighteenth centuries, at least in terms of animal resources important to the commerce of the Lower Mississippi Valley (Rollings 1995; see also Le Page du Pratz 1774; Surrey 1916). The French and Spanish governments in Louisiana thus periodically maintained a military garrison near the Quapaw villages, around which European settlers congregated (Arnold 1991:5–17). There, at Arkansas Post, interdependent economic ties and other middle ground relationships developed between the Quapaws and their European neighbors. These two factors—political alliances and the development of a "frontier exchange economy" (Usner 1992)—provided several opportunities for the Quapaws to acquire trade goods.

The establishment in 1686 of Tonti's trading house near Osotuoy was the first in a series of events that would draw Quapaws into the frontier exchange economy of the Lower Mississippi Valley. Both La Salle and Tonti were interested in developing the buffalo hide trade, but this plan failed due to the lack of a market (Murphy 1941:86). Subsequently, Quapaw participation in the frontier exchange economy turned to provision of foodstuffs for Europeans and Americans living in and around their villages; service as guides for explorers, hunters, and traders; and production of forest commodities for exchange with traders and merchants operating out of Arkansas Post and New Orleans.

Provision of foodstuffs for European consumption began early on, as indicated by Joutel's remark that he was supplied with bags of "Indian corn" from the stores of the Frenchmen stationed at Tonti's post (Margry 1876–86 3:441). Quapaws supplied meat and produce to soldiers garrisoned at the post and to local settlers throughout the eighteenth century. It is not possible to measure the extent of this trade from existing records, but it is likely that the European denizens of Arkansas Post—like their counterparts at other interior posts—probably were forced to rely on their Indian neighbors for most of their dietary staples (Usner 1992:198). In return for these provisions and for their service as guides, Quapaws received a variety of trade goods, including guns, powder and shot, hatchets, knives, awls, needles, bracelets, rings, glass beads, cloth, and articles of clothing (Margry 1876–86 3:428–37).

Commercial production of forest commodities developed steadily. By 1765, Arkansas was described as a place where "people subsist mostly by hunting, and every season send to New Orleans great quantities of bear's oil, tallow, salted buffalo meat, and a few skins" (Pittman 1770:40). Quapaws joined Europeans in the production of these goods. Bossu, for example, witnessed Quapaw women making tallow cakes which were then sold or traded to Europeans (Bossu 1982:42). Preserved meat was another commodity produced in great quantities; Father du Poisson noted that buffalo (or "cattle," as he called them) were scarce between New Orleans and Arkansas, so dried and salted meat from Arkansas was sent down the Mississippi "to supply the colony" (Thwaites 1896–1901 67:285).

The trade in deerskins, which represented an important component of the frontier exchange economy elsewhere in the Lower Mississippi Valley (Usner 1992:244–75), drew little commerce in Arkansas. Bienville, for example, lamented that the Quapaws "can scarcely furnish from their hunting one thousand deerskins per year." This was a paltry amount compared, for example, to the numbers obtained by the Talapoosas, who, he noted, annually traded 5,000 deerskins to the English, or by the Abihkas, whom he believed capable of supplying 8,000 skins per year (Rowland and Sanders 1927–84 3:532–37).

Despite this attenuated commitment to the frontier exchange economy, the Quapaws became increasingly dependent on trade goods acquired from Europeans. Mercenary service in French and Spanish military campaigns became an important adjunct to production of forest commodities. Quapaw actions in the First Chickasaw War of 1736, the Second Chickasaw War of 1738, and in numerous attacks on the Chickasaws during the 1740s brought them periodic rewards of trade goods sent by French governors (see, for example, Pierre Vaudreuil to the minister, October 30, 1745, ANC, $C^{13}A$ 29:57; see also Shea 1854).

During the second half of the eighteenth century, however, the "battle-front" shifted from the east toward the north. Following the establishment of a French trade entrepôt at St. Louis in 1764, the Osages captured the "middleman" position in the flow of goods between St. Louis traders and tribes on the Great Plains. Defense of this position brought the Osages into frequent conflict with their neighbors, including the Quapaws (Rollings 1992). When expansion of the Osage domain encroached on the Arkansas and Red rivers, posing a serious threat to Spanish posts in the region, the Quapaws were urged to attack the Osages and were periodically rewarded for their actions (Arnold 1991:112–24).

To hold Quapaws and other Mississippi Valley tribes to their alliances in the face of unremitting English enticements, French officials in New Orleans developed a policy of delivering annual presents. At first, these often arrived late to Arkansas Post and sometimes failed to arrive at all. During the Spanish era, presents were distributed on a more regular basis, in amounts perhaps sufficient to supply most of the Quapaws' needs (Morris S. Arnold, personal communication 1998). The variety of Spanish goods sent to the tribes was even greater than that which the French had provided, and the Quapaws received an expanded inventory of goods (see, e.g., AGI, PC, *leg.* 107:225 for the 1775 present, and AGI, PC, *leg.* 189B:52 for the 1776 present). Like the French before them, the Spaniards realized that annual presents were important to the maintenance of cooperative relationships. Commandant Alexandre de Clouet said of the Quapaws: "It is true that they remain faithful to Spain and France; but deprived of strong liquor, bread, and their present, one cannot count on them" (Alexandre de Clouet to Mon General, May 21, 1768, AGI, PC, *leg.* 107:44).

A third sphere of interaction with Europeans involved periodic discourse with missionaries. From the time they first welcomed Marquette, the Quapaws tirelessly petitioned for missionaries to serve in their villages. Other regions of the Lower Mississippi Valley supporting larger indigenous populations were deemed more fertile ground for the mission effort, so the Quapaws had to wait until 1700, when Nicolas Foucault was sent by the Seminary of Foreign Missions in Quebec. Foucault established himself among the Quapaws in 1701, but left in disgust the following year and was murdered by Koroa guides en route to New Orleans (O'Neill 1966:15–19, 38). The Quapaws retaliated with an attack that convinced Bienville that the Koroas had been "entirely destroyed" (Rowland and Sanders 1927–84 3:22–23). The Quapaws put on a grand welcome for Father Paul du Poisson when he arrived in 1727, and similar receptions were given to other Jesuit priests sent to Arkansas (Delanglez 1935). Despite their friendly disposition toward missionaries, the Quapaws were notoriously poor converts (Dickinson 1991; Jones 1997). When the American colonial era commenced at the beginning of the nineteenth century, traditional religious beliefs and practices remained intact (Nuttall 1980:96–99). What, then, can explain the Quapaws' active pursuit of missionary ties?

An attempt by the Quapaws to bring Poisson into the compass of their social system provides important clues about their disposition toward missionaries in general. Two days after Poisson arrived in their village, two Quapaw "chiefs" attempted to perform the calumet ceremony, assuring him that the performance was "without design"—that is, "without any anticipation of return." But it was revealed that a kinship link would be created, the obligations of which the Quapaws spelled out in this exchange recorded by Poisson:

[A] man asked me if I were inclined to adopt him as my son; if so, when he returned from the hunt he would cast, *without design,* his game at my feet and I should not say to him as other Frenchmen did: *For what dost thou hunger?* (this means, "What dost thou wish me to give for that?"), but I should make him sit down, and should give him food as to my own son; and when he returned a second time to me I should say: "Sit down, my son; look, here are vermillion and powder." (Thwaites 1896–1901 67:255–57)

The Quapaws' intentions seem clear enough: the father-son relationship they caricatured had material obligations based on generalized reciprocity in which goods are given without expectation of a return of equal value at any specified time. Also embedded within this dialogue is reference to an alternative form of exchange based on a negotiation of values: "What dost thou wish me to give for that?" This, of course, refers to the barter on which the frontier exchange economy was based, so here the Quapaws made a clear distinction between reciprocal gift giving and economic exchange. There is more: the fact that they were determined to center their relationship with Poisson on this distinction suggests that the importance they attached to the missionary presence had more to do with the structure of the frontier economy than with a desire to learn about the European's religious beliefs. At the risk of drawing too large an interpretation from too small an example, the Quapaws may have viewed the presence of a missionary in their villages mainly as another link in a chain of relationships binding them ever more strongly to the frontier exchange economy.

A fourth mode of Quapaw interaction with Europeans involved diplomatic negotiations, mostly at Arkansas Post or New Orleans. A frequently cited example took place at New Orleans in 1756 when the Quapaw leader Guedelonguay met with Governor Kerlérec to settle the fate of four Frenchmen captured by the Quapaws but accused by French authorities of smuggling and murder (see, for example, Arnold 1985:24–28). For reasons that can only be imagined but which must have been related to the largely undocumented interpersonal ties that knit together Quapaws and Europeans in an isolated frontier community, Guedelonguay petitioned Kerlérec for release of the malefactors into his own safekeeping. To support his appeal, Guedelonguay mentioned the help the Quapaws had given the French in their wars against the Chickasaws (during which Guedelonguay lost a son and had a daughter wounded), and the fact that the Quapaws had recently handed over to the French six slaves and five Choctaws they had captured. When Kerlérec refused this request, Guedelonguay played his trump card: he stated that the four deserters had taken refuge in the "sacred cabin where they practice their religion," so now according to Quapaw custom they were absolved of their crime. Moreover, "the man who is chief of the said cabin would sooner lose his life than allow the refugee to suffer the penalty for his crime," and Guedelonguay himself "could not answer for the dangerous attacks and the rebellions that the chief of the sacred cabin could bring about and that would not fail to take place," should the Quapaws be denied their petition. At this, Kerlérec relented, but only after gaining a promise that the request would be the last of its kind (Rowland and Sanders 1927–84 5:173–75).

This case raises a number of interesting points. It is one of several complaints brought before colonial officials by Indian leaders increasingly perturbed by the government's harsh treatment of soldiers who at midcentury were deserting their posts or committing other infractions in record numbers (Usner 1992:241–43). Chronic shortages of provisions were partly to blame for this state of affairs, and these shortages must have impacted Indian villages as well. In 1745, for example, Governor Vaudreuil documented Quapaw complaints about the quality and prices of the goods they were receiving (Pierre Vaudreuil to the minister, October 30, 1745, ANC, C^{13}A 29:57). The Guedelonguay case provides evidence that the multiethnic, Indian and European community at Arkansas found it necessary to strengthen their local networks of reciprocal social ties in an effort to counter mounting economic stresses. If this was indeed the case, it is no wonder that Indian leaders reacted negatively to government persecution of their European neighbors for crimes external to the immediate concerns of maintaining the viability of the local community.

Another interesting feature of the exchange between Guedelonguay and Kerlérec is the mention of a "sacred cabin" (*cabanne de valeur*) whose "chief" seemed to enjoy some kind of unchallenged authority over events and circumstances that transpired therein. The existence of such an institution among the Quapaws is intriguing, to say the least, in light of their otherwise nonhierarchical social and political institutions. This egalitarian pose was pervasive. Village leaders' lack of authority over warriors has already been mentioned, and commandant Leyba, writing in 1771, pointed out that "among these people every voice is equal—the great and the small" (Fernando de Leyba to Luis de Unzaga y Amezaga, June 6, 1771, AGI, PC, *leg.* 107:247). How can the existence of this seemingly unusual institution and its hierarchical mode of authority be explained?

Possibly Guedelonguay, for the purposes of the moment, resurrected a practice of hierarchical authority that had not recently been in use but which remained in the reservoir of cultural knowledge maintained in Quapaw lore. This accords with other evidence of attenuated authority hierarchies, such as Bénard de La Harpe's previously mentioned comments about the Kappa "great chief." Alternatively, the European practice of conferring medals of honor on favored Indian leaders to foster their cooperation and to provide a single tribal representative seems to have created a new form of political office based on the European model of hierarchical authority (Sabo 1991: 127–28). There is some evidence that Quapaws distinguished European-appointed medal chiefs from the holders of traditional leadership positions (even if this had not been the original European intent). In 1789, for example, a Quapaw named Pasemony refused to accept a medal offered by Captain Vallière on the grounds that it might offend others in his community (Joseph Vallière to Esteban Miró, April 4, 1789, AGI, PC, *leg.* 15:342).

Guedelonguay's performance in the diplomatic exchange considered here is consistent with both of these explanations. What is most interesting is Guedelonguay's combining elements of French and Quapaw legal concepts to resolve a diplomatic dispute (see Arnold 1997 for additional examples). In this context of willful manipulation and change, continuity in the use of kinship and reciprocity concepts as idioms for structuring relationships with the French seems all the more significant.

Cultural Consequences of Quapaw Interactions with Europeans

The main conclusion of the foregoing discussion of Quapaw modes of interaction with Europeans is that a multiethnic community developed in Arkansas, made possible by shared social, economic, and political arrangements. Nowhere are these shared middle ground arrangements more provocatively expressed than in their depiction on the fascinating "Three Villages" painted hide at the Musée de l'Homme in Paris (Arnold 1994). Produced by one or more anonymous Quapaw artists, this hide is illustrated with images of the sun and moon, two calumets, a battle scene involving two groups of Indians, a scalp dance performed by men and women, three Indian villages alongside four French buildings, and a fourth Indian village shown opposite the other three. The words *Ackansas* (referring to the tribe as a whole), plus the village names *Ouzovtovovi, Tovarimon,* and *Ovoappa* are written above the three villages shown adjacent to the French buildings, which in turn bear an almost uncanny resemblance to a 1734 description of four structures built at Arkansas Post by Pierre Petit de Coulange (Rowland and Sanders 1927–84 3:665–66). This hide is a singularly important *native* text, and as we gain the facility to decipher its pictographic imagery it will undoubtedly yield unprecedented insights into Quapaw perspectives on events of the colonial era. Until that decipherment becomes possible, however, we will have to rely on European texts to shed light on the question of what were the impacts on the Quapaws of their participation in middle ground arrangements.

The first impact of European presence in the Lower Mississippi Valley was consolidation and relocation of Quapaw villages in response to changing geopolitical circumstances. The residents of Tongigua had abandoned their location on the eastern bank of the Mississippi River, apparently joining the village of Kappa, by the time of Gravier's visit in 1700. By 1727, all three Quapaw villages were located along the Arkansas River, although the original four communities could still be distinguished (Thwaites 1896–1901 67:319). When Father Vitry visited in 1739, however, the Tongigua community had evidently lost its identity (Delanglez 1964:262). Following a 1748 flood, the Quapaws moved their villages to the higher ground at Écores Rouges (Rowland and Sanders 1927–84 5:33).

Unfortunately for the French, this last move left Arkansas Post vulnerable to the devastating attack the Chickasaws made on it the following year. The post settlement was then also moved to Écores Rouges, to take advantage of the protection afforded by closer proximity to the Quapaws. The Quapaws followed the post when it was relocated farther down the Arkansas River in 1756, only to return upriver when it was again moved in 1779. This suggests that they held a similar view of the safety afforded by living near their French neighbors. Osage aggression threatened Quapaw and French settlements alike during the latter half of the eighteenth century.

What we see in eighteenth-century Arkansas is the emergence of a multi-ethnic, French and Quapaw community making settlement decisions in tandem. The movement of this community remained within the territory adjacent to the Arkansas/Mississippi River confluence, which the Quapaws defined as their homeland via reference to the burial sites of their ancestors.

Within this traditional eastern Arkansas homeland, population declines resulting from disease and warfare represent a second major consequence of Quapaw interaction with Europeans. From an estimated population of 6,000 to 8,000 people in 1682, the Quapaws numbered fewer than 700 in 1763, mainly as a result of epidemics suffered in 1698, 1747, and 1751 (Baird 1980:37). Throughout the Spanish period, their numbers seem to have remained at about this level. (For example, the 1777 census of Arkansas Post, AGI, PC, *leg.* 190:111, lists 509 Quapaws living in three villages.). Little is known about the impacts of this demographic decline on Quapaw social organization, political and religious institutions, economic arrangements, or other cultural features. This is another area where additional research is needed.

A third consequence of Quapaw interaction with Europeans was a shift in economic organization in which traditional agricultural, hunting, and fishing activities were displaced by participation in the frontier exchange economy. As shown previously, the Quapaw mode of participation in this economy involved provision of foodstuffs for local settlers, production of forest commodities for exchange, and service as guides. Service as mercenaries in European military campaigns was an important adjunct occupation. To a large degree, these new economic endeavors involved traditional skills of travel, warfare, hunting, and processing of various animal products, and modes of exchange were undoubtedly based on pre-European strategies. The employment of these skills in the context of the frontier exchange economy still may have introduced some changes in the division of labor and in the scheduling of village activities, to a degree that we are presently unable to measure. More important, participation in this new economy gave added importance to the distinction between production for consumption and production for exchange. As the status of trade goods evolved from novelty items to necessities, greater investments of time and effort were directed toward production for exchange. In short, Quapaws transformed themselves from a community of self-sufficient agriculturalists and part-time traders to a community supported by a more diversified economy that became inextricably tied to international commodities markets.

Political realignments and adjustments in the methods of diplomacy represent a fourth circumstance affecting the Quapaw cultural system. The accounts of the Marquette and La Salle expeditions make it clear that Quapaw villagers had other allies among Lower Mississippi Valley tribes, notably the Illinois and the Taensas, prior to the arrival of Europeans. However important these alliances may have been, with the appearance of

Europeans it was necessary to establish a new series of external relationships, which often resulted in changes in the nature or strength of previous alliances.

Early diplomatic interactions with Europeans involved use of the calumet ceremony. The purpose of this ceremony, as noted, was to bring important European representatives (explorers, government officials, missionaries, et cetera) into the social world of the Quapaws. The kinship idiom conferred by this ceremony seems to have been a prerequisite for meaningful dialogue and cooperative interaction. The willingness of the French to participate in this ceremony was crucial to the development of middle ground arrangements that brought about the subsequent coalescence of a multicultural community in eastern Arkansas.

By the 1720s, the French had begun to tamper with this relationship by awarding medals decorated with the image of the king to favorite Indian leaders. This served to strengthen ties with those leaders and had the effect of singling them out as tribal representatives. This practice became even more prevalent during the Spanish era. Among the Quapaws, a new political office of "medal chief" emerged, in which the major, if not primary, responsibility seems to have been the management of negotiations with Europeans. The advent of this new political office does not mean that traditional leadership positions were replaced; we have already cited evidence to the contrary. Although conflicts between traditional leaders and medal chiefs must have arisen from time to time, it may also have been the case that the duties of medal chiefs sometimes shielded traditional leaders from contact with Europeans, thereby helping to preserve the integrity of cultural institutions managed by traditional leaders. In any event, it is likely that pragmatic concerns of the moment determined which of these leaders' views would prevail, if and when there were differences of opinion.

When Quapaw medal chiefs exercised their authority, as illustrated in the confrontation between Guedelonguay and Kerlérec, it seems clear that the interdependency and complementary opposition metaphors formerly associated with the calumet ceremony were no longer employed. Replacing those old metaphors were new ones reflecting hierarchical forms of authority similar to European modes of political discourse. We cannot be certain if these new metaphors represent an assimilation of European concepts or a resuscitation of indigenous institutions. We have observed, however, that the use of these new metaphors in diplomatic exchanges continued to be framed within the traditional idiom of kinship relations.

Finally, it needs to be mentioned that the middle ground arrangements examined here represent a phenomenon that persisted only during the era of Quapaw interaction with European colonists. With the advent of U.S. control of the region, which began with purchase of the Louisiana Territory in 1803, the Quapaws came to be dominated by more forceful government policies that led ultimately to the loss of their homelands and removal to Oklahoma.

Summary: Continuity and Change on the Middle Ground

The preceding reconstruction, selectively illustrated from a much larger series of examples, permits identification of several phenomena that developed in the context of middle ground relationships between Quapaws and Europeans in Arkansas. Although this reconstruction ignores many other phenomena, it permits identification of major aspects of continuity and change in the Quapaw cultural system.

We begin with identification of three core features of the Quapaw cultural system that appear to be resilient in the face of sociocultural and environmental pressures that accompanied European presence in the Lower Mississippi Valley. The first is the geographic position Quapaws were able to maintain within a traditional homeland defined by ancestral burial grounds. Second is their dualistic social organization, in which unilineal descent groups were partitioned into two moieties connected by reciprocal ties of responsibility and obligation. These ties conferred a common order of egalitarian interdependency and complementary opposition on other aspects of the cultural system, including village settlement patterns, political leadership, and ritual regulation of the material and spiritual affairs of the community. Third is the religious concept of Wakonda, the invisible creative force that joined primordial male and female life forces to make possible the biological and social reproduction of the Quapaw community. This belief system provided a philosophical basis connecting the interdependency and complementary opposition metaphors with the Dhegiha theme of interconnected cultural units creating a whole that is greater than the sum of its parts.

To sustain an argument that these features comprised an integrated whole, it is necessary to demonstrate that none existed independently from the others. We cannot make such a demonstration on the basis of native *statements* recorded in colonial European documents, but Quapaw *actions* provide the basis for a supporting reconstruction. First, the status of unilineal descent groups as fundamental social units representing cultural continuity through time was evidently dependent on the spiritual relationship between living members and ancestors symbolically represented in the distribution of local burial sites. This relationship was fundamental to the concept of a homeland. Second, the thematic significance of descent groups as interdependent parts of a greater whole was related in turn to religious beliefs involving primordial male and female life forces brought together by Wakonda to sustain biological and social reproduction. Finally, the ancestor soul/homeland complex of ideas gained prominence as a metaphor of temporal continuity via its connection with Wakonda, the eternal force that created humans in the first instance and whose presence served to sanctify the relationship between the living and the dead whenever burial rituals were performed. In sum, each element of this triad of beliefs and behaviors derived at least part of its meaning from its relationship with one or both of the other features. It is in this specific sense that we can refer to the interrelationships among geographic location, social organization, and religious beliefs as a cultural core.

If these features of the eighteenth-century Quapaw cultural system did in fact exist as a resilient complex of associated beliefs and behaviors, it may follow that the changes witnessed in political organization and diplomatic strategy came about in ways that served to maintain the integrity of the core features. Political organization was altered when a new office, that of medal chief, was created. Diplomatic strategy, as we have seen, changed from its earlier emphasis on the interdependency and reciprocity metaphors reflected in the calumet ceremony to an emphasis on hierarchical modes of authority displayed in the exchanges between medal chiefs and colonial officials. On a more abstract level, the discourse of political organization and diplomacy continued to employ the idiom of kinship relations, which also underpinned the complex of beliefs and behaviors representing the core features of the Quapaw cultural system. Even if these changes were not intentionally made in order to preserve core features, the transformed system still maintained an overall coherence with the structural persistence of kinship as the basic conceptual framework in relation to other cultural phenomena.

Future archaeological and ethnohistorical research can do much to enlarge on the issues addressed in this essay. One of the most important to be resolved is the question of Quapaw origins. As we achieve a better understanding of these origins, it may be possible to combine information about prehistoric and historic developments to reconstruct a "native history" of the Quapaws (Trigger 1983). Continued investigation of Quapaw interactions with Europeans and Americans will do much to advance our knowledge of subsequent Quapaw history, including the question of how the native history differed from the western histories more familiar to modern scholars. What may advance our prospects most for gaining new insights into these issues is recognition that historic Quapaws were not autonomous culture-bearers but participants in the creation of an intercultural middle ground in colonial Arkansas.

Acknowledgments

I thank Morris S. Arnold, Michael P. Hoffman, John H. House, and Jeffrey M. Mitchem for helpful comments on this essay.

Bibliography

AGI, PC Archivo General de Indias, Seville, Papeles de Cuba (various *legajos*)
ANC, C¹³A Archives Nationales, Paris, Archives des Colonies, sous-série C¹³A.
Arnold, Morris S.
1985   *Unequal Laws unto a Savage Race: European Legal Traditions in Arkansas, 1686–1836*. Fayetteville: University of Arkansas Press.
1991   *Colonial Arkansas, 1684–1804: A Social and Cultural History*. Fayetteville: University of Arkansas Press.
1994   Eighteenth-Century Arkansas Illustrated. *Arkansas Historical Quarterly* 53 (2):119–36.
1997   Cultural Imperialism and the Legal System: The Application of European Law to Indians in Colonial Louisiana. *Loyola Law Review* 42:727–44.
2000   *The Rumble of a Distant Drum: The Quapaws and the Old World Newcomers, 1673–1804*. Fayetteville: University of Arkansas Press.
Ashe, Thomas
1808   *Travels in America, Performed in 1806, for the Purpose of Exploring the Rivers Alleghany, Monongahela, Ohio, and Mississippi and Ascertaining the Produce and Condition of Their Backsand Vicinity*. London: Reprinted by E. M. Blunt for W. Sawyer and Company.
Baird, W. David
1980   *The Quapaw Indians: A History of the Downstream People*. Norman: University of Oklahoma Press.
Barnes, R. H.
1984   *Two Crows Denies It: A History of Controversy in Omaha Sociology*. Lincoln: University of Nebraska Press.

Bizzell, David W. (editor)
1981   A Report on the Quapaw: Letters of Governor George Izard to the American Philosophical Society, 1825–1827. *Pulaski County Historical Review* 29 (4):66–79.
Bossu, Jean-Bernard
1771   *Travels through That Part of North America Formerly Called Louisiana.* Translated by J. R. Forster. London: T. Davies.
1962   *Travels in the Interior of North America, 1751–1762.* Translated and edited by Seymour Feiler. Norman: University of Oklahoma Press. Originally published 1768.
1982   *New Travels in North America, 1770–1771.* Translated and edited by Samuel Dorris Dickinson. Natchitoches, La.: Northwestern State University Press. Originally published 1777.
Charlevoix, Pierre Xavier
1923   *Journal of a Voyage to North America.* 2 vols. Translated and edited by L. P. Kellogg. Chicago: Caxton Club.
Delanglez, Jean
1935   *The French Jesuits in Lower Louisiana, 1700–1763.* Washington, D.C.: Catholic University Press.
Delanglez, Jean (editor and translator)
1964   The Journal of Pierre Vitry, S.J., 1738–1740. *Louisiana Studies* 3(1):250–309.
Dickinson, Samuel D.
1991   Shamans, Priests, Preachers, and Pilgrims at Arkansas Post. In *Arkansas before the Americans,* edited by H. A. Davis, 95–104. Research Series 40. Arkansas Archeological Survey, Fayetteville.
Dorsey, James Owen
1885   *On the Comparative Phonology of the Four Siouan Languages.* Annual Report of the Smithsonian Institution for 1883:919–29. Washington, D.C.
1894   *A Study of Siouan Cults.* Annual Report of the Bureau of American Ethnology 11:361–544. Washington, D.C.
1897   *Siouan Sociology: A Posthumous Paper.* Annual Report of the Bureau of American Ethnology 15:213–50. Washington, D.C.
Fletcher, Alice, and Francis La Flesche
1911   *The Omaha Tribe.* Annual Report of the Bureau of American Ethnology 27:17–660. Washington, D.C.
Ford, James A.
1961   *Menard Site: The Quapaw Village of Osotouy on the Arkansas River.* Anthropological Papers 48(2):133–91. American Museum of Natural History, New York.
González López-Briones, M. Carmen
1983   Spain in the Mississippi Valley: Spanish Arkansas, 1762–1804. Ph.D. diss., Purdue University, Lafayette, Indiana.
Henning, Dale R.
1993   The Adaptive Patterning of the Dhegiha Sioux. *Plains Anthropologist* 38 (146):253–64.

Hoffman, Michael P.
1986   Protohistory of the Lower and Central Arkansas River Valley in Arkansas. In *The Protohistoric Period in the Mid-South: 1500–1700*, edited by D. H. Dye and R. C. Brister, 24–37. Archaeological Report no. 18. Mississippi Department of Archives and History, Jackson.
1990   The Terminal Mississippian Period in the Arkansas River Valley and Quapaw Ethnogenesis. In *Towns and Temples along the Mississippi*, edited by D. H. Dye and C. A. Cox, 208–26. Tuscaloosa: University of Alabama Press.
1991   Quapaw Structures, 1673–1834, and Their Comparative Significance. In *Arkansas before the Americans*, edited by H. A. Davis, 55–68. Research Series 40. Arkansas Archeological Survey, Fayetteville.
1993a   The Depopulation and Abandonment of Northeastern Arkansas in the Protohistoric Period. In *Archaeology of Eastern North America: Papers in Honor of Stephen Williams*, edited by J. B. Stoltman, 261–76. Archaeological Report no. 25. Mississippi Department of Archives and History, Jackson.
1993b   Identification of Ethnic Groups Contacted by the de Soto Expedition in Arkansas. In *The Expedition of Hernando de Soto West of the Mississippi, 1541–1543*, edited by G. A. Young and M. P. Hoffman, 132–42. Fayetteville: University of Arkansas Press.
1994   Ethnic Identities and Cultural Change in the Protohistoric Period of Eastern Arkansas. In *Perspectives on the Southeast*, edited by P. B. Kwachka, 61–70. Southern Anthropological Society Proceedings no. 27. Athens: University of Georgia Press.
1995   Protohistoric Tunican Indians in Arkansas. In *Cultural Encounters in the Early South*, compiled by J. Whayne, 61–75. Fayetteville: University of Arkansas Press.
Hollow, Robert C., and Douglas R. Parks
1980   Studies in Plains Linguistics: A Review. In *Anthropology on the Great Plains*, edited by W. R. Wood and M. Liberty, 68–97. Lincoln: University of Nebraska Press.
House, John H.
1991   The Mississippian Sequence in the Menard Locality, Eastern Arkansas. In *Arkansas before the Americans*, edited by H. A. Davis, 6–39. Research Series 40. Arkansas Archeological Survey, Fayetteville.
1997   Noble Lake: A Protohistoric Archaeological Site on the Lower Arkansas River. *Arkansas Archeologist* 36:47–97.
Jeter, Marvin D.
1986   Tunicans West of the Mississippi: A Summary of Early Historic and Archaeological Evidence. In *The Protohistoric Period in the Mid-South: 1500–1700*, edited by D. H. Dye and R. C. Brister, 38–63. Archaeological Report no. 18. Mississippi Department of Archives and History, Jackson.
Jeter, Marvin D., Kathleen M. Cande, and John J. Mintz (editors)
1990   *Goldsmith Oliver 2 (3PU306): A Protohistoric Archeological Site near Little Rock, Arkansas*. Report submitted to Federal Aviation Administration, Southwest Region, Fort Worth, Texas, by the Arkansas Archeological Survey, Fayetteville.

Jeter, Marvin D., Jerome C. Rose, G. Ishmael Williams, Jr., and Anna M. Harmon
1989   *Archeology and Bioarcheology of the Lower Mississippi Valley and Trans-Mississippi South in Arkansas and Louisiana.* Research Series 37. Arkansas Archeological Survey, Fayetteville.

Jones, Linda Carol
1997   Conversion of the Tamaroas and the Quapaws: An Unlikely Outcome in the Missions of the Seminary of Québec, 1698–1707. Master's thesis, University of Arkansas, Fayetteville.

Kellogg, Louise Phelps (editor)
1917   *Early Narratives of the Northwest, 1634–1699.* New York: Barnes and Noble.

Le Page du Pratz, M.
1774   *The History of Louisiana.* London: T. Becket.

Margry, Pierre (editor)
1876–86 *Découvertes et Établissements des Français dans l'Ouest et dans le Sud l'Amérique Septentrionale, 1614–1754* (Discoveries and settlements of the French in the west and the south of North America, 1614–1754). 6 vols. Paris: Maisonneuve.

McGee, W. J.
1894   *The Siouan Indians: A Preliminary Sketch.* Annual Report of the Bureau of American Ethnology 15:157–212. Washington, D.C.

Morse, Dan F.
1991   On the Possible Origin of the Quapaws in Northeast Arkansas. In *Arkansas before the Americans,* edited by H. A. Davis, 40–54. Research Series 40. Arkansas Archeological Survey, Fayetteville.

Morse, Dan F., and Phyllis A. Morse
1983   *Archaeology of the Central Mississippi Valley.* New York: Academic Press.

Murphy, Edmund R.
1941   *Henry de Tonty: Fur Trader of the Mississippi.* Baltimore: Johns Hopkins University Press.

Murray, Katherine A.
1989   Bioarchaeology of the Post Contact Mississippi and Arkansas River Valleys, A.D.1500–1700. Master's thesis, University of Arkansas, Fayetteville.

Nuttall, Thomas
1980   *A Journal of Travels into the Arkansas Territory during the Year 1819.* Edited by S. Lottinville. Norman: University of Oklahoma Press.

O'Neill, Charles Edwards
1966   *Church and State in French Colonial Louisiana.* New Haven: Yale University Press.

Phillips, Philip
1970   *Archaeological Survey in the Lower Yazoo Basin, Mississippi, 1949–1955.* Papers of the Peabody Museum of Archaeology and Ethnology no. 60. Harvard University, Cambridge.

Pittman, Philip
1770   *The Present State of European Settlements on the Mississippi.* London.

Rankin, Robert L.
1993   Language Affiliations of Some de Soto Place Names in Arkansas. In *The Expedition of Hernando de Soto West of the Mississippi, 1541–1543,* edited by G. A. Young and M. P. Hoffman, 210–21. Fayetteville: University of Arkansas Press.

n.d.   Quapaw as a Historically Dhegiha Language: Grammar. Unpublished manuscript, University of Arkansas, Fayetteville.

Rollings, Willard H.
1992   The Osage: An Ethnohistorical Study of Hegemony on the Prairie-Plains. Columbia: University of Missouri Press.
1995   Living in a Graveyard: Native Americans in Colonial Arkansas. In Cultural Encounters in the Early South, compiled by J. Whayne, 38–60. Fayetteville: University of Arkansas Press.

Rowland, Dunbar, and Albert G. Sanders (editors and translators)
1927–84 Mississippi Provincial Archives. 5 vols. Mississippi Department of Archives and History, Jackson.

Sabo, George, III
1991   Inconsistent Kin: French-Quapaw Relations at Arkansas Post. In Arkansas before the Americans, edited by H. A. Davis, 105–30. Research Series 40. Arkansas Archeological Survey, Fayetteville.
1995   Rituals of Encounter: Interpreting Native American Views of European Explorers. In Cultural Encounters in the Early South, compiled by J. Whayne, 76–87. Fayetteville: University of Arkansas Press.

Shea, John Gilmary (editor)
1854   Journal de la Guerre du Micissippi contre les Chicashas (Journal of the war on the Mississippi against the Chickasaws). New York: Cramoissy Press.

Smith, Ralph
1951   Exploration of the Arkansas River by Bénard de la Harpe, 1721–22. Arkansas Historical Quarterly 10(4):339–63.

Stahle, David W., Malcolm K. Cleaveland, and John G. Hehr
1985   A 450-Year Drought Reconstruction for Arkansas, United States. Nature 316(6028):530–32.

Surrey, N. M. Miller
1916   The Commerce of Louisiana during the French Regime, 1699–1763. New York: Columbia University Press.

Swanton, John R.
1911   Indian Tribes of the Lower Mississippi Valley and Adjacent Coast of the Gulf of Mexico. Smithsonian Institution, Bureau of American Ethnology Bulletin 43. Washington, D.C.

Thwaites, Reuben Gold (editor)
1896–1901 The Jesuit Relations and Allied Documents. 73 vols. Cleveland: Burrows Brothers.

Trigger, Bruce G.
1983   American Archaeology as Native History: A Review Essay. William and Mary Quarterly 40(3):413–52.

Usner, Daniel H., Jr.
1992   Indians, Settlers, and Slaves in a Frontier Exchange Economy: The Lower Mississippi Valley before 1783. Chapel Hill: University of North Carolina Press.

White, Richard
1991   The Middle Ground: Indians, Empires, and Republics in the Great Lakes Region, 1650–1815. Cambridge: Cambridge University Press.

8

Cherokee Ethnohistory and Archaeology from 1540 to 1838

GERALD F. SCHROEDL

At the beginning of the eighteenth century, Cherokee settlements were found in five geographically distinctive areas that each contained ten to twelve politically independent towns (fig. 8.1) (Goodwin 1977; Smith 1979). The Lower towns were located along the upper reaches of the Savannah River drainage on the Tugaloo, Chattooga, Keowee, and Toxaway rivers in northwestern South Carolina and northeastern Georgia, while the Middle towns were situated on the upper reaches of the Little Tennessee River in western North Carolina. The Valley towns were found on the upper Hiwassee, Valley, and Cheoah rivers, and the Out towns were located in the Tuckasegee and Oconaluftee river valleys. The Overhill towns occupied the Hiwassee and Little Tennessee river valleys in eastern Tennessee. Overhill and Valley town residents spoke the western or Otali dialect. The middle or Kituhwa dialect was spoken in the Middle and Out towns, while the Lower town inhabitants spoke the Lower or Elati dialect (Mooney 1900).

Cherokee population totaled around 20,000 persons at the time of contact with Europeans, but this number was reduced to 12,000 or less during the eighteenth century, because of epidemics and hostilities with Anglo Americans and other Native Americans (Thornton 1990:13–46). For the same reasons, the total number and location of villages and their populations also fluctuated, with variations becoming particularly acute in the second half of the eighteenth century (see Goodwin 1977; Smith 1979).

Cherokee towns included an octagonal townhouse or council house measuring 14 to 18 meters across, a rectangular summer townhouse or pavilion about 4 by 16 meters on a side, and a surrounding village plaza, covering not more than about 1 hectare, where public meetings and ceremo-

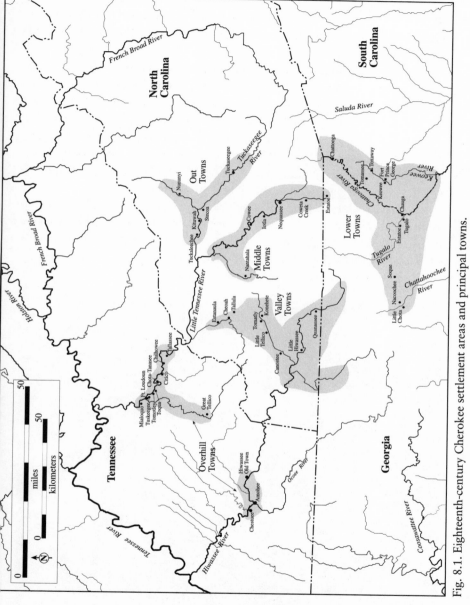

Fig. 8.1. Eighteenth-century Cherokee settlement areas and principal towns.

nial activities took place (fig. 8.2) (Schroedl 1986b, 1989). Individual villages contained ten to sixty domestic structures, with populations ranging from 100 to 600 people. Smaller settlements and individual farmsteads were found in more remote locations throughout Cherokee territory. Households consisted of a circular winter house about 7 to 8 meters in diameter (Schroedl 1989). These buildings had four central support posts and a central hearth. Adjacent rectangular summer houses measuring 4 by 10 meters had less well defined open walls and gable roofs. Around these structures were pits for storage and for obtaining clay. Human burials were often placed in pits in and around the summer house. Dwellings were spaced 25 to 50 meters apart, and villages covered 10 to 80 hectares, depending on local topography, population, and the amount of land in agricultural production. Cherokee villages were not palisaded in the eighteenth century.

Cherokee social and political activities were organized according to seven matrilineal clans, as well as a civil or white division and a red or military division (Gearing 1962; Gilbert 1943). Unlike other southeastern groups such as the Creeks (Swanton 1928), the civil and military divisions of the Cherokee did not constitute kin-based moieties.

Fig. 8.2. Artist's depiction of the Overhill Cherokee town of Chota ca. 1760.

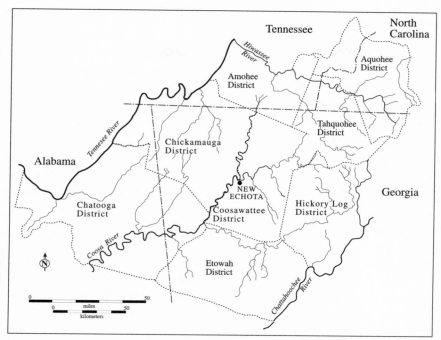

Fig. 8.3. Cherokee Nation, 1820–38.

Cherokee subsistence relied on hunting deer, bear, turkey, and a variety of smaller animals and on growing several varieties of corn, beans, and squash (Goodwin 1977:49–82). European-introduced animals and crops took on greater importance in Cherokee subsistence through the mid-eighteenth century (Bogan 1982).

After the American Revolutionary War, the pattern of Cherokee settlement and its attendant economic, social, political, and religious patterns were greatly altered. The pattern of highly organized nucleated towns was largely replaced by dispersed communities consisting of small log cabins, with associated outbuildings and individual family agricultural lands (Pillsbury 1983; Riggs 1996; Wilms 1974). Townhouses served the political and religious needs of these communities, but Anglo American commerce and Christian missions came to have greater influence in Cherokee life. As the traditional towns of the eighteenth century were abandoned, Cherokee population and new settlements were established primarily in northern Georgia. Here the Cherokee Nation became fully established in the early nineteenth century, only to be relocated to the west by forced removal by the United States in 1838 (fig. 8.3)(Brown 1938; Mooney 1900).

Documentary Sources

The Spanish explorers de Soto in 1540 and Juan Pardo in 1566 traveled into the historic territory of the Cherokee (Hudson 1987, 1990, 1994). The
precise routes they followed, the exact locations of the native towns they
visited, and the ethnic groups they encountered remain a source of debate
(Beck 1997; Boyd and Schroedl 1987; Brain 1998). Nevertheless, there
seems little doubt that the Spanish contacted the ancestors of the historic
Cherokee in western North Carolina and in eastern Tennessee. In some
cases, the ancestors of the Cherokee occupied towns in the same regions,
such as the Middle and Out towns, where they lived in the eighteenth century. In other cases, their towns were located where no Cherokee towns
existed in the eighteenth century. For example, Pardo and de Soto may have
encountered Cherokee ancestors on the Tennessee River and its tributaries
north and east of Knoxville. In other instances eighteenth-century Cherokee
towns are found in places that may have been settled by other culture groups
in the sixteenth century. Some researchers, for example, suggest that Muskogean speakers occupied the lower Little Tennessee River valley at the time of
Spanish contact (Booker et al. 1992). Following the sixteenth-century Spanish incursions, there are few ethnohistoric sources from which to trace the
history of the Cherokee until the late seventeenth century.

Once the South Carolina colony was established at Charleston in 1670,
the British initiated a nearly uninterrupted chronicle of Cherokee culture
that can be directly related with considerable reliability to the archaeological
record. The British produced numerous colonial government documents
recording their relationships with the Cherokee (McDowell 1955, 1958,
1970), and there is an equally abundant record kept by the U.S. government
after 1776 (see, for example, Lowrie et al. 1832, 1834; U.S. Department of
Interior 1800–1880). In addition, there are excellent eyewitness descriptions
of the Cherokee by diplomats (for example, John Herbert [Salley 1936]),
soldiers (for example, Henry Timberlake [Williams 1927]), missionaries (for
example, William Richardson [Williams 1931]), traders (for example, James
Adair [Williams 1930]), and travelers (for example, William Bartram [Van
Doran 1928]). Many of these individuals also produced important historic
maps from which we can reconstruct and interpret Cherokee social and
economic geography (Cumming 1958). Contemporary drawings and paint-
ings document individual dress and physical characteristics (Fundaburk
1958; Horan 1972). Historical syntheses of the Cherokee from a colonial

perspective are well represented, for example, in the works of Crane (1929), Alden (1944), and Williams (1937). Greater emphasis on Cherokee social, political, economic, and ideological organization are found, for example, in Mooney (1900), Gilbert (1943), Gearing (1962), and Goodwin (1977). The abundance of ethnohistorical data on the Cherokee is illustrated by Fogelson's (1978) bibliography that lists nearly 350 references, and surely this has more than doubled since its publication twenty-two years ago.

Archaeological Sources

Archaeological interest in the Cherokee began in the late nineteenth and early twentieth centuries when Cyrus Thomas working in east Tennessee (Thomas 1890) and researchers from the Valentine Museum (of Richmond, Virginia) and the Smithsonian Institution working in western North Carolina (see Dickens 1979) attempted to identify mounds and other archaeological remains as representing the prehistoric Cherokee. They concluded that Cherokee culture had developed in place from prehistoric antecedents identified in the archaeological record. In the 1930s, influenced by the ethnographic and ethnohistoric work of John Swanton (for example, 1932, 1985; see Smith 1984), Lewis and Kneberg (1946) concluded, from their work primarily at late prehistoric sites on the Tennessee River and its tributaries, that the Cherokee had migrated to eastern Tennessee, replacing Muskogean people in the late seventeenth century. Except for small excavations at Chota and Tanasee (see Schroedl and Russ 1986), however, they conducted little work at historically documented Cherokee towns, relying on scattered Cherokee occupations they identified at Mississippian period sites to reach their conclusions.

In the 1960s, the University of North Carolina began research in western North Carolina that sought to demonstrate uninterrupted development from prehistoric to historic Cherokee cultures (Coe 1961). Surface collections or test pit excavations were made at five Cherokee towns, including Nequassee, Joree, Cowee, Nununyi, and Kituhwa (Egloff 1967), but excavations of only single domestic structures were conducted at the eighteenth-century Townsend and Tuckasegee sites (Dickens 1967; Keel 1976). The only large-scale excavations were at the Coweeta Creek site, which revealed extensive occupation dating to the sixteenth or seventeenth century (Rodning 1996). Investigations at the Cherokee Lower towns of Estatoe, Chauga, and Tugalo by the University of Georgia focused on the mounds at these sites and produced only sparse evidence of eighteenth-century occupations (Kelly and DeBaillou 1960; Kelly and Neitzel 1961; Smith and Williams 1978; Williams and Branch 1978). Excavations at the eighteenth-century towns of Keowee and Toxaway as well as the contemporary British military post, Fort Prince George (1753–68), were also made by the University of South Carolina in the 1950s and 1960s (see Harmon 1986). While directed at understanding the origins of Cherokee culture, the work in Georgia, South Carolina, and North Carolina began to form the core of a description of eighteenth-century Cherokee archaeological culture grounded in ethnographic and ethnohistoric descriptions.

By far the most ambitious and extensive investigation of eighteenth-century Cherokee sites is the work by the University of Tennessee at the Overhill towns in the lower Little Tennessee River valley (Baden 1983; Chapman and Newman 1979; Guthe and Bistline 1981; Polhemus 1987; Russ and Chapman 1983; Schroedl [ed.] 1986). Guided primarily by Lieutenant Henry Timberlake's diary and his remarkably accurate map of these villages (fig. 8.4) (Williams 1927), large-scale archaeological excavations were conducted at Citico, Chota, Tanasee, Toqua, Tomotley, Tuskegee, Mialoquo, and several smaller related sites. These investigations recorded six townhouses, two summer pavilions, seventy-six domestic structures, 1,351 pit features, and 212 human burials (Schroedl 1986c). Contemporary British and Anglo American sites, particularly Fort Loudoun (1756–60) (Kutruff and Bastian 1977) and the Tellico Blockhouse (1794–1807) (Polhemus 1979), were also investigated. In addition to the established goals of identifying Cherokee origins and describing eighteenth-century Cherokee culture, for the first time explaining Cherokee culture change during the historic period became an explicit research goal of Cherokee archaeological research.

The first step in addressing the question of Cherokee culture change was to use ethnohistoric data to define a sequence of time periods representing distinctive military, economic, political, and diplomatic relationships between Cherokee and Anglo American cultures. The second step was to identify distinctive archaeological assemblages for each time period. Comparison of the assemblages was used to describe the kind and degree of change in Cherokee culture (Ford 1982; Newman 1977; Riggs 1987b; Russ 1984; Schroedl 1986c). More recent excavations at Hiwassee Old Town in eastern Tennessee (Riggs 1987a) and the Lower towns of Tomassee and Chattooga in South Carolina (Schroedl 1994; Smith et al. 1988), as well as surface

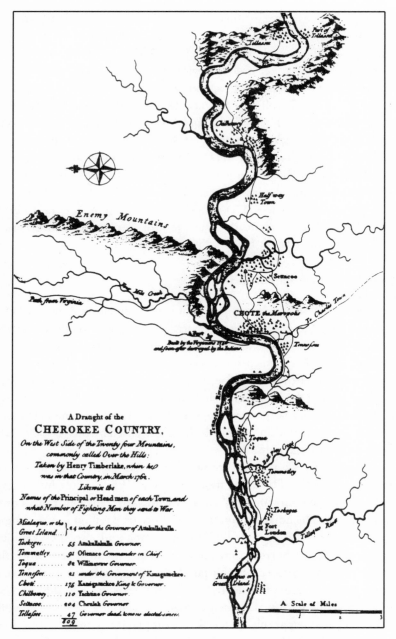

Fig. 8.4. Lieutenant Henry Timberlake's map of the Overhill Cherokee towns on the lower Little Tennessee River in 1762.

collections and test excavations at the Valley and Out towns, including numerous nineteenth-century cabin sites, have further elaborated or expanded this fundamental model (Greene 1996; Riggs 1996).

Presently the Cherokee archaeological and ethnohistoric data are organized according to seven periods spanning the time A.D. 1540 to the present. These periods are as follows: Spanish exploration (1540–1670), English contact (1671–1745), English colonial (1746–75), American Revolutionary War (1776–94), American federal (1795–1818), Cherokee removal (1819–38), and Cherokee post-removal (1839 to present). In western North Carolina this chronology includes the early Qualla (1450–1650) and late Qualla (1650–1838) archaeological phases (Dickens 1979, 1986). The Tugalo (1450–1600) and Estatoe (1700–1838) phases account for the Cherokee archaeological record in northwestern South Carolina and northeastern Georgia (Anderson 1994; Hally 1986).

Period of Spanish Exploration

Cherokee archaeology during the period of Spanish exploration (1540–1670) is difficult to characterize, because of differences in interpretation of the Spanish chronicles and difficulties making unambiguous identifications of sixteenth- and seventeenth-century occupations in the absence of historic artifacts. Chattooga, Estatoe, Tugalo, Chauga, and especially Coweeta Creek are among the sites from which to address the sixteenth- and seventeenth-century Cherokee archaeological record. These sites indicate that the use of platform mounds probably declined or ceased by the period's end, as did the use of village palisades.

At Coweeta Creek at least six townhouses that measure 14 meters on a side are superimposed on a low mound (Moore 1990). These buildings are square or square with truncated corners with wall trench entrances on the southeast side. The adjacent summer structure or pavilion is a rectangular building about 6 meters wide by 14 meters long and also shows multiple rebuilding episodes. Surrounding the village plaza are dense concentrations of postmolds, pit features, and burials defining at least nine distinctive domestic structure areas. Residential structures are square buildings 6 to 7 meters on a side with wall trench entrances (Rodning 1996). The village architecture is comparable to late Mississippian structures dating to the fifteenth and sixteenth centuries elsewhere in the region. The village plan at

Coweeta Creek, except for the placement of the townhouse on a mound, is comparable to fifteenth-century Mouse Creek villages, particularly Ledford Island in eastern Tennessee (Sullivan 1987).

Cherokee presence at Chauga, Estatoe, and Tugalo is difficult to interpret because these sites are poorly reported or because they contain multiple Woodland and Mississippian period occupations. Excavations focused on platform mounds at these sites where the later construction stages, attributed to Cherokee occupation, are poorly preserved. It is possible that early historic era community buildings were associated with the occupations on the mound summit. Village deposits excavated at Tugalo (Williams and Branch 1978) and Chauga (Kelly and Neitzel 1961) apparently contain evidence of eighteenth-century occupation, but there are no domestic structure patterns. There are fences or walls associated with the mound structures, and there may have been a village palisade at Chauga, but it is impossible to establish the association of these features with Cherokee occupation. Anderson (1994:305) suggests that these sites may not have been occupied by the Cherokee until the eighteenth century. Evidence from Chattooga suggests otherwise. Although no mound is present at Chattooga, there are five townhouses, four of which are superimposed. The final townhouse was destroyed in the mid-1730s, and preceding community structures could date to the mid-seventeenth century or earlier.

Grit-tempered complicated stamped ceramics characteristic of the early Qualla and Tugalo phases occur in North and South Carolina during this period (Dickens 1979; Hally 1986). These phases are distinguished by the occurrence of particular stamped motifs, substantial numbers of incised wares, and the absence of check-stamped wares. In eastern Tennessee shell-tempered ceramics of the late Dallas phase are present at this time.

English Contact Period

During the contact period (1671–1745), the Cherokee established sustained diplomatic and economic relationships primarily, but not exclusively, with the South Carolina colony. French attempts to influence the Cherokee, although persistent and a constant concern of the British, enjoyed only intermittent and limited success. Diplomacy was marked by Indian leaders traveling to Charleston to negotiate requests and lodge complaints and by English emissaries, most notably Colonel George Chicken (Williams 1928),

John Herbert (Salley 1936), and Alexander Cumming (Williams 1928) visiting Cherokee towns to enlist the aid and support of the Cherokee. For the first time, Europeans traveled throughout the full extent of Cherokee territory and produced firsthand descriptions of their experiences. The strength of British influence at this time is illustrated by the large contingent of Cherokee who pledged their loyalty at Charleston during the Yamasee War of 1715 (see Milling 1969:135–64). The Cherokee in turn benefited from increased access to European technology (Hatley 1993).

The deerskin trade became the context for economic relationships during this period. Although English traders initially were financed by plantation owners, trade was soon regulated by the colonial government and resident traders became established at many Cherokee villages (McDowell 1955). Utilitarian items, especially cloth, blankets, beads, guns, hoes, axes, and knives, dominated the trade during the contact period.

The Cherokee had established villages in all the areas that they were known to occupy in succeeding decades prior to the American Revolutionary War. In 1738 they were devastated by a smallpox epidemic that probably reduced their population of 20,000 by nearly half (Thornton 1990). It is believed that many Lower towns, particularly in northwestern South Carolina and northeastern Georgia, were abandoned because of population losses (Goodwin 1977). Eventually, some were reoccupied, but smaller villages in this area, and perhaps in other areas as well, were never resettled.

The archaeological record of the contact period is best known from the Chattooga site in South Carolina and from work at the Overhill towns (Schroedl 1986c, 1989, 1994). The data suggest that village patterning—consisting of a townhouse, summer townhouse, village plaza, and paired winter and summer structures—was widely in place by this time. Of the four superimposed townhouses at Chattooga, the two earlier buildings have four major roof support posts and are 14 to 16 meters in diameter, while the later two are about 17 meters in diameter with eight major support posts (see fig. 8.5). The final use of this building occurred in the mid-1730s and probably corresponds to the abandonment of the settlement. Posthole patterns represent multiple summer pavilions measuring 4 to 5 meters wide and 12 meters long. Much of the village plaza area was covered with pea-sized gravel. Excavation in two areas indicates the use of paired winter and summer structures, and surface collections suggest the widely dispersed occurrence of additional domestic households (Howard 1997; Schroedl 1994).

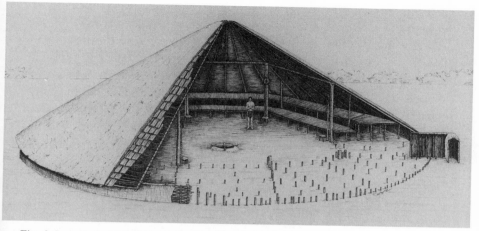

Fig. 8.5. Artist's depiction of the Chota townhouse ca. 1760.

Intense occupation during subsequent periods makes it more difficult to identify specific contact period occupational features at the Overhill towns. Nevertheless, there are four pit features and numerous trade goods that are unambiguously dated to the period at Chota-Tanasee (Newman 1986:448). The predominance of paired winter and summer houses and the occurrence of an early style townhouse with four major roof support posts also suggest early eighteenth-century occupation at this site (Schroedl 1986b). Similar evidence is present at Citico (Chapman and Newman 1979) and Toqua (Polhemus 1987; Schroedl 1978), although no townhouses were excavated at Citico and there are two townhouses at Toqua. Chota, Tanasee, and Citico are among the Overhill towns identified and visited by the British in the early eighteenth century (see Williams 1928); Toqua is not documented until the mid-eighteenth century.

Overhill ceramics are predominantly shell tempered and plain with folded rims (Bates 1986), while at Chattooga and elsewhere in the Cherokee country grit-tempered, complicated stamped Qualla ceramics predominate (Keel 1976). Fatherland Incised ceramics recovered at Chota-Tanasee (Bates 1986) are clear evidence for the Natchez, who were dispersed by the French in the Lower Mississippi River Valley and settled among the Creeks and Cherokee in the 1730s (Crane 1929; Woods 1980). At Chattooga there is abundant evidence for the manufacture and use of steatite pipes, suggesting that this industry was accelerated by the acquisition of iron implements for cutting stone. The few trade objects recovered at Chattooga, however, suggest that not all Cherokee settlements had equal access to European-made goods. On the other hand, the uncommon occurrence of stone tools and chipping debris at Chattooga suggests that European metal tools, even though not available in large numbers, rapidly replaced much of the native lithic technologies. The comparatively greater abundance of trade goods in the Overhill sites shows that British efforts to expand the flow and availability of trade goods were increasingly directed toward the Overhill towns. The success of this strategy, however, was not fully realized until the mid-eighteenth century.

There is no evidence for fundamental changes in Cherokee social institutions during this time, although military and political leadership roles surely took on greater importance in response to British economic and political alliances with the Cherokee (Gearing 1962). Few references to Cherokee belief systems are attributed to this period, but Alexander Longe's observations circa 1725 indicate the presence of religious specialists, including priests and their apprentices, and suggest that their role in ritual activity may have been more distinctly defined than in subsequent times (Corkran 1969). At Chattooga remains of domestic pigs and peaches indicate the use of these introduced species, but no archaeological or ethnohistoric data suggest dramatic alterations to Cherokee subsistence (Goodwin 1977; Walker 1995). Patterns in the organization of labor and the roles of men and women in economic activities must have been modified, especially as the deerskin trade became fully established (Hatley 1993). Demographic changes resulting from disease epidemics, economic conditions, and the military and political rivalry between the English and French are evidenced in the ethnohistoric data from the contact period. Such changes except for the abandonment of Chattooga circa 1730, are more difficult to document in the archaeological record.

English Colonial Period

The English Colonial period (1746–75) is well documented ethnohistorically and is well represented in the archaeological record particularly at the Overhill towns (see, for example, Corkran 1962; Crane 1929; Schroedl [ed.] 1986). During this time, political and economic dependence on the deerskin trade became paramount to both the Cherokee and English. The South Carolina colonial government devoted a greater proportion of its energy to securing and maintaining its relationship with the Overhill towns, because of their strategic location on the French and Creek frontier. The French intensified their efforts to influence the Cherokee by sending their agents into the Overhill country to exploit political differences among Cherokee leaders. For their allegiance against the British, the Cherokee demanded large shipments of trade goods, which the French were never able to supply, and by 1760 the French threat to British domination had ended in the Cherokee country. Cherokee political power became focused in a few prominent individuals, and the Overhill towns developed greater political, military, and economic influence over the other Cherokee towns. For example, Old Hop, Standing Turkey, and subsequently the Great Warrior Oconastota assumed the position of tribal leader in the 1760s. Efforts by Christian missionaries such as John Martin and William Richardson had little impact on changing Cherokee religious beliefs (Alden 1944:351; Williams 1931).

Resident traders became even more firmly established throughout the Cherokee country (Rothrock 1929). To protect their military and economic interests and to maintain their alliance with the Cherokee, the British constructed Fort Prince George (1753–68) in the Lower towns and Fort Loudoun (1756–60) in the Overhills (Ivers 1970) as buffers against incursions by the French and their Indian allies. This made it possible for the Cherokee to interact and negotiate with British officers and soldiers almost daily. The number and kinds of trade goods increased everywhere, but became especially abundant in the Overhills. Additional items of clothing were imported, a larger variety of items of personal adornment were traded, and a greater diversity and abundance of general hardware and utensils became available (McDowell 1958, 1970). The Cherokee clearly recognized their dependence on the British to supply them with the technology they needed to survive (Corkran 1962; Crane 1929).

Direct conflict with the British, including the Cherokee siege and destruction of Fort Loudoun, occurred in the late 1750s (Kelley 1961; Williams 1937). This conflict was precipitated when white settlers attacked and killed several Cherokee warriors who had abandoned military expeditions against the French because the British had not rewarded them as promised. The Indians retaliated by destroying several colonial settlements and killing a number of settlers. The British responded by restricting trade and organizing military campaigns against the Cherokee. Attempting to sue for peace, a contingent of Cherokee was taken hostage and eventually murdered at Fort Prince George. The Cherokee, led by Oconastota, who had been released before the Fort Prince George massacre, laid siege to Fort Loudoun (Kelley 1978). When its garrison surrendered, most of the soldiers were killed and the fort was never reoccupied. In response to the siege, punitive expeditions led by Colonel Archibald Montgomery destroyed the Lower towns (Hatley 1993:119–40), and Colonel James Grant burned most of the Middle and Out towns (King and Evans 1977). Although these towns were reoccupied or relocated, their number, size, and population diminished. Refugees added to the populations of the Overhill towns, which had been spared destruction.

In 1761 Lieutenant Henry Timberlake came as a peace emissary to the Overhill towns, where he recorded the most comprehensive observations on Cherokee culture available for the mid-eighteenth century (Williams 1927). His map of the lower Little Tennessee River valley provides remarkably accurate information on the size, location, and population of each of the Cherokee towns (see fig. 8.4).

Direct archaeological evidence for the military destruction of the Lower and Middle towns has not been documented. Large rectangular domestic structures, measuring 9 to 12 meters long and 4 meters wide, at Chota and especially Tomotley, however, may represent Cherokee architectural patterns more commonly found in the Lower towns, indicating the influence of refugee populations among the Overhills (Baden 1983; Schroedl 1989). Similar structures, for example, were recorded at Toxaway (Harmon 1986: fig. 5). The arrangements of these buildings in groups of two or three at right angles to one another resemble patterns seen in Upper Creek villages (Waselkov and Braund 1995). Similarly, the greater abundance of Qualla ceramics and complicated and check-stamped surface treatments in the Overhill archaeological collections at all sites, but especially Tomotley, may also represent this influence (Baden 1983; Schroedl 1986c). The numerous British personal and military artifacts found at the Overhill sites, such as sword fragments, artillery shell pieces, military issue gun parts, and British-made ceramics, unquestionably came from the looting of Fort Loudoun rather than normal acquisition through traders (Carnes 1983; Newman 1986). The destruction of Cherokee settlements, as well as the accompanying loss and dislocation of population, was exacerbated by the smallpox epidemic of 1759–60 (Thornton 1990:33). Measles and influenza outbreaks caused

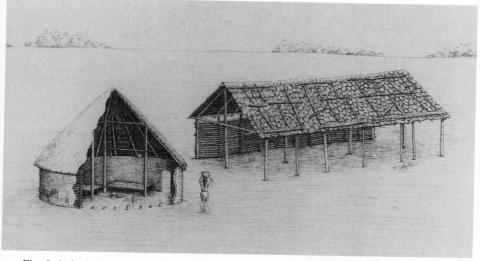

Fig. 8.6. Artist's reconstruction of winter-summer dwellings.

even greater devastation because the Cherokee probably had no previous exposure to these diseases. Together disease and hostilities may have reduced the population by 2,000 to 3,000 persons.

During the colonial period, European domestic animals, especially chickens and pigs, represent a marked change in subsistence, which was also surely accompanied by greater use of introduced plants, particularly peaches, additional legumes, and both Irish and sweet potatoes (Bogan et al. 1986; Goodwin 1977:125–46). The patterning of individual settlements—consisting of a townhouse, summer pavilion, village plaza, and associated domestic structures as documented at Chota-Tanasee, for example—remained virtually identical to that for the earlier contact period. Domestic architecture at villages like Chota-Tanasee, Citico, and Toqua included primarily paired winter and summer structures, with each household having its own complement of pits for soil recovery and storage, food processing and manufacturing areas, and burial places in and around the summer structure (fig. 8.6) (Schroedl 1986a, 1989). In the vicinity of most domestic structures is a rectangular or oval pit measuring 1–2 meters wide, 2–3 meters long, and up to 1 meter deep. These pits have single or paired posts on the interior at either end for supporting a roof or cover and are considered storage facilities (Schroedl 1986a). Presently these features are nearly exclusive to the Overhill archaeological record, where they are especially prevalent in the colonial period. As evidenced at Chota-Tanasee, Toqua, and Tomotley, a small number of rectangular and circular structures, which are consistent in size and plan with domestic houses, incorporate a rectangular cellar pit at the structure center. This use of pits within structures and individual rectangular or oval pits with a cover or a roof may represent European influence in architecture related to the storage of European root crops.

After the mid-eighteenth century, Cherokee townhouses are octagonal structures with eight rather than four major roof supports (fig. 8.5). This change took place at Chattooga in the early eighteenth century (Schroedl 1994) and at Chota-Tanasee probably in the 1740s or 1750s (Schroedl 1986c). Contemporary structures with eight major roof support posts were recorded at Tomotley and Mialoquo (Baden 1983; Russ and Chapman 1983). Using eight roof support posts makes it possible to create interior space for accommodating larger groups of people. This probably became more important in the mid-eighteenth century as the populations of Cherokee towns fluctuated. Perhaps more important, an architectural change of this kind altered the spatial representation of Cherokee social and ideological patterns: townhouse interior space was now divided into eight equal-sized sections. One section accommodated the structure's entrance, and each one of the other seven was reserved for a different Cherokee clan (Gilbert 1943; Schroedl 1986b). Consequently, clear demarcation of clan social and ritual space occurred within the townhouse. The reasons for this architectural change or its relationship to Anglo American contact are not obvious in either the ethnohistoric nor archaeological records. Perhaps it occurred as clans assumed greater roles in town social integration as a response to escalating conflict between clans precipitated by demographic disruptions, population movements, and the intensification of political and economic relationships with the British.

By the end of the colonial period, Cherokee political, economic, and military power were diminished or seriously compromised. The French threat to British dominance and influence over the Cherokee was virtually eliminated. The center of Cherokee population, political influence, and military power was concentrated in the Overhill towns. The destruction of the Lower, Middle, and Out towns, the deprivations caused by trade restrictions, and increased mortality from disease placed the Cherokee at a distinc-

Fig. 8.7. Dwellings observed by Louis-Philippe at Toqua in 1797.

tive disadvantage in their relationships with the British. Cherokee strength was further reduced as increasingly large numbers of white settlers encroached on their land and the Cherokee were forced by treaties in 1768, 1770, and 1772 to surrender large tracts of land in Virginia, West Virginia, eastern Kentucky, and northeastern Tennessee (Royce 1888, 1900).

American Revolutionary War Period

As a result of Cherokee support of the British during the American Revolutionary War (1776–94), destructive changes were initiated in virtually all realms of their society (Brown 1938; Williams 1925–26, 1944). The flow of British trade goods, upon which Cherokee were dependent, was cut off, and Cherokee settlements were subject to repeated attacks by American forces. Assaults were led against the Lower towns in 1776 by Colonel Andrew Williamson's forces, and against the Middle, Valley, and Out towns by General Griffith Rutherford and Colonel William Moore. The burned remains of a single rectangular structure excavated at the Townsend site may represent Rutherford's destruction (Dickens 1967). Most Cherokee casualties, as with previous conflicts with the British, resulted from starvation, exposure, and related disease rather than military action. As survivors from many different towns found refuge in a few settlements, towns like Cowee and perhaps others, especially in the Overhills, increased in size and population (Van Doran 1928). The Overhill towns absorbed additional Cherokee who fled while their villages were under attack, and although the Overhills themselves were repeatedly attacked, their villages were able to survive for a longer time.

In November 1776, American forces under the command of Colonel William Christian, while sparing Chota and several other towns, burned five of the Overhill towns and their crops. One of the towns destroyed by Christian was Mialoquo, the primary village of Chief Dragging Canoe, who opposed the peace accords being negotiated by other Cherokee leaders (Williams 1944). Cherokee support for Dragging Canoe and the growth of Mialoquo at the time of the American Revolution are reflected in the archaeological record, where there are many more than the fourteen domestic dwellings recorded by Timberlake in 1761 and where a townhouse was built after his visit (Russ and Chapman 1983; Schroedl 1989). The excavated buildings reflect further change in architecture and patterning in domestic structures. Paired winter and summer houses are not found at Mialoquo. Instead there are isolated circular winter houses, large rectangular dwellings like those at Tomotley, and smaller cabins (approximately 7 meters long by 3 meters wide) whose walls were formed by flexible saplings or rails. These later dwellings are comparable to ones observed by Louis-Philippe and drawn by his brother at Toqua in 1797 (fig. 8.7) (Louis-Philippe 1977; Sturtevant 1978:198).

Despite the truce and further land cessions in 1777, hostilities with the Americans were renewed in 1780 when expeditions led by Colonels John Sevier and Arthur Campbell destroyed ten Overhill towns including Chota. Additional attacks were carried out in 1782, 1786, and 1788 (Brown 1938; Williams 1944). In 1761 Timberlake had counted sixty-four domestic dwellings at Chota and Tanasee; in 1784 only thirty were observed (Williams 1927, 1928). With their population depleted, many Cherokee, following Dragging Canoe and other leaders, retreated to establish the seven Chickamauga towns in southern Tennessee, northern Alabama, and northern Georgia. There has been no archaeological confirmation of the precise location of these towns.

Evidence of Cherokee movement to the south and of the ravages of warfare with the Americans is found in the archaeological record at Hiwassee Old Town, located on the lower Hiwassee River (Riggs 1987a; Riggs et al. 1989). Ethnohistoric sources suggest that the population of this town increased substantially at the time of the Revolutionary War. Only small cabins and large rectangular houses are represented among the six buildings excavated here. Several buildings were burned, but these events cannot be directly linked to American assaults on the village in the 1780s. Recovered artifacts document reductions in the numbers and kinds of trade goods and increased evidence for the repair, recycling, and native manufacture of iron, lead, and pewter objects. Production of lithic tools also was renewed, but at Hiwassee Old Town they were more often made of bottle glass than chert. Frequencies of grit-tempered ceramics, the occurrence of shallow, flat bottom pans, and the varieties of stamped motifs are greater here than in villages along the lower Little Tennessee River. Use of domestic animals also is less evident in the faunal remains from the site, while the butchered remains of a small horse or pony represent an animal that the Cherokee would have eaten only as a last resort (Williams 1927:66–67).

During the American Revolutionary War, the Valley, Out, Lower, and Middle towns were destroyed, and most were never occupied again. The Overhill towns were barely able to survive, and Ustenalli in northern Georgia replaced Chota as the Cherokee capital in 1788 (Woodward 1963:109). The Cherokee found refuge in the establishment of the Chickamauga towns, but American militias eventually attacked and burned these towns, too, and additional settlements in northern Georgia and Alabama (Malone 1956; Mooney 1900). Small remnant populations of the Valley, Middle, and Out towns managed to survive in western North Carolina, where they formed distinctive communities in the late eighteenth and early nineteenth centuries. Smallpox epidemics in 1780 and 1783 further compounded the Cherokee dilemma (Thornton 1990:33–34). Protracted hostilities, which continued until 1794, reduced and disseminated the Cherokee population and disrupted their cultural institutions. Much of their territory was occupied by white settlers, they had ceded nearly 50,000 square miles of land to the United States, virtually all their villages were in ruins, and thousands of Cherokees had died. The Cherokee were on the verge of extinction.

Federal Period

The federal period (1795–1818) is marked by the policies of Cherokee acculturation initiated by the U.S. government. These policies were intended to revitalize the Cherokee economy and restructure their political and social organization to conform with Anglo American patterns (Prucha 1962). Trade goods were abundant and diverse, representing most previously available artifacts but including many more agricultural implements, construction tools, and household goods. Cherokee men were instructed in agriculture and animal husbandry and given the tools for this work; women were provided instruction and technology for spinning yarn and weaving cloth. The government demanded that the Cherokee abandon their communal village way of life and become a nation of individual family farmsteads.

To monitor the implementation of their program, the government stationed agents and military personnel at various locations, including Tellico Blockhouse (1794–1807), Hiwassee Garrison (1807–15), Hiwassee Indian Agency (1816–21), and Fort Southwest Point (1792–1807) (Ford 1982). Comprehensive archaeological studies have been conducted at the Tellico Blockhouse (Polhemus 1979) and Fort Southwest Point (Smith 1993). Some Cherokee, mostly of mixed blood, who embraced the policies of culture change became wealthy merchants and planters and came to dominate Cherokee political institutions. Cherokee who attempted to maintain their traditional way of life were mostly full bloods and because of their resistance to change remained economically impoverished (see Anderson 1991; McLoughlin 1986).

Especially evident in Cherokee archaeological assemblages, when compared to earlier periods, are increased frequencies of containers and ceramics made by Anglo Americans and correspondingly reduced numbers of aboriginal vessels, with shallow pans and large jars the predominant vessel forms. Ornaments are less frequent and there is a greater variety of trade goods than in earlier periods. Comparisons among federal period archaeological assemblages from Chota, Citico, and the Bell Rattle Cabin sites, however, show differences in the degree of Cherokee material acculturation (Riggs 1987b, 1989). The Citico and Chota sites are characterized by few Anglo American household furnishings, kitchen wares, and architectural hardware, indicating a more traditional lifeway than at the Bell Rattle Cabin site, where increased frequencies of these artifacts suggest greater use of Anglo American technology for food preparation and serving and the incorporation of nontraditional architectural materials into house construction. Federal period Cherokee assemblages are distinguished from contemporary Anglo American farmsteads by the occurrence of aboriginal ceramics and ornaments, fewer numbers and varieties of Anglo American ceramics and glassware, and smaller amounts of architectural hardware. During the federal period overall use of domestic animals increased dramatically, and the Cherokee began to raise both pigs and cattle for commercial markets (Bays 1991; Newman 1979). Faunal remains, however, indicate that the Cherokee continued to exploit native animals, and that their consumption of domestic stock probably was less than that of their Anglo American neighbors (Ford 1982).

Cherokee architecture includes the construction of small single-family rectangular rail cabins and small single-room cribbed log houses. These incorporated exterior chimneys, doors, and interior cellars. Many families continued to build circular winter houses as cold-weather retreats and for the practice of traditional social, ceremonial, and medical activities.

Many Cherokee communities were composed of individual households widely dispersed along 10 to 20 kilometers of smaller streams or rivers. For example, at least fifteen distinctive Cherokee communities, representing remnants of the Valley, Middle, and Out towns, were established in the Hiwassee, Valley, and Notley River valleys in southwestern North Carolina after the Revolutionary War (Riggs 1988, 1996). Each community included 15 to 100 households consisting of a single cabin or multiple cabins, sometimes a circular winter house, and possibly a corncrib situated on 1 to 5 hectares. Seven communities had townhouses. Excavations at Hickory Log town in northern Georgia suggest that the density of settlements was greater in this area, even though houses were distributed for several kilometers along a stream or river just as in southwestern North Carolina (Webb 1995). Former eighteenth-century village sites, if occupied at all, had small populations of one or two families. Townhouses were constructed at some of these sites to serve the surrounding community (Schroedl 1989). Although townhouses maintained the octagonal plan of earlier structures and were similar to them in size, townhouse architecture replaced vertical post walls with horizontal log construction. In 1799 only five dwellings were occupied at Chota (Williams 1928); at Toqua there were ten dwellings and a townhouse in 1797 (Sturtevant 1978).

During the federal period, Christian missionaries became firmly established among the Cherokee. Examples include the Valley Towns mission near Murphy, North Carolina, founded in 1820, the Brainerd mission established near Chattanooga in 1817, and the Moravian mission at Spring Place in northern Georgia founded in 1802 (McLoughlin 1984, 1990, 1994; Walker 1931). The opportunity for their children to attend school at the missions contributed greatly to Cherokee support for these institutions. Some Cherokee converts became preachers, and many others accommodated their beliefs to Christian teachings. Traditional beliefs were by no means lost, nor was the matrilineal kinship system completely eliminated. During this time, Sequoyah developed his syllabary for writing the Cherokee language, which was quickly adopted and brought widespread literacy to the Cherokee (Mooney 1900; Perdue 1994).

Cherokee political organization coalesced around the lineage rivalries that had characterized the mid-eighteenth century and the growing division between conservative full-blood Cherokee, who wanted to limit the effects of acculturation and preserve their traditional culture, and progressive mixed-blood Cherokee, who wanted to accommodate and prosper in the context of American culture. By the early years of the nineteenth century, the Cherokee population had rebounded to about 16,000 (Thornton 1990:43).

Removal Period

During the removal period (1819–38) the Cherokee Nation was formally established, and the policy of Indian removal, first formulated in the early nineteenth century, was fully implemented by the United States. The Cherokee Nation was centered at its capital, New Echota in northern Georgia, and except for remnants of the Valley, Middle, and Out towns in western North Carolina, the core of former Cherokee territory was now occupied by American frontier culture. In 1802 the state of Georgia gave up its claims to land in Alabama and Mississippi to the U.S. government in exchange for the latter's promise to nullify Indian claims to land in Georgia. Prompted by the discovery of gold in 1828 and the passage of the Indian Removal Act of 1830, Georgia acted on its own, and Cherokee land was confiscated and disbursed to Georgia citizens by lottery in 1832. The Treaty of New Echota, by which the Cherokee would give up all lands in the east in exchange for resettlement in the west, was signed by a small group of Cherokee leaders in 1835 (Mooney 1900). This exacerbated the political divisiveness that had taken shape during the previous decades as traditional Cherokee struggled to retain possession of their land while finding an acceptable balance between the social, economic, and ideological pressures of American culture and the traditional cultural institutions that distinguished them as Cherokee (Perdue 1991). In the end, about 16,000 to 17,000 Cherokee were forcibly removed to the west, and as many as 8,000 of them died as a direct result of the removal (Thornton 1991).

The Cherokee removal created a rich documentary record, including maps, property assessments, spoliation claims (or claims for property losses), census data, and eyewitness accounts, that describes with remarkable detail individual Cherokee, their families, their communities, their households, and even their household contents (see, for example, Armstrong 1819–20; Cherokee Claims Papers 1838–42; Klinck and Talman 1970; United States War Department 1835; Welch and Jarrett 1836–37). The archaeological record for the removal period is similar to that for the preceding federal period, except that the extraordinary details found in the historical materials permit fine-scale interpretations of individual sites and their assemblages, patterns of site densities and distributions, and multiple dimensions of Cherokee life and culture rarely possible in other situations. Historical analysis of more than 600 Cherokee households in southwestern North Carolina documents the social and economic differences between full-blood and mixed-blood Cherokee and reflects how they adapted to the external pressure for removal and internal conflict between Anglo and Indian lifestyles (Riggs 1996).

On the Hiwassee, Notley, and Valley rivers archaeological studies using surface collections were conducted at the locations of sixty-two Cherokee farmsteads. Of thirty-five occupations dated to the nineteenth century, eighteen represent removal period occurrences and twelve of these are correlated with their specific historically documented Cherokee occupants (Riggs 1996; Riggs and Kimball 1996). Archaeological assemblages of the period show that traditional households possessed fewer and less diverse American-made goods while retaining aboriginal technology, especially ceramics for making hominy. More westernized Cherokee household assemblages indicate greater participation in American economic institutions. On the other hand, the ethnohistoric record clearly shows that traditional Cherokee were unwilling to become full participants in American social, political, and ideological institutions, while westernized Cherokee were unable to do this because of white prejudice.

The study of removal period Cherokee households is best illustrated by the John Christie family and the excavation of one of their cabins on the Hiwassee River (Riggs 1997). A surface collection and excavation of a cellar measuring 2 meters square and 70 centimeters deep produced sherds representing an assortment of thirty-four Euro-American ceramic vessels and six aboriginal pans and large jars. Personal items, including beads, buttons, mirrors, smoking pipes (aboriginal and Euro-American), occur at the site. There are numerous examples of household goods such as tableware and glass bottle fragments, and of construction and agricultural tools such as axes and plowshares. The food remains are mostly from domestic animals, but wild turkey and several fish species also were recovered at the site. The Christies were a comparatively westernized Anglo Cherokee family whose lifestyle was more like their Anglo American than their Cherokee neighbors. The Christie cabin archaeological assemblage is comparable to items that were purchased at local stores and to those for which the Christies filed claims against the government following their removal to Oklahoma. The Christie assemblage reflects a pattern of Anglo American material consumption, while expressing cultural ambiguity in retaining aboriginal elements such as ceramics. Although very much Anglo American in their economic and subsistence patterns, the Christies were excluded from Anglo American society because they were Cherokee.

Wilms (1974, 1991) and Pillsbury (1983) studied the cultural geography of the Cherokee removal period in northern Georgia, but comprehensive studies of the associated archaeological record are poorly developed. Excavations at New Echota and the Vann House conducted in the 1950s, for example, are not adequately reported (DeBaillou 1955, 1957; Smith 1992), and more recent work has not been fully studied regarding the differentiation of Cherokee traditionalists, acculturated Cherokee like the Christies, and the comparatively wealthy Cherokee planters of northern Georgia (see, for example, Alvey et al. 1993; Baker 1970; Garrow 1979; Wood and Wood 1995). To facilitate removal of the Cherokee, the U.S. Army established compounds to garrison troops and to temporarily inter Indians before their deportation (Evans 1977). Archaeological and historical interest is now developing in these camps and the actual routes used to move the Cherokee west (National Park Service 1994).

In some cases specific Cherokee households and the individuals who occupied them can be linked to the places where they settled in Oklahoma or to their descendants living in Oklahoma and North Carolina today. An archaeological record of the Cherokee in Arkansas has been acknowledged (Davis 1987). The best documented settlements, however, probably have been destroyed by highway, reservoir, and urban-related construction. No sustained effort has been made to locate additional Cherokee occupations in the state, and no nineteenth-century Cherokee sites have been reported to date in the course of more general cultural resource surveys. Attempts to locate sites associated with the Texas Cherokee have met with some success (Jurney 1995), and efforts to conduct archaeological survey and excavation of removal period Cherokee sites in Oklahoma have been initiated (Townsend 1993, 1995).

Conclusion

For the period 1670–1838 there is a remarkable ethnohistoric and archaeological record of culture change and survival among the Cherokee. Before the American Revolutionary War, Cherokee technological, economic, and subsistence patterns were altered, but traditional patterns of social organization, belief systems, and the occupation of nucleated towns were maintained despite demographic changes caused by epidemics and military conflicts with the British. Cherokee political institutions were not fundamentally changed, although the autonomy of individual towns was compromised as a small number of strong diplomatic and military leaders responded to British interests on behalf of many settlements. The Overhill settlements and their leaders dominated relationships with the British.

Towns were composed of a townhouse, summer pavilion, a village plaza, their associated domestic dwellings, and accompanying activity areas. Domestic architecture consisted of paired winter and summer dwellings, but long rectangular structures also form distinctive patterns at some towns. Cherokee subsistence and patterns of agricultural production also remained largely intact, although domestic animals, particularly pigs and chickens, and introduced root crops increasingly contributed to their diet by the mid-eighteenth century. The adoption of sweet potatoes, Irish potatoes, and other plants is possibly related to the use of large rectangular or oval covered storage pits and the placement of cellar pits in some domestic structures. Qualla and Overhill ceramic traditions remained distinctive until population dispersal in the mid-eighteenth century, when Qualla motifs and types became more frequent in the Overhill towns. Except for brass kettles and perhaps glass bottles, British-made ceramics are rare in the Cherokee archaeological record before the American Revolutionary War. There was widespread adoption of other European technology, however, such as guns, knives, and hoes, and personal items such as beads, smoking pipes, sheet and wire arm bands, and mirrors. The use of lithic tools, although never totally lost, was greatly reduced early in the eighteenth century. The production of steatite pipes was probably accelerated because metal carving tools became available.

Because of the American Revolutionary War, the Cherokee lost most of their traditional lands, and most of their ancient town sites were abandoned or severely reduced in population. As a whole, the Cherokee were displaced to southwestern North Carolina, southeastern Tennessee, and northern Georgia, where new towns and the nucleus of the Cherokee Nation was established in the early nineteenth century. Large nucleated towns were replaced by dispersed communities consisting of individual farmsteads and isolated townhouses. In northern Georgia some towns may have been more densely settled, and wealthier Cherokee prospered as merchants and plantation owners. The use of townhouses and winter hothouses served to maintain traditional values and community solidarity. Log crib construction replaced traditional vertical post architecture for both domestic and public buildings.

Archaeological assemblages are dominated by Euro-American artifacts including farming implements, construction tools, household utensils, and personal items rarely found in earlier times. Aboriginal ceramics were largely restricted to shallow pans and to large jars for the processing of corn. Cherokee subsistence, while including native animals and plants, relied to a greater degree on European-introduced plants and animals. Because the deerskin trade era ended and participation in warfare was virtually eliminated, the economic role of Cherokee men focused more on agricultural production, particularly livestock raising. Traditional matrilineal kinship and clan organization were compromised but not entirely eliminated as the Cherokee adjusted to Anglo American economic, political, and legal institutions. Christian missionaries converted many Cherokee, but traditional religious beliefs and values remained deeply held. Literacy was widely achieved because of missionary schools and the widespread adoption and use of the Sequoyah syllabary.

Internal conflict and social differences within Cherokee society are reflected in the assemblages of individual households. Despite Cherokee efforts to participate in Anglo American culture as well as to retain their traditional culture, they were exiled to the west by the United States. Because small numbers of Cherokee were able to remain in western North Carolina, two distinctive political groups, the eastern and western bands, were created. The Cherokee archaeological record for the period after 1838 is poorly known.

Removal period historical data are exceptional for the richness of detail they contain, connecting specific Cherokee and their families with their descendants now living in western North Carolina and eastern Oklahoma. This relationship has special meaning and significance to Cherokee people today as they seek to further understand and appreciate their political, social, and ideological heritage.

Acknowledgments

I thank Bonnie McEwan for asking me to contribute this chapter. I also thank her for inviting me to present a shorter version of this essay at the Society for Historical Archaeology conference, and I am grateful for Charles Ewen's comments which helped me improve the final essay. Brett Riggs has assisted me in numerous ways in the course of sharing our mutual interests in the ethnohistory and archaeology of the Cherokee. I especially appreciate his review of this essay and his production of figures 8.1 and 8.3. Figure 8.2 is reproduced with permission of Tig Productions, and figures 8.4, 8.5, and 8.6 are courtesy of the Frank H. McClung Museum. Figure 8.7 is reproduced from Louis-Philippe 1977.

Bibliography

Alden, John R.
1944   *John Stuart and the Southern Colonial Frontier: A Study of Indian Relations, War, Trade, and Land Problems in the Southern Wilderness, 1753–1775.* Ann Arbor: University of Michigan Press.

Alvey, Richard, Harley Lanham, Sean Coughlin, Gary Crites, and Brett Riggs
1993   *Intensive Archaeological Survey for Cultural Resources and Testing of Site 9Ck51 in the I-75 to State Route 371 Connector, Section NH–208–1(5) Bartow, Forsyth, and Cherokee Counties, Georgia.* Report submitted to the Georgia Department of Transportation, Atlanta.

Anderson, David G.
1994   *The Savannah River Chiefdoms: Political Change in the Late Prehistoric Southwest.* Tuscaloosa: University of Alabama Press.

Anderson, William L. (editor)
1991   *Cherokee Removal, Before and After.* Athens: University of Georgia Press.

Armstrong, Robert
1819–20 Plats and Surveys of Cherokee Reservations, by Robert Armstrong, surveyor. U.S. National Archives Record Group 75. Washington, D.C.

Baden, William W.
1983   *Tomotley: An Eighteenth-Century Cherokee Village.* Report of Investigations 36. Department of Anthropology, University of Tennessee, Knoxville.

Baker, Steven G.
1970   Selective Analysis of Two Historic Indian Trash Pits from New Echota. *Conference on Historic Sites Archaeology Papers* 5:122–37.

Bates, James F.
1986   Aboriginal Ceramic Artifacts. In *Overhill Cherokee Archaeology at Chota-Tanasee,* edited by G. F. Schroedl, 289–331. Report of Investigations 38. Department of Anthropology, University of Tennessee, Knoxville.

Bays, Brad Alan
1991   The Historical Geography of Cattle Herding among the Cherokee Indians. Master's thesis, Department of Geography, University of Tennessee, Knoxville.

Beck, Robin A.
1997   From Joara to Chiaha: Spanish Exploration of the Appalachian Summit Area, 1540–1568. *Southeastern Archaeology* 16:162–69.

Bogan, A. E.
1982   Archaeological Evidence of Subsistence Patterns in the Little Tennessee River Valley. *Tennessee Anthropologist* 7:38–50.

Bogan, A. E., L. LaValley, and G. F. Schroedl
1986   Faunal Remains. In *Overhill Cherokee Archaeology at Chota-Tanasee,* edited by G. F. Schroedl, 469–514. Report of Investigations 38. Department of Anthropology, University of Tennessee, Knoxville.

Booker, Karen M., Charles M. Hudson, and Robert L. Rankin
1992   Place Name Identification and Multilingualism in the Sixteenth-Century Southeast. *Ethnohistory* 39:399–451.

Boyd, C. Clifford, Jr., and G. F. Schroedl
1987   In Search of Coosa. *American Antiquity* 52:840–44.

Brain, Jeffrey P.
1998   The DeSoto Entrada into the Southeastern United States. *Review of Archaeology* 19:30–35.

Brown, John P.
1938   *Old Frontiers, The Story of the Cherokee Indians from Earliest Times to the Removal to the West, 1838.* Kingsport, Tenn.: Southern Publishers.

Carnes, Linda F.
1983   Appendix II: Identification of the Euro-American Artifacts. In *Tomotley: An Eighteenth-Century Cherokee Village*, by W. W. Baden, 173–209. Report of Investigations 36. Department of Anthropology, University of Tennessee, Knoxville.
Chapman, Jefferson, and Robert Newman
1979   Archaeological Investigations at the Citico Site. In *The 1978 Archaeological Investigations at the Citico Site (40Mr7)*, edited by J. Chapman, 1–4. Report submitted to the Tennessee Valley Authority, Knoxville.
Cherokee Claims Papers
1838–42 Cherokee Spoliation and Improvement Claims. In Cherokee Collection [Penelope Allen Papers]. Microfilm Record 815. Tennessee State Library and Archives, Nashville.
Coe, Joffre
1961   Cherokee Archaeology. In *Symposium on Cherokee and Iroquois Culture*, edited by W. Fenton and J. Gulick, 53–60. Smithsonian Institution, Bureau of American Ethnology Bulletin 180. Washington, D.C.
Corkran, David
1962   *The Cherokee Frontier: Conflict and Survival, 1740–1762*. Norman: University of Oklahoma Press.
Corkran, David (editor)
1969   A Small Postscript on the Ways and Manners of the Indians Called Cherokees, the Contents of the Whole So That You May Find Everything by the Pages [by Alexander Longe, 1725]. *Southern Indian Studies* 21:6–49.
Crane, Verner
1929   *The Southern Frontier, 1670–1732*. Durham, N.C.: Duke University Press.
Cumming, William P.
1958   *The Southeast in Early Maps*. Chapel Hill: University of North Carolina Press.
Davis, Hester
1987   The Cherokee in Arkansas: An Invisible Archaeological Resource. In *Visions and Revisions: Ethnohistoric Perspectives on Southern Culture*, edited by G. Sabo III and W. M. Schneider, 48–58. Southern Anthropological Society Proceedings 20. Athens: University of Georgia Press.
DeBaillou, Clemens
1955   Excavations at New Echota in 1954. *Early Georgia* 1:18–29.
1957   The Chief Vann House, The Vann's Tavern and Ferry. *Early Georgia* 2:3–11.
Dickens, Roy S., Jr.
1967   The Route of Rutherford's Expedition against the North Carolina Cherokees. *Southern Indian Studies* 19:3–24.
1979   The Origins and Development of Cherokee Culture. In *The Cherokee Nation: A Troubled History*, edited by D. King, 3–32. Knoxville: University of Tennessee Press.
1986   An Evolutionary-Ecological Interpretation of Cherokee Development. In *The Conference on Cherokee Prehistory*, assembled by D. G. Moore, 81–94. Swannanoa, N.C.: Warren Wilson College.

Egloff, Brian J.
1967   An Analysis of Ceramics from Historic Cherokee Towns. Master's thesis, Department of Anthropology, University of North Carolina, Chapel Hill.
Evans, E. Raymond
1977   Fort Marr Blockhouse: The Last Evidence of America's First Concentration Camp. *Journal of Cherokee Studies* 2:257–63.
Fogelson, Raymond D.
1978   *The Cherokees: A Critical Bibliography.* Newberry Library Center for the History of the American Indian Bibliographical Series, Indiana University, Bloomington.
Ford, Thomas B.
1982   An Analysis of Anglo-American–Cherokee Culture Contact during the Federal Period, the Hiwassee Tract, Eastern Tennessee. Master's thesis, Department of Anthropology, University of Tennessee, Knoxville.
Fundaburk, Emma Lila
1958   *Southeastern Indians' Life Portraits: A Catalogue of Pictures, 1564–1860.* Fairhope, Ala.: American Bicentennial Museum.
Garrow, Patrick H.
1979   The Historic Cabin Site: The Last Trace of the Cherokee Town of Coosawattee. *Early Georgia* 7:1–28.
Gearing, Fred
1962   *Priests and Warriors: Structures for Cherokee Politics in the Eighteenth Century.* American Anthropological Association Memoir 93. Menasha, Wisconsin.
Gilbert, William H.
1943   *The Eastern Cherokee.* Anthropological Paper 23. Smithsonian Institution, Bureau of American Ethnology Bulletin 133, 169–413. Washington, D.C.
Goodwin, Gary C.
1977   *Cherokees in Transition: A Study of Changing Culture and Environment Prior to 1775.* Research Paper 181. Department of Geography, University of Chicago.
Greene, Lance K.
1996   The Archaeology and History of the Cherokee Out Towns. Master's thesis, Department of Anthropology, University of Tennessee, Knoxville.
Guthe, Alfred K., and Marian Bistline
1981   *Excavations at Tomotley, 1973–74, and the Tuskegee Area: Two Reports.* Report of Investigations 24. Department of Anthropology, University of Tennessee, Knoxville.
Hally, David J.
1986   The Cherokee Archaeology of Georgia. In *The Conference on Cherokee Prehistory,* assembled by D. G. Moore, 95–121. Swannanoa, N.C.: Warren Wilson College.
Harmon, Michael
1986   *Eighteenth-Century Lower Cherokee Adaptation and Use of European Material Culture.* Volumes in Historical Archaeology 2. South Carolina Institute of Archaeology and Anthropology, University of South Carolina, Columbia.

Hatley, Tom
1993   *The Dividing Paths, Cherokees and South Carolinians through the Era of Revolution.* New York and Oxford: Oxford University Press.
Horan, James D.
1972   *The McKenney-Hall Portrait Gallery of American Indians.* New York: Bramhall House.
Howard, A. Eric
1997   An Intrasite Spatial Analysis of Surface Collections at Chattooga: A Lower Town Cherokee Village. Master's thesis, Department of Anthropology, University of Tennessee, Knoxville.
Hudson, Charles
1987   Juan Pardo's Excursion beyond Chiaha. *Tennessee Anthropologist* 12:74–87.
1990   *The Juan Pardo Expeditions.* Washington, D.C.: Smithsonian Institution Press.
1994   The Hernando de Soto Expedition, 1539–1543. In *The Forgotten Centuries: Indians and Europeans in the American South, 1521–1704,* edited by C. Hudson and C. Tesser, 74–103. Athens: University of Georgia Press.
Ivers, Larry E.
1970   *Colonial Forts of South Carolina.* Tricentennial Booklet 3. Columbia: University of South Carolina.
Jurney, David
1995   The Western Cherokee Migrations to Texas, 1820–1839. Paper presented at the Southeastern Archaeological Conference, Knoxville.
Keel, Bennie C.
1976   *Cherokee Archaeology: A Study of the Appalachian Summit.* Knoxville: University of Tennessee Press.
Kelley, James C.
1978   Oconostota. *Journal of Cherokee Studies* 3:221–38.
Kelley, Paul
1961   *Historic Fort Loudoun.* Fort Loudoun Association, Vonore, Tenn.
Kelly, Arthur R., and Clemens DeBaillou
1960   Excavation of the Presumptive Site of Estatoe. *Southern Indian Studies* 12:3–30.
Kelly, A. R., and R. S. Neitzel
1961   *The Chauga Site in Oconee County, South Carolina.* Laboratory of Archaeology Series 3. Department of Anthropology, University of Georgia, Athens.
King, Duane, and Raymond Evans (editors)
1977   Memoirs of the Grant Expedition against the Cherokees in 1761. *Journal of Cherokee Studies* 2:271–338.
Klinck, Carl F., and James J. Talman (editors)
1970   *The Journal of Major John Norton, 1816.* Toronto: Champlain Society.
Kutruff, Carl, and Beverly Bastian
1977   Fort Loudoun Excavations: 1975 Season. *Conference on Historic Site Archaeology Papers* 10:11–23.
Lewis, T. M. N., and Madeline D. Kneberg
1946   *Hiwassee Island: An Archaeological Account of Four Tennessee Indian Peoples.* Knoxville: University of Tennessee Press.

Louis-Philippe, King of France (1830–48)
1977   *Diary of My Travels in America.* Translated from the French by Stephen Becker. New York: Delacorte Press.
Lowrie, Walter, Walter S. Franklin, and Mathew St. Clair Clark (editors)
1832,   *American State Papers: Indian Affairs.* Vols. 1 and 2. *Documents, Legislative*
1834   *and Executive of the Congress of the United States.* Washington, D.C.: Gales and Seaton.
Malone, Henry
1956   *Cherokees of the Old South.* Athens: University of Georgia Press.
McDowell, W. L., Jr. (editor)
1955   Journals of the Commissioners of the Indian Trade, September 20, 1710–August 29, 1718. South Carolina Archives Department, Columbia.
1958   Documents Relating to Indian Affairs, May 21, 1750–August 7, 1754. South Carolina Archives Department, Columbia.
1970   *Documents Relating to Indian Affairs, 1754–1765.* Columbia: University of South Carolina Press.
McLoughlin, William G.
1984   *Cherokees and Missionaries, 1789–1839.* New Haven: Yale University Press.
1986   *Cherokee Renascence in the New Republic.* Princeton, N.J.: Princeton University Press.
1990   *Champions of the Cherokees: Evan and John B. Jones.* Princeton, N.J.: Princeton University Press.
1994   *The Cherokee and Christianity, 1794–1870.* Athens: University of Georgia Press.
Milling, Chapman J.
1969   *Red Carolinians.* Columbia: University of South Carolina Press.
Mooney, James
1900   *Myths of the Cherokee.* Nineteenth Annual Report of the Bureau of American Ethnology. Washington, D.C.
Moore, David G.
1990   An Overview of Historic Aboriginal Public Architecture in Western North Carolina. Paper presented at the Southeastern Archaeological Conference, Mobile, Alabama.
National Park Service (NPS)
1994   Certification Guide: Trail of Tears National Historic Trail. National Park Service, Long Distance Trails Group Office. Santa Fe, New Mexico.
Newman, Robert D.
1977   An Analysis of the European Artifacts from Chota-Tanasee: An Eighteenth-Century Overhill Cherokee Town. Master's thesis, Department of Anthropology, University of Tennessee, Knoxville.
1979   The Acceptance of European Domestic Animals by the Eighteenth Century Cherokee. *Tennessee Anthropologist* 4:101–7.
1986   Euro-American Artifacts. In *Overhill Cherokee Archaeology at Chota-Tanasee,* edited by G. F. Schroedl, 415–68. Report of Investigations 38. Department of Anthropology, University of Tennessee, Knoxville.

Perdue, Theda
1991   The Conflict Within: Cherokees and Removal. In *Cherokee Removal, Before and After,* edited by W. L. Anderson, 55–74. Athens: University of Georgia Press.
1994   The Sequoyah Syllabary and Cultural Revitalization. In *Perspectives on the Southeast, Linguistics, Archaeology, and Ethnohistory,* edited by P. B. Kwachka, 116–25. Southern Anthropology Society Proceedings 27. Athens: University of Georgia Press.

Pillsbury, Richard
1983   The Europeanization of the Cherokee Settlement Landscape Prior to Removal: A Georgia Case Study. In *Historical Archaeology of the Eastern United States, Papers from the R. J. Russell Symposium,* edited by R. W. Neuman, 59–69. Geosciences and Man 23. Baton Rouge, Louisiana.

Polhemus, Richard
1979   *Archaeological Investigation of the Tellico Blockhouse Site: A Federal Military and Trade Complex.* Report of Investigations 26. Department of Anthropology, University of Tennessee, Knoxville.
1987   *The Toqua Site: A Late Mississippian Dallas Phase Town.* 2 vols. Report of Investigations 41. Department of Anthropology, University of Tennessee, Knoxville.

Prucha, Francis P.
1962   *American Indian Policy in the Formative Years: The Indian Trade and Intercourse Acts, 1790–1834.* Cambridge: Harvard University Press.

Riggs, Brett H.
1987a   Archaeological Investigations at Hiwassee Old Town (40Pk3), Polk County, Tennessee. Paper presented at the Southeastern Archaeological Conference, Charleston, South Carolina.
1987b   Socioeconomic Variability in Federal Period Overhill Cherokee Archaeological Assemblages. Master's thesis, Department of Anthropology, University of Tennessee, Knoxville.
1988   *An Historical and Archaeological Reconnaissance of Citizen Cherokee Reservations in Macon, Swain, and Jackson Counties, North Carolina.* Report submitted to the North Carolina Division of Archives and History, Raleigh.
1989   Interhousehold Variability among Early-Nineteenth-Century Cherokee Artifact Assemblages. In *Households and Communities: Proceedings of the Twenty-first Annual Chacmool Conference,* edited by S. MacEachern, D. Archer, and R. Garvin, 328–38. Calgary, Alberta, Canada.
1996   *Removal Period Cherokee Households and Communities in Southwestern North Carolina (1835–1838).* Report submitted to the North Carolina Division of Archives and History, Raleigh.
1997   The Christie Cabin Site: Historical and Archaeological Evidence of the Life and Times of a Cherokee Métis Household (1835–1838). In *May We All Remember Well,* vol. 1, *A Journal of the History and Cultures of Western North Carolina,* edited by R. S. Brunk, 228–48. Asheville, N.C.: Robert S. Brunk Auctions Service.

Riggs, Brett H., George M. Crothers, and Norman Jefferson
1989   Conflict and Stress at Hiwassee Old Town during the American Revolution. Paper presented at the Society for American Archaeology, Atlanta, Georgia.
Riggs, Brett H., and Larry R. Kimball
1996   *The 1993–1994 Archaeological Survey of Hiwassee Reservoir, Cherokee County, North Carolina.* Report submitted to the Tennessee Valley Authority, Norris, Tennessee.
Rodning, Christopher B.
1996   Trends in Intrasite Settlement Patterning in the Appalachian Summit Region during Late Precontact and Early Postcontact Times. Paper presented at the Conference on Appalachian Highlands Archaeology, Albany, N.Y.
Rothrock, Mary
1929   Carolina Traders among the Overhill Cherokees, 1690–1760. *East Tennessee Historical Society's Publications* 1:3–18.
Royce, Charles
1888   *The Cherokee Nation of Indians.* Fifth Annual Report of the Bureau of American Ethnology. Washington, D.C.
1900   *Indian Land Cessions in the U.S.* Eighteenth Annual Report (Part 2) of the Bureau of American Ethnology. Washington, D.C.
Russ, Kurt C.
1984   Exploring Overhill Cherokee Material Culture Patterning. Master's thesis, Department of Anthropology, University of Tennessee, Knoxville.
Russ, Kurt C., and Jefferson Chapman
1983   *Archaeological Investigations at the Eighteenth-Century Overhill Cherokee Town of Mialoquo.* Report of Investigations 37, Department of Anthropology, University of Tennessee, Knoxville.
Salley, A. S. (editor)
1936   Journal of Colonel John Herbert, Commissioner of Indian Affairs for the Province of South Carolina, October 17, 1727, to March 19, 1727/8. South Carolina Historical Commission, Columbia.
Schroedl, Gerald F.
1978   Louis-Philippe's Journal and Archaeological Investigations at the Overhill Cherokee Town of Toqua. *Journal of Cherokee Studies* 3:206–20.
1986a   Features, Postmolds, and Burial Pits. In *Overhill Cherokee Archaeology at Chota-Tanasee,* edited by G. F. Schroedl, 43–124. Report of Investigations 38. Department of Anthropology, University of Tennessee, Knoxville.
1986b   Structures. In *Overhill Cherokee Archaeology at Chota-Tanasee,* edited by G. F. Schroedl, 217–72. Report of Investigations 38. Department of Anthropology, University of Tennessee, Knoxville.
1986c   Overhill Cherokee Archaeology from the Perspective of Chota-Tanasee. In *Overhill Cherokee Archaeology at Chota-Tanasee,* edited by G. F. Schroedl, 531–51. Report of Investigations 38. Department of Anthropology, University of Tennessee, Knoxville.
1989   Overhill Cherokee Household and Village Patterns in the Eighteenth Century. In *Households and Communities: Proceedings of the Twenty-first Annual Chacmool Conference,* edited by S. MacEachern, D. Archer, and R. Garvin, 350–60. Calgary, Alberta, Canada.

Cherokee Ethnohistory and Archaeology from 1540 to 1838 239

1994   A *Summary of Archaeological Studies Conducted at the Chattooga Site, Oconee County, South Carolina, 1989–1994.* Report submitted to the U.S. Forest Service, Francis Marion and Sumter National Forests. Columbia, S.C.

Schroedl, Gerald F. (editor)
1986   *Overhill Cherokee Archaeology at Chota-Tanasee.* Report of Investigations 38. Department of Anthropology, University of Tennessee, Knoxville.

Schroedl, Gerald F., and Kurt C. Russ
1986   An Introduction to the Ethnohistory and Archaeology of Chota and Tanasee. In *Overhill Cherokee Archaeology at Chota-Tanasee,* edited by G. F. Schroedl, 1–42. Report of Investigations 38. Department of Anthropology, University of Tennessee, Knoxville.

Smith, Betty A.
1979   Distribution of Eighteenth-Century Cherokee Settlements. In *The Cherokee Indian Nation: A Troubled History,* edited by D. H. King, 46–60. Knoxville: University of Tennessee Press.

Smith, Bruce D.
1984   Mississippian Expansion: Tracing the Historical Development of an Explanatory Model. *Southeastern Archaeology* 3:13–32.

Smith, Marvin T.
1992   *Historic Period Indian Archaeology of Northern Georgia.* Report no. 30. Laboratory of Archaeology Series, University of Georgia, Athens.

Smith, Marvin T., and J. Mark Williams
1978   European Trade Material from Tugalo, 9ST1. *Early Georgia* 6:38–53.

Smith, Marvin, Mark Williams, Chester DePratter, Marshall Williams, and Mike Harmon
1988   *Archaeological Investigations at Tomassee (38OC186), a Lower Cherokee Town.* Research Manuscript Series 206. South Carolina Institute of Archaeology and Anthropology, University of South Carolina, Columbia.

Smith, Samuel D. (editor)
1993   *Fort Southwest Point Archaeological Site, Kingston, Tennessee: A Multidisciplinary Interpretation.* Research Series no. 9. Division of Archaeology, Tennessee Department of Environment and Conservation, Nashville.

Sturtevant, William C.
1978   Louis Philippe on Cherokee Architecture and Clothing in 1797. *Journal of Cherokee Studies* 3:198–205.

Sullivan, Lynne P.
1987   The Mouse Creek Phase Household. *Southeastern Archaeology* 6:16–29.

Swanton, John R.
1928   *Social Organization and Social Usages of the Indians of the Creek Confederacy.* Forty-second Annual Report of the Bureau of American Ethnology. Washington, D.C.
1932   The Relation of the Southeast in General Culture Problems of American Prehistory. In *Conference on Southern Pre-history,* 60–74. Washington, D.C.: National Research Council.
1985   *Final Report of the United States DeSoto Expedition Commission.* Reprint of the 1939 report. Washington D.C.: Smithsonian Institution Press.

Thomas, Cyrus
1890   *The Cherokee in Pre-Columbian Times.* New York: N.D.C. Hodges.
Thornton, Russell
1990   *The Cherokees: A Population History.* Lincoln: University of Nebraska Press.
1991   The Demography of the Trail of Tears Period: A New Estimate of Cherokee Population Losses. In *Cherokee Removal, Before and After,* edited by W. L. Anderson, 1–28. Athens: University of Georgia Press.
Townsend, Russell
1993   The Study of Cherokee Log Houses in Eastern Oklahoma. Master's thesis, Department of Anthropology, University of Tulsa, Tulsa, Okla.
1995   A Brief Synopsis of Cherokee Archaeology in Northeastern Oklahoma. Paper presented at the Southeastern Archaeological Conference, Knoxville, Tennessee.
U.S. Department of Interior
1800–   Records of the Bureau of Indian Affairs. U.S. National Archives Record Group
  1880 75. Washington, D.C.
U.S. War Department
1835   Census Roll of the Cherokee Indians East of the Mississippi. Microcopy T-496, U.S. National Archives Record Group 75. Washington, D.C.
Van Doran, Mark (editor)
1928   *Travels of William Bartram.* New York: Dover Press.
Walker, Renee
1995   Faunal Remains from the Chattooga Site (38Oc18), Oconee County, South Carolina. Manuscript on file, Department of Anthropology, University of Tennessee, Knoxville.
Walker, William S.
1931   *Torchlights to the Cherokees, The Brainerd Mission.* New York: Macmillan.
Waselkov, Gregory A., and Kathryn H. Braund (editors)
1995   *William Bartram on the Southeastern Indians.* Lincoln: University of Nebraska Press.
Webb, Paul A.
1995   Hickory Log: Investigations at a Cherokee Homestead in North Georgia. Paper presented at the Southeastern Archaeological Conference, Knoxville, Tennessee.
Welch, William, and Nimrod Jarrett
1836–37 Valuations of Cherokee Property in North Carolina. U.S. National Archives Record Group 75. Washington, D.C.
Williams, Marshall, and Carolyn Branch
1978   The Tugalo Site, 9ST1. *Early Georgia* 6:32–37.
Williams, Samuel Cole
1925–26 Colonel Joseph Williams' Battalion in Christians Campaign. *Tennessee Historical Magazine* 9:102–16.
1931   An Account of the Presbyterian Mission to the Cherokees, 1757–1759. *Tennessee Historical Magazine* 1:125–38.
1937   *Dawn of Tennessee Valley and Tennessee History.* Johnson City: Watauga Press.

1944   *Tennessee during the Revolutionary War.* Tennessee Historical Commission, Nashville.

Williams, Samuel Cole (editor)
1927   *Lieutenant Henry Timberlake's Memoirs, 1756–1765.* Johnson City, Tenn.: Watauga Press.
1928   *Early Travels in the Tennessee Country, 1540–1800.* Johnson City, Tenn.: Watauga Press.
1930   *Adair's History of the American Indians.* Johnson City, Tenn.: Watauga Press.

Wilms, Douglas C.
1974   Cherokee Settlement Patterns in Nineteenth-Century Georgia. *Southeastern Geographer* 14:46–53.
1991   Cherokee Land Use in Georgia before Removal. In *Cherokee Removal, Before and After,* edited by W. L. Anderson, 1–28. Athens: University of Georgia Press.

Wood, Karen G., and W. Dean Wood
1995   Cherokee Settlement at the Time of Removal in Northern Georgia. Paper presented at the Southeastern Archaeological Conference, Knoxville, Tennessee.

Woods, Patricia Dillon
1980   *French-Indian Relations on the Southern Frontier, 1699–1762.* Studies in American History and Culture 18. Ann Arbor: University of Michigan Research Press.

Woodward, Grace Steele
1963   *The Cherokees.* Norman: University of Oklahoma Press.

9

Upper Creek Archaeology

GREGORY A. WASELKOV AND MARVIN T. SMITH

During the eighteenth and early nineteenth centuries, people referred to as Upper Creeks lived in parts of today's Alabama along the Coosa, Tallapoosa, and Alabama rivers. The term *Upper Creeks* included natives of east-central Alabama who coalesced with a complex amalgam of peoples that formerly lived in eastern Tennessee, northwestern Georgia, and even as far afield as the present state of Mississippi. They fled those regions in the seventeenth century as refugees from European-introduced epidemics and from warfare brought about by the English-sponsored slave trade. The label was imposed on these diverse groups by English traders and political leaders who either failed to grasp or chose to gloss over the ethnic complexity subsumed by the all-encompassing term *Upper Creeks*. They no doubt preferred to be known by their *talwa* (which roughly translates as "town") names or perhaps as Abihkas, Alabamas, Tallapoosas, and Okfuskees, referring to the major regional affiliations of *talwas* (Waselkov and Cottier 1985). During the eighteenth century, the Abihkas occupied the Coosa River valley approximately 60 miles north of the Fall Line at present-day Montgomery, the Alabamas lived around the headwaters of the Alabama River, Tallapoosa *talwas* were distributed along the lower Tallapoosa River just east of the Alabamas, and the Okfuskees lived farther upstream on the Tallapoosa (fig. 9.1). Each of these groups has a complex history (Braund 1993; Corkran 1967; Swanton 1922), but during the last century they have received varying levels of attention from archaeologists. This chapter summarizes the state of archaeological knowledge for each of these four groups. (For a discussion of the closely related Lower Creeks, see Worth, this volume.)

Nearly 250 historic Upper Creek archaeological sites have so far been reported from surveys in Alabama. Many of these have been attributed to

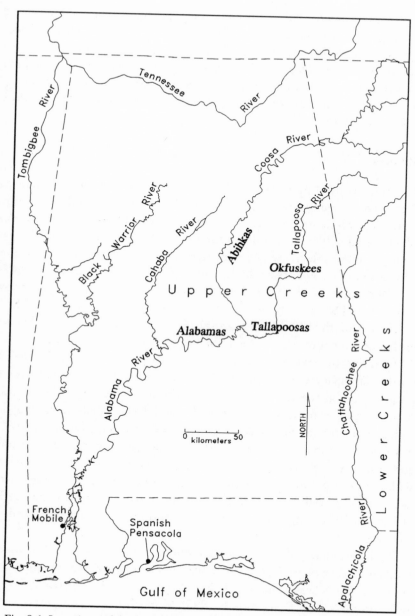

Fig. 9.1. Locations of the four regional divisions of Upper Creek *talwas* in the mid-eighteenth century (superimposed on a map of modern-day Alabama).

specific *talwas*, including numerous isolated household sites presumably affiliated with nearby village sites. In a recent study, Lolley (1996) presented a map method for identifying the historic names of Upper Creek archaeological sites. No one has yet attempted to analyze in detail the evolving settlement pattern of a particular *talwa*. There does seem, however, to have been a general trend toward settlement decentralization and dispersal during the late eighteenth and early nineteenth centuries (Waselkov 1981; Waselkov and Wood 1986).

Abihkas

The Abihkas lived on the Coosa River and its major tributary, Talladega Creek. They seem to have consisted primarily of remnants of the sixteenth-century chiefdom of Coosa, a native polity of northwestern Georgia. Abihka villages gradually migrated down the Coosa River throughout the seventeenth century, and there they apparently joined an indigenous people, known to archaeologists as the Kymulga phase (Knight 1985a, 1990:47–48). During the 1730s and 1740s, the Abihkas were joined by Chickasaw, Natchez, and Shawnee refugee villages (Corkran 1967; Swanton 1922).

Marvin Smith (1987, 1989a, 1989b, 1993) has detailed what is known of the movement of the Coosa-Abihka people down the Coosa River (fig. 9.2). During the sixteenth century, the Coosa population was located in northwestern Georgia in three major settlement concentrations. The Coosas proper lived on the Coosawattee River, the Itabas occupied the Etowah River valley near present-day Cartersville, and the Ulibahalis (including the Apicas, ancestors of the Abihkas) lived along the Coosa River near present-day Rome, Georgia. Hereditary chiefs of Coosa ruled over all these people and others far into present-day Tennessee. Other people, perhaps affiliated with the Coosas and now identified by their Kymulga phase culture, lived in present-day Alabama on Ogletree Island (Morrell 1964; Walling 1993), at site 1Ce308 (Little and Curren 1981), and farther south near modern Childersburg.

By the beginning of the seventeenth century, most if not all of the inhabitants of northwestern Georgia had migrated downstream into present-day Alabama. There was a small, little-known population in the area of Coates Bend on the Coosa River (Smith 1993). A much larger concentration of sites—known as the Weiss phase—existed in the area of the Weiss Reservoir in Cherokee County (Holstein et al. 1990; Holstein, Hill, and Little 1997;

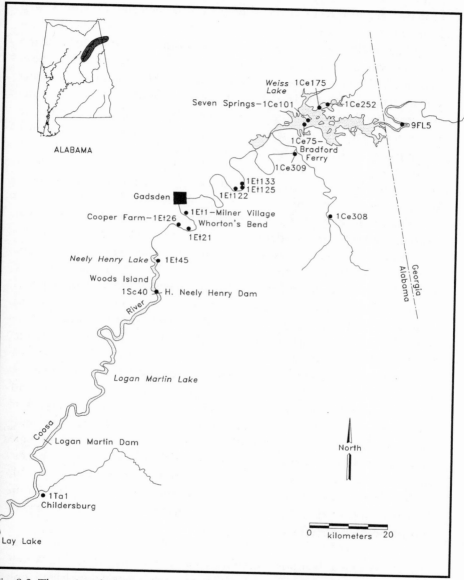

Fig. 9.2. The series of Abihka sites on the Coosa River occupied from the mid-sixteenth to the late eighteenth century.

Smith 1987, ms.). Overall population, however, appears to have decreased, probably due to the effects of European disease epidemics (Smith 1987). Mound building, once such an important element of prehistoric Mississippian ritual, ended, and storage in belowground pits was reintroduced. Little else is known about sites of the Weiss phase. No complete houses have been excavated, although Holstein, Hill, and Little (1997) report a partial structure from the Hurley site, 1Ce137, with an anomalous wall-trench construction technique unknown from earlier or later sites. Subsistence remains are not documented, and little is known of village plan. Burials are frequently accompanied by European artifacts, especially glass beads, brass disk ornaments, and (rarely) iron tools. Clarksdale bells have been documented from sites of this phase. Shell gorgets are absent, and shell beads have been reported from only one site.

By approximately 1630, the Coosa-Abihka people had again migrated south to the area of present-day Gadsden, Alabama, at Whorton's Bend. The Whorton's Bend phase is best known from the Milner Village and Cooper Farm sites (Smith 1987; Smith et al. 1993), where burials were salvaged over a number of years by avocational archaeologists. Almost nothing was learned about community size and plan, house types, and other aspects of culture. At least three villages and several farmsteads are documented. Pottery by this time is now commonly shell tempered, and finished with a brushed surface treatment and decorative incising. Other aboriginal items have decreased in abundance, but stone pipes and a discoidal stone are known. The presence of many stone arrowpoints indicates that firearms had not yet been introduced. These sites contain many newly acquired types of European trade goods. Iron axes are common and often greatly worn, indicating everyday use as tools. Brass harness bells are numerous, as are some new forms of brass ornaments: neck collars and wide sheet metal armbands. Most, if not all, European trade goods are probably derived from Spanish trade sources to the south and east. Bison remains have been reported from Milner (Smith et al. 1993), suggesting a change from the Mississippian subsistence reliance on white-tailed deer.

By around 1670 the Coosa-Abihka people again migrated farther south and concentrated their population into one community located on Woods Island (Morrell 1965; Smith 1987, 1995). Excavations at Woods Island took place in the early 1960s as a reservoir salvage project. Although house remains were encountered by the archaeologists, their descriptions are not clear. Apparently houses were of the less substantial "summer house" variety, and no semisubterranean "winter houses" were documented, although both types of structures are known from late prehistoric and earlier historic contexts. The loss of this architectural type occurred simultaneously on Tallapoosa sites, suggesting to Waselkov that the abandonment of substantial winter structures reflects a shift to large-scale winter hunts conducted at upland camps for the commercial deerskin trade (Waselkov 1990). Houses at Woods Island were widely scattered on the 10.4-hectare site, reflecting a population of only a few hundred people (Smith 1995:98).

Although recovery techniques for plant remains were in their infancy when Woods Island was excavated, peach pits were recovered, documenting the addition of this Old World crop to the native diet. European-produced grave goods continued to dominate burial accompaniments. Newly introduced items included brass kettles, firearms, iron hoes of the Spanish lugged type, scissors, and new styles of glass beads. Some of these items were certainly obtained from English trading sources. Pottery continues to be shell tempered, with brushing the primary surface treatment and incising present on many vessels. Shell-tempered cordmarked pottery appeared for the first time in the Coosa River sequence, perhaps reflecting the arrival of refugees from the Tennessee River area (Smith 1995:100). Smith (1995) suggested that Woods Island represents the Abihka town of this period, and Crane (1981:46) noted that an English trading post was established among the Abihkas in the last years of the seventeenth century.

By the eighteenth century most of the Coosa-Abihkas had moved still farther south to join remnants of the Kymulga phase people in present-day Talladega County, Alabama. Much is known of the settlement of these people through surveys conducted by Knight (1985a; Knight et al. 1984) and Waselkov (1980). Eighteenth-century occupation by the Coosa-Abihkas is best known from excavations at the Childersburg site (DeJarnette and Hansen 1960). Major excavations revealed fifty-two midden pits, four fire pits, thirty-seven postholes, two trenches, and twelve burials. Some of the features labeled as postholes were corncob-filled smudge pits. Features contained an abundance of ceramics, trade materials, and such introduced subsistence items as eggshells from domesticated chickens and peach seeds (Sheldon 1978).

Early nineteenth-century occupation of this region is best known from the site of Fort Leslie (Knight 1997), a stockade erected by Creek Indians during the Creek Civil War of 1813–14. The fort was located within Talladega town and was named for Alexander Leslie, a trader of Creek-English descent. The site is noteworthy for its abundant European ceramic specimens and sparse native wares, primarily grit-tempered Chattahoochee Roughened (formerly Chattahoochee Brushed) and Lamar Incised *var. Ocmulgee Fields.*

Alabamas

The Alabamas lived near the headwaters of the Alabama River near present-day Montgomery. For the most part, the group had not lived in this area in prehistoric times (Sheldon 1974). Based on a reconstruction of the route of Hernando de Soto by Charles Hudson and his associates (Hudson 1997), the Alabamas proper apparently lived in eastern Mississippi in the mid-sixteenth century. Other people, most importantly the Koasatis, joined them in central Alabama from their homeland in the eastern Tennessee River valley late in the seventeenth century (Webb and Wilder 1951). All were speakers of western Muskogean languages. Their sites are poorly known archaeologically. Digging by members of the Alabama Anthropological Society in the early twentieth century, particularly at the site of Taskigi, uncovered many burials. Some society members kept notes on grave lot associations, and their collections at the Department of Archives and History are proving useful to modern archaeologists (Waselkov 1994; Waselkov and Sheldon 1987). More recently, excavations at Fort Toulouse, a French military and trading outpost (1717–63) located immediately adjacent to Taskigi, have yielded an abundance of Alabama artifacts from French colonial contexts (Waselkov 1984a; Waselkov et al. 1982).

By the mid-seventeenth century, the Alabamas were heavily engaged in trade to obtain brass ornaments, iron tools, and glass beads from Spanish missions in Florida. Little direct historical documentation of this trade exists. But circumstantial evidence in the form of artifact distributions focused on the province of Apalachee suggests strongly that Apalachees served as middlemen in a trade network that obtained deerskins and other native products in exchange for desirable new materials and commodities (Smith 1987; Waselkov 1989b). English traders began to compete for deerskins in the 1680s or 1690s, eventually stimulating a huge demand for firearms, cloth, and other European goods among the Alabamas and other Upper Creek divisions (Waselkov and Sheldon 1987).

Trade with Spanish Florida ended abruptly in 1704, when Creek-English raids destroyed the Apalachee missions; soon afterward the Alabamas became embroiled in a war with the newly founded French colony at Mobile. When British trade abuses led to the Yamasee War of 1715, during which the Creeks temporarily evicted British traders from the interior Southeast, the "Grand Chief of the Alabamas" invited the French to establish Fort Toulouse in their midst (Waselkov 1989a:ix-x, 1992). Creek leaders then encouraged the development of competing pro-French and pro-British factions among their peoples. The ensuing political factionalism, far from being a source of division and weakness, enabled Creek leaders to maintain diplomatic neutrality between the often warring European colonies while reaping economic benefits in the form of lavish presents and favorable trading terms from colonial agents ever hopeful of military alliances. The material rewards of this balanced factionalism are manifest in the goods placed in Alabama and Tallapoosa graves between 1720 and 1760, with approximately equal numbers of individuals buried exclusively with French-made or British-made goods (Waselkov 1993).

In the absence of modern excavations at their village sites, we still know little archaeologically about Alabama culture during the eighteenth century. Ceramics made by Alabama potters have been found at Fort Toulouse, however, where they greatly outnumber European-made ceramics. Nearly all are from large Chattahoochee Roughened jars, which evidently were obtained by the French soldiers and colonists for food storage. The Alabamas also produced Colono vessel forms—jars, bowls, and plates modeled on European styles—specifically for trade to the French (Sheldon 1985; Waselkov 1992:43–44).

The native ceramic assemblage from Fort Toulouse further indicates that Alabama potters had largely abandoned their traditional shell-tempered wares by midcentury and adopted the sand-tempered wares of the Tallapoosas, perhaps one overtly material sign of social coalescence with their eastern Muskogean neighbors (Knight 1994). A significant minority of ceramics contain mixtures of shell and sand tempering, which one would expect near the end of a transitional period (Waselkov 1984a:26–27; Waselkov et al. 1982:27). Many Alabamas and Koasatis moved away when the French withdrew from Fort Toulouse, abandoning their colony to the Spanish and British in 1763. Chattahoochee Roughened pottery remained in use at Alabama-Koasati sites in Louisiana and Texas as late as the 1830s (Jurney and Perttula 1995).

250 Gregory A. Waselkov and Marvin T. Smith

Tallapoosas

The Tallapoosas lived on the lower Tallapoosa River where the river follows along the Fall Line ecotone just east of present-day Montgomery, Alabama (fig. 9.3). The core towns of these people appear to be descended from local prehistoric populations, but other refugees, particularly some of the Abihka people, joined them during the eighteenth century. Through archaeology, much more is known of this Upper Creek group than of any other. During the early twentieth century, excavations by the Alabama Anthropological Society recovered a wealth of Tallapoosa material culture. Unfortunately, the society's methods were geared entirely toward locating and excavating graves to collect grave goods (Brannon 1935; also see Heldman and Ray 1975). Many of those early collections, biased though they are, still retain research value and have recently been reanalyzed (Waselkov and Sheldon 1987). Modern excavations have been conducted at Big Tallassee (Fairbanks 1962a, 1962b; Knight and Smith 1980), Tukabatchee (Knight 1985b), Hoithlewaulee (Waselkov 1985), Hickory Ground (Cottier and Sheldon 1992; Sheldon et al. 1988, 1990; Silvia Mueller 1991, 1992, 1995), and especially at the town of Fusihatchee (Waselkov et al. 1990).

Knight (1985b) suggested a three-phase cultural sequence, beginning with the Shine II phase (1400–1550), followed by the Atasi phase (1600–1715) and the Tallapoosa phase (1715–1837). The gap from 1550 to 1600 in this sequence, Knight thinks, is due to a lack of data at present and does not reflect a discontinuity in the valley's occupation.

The Shine II phase is a variant of Lamar culture characterized by primarily plain undecorated pottery (about 85 percent, according to Knight). Minority types include Lamar Complicated Stamped, Mercier Check Stamped, and infrequent bold incising. Tempering is primarily coarse sand or grit, but shell and/or grog tempering is known (Knight 1985b:10).

The Atasi phase is best known from a reported structure at Tukabatchee (Knight 1985b), test excavations at Big Tallassee (Knight and Smith 1980), and the incompletely reported Fusihatchee excavations. Ceramic characteristics from this phase include the replacement of complicated stamping with brushing as the new style of surface treatment, the appearance of bold incising with widely spaced line elements, and a continued preeminence of grit over shell as tempering material. European trade goods, which are entirely Spanish in origin early in the seventeenth century and gradually augmented by English goods beginning in the 1680s, are common. But they occur most

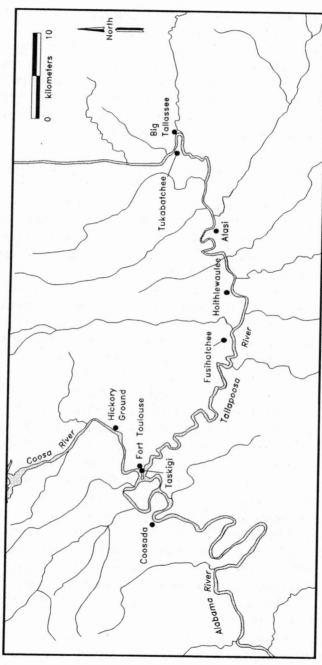

Fig. 9.3. The lower Coosa and Tallapoosa valleys, with Upper Creek sites dating from the seventeenth to the nineteenth century.

often as burial accompaniments and rarely have been recovered from domestic contexts. During excavations at Tukabatchee, Knight (1985b) reported excavation of a round winter house identified from a maze of postholes. The round house would be unique for the Upper Creek area; it was probably, in fact, square with rounded corners, which is the post pattern observed in several dozen semisubterranean winter houses excavated at Fusihatchee. Villages appear to have been densely nucleated settlements, although palisades are absent and no platform mound construction has been documented.

The Tallapoosa phase includes most of the eighteenth-century occupation of the lower Tallapoosa Valley. This phase is best known from work at Tukabatchee, Hoithlewaulee, Fusihatchee, and Hickory Ground. Ceramic traits include brushing as the most common surface treatment, narrower incising occupying a smaller area of the vessel, and the appearance of the type Kasihta Red Filmed. Minority shell tempering gradually disappears during this phase (Knight 1985b:12–13).

The presence of readily dated European-made artifacts, such as glass beads, at these historic sites usually permits excavated contexts to be dated quite precisely, often within a quarter century. So Knight's three-phase system, with its coarser temporal resolution, has proven most useful in organizing surface collections obtained from regional surveys. Waselkov (1981) presented a settlement pattern study based on surface collections in the lower Tallapoosa Valley, and additional survey data were provided by Dimmick (1989). From these surveys, spatial limits of *talwas* can be identified that correspond to historically described boundaries. There is also a steady trend toward settlement dispersal that culminates, by the 1830s, in most town centers being occupied only by a council house and square ground.

Changes in settlement pattern reflect a transition from traditional farming methods to the adoption of cattle raising and plow agriculture. Cultivation of large communal fields in floodplain bottomlands, combined with household gardening in or near villages, began to disappear in the 1790s as individual families moved into adjacent uplands looking for grazing range for their cattle. The effects of this rearrangement on Creek social life were profound, as traditional matrilineages lost control of communal fields and private livestock replaced free-ranging deer as a principal subsistence resource (Waselkov 1997).

Analyses of plant remains from Fusihatchee and Tukabatchee (Gremillion 1993, 1995; Lentz 1985) document the selective incorporation of

Old World domesticates into the native agricultural system. Indigenous farmers practiced traditional maize agriculture, supplemented with a heavy reliance on hickory nuts and acorn collecting and a variety of other crops, including beans, squash/gourd, chenopod, knotweed, and little barley. Contact with Spanish colonists in Florida introduced cowpeas (black-eyed peas), peaches, and watermelons, crops that may have been chosen from among the wide array of available Old World domesticates for their similarity to New World counterparts (Gremillion 1995:13).

Cattle, hogs, and chickens appear in the archaeological record by the middle of the eighteenth century, but they were only a minor component of the diet until half a century later. Unfortunately, few analyses are available yet on Upper Creek faunal remains. Preliminary studies of Fusihatchee animal bones suggest that the Tallapoosas exploited a diverse resource base, but that deer contributed most of the biomass—three-quarters of the total during the late seventeenth century, and half by the mid-eighteenth century (Reitz 1997). Horses were acquired early for transport (replacing human bearers in the deerskin trade soon after the Yamassee War), and saddles and other tack are present as grave goods (Waselkov 1998:196–97).

Extensive excavations at Fusihatchee revealed a range of public and private architectural forms (fig. 9.4). A series of six sequentially occupied winter council houses or rotundas (Sheldon 1990) and a square ground compound of four open-sided cabins comprise the sample of public structures. Early examples of winter council houses were large square, semisubterranean structures (from 11.5 to 15.5 meters in width) with rounded corners. Mid- and late eighteenth-century examples have circular floor plans and no evidence of a sunken floor. Two vacant areas near these council houses may be ball grounds or chunkey game yards (a feature also noted from surface collection data at Hoithlewaulee; Cottier 1985). Also nearby were two very large pits that served as clay sources for domestic and public building construction and for potting clay. William Bartram mentioned the existence, at several Upper Creek towns in 1775, of such pits or artificial ponds where medicinal plants were grown (Waselkov and Braund 1995:106). A large fenced area on the periphery of the site may be a white trader's compound.

Sheldon (1997) studied a large sample of 124 domestic structures at Fusihatchee. Two dozen of these are seventeenth-century semisubterranean winter houses, all of which were destroyed by fire upon abandonment. Some were paired with rectangular summer houses. Around the turn of the eighteenth century, winter house–style construction ended, and all subsequent

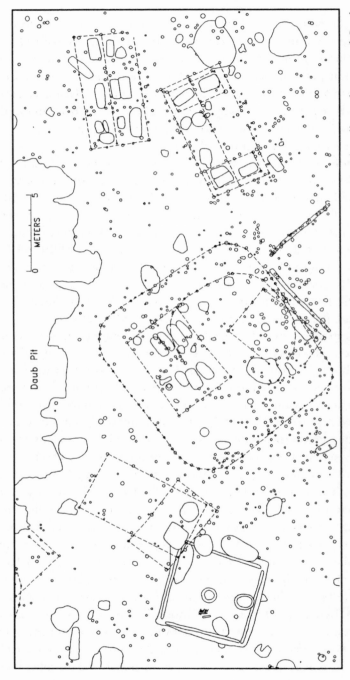

Fig. 9.4. A portion of the Fusihatchee site (1EE191) excavations, showing two Mississippian houses with wall trenches, several Creek "summer" houses with rectangular floor plans, a large eighteenth-century council house (square with rounded corners) over a roughly circular protohistoric "winter" house, and part of an extensive clay pit that was mined for construction daub and potters' clay.

Daub Pit

METERS

private domiciles took the form of aboveground rectangular buildings with subfloor storage/refuse pits and burials (several examples of which are also known from the Hickory Ground site; Silvia Mueller 1995). Many of these were grouped, together with rectangular open-sided arbors, into household compounds of two, three, or four structures (Meyers 1996; Sheldon 1997). Small smudge pits filled with charred corncobs were frequently found in clusters near the arbors, perhaps indicating areas of hide processing. The transition from semisubterranean houses to household compounds seems to be related to the increased importance of the deerskin trade in the eighteenth century (Waselkov 1990).

The correlation of subfloor storage/refuse pits and burials with particular structures permits comparisons of artifacts from different households as well as comparisons of grave goods among members of the same household (Waselkov 1985:34–54). Study of the 342 burials excavated at Fusihatchee should produce a wealth of information on population health and family organization. A preliminary analysis indicates high mortality rates throughout the village's occupation, with few individuals reaching their fifties (Reeves and Larsen 1997).

During the early nineteenth century (circa 1815–35), the Tallapoosas and other Upper Creeks began to adopt elements of log house architecture from intruding American settlers. Excavations at the site of one such house, 1MC120, situated on an upland terrace overlooking Calebee Creek, uncovered no subsurface features of any kind. The associated ceramic assemblage includes imported pearlware and Chattahoochee Roughened sherds, with a few pieces of redware and stoneware. The single Colono sherd is a plate base with foot ring (Waselkov 1984b). Sites of this period suggest a growing economic rift between the few wealthy elite families and the materially impoverished balance of the population (Saunt 1999), represented by the occupants of 1MC120.

Okfuskees

The Okfuskees lived along the upper Tallapoosa River, upstream from the Tallapoosas. Little is known of the prehistory and seventeenth-century lifeways of this group through archaeology. Using historic documents, ethnologist John Swanton decided that the Okfuskees were closely related to the Coosa-Abihka people (Swanton 1922). The most thorough excavation of an

Okfuskee town was conducted at Nuyaka by Roy Dickens (1979:77–100; Dickens and Chapman 1978), based on earlier work by Charles Fairbanks (1962a, 1962b). Nuyaka was founded in 1777 and burned by the Georgia militia in 1813. Excavations failed to locate any houses, but eighteen sub-plowzone features were revealed. Creek ceramics were the most commonly recovered artifacts, and these appear to be closely related to the Tallapoosa phase material found downstream (Knight 1985a; Knight, Cole, and Walling 1984). Remains of chickens and cattle were present, but deer continued to provide much of the available meat (Edmiston 1979:190; Fairbanks 1962a:54).

Dickens also investigated the nearby Creek War battlefield site of Horse-shoe Bend (Dickens 1979:18–76). By the early nineteenth century, pressures to adopt American-style agriculture and to abandon traditional cultural values led to a violent fission of the Upper Creeks into a pro-American faction and a nativist one, called the Red Sticks. After an initial Red Stick success in 1813 and the battle of Fort Mims, American armies converged on the Upper Creek country. Following the destruction of Nuyaka, Okfuskee refugees from several *talwas* constructed a barricade across the narrowest part of a nearby bend in the Tallapoosa River, behind which grew a new community called Tohopeka. In the final major battle of the war in 1814, General Andrew Jackson's army stormed the barricade and destroyed the village. Excavated portions of the barricade revealed a sophisticated struc-ture consisting of a trench, stacked log wall, and fraising (Waselkov 1986). Silver, brass, and glass ornaments that had been so popular before the war were completely absent, and the fragments of bottle glass recovered at Toho-peka were mostly small flakes reused as scrapers or carefully cached for later use as tools (Dickens 1979:162). The few Euro-American trade goods found at Tohopeka probably reflect not only the impoverished condition of the refugee inhabitants but overt rejection of non-native technology by the re-ligious leaders of the anti-American faction during the Creek War (Waselkov and Wood 1986:16).

Conclusions

Recent archaeological studies have provided a wealth of information on the people known as the Upper Creeks. The Coosa-Abihkas and Tallapoosas are the best documented through archaeology, followed by the Okfuskees and

Alabamas. From the available information, some general trends can be identified. Settlement patterns shifted from compact, often fortified, towns in the sixteenth century to more dispersed settlement around ceremonial centers by the eighteenth century, and finally to widely dispersed individual house sites affiliated with isolated council houses by the time of forced removal from the Southeast in the 1830s. House styles also underwent dramatic change. Protohistoric occupants of this region regularly constructed semisubterranean "winter" houses and less elaborate rectangular "summer" houses. By roughly A.D. 1700, the semisubterranean house style had been abandoned, although this style of construction continued to be utilized for public buildings. Log houses eventually replaced the summer-style house forms, as well, by the 1830s.

Traditional subsistence practices changed from an emphasis on hunting deer for food and raising corn, beans, squash, and other plants during the protohistoric period toward the incorporation of certain select European domesticates, plant and animal, into the Upper Creek agricultural system. During the seventeenth century, some Old World cultigens such as peaches, watermelons, and cowpeas were adopted, and during the eighteenth century domesticated pigs, cattle, and chickens became increasingly common around Upper Creek households. European demand for deerskins first drew the Upper Creeks into trade with Spanish colonists in Florida, from whom they obtained ornaments, tools, and cloth made from previously unobtainable materials, such as brass, iron, glass, and wool (Smith 1987; Waselkov 1989b). Replacement of native material culture with items of European manufacture occurred gradually. The first items to be accepted were ornamental in nature, followed by iron cutting tools like axes and knives. All were common by the middle of the seventeenth century.

With the arrival of English traders in the late seventeenth century (and French traders a few decades later), access to trade goods—including firearms—increased exponentially, and within a century the Upper Creeks found themselves dependent on this trade (Waselkov 1998). By the early eighteenth century, firearms had largely replaced the bow and arrow for hunting and warfare. At about this time, glass bottles and occasional European ceramics begin to appear at Upper Creek sites, but native pottery continued to be made well into the nineteenth century. The persistence of traditional pottery manufacture and use may reflect continuing control of the village-level economy by matrilineages long after Creek men's labor had been co-opted by the European deerskin trade. Silver ornaments became the style of decoration by the late 1760s, and by roughly the time of the American Revolution, domesticated horses were common in the Upper Creek country.

Increasing demands for land cessions and extreme hunting pressure on the region's deer population eventually forced the Creeks to adopt cattle raising and plow agriculture in an effort to assimilate their economy with that of the encroaching Americans (Ethridge 1997; Usner 1985). Individual households also attempted to escape the authority of elite lineages to achieve greater social and economic independence (Wesson 1997). Internal social conflicts between traditionalists and those who favored accommodation with the Americans eventually led to the appearance of a religious revitalization movement and finally to civil war (Martin 1991). By the war's end in 1814, every Upper Creek village had been abandoned or destroyed (Waselkov and Wood 1986:12–14), and the stage was set for removal of nearly the entire Upper Creek population in 1836–37.

Forced removal of the Creeks in the early nineteenth century effectively ends their archaeological record in their homeland. A few Creeks managed to avoid removal, including some in southern Alabama whose descendants eventually became the modern Poarch Band of Creeks. Others adopted an American lifestyle and thus became essentially invisible in the archaeological record. The majority moved west to the present-day Oklahoma area, where they continued to adapt their culture much as they had during the previous centuries. Even after centuries of intimate contact with Europeans and Americans, the Creeks retained distinctive elements of traditional material culture that they continued to practice in their new homeland (Schmitt 1950; Schmitt and Bell 1954; Wyckoff and Barr 1968).

Acknowledgments

Sarah Mattics drafted figures 9.1 and 9.3. Figure 9.2 is based on an original map by Julie Barnes Smith. The partial Fusihatchee site plan in figure 9.4 is reproduced courtesy of Craig T. Sheldon, Jr., and John W. Cottier.

Bibliography

Brannon, Peter A.
1935   *The Southern Indian Trade.* Montgomery: Paragon Press.

Braund, Kathryn E. Holland
1993   *Deerskins and Duffels: Creek Indian Trade with Anglo-America, 1685–1815.* Lincoln: University of Nebraska Press.

Corkran, David H.
1967   *The Creek Frontier, 1540–1783.* Norman: University of Oklahoma Press.

Cottier, John W.
1985   Display and Analysis of Spatial Data from Hoithlewaulee. In *Culture Change on the Creek Indian Frontier,* edited by G. A. Waselkov, 17–33. Report to the National Science Foundation, Washington, D.C. Grant BNS-83054437.

Cottier, John W., and Craig T. Sheldon, Jr.
1992   *The Archaeology of the Coosa Bluff Development Project, Wetumpka, Elmore County, Alabama.* Report submitted to the Alabama Historical Commission, Montgomery.

Crane, Verner W.
1981   *The Southern Frontier, 1670–1732.* New York: W. W. Norton. Originally published 1929.

DeJarnette, David L., and Asael T. Hansen
1960   *The Archaeology of the Childersburg Site, Alabama.* Notes in Anthropology 4. Florida State University, Tallahassee.

Dickens, Roy S., Jr.
1979   *Archaeological Investigations at Horseshoe Bend.* Special Publication 3. Alabama Archaeological Society, Tuscaloosa.

Dickens, Roy S., Jr., and James H. Chapman
1978   Ceramic Patterning and Social Structure at Two Late Historic Upper Creek Sites in Alabama. *American Antiquity* 43(3):390–98.

Dimmick, Fredericka R.
1989   A Survey of Upper Creek Sites in Central Alabama. *Journal of Alabama Archaeology* 35:1–86.

Edmiston, Paula F.
1979   Zooarchaeological Remains. In *Archaeological Investigations at Horseshoe Bend,* by Roy S. Dickens, Jr., 187–94. Special Publication 3. Alabama Archaeological Society, Tuscaloosa.

Ethridge, Robbie F.
1997   A Contest for Land: The Creek Indians on the Southern Frontier, 1796–1816. Ph.D. diss., Department of Anthropology, University of Georgia. University Microfilms 9722463.

Fairbanks, Charles H.
1962a   Excavations at Horseshoe Bend, Alabama. *Florida Anthropologist* 15(2):41–56.
1962b   Late Creek Sites in Central Alabama. *Southeastern Archaeological Conference Newsletter* 9(1):64–68.

Gremillion, Kristen J.
1993   Adoption of Old World Crops and Processes of Cultural Change in the Historic Southeast. *Southeastern Archaeology* 12(1):15–20.
1995   Comparative Paleoethnobotany of Three Native Southeastern Communities of the Historic Period. *Southeastern Archaeology* 14(1):1–16.
Heldman, Donald P., and R. Craig Ray
1975   A Late Historic Burial in Montgomery County, Alabama. *Journal of Alabama Archaeology* 21(1):79–97.
Holstein, Harry O., Curtis E. Hill, and Keith J. Little
1997   The Hurley Site (1Ce137): A Protohistoric Habitation Site in the Weiss Lake Basin, Cherokee County, Alabama. *Journal of Alabama Archaeology* 43(1):1–34.
Holstein, Harry O., Curtis E. Hill, Keith J. Little, and Caleb Curren
1990   *Ethnohistoric Archaeology and Hypothesis Testing: Archaeological Investigation of the Terrapin Creek Site.* Report submitted to the Alabama De Soto Commission, Tuscaloosa.
Hudson, Charles M.
1997   *Knights of Spain, Warriors of the Sun: Hernando de Soto and the South's Ancient Chiefdoms.* Athens: University of Georgia Press.
Jurney, David H., and Timothy K. Perttula
1995   Nineteenth-Century Alibamu-Koasati Pottery Assemblages and Culinary Traditions. *Southeastern Archaeology* 14(1):17–30.
Knight, Vernon J., Jr.
1985a   *East Alabama Archaeological Survey 1985 Season.* Report of Investigations 47. Office of Archaeological Research, University of Alabama, Tuscaloosa.
1985b   *Tukabatchee: Archaeological Investigations at an Historic Creek Town, Elmore County, Alabama.* Office of Archaeological Research, Report of Investigations 45. Alabama State Museum of Natural History, Tuscaloosa.
1990   Phase Characteristics, Middle Coosa River, Upper Tallapoosa River, and Lower Tallapoosa River. In *Lamar Archaeology: Mississippian Chiefdoms in the Deep South,* edited by M. Williams and G. Shapiro, 46–51. Tuscaloosa: University of Alabama Press.
1994   The Formation of the Creeks. In *The Forgotten Centuries: Indians and Europeans in the American South, 1521–1704,* edited by C. Hudson and C. Tesser, 373–92. Athens: University of Georgia Press.
1997   Fort Leslie, and Upper Creek Ceramics of the Early Nineteenth Century. *Journal of Alabama Archaeology* 43(1):35–47.
Knight, Vernon J., Jr., and Marvin T. Smith
1980   Big Tallassee: A Contribution to Upper Creek Site Archaeology. *Early Georgia* 8(1–2):59–74.
Knight, Vernon J., Jr., Gloria Cole, and Richard Walling
1984   *An Archaeological Reconnaissance of the Coosa and Tallapoosa River Valleys, East Alabama: 1983.* Report of Investigations 43. Office of Archaeological Research, University of Alabama, Tuscaloosa.
Lentz, David L.
1985   Archaeobotanical Remains from the Tukabatchee Sites. *Journal of Alabama Archaeology* 31(2):91–100.

Little, Keith, and Cailup B. Curren
1981   Site 1Ce308: A Protohistoric Site on the Upper Coosa River in Alabama. *Journal of Alabama Archaeology* 27:117–24.
Lolley, Terry L.
1996   Ethnohistory and Archaeology: A Map Method for Locating Historic Upper Creek Indian Towns and Villages. *Journal of Alabama Archaeology* 42:1–93.
Martin, Joel W.
1991   *Sacred Revolt: The Muskogees' Struggle for a New World.* Boston: Beacon Press.
Meyers, Allan D.
1996   Household Organization and Refuse Disposal at a Cultivated Creek Site. *Southeastern Archaeology* 15(2):132–44.
Morrell, L. Ross
1964   Two Historic Island Sites in the Coosa River. *Florida Anthropologist* 27 (2):75–76.
1965   *The Woods Island Site in Southeastern Acculturation, 1625–1800.* Notes in Anthropology 11. Florida State University, Tallahassee.
Reeves, Marianne E., and Clark Spencer Larsen
1997   *Archaeological Human Skeletal Remains Inventory of the Fusihatchee Town Site (1EE191): Summary Report.* Research Laboratories of Anthropology, University of North Carolina, Chapel Hill.
Reitz, Elizabeth J.
1997   *Vertebrate Fauna from Fusihatchee (1EE191).* Zooarchaeology Laboratory, Museum of Natural History, University of Georgia, Athens.
Saunt, Claudio
1999   *A New Order of Things: Property, Power, and the Transformation of the Creek Indians, 1733–1816.* Cambridge: Cambridge University Press.
Schmitt, Karl
1950   Two Creek Pottery Vessels from Oklahoma. *Florida Anthropologist* 3(1–2):3–8.
Schmitt, Karl, and Robert E. Bell
1954   Historic Indian Pottery from Oklahoma. *Oklahoma Anthropological Society Bulletin* 2:19–30.
Sheldon, Craig T., Jr.
1974   The Mississippian-Historic Transition in Central Alabama. Ph.D. diss., Department of Anthropology, University of Oregon. University Microfilms International 375–4526.
1985   Colono-Indian Vessels from Central Alabama. In *Culture Change on the Creek Indian Frontier,* edited by G. A. Waselkov, 121–37. Report to the National Science Foundation, Washington, D.C. Grant BNS-8305437.
1990   The Council Houses of Fusihatchee. In *Archaeological Excavations at the Early Historic Creek Indian Town of Fusihatchee (Phase I, 1988–1989),* by G. A. Waselkov, J. W. Cottier, and C. T. Sheldon, Jr., 45–76. Report to the National Science Foundation, Washington, D.C. Grant BNS-8718934.
1997   Historic Creek "Summer" Houses of Central Alabama. Paper presented at the Annual Meeting of the Society for American Archaeology, April 4, 1997. Nashville.

Sheldon, Craig T., Jr., John W. Cottier, and Gregory A. Waselkov
1988   A Preliminary Report on the Subsurface Testing of a Portion of the Creek
        Indian Property at Hickory Ground. Report submitted to the Poarch Band of
        Creek Indians, Poarch, Ala.
1990   Additional Archaeological Investigations of the Hickory Ground Site, Elmore
        County, Alabama. Report submitted to the Poarch Band of Creek Indians,
        Poarch, Ala.
Sheldon, Elizabeth S.
1978   Childersburg: Evidence of European Contact Demonstrated by Archaeologi-
        cal Plant Remains. Southeastern Archaeological Conference Special Publica-
        tion 5:28–29.
Silvia Mueller, Diane
1991   Report on the Archaeological Investigations at the Hickory Ground (1EE89),
        Elmore County, Alabama (1990–1991). Part 1: Areas A and C. Report sub-
        mitted to the Poarch Band of Creek Indians, Poarch, Ala.
1992   Report on the Archaeological Investigations at the Hickory Ground (1EE89),
        Elmore County, Alabama (1990–1991). Part 2: Parcel 21 and a Planned Road
        and Sewer Line. Report submitted to the Poarch Band of Creek Indians,
        Poarch, Ala.
1995   Intrasite Settlement at the Historic Creek Town of Hickory Ground (1EE89),
        Elmore County, Alabama (1990–1991). Journal of Alabama Archaeology
        41(2):107–34.
Smith, Marvin T.
1987   Archaeology of Aboriginal Culture Change in the Interior Southeast: Depopu-
        lation during the Early Historic Period. Ripley P. Bullen Monographs in An-
        thropology and History. Gainesville: University Presses of Florida.
1989a   Aboriginal Population Movements in the Early Historic Period Interior South-
        east. In Powhatan's Mantle: Indians in the Colonial Southeast, edited by P. H.
        Wood, G. A. Waselkov, and M. T. Hatley, 21–34. Lincoln: University of Ne-
        braska Press.
1989b   In the Wake of De Soto: Alabama's Seventeenth-Century Indians on the Coosa
        River. Report Submitted to the Alabama De Soto Commission, Tuscaloosa.
1993   Seventeenth-Century Aboriginal Settlement on the Coosa River. In Archaeo-
        logical Survey and Excavations in the Coosa River Valley, Alabama, edited by
        V. J. Knight, Jr., 63–70. Alabama Museum of Natural History Bulletin 15.
        Tuscaloosa.
1995   Woods Island Revisited. Journal of Alabama Archaeology 41(2):93–106.
Smith, Marvin T., Vernon J. Knight, Jr., Julie B. Smith, and Kenneth R. Turner
1993   The Milner Village: A Mid-Seventeenth-Century Site near Gadsden, Alabama.
        In Archaeological Survey and Excavations in the Coosa River Valley, Ala-
        bama, edited by V. J. Knight, Jr., 49–61. Alabama Museum of Natural History
        Bulletin 15. Tuscaloosa.
Swanton, John R.
1922   Early History of the Creek Indians and Their Neighbors. Smithsonian Insti-
        tution, Bureau of American Ethnology Bulletin 73. Washington, D.C.

Usner, Daniel H., Jr.
1985   American Indians on the Cotton Frontier: Changing Economic Relations with Citizens and Slaves in the Mississippi Territory. *Journal of American History* 72(2):297–317.

Walling, Richard
1993   Lamar in the Middle Coosa River Drainage: The Ogletree Island Site (1Ta238), a Kymulga Phase Farmstead. In *Archaeological Survey and Excavations in the Coosa River Valley, Alabama,* edited by V. J. Knight, Jr., 33–48. Alabama Museum of Natural History Bulletin 15. Tuscaloosa.

Waselkov, Gregory A.
1980   *Coosa River Archaeology.* 2 vols. Auburn University Archaeological Monograph 2. Auburn, Alabama.

1981   *Lower Tallapoosa River Cultural Resources Survey: Phase I Report.* Report submitted to the Alabama Historical Commission. Montgomery.

1984a   *Fort Toulouse Studies.* Auburn University Archaeological Monograph 9. Montgomery, Alabama.

1984b   *Intensive Subsurface Archaeological Investigations at the I-85 Shorter-Milstead Interchange, Alabama.* Report submitted to the Alabama Highway Department, Montgomery.

1985   *Culture Change on the Creek Indian Frontier.* Report to the National Science Foundation, Washington, D.C. Grant BNS-8305437.

1986   A Reinterpretation of the Creek Indian Barricade at Horseshoe Bend. *Journal of Alabama Archaeology* 32(2):95–107.

1989a   Introduction: Recent Archaeological and Historical Research. In *Fort Toulouse: The French Outpost at the Alabamas on the Coosa,* by Daniel H. Thomas, vii–xlii. Tuscaloosa: University of Alabama Press.

1989b   Seventeenth-Century Trade in the Colonial Southeast. *Southeastern Archaeology* 8(2):117–33.

1990   Historic Creek Architectural Adaptations to the Deerskin Trade. In *Archaeological Excavations at the Early Historic Creek Indian Town of Fusihatchee (Phase 1, 1988–1989),* by G. A. Waselkov, J. W. Cottier, and C. T. Sheldon, Jr., 39–44. Report submitted to the National Science Foundation, Washington, D.C.

1992   French Colonial Trade in the Upper Creek Country. In *Calumet and Fleur-de-Lys: Archaeology of Indian and French Contact in the Midcontinent,* edited by J. A. Walthall and T. E. Emerson, 35–53. Washington, D.C.: Smithsonian Institution Press.

1993   Historic Creek Indian Responses to European Trade and the Rise of Political Factions. In *Ethnohistory and Archaeology: Approaches to Postcontact Change in the Americas,* edited by J. D. Rogers and S. M. Wilson, 123–31. New York: Plenum Press.

1994   A History of the Alabama Anthropological Society. *Southeastern Archaeology* 13(1):64–76.

1997   Changing Strategies of Indian Field Location in the Early Historic Southeast. In *People, Plants, and Landscapes: Studies in Paleoethnobotany,* edited by K. J. Gremillion, 179–94. Tuscaloosa: University of Alabama Press.

1998   The Eighteenth-Century Anglo-Indian Trade in Southeastern North America. In *New Faces of the Fur Trade: Selected Papers of the Seventh North American Fur Trade Conference, Halifax, Nova Scotia, 1995*, edited by J. Fiske, S. Sleeper-Smith, and W. Wicken, 193–222. East Lansing: Michigan State University Press.

Waselkov, Gregory A., and Kathryn E. Holland Braund (editors)
1995   *William Bartram on the Southeastern Indians*. Lincoln: University of Nebraska Press.

Waselkov, Gregory A., and John W. Cottier
1985   European Perceptions of Eastern Muskogean Ethnicity. In *Proceedings of the Tenth Meeting of the French Colonial Historical Society, April 12–14, 1984*, edited by P. P. Boucher, 23–45. Lanham, Md.: University Press of America.

Waselkov, Gregory A., and Craig T. Sheldon, Jr.
1987   *Cataloguing and Documenting the Historic Creek Archaeological Collections of the Alabama Department of Archives and History*. Report to the National Science Foundation, Washington, D.C. Grant BNS-8507469.

Waselkov, Gregory A., and Brian M. Wood
1986   The Creek War of 1813–1814: Effects on Creek Society and Settlement Pattern. *Journal of Alabama Archaeology* 32(1):1–24.

Waselkov, Gregory A., John W. Cottier, and Craig T. Sheldon, Jr.
1990   *Archaeological Excavations at the Early Historic Creek Indian Town of Fusihatchee (Phase 1, 1988–1989)*. Report to the National Science Foundation, Washington, D.C. Grant BNS-8718934.

Waselkov, Gregory A., Brian M. Wood, and Joseph M. Herbert
1982   *Colonization and Conquest: The 1980 Archaeological Excavations at Fort Toulouse and Fort Jackson, Alabama*. Auburn University Archaeological Monograph 4. Auburn, Alabama.

Webb, William S., and Charles G. Wilder
1951   *An Archaeological Survey of Guntersville Basin on the Tennessee River in Northern Alabama*. Lexington: University Press of Kentucky.

Wesson, Cameron B.
1997   Households and Hegemony: An Analysis of Historic Creek Culture Change. Ph.D. diss., Department of Anthropology, University of Illinois at Urbana-Champaign. University Microfilms International 9737286.

Wyckoff, Don G., and Thomas P. Barr
1968   *The Posey Site (Wg-19): A Historic Site in the Three Forks Locale, Eastern Oklahoma*. Oklahoma River Basin Survey, Archaeological Site Report 10. University of Oklahoma Research Institute, Norman.

10

The Lower Creeks

Origins and Early History

JOHN E. WORTH

The Lower Creeks were one of the most important and influential Native American groups in the historic period Southeast, and have justifiably received considerable attention from modern scholars, including a wide range of historians and anthropologists. During the past seven decades, archaeology has made significant contributions to our present-day understanding of their origins, culture, and history. Despite this fact, however, surprisingly few overall syntheses of this work have ever been published, and most of the literature that does exist is not widely accessible, either to archaeologists and other researchers or to the general public. Even today, the most comprehensive archaeological list of eighteenth-century Lower Creek town identifications along the lower Chattahoochee River is still a pair of typescript manuscripts written by Harold Huscher some four decades ago (Huscher 1958, 1959; Knight and Mistovich 1984:227), and the identities of earlier Lower Creek towns along the Ocmulgee River are still being debated (see, for example, Pluckhahn 1997: 353–60; Smith 1992:39–45). Moreover, despite the fact that Works Progress Administration excavations of the Lower Creek town and English stockade at Macon Plateau during the 1930s were among the earliest scientific archaeological projects in the Southeast (see Hally 1994a), the final report on this project was delayed three decades, and this manuscript is still only available as a microform dissertation, despite more recent compilations and summaries of these data (Mason 1963a; Pluckhahn 1997; Powell 1994; Waselkov 1994). Even with the release of this delayed report, however, the archaeological phase (Blackmon) associated with the seventeenth-century antecedents of these Lower Creek towns was only formally defined in the 1980s (Knight and Mistovich 1984; Mistovich and Knight 1986; Schnell 1990).

For these reasons, the present chapter was assembled in large part from a diversity of primary archaeological site reports (several of which are unpublished), as well as the secondary summaries and overviews that are available. I have intentionally focused my attention on the earliest phases of Lower Creek history (that is, their origins and early migrations through about 1716), since this is undoubtedly the least well-known period, and since I believe that it is here that archaeology will ultimately make many of its most important contributions. Nevertheless, my overview also includes selected sites occupied through the removal era (1836), since a considerable amount of work has been (and continues to be) carried out regarding Lower Creek culture change and population expansion during the late eighteenth and early nineteenth centuries.

Lower Creek Origins through 1692

Archaeological research holds considerable promise as a pivotal source of direct information on the ultimate origins of the Lower Creeks, particularly since many of the earliest transformations of the historic period occurred beyond the light of ethnohistoric documentation. Early archaeological work resulted in several theories concerning the archaeological identity and roots of historic Indian groups such as the Creeks and Cherokees, much of which has now been either rejected outright or substantially revised in the light of more recent data. Comprehensive reviews of this early literature are given elsewhere (for example, Knight 1994b; Russell 1975), and for my purposes here it suffices to note that following several decades of additional research, the earliest debates on the stylistic and historical connection between prehistoric Lamar material culture (principally ceramics) and that of the historic Creeks and Cherokees have been effectively resolved; the ceramic assemblages of *both* historic Indian groups have their origins in prehistoric Lamar-related assemblages, though the actual connections are somewhat more convoluted than originally envisioned by early researchers (such as Fairbanks 1952, 1958; Sears 1955; Willey and Sears 1952). In point of fact, the ultimate roots of the Lamar-derived material culture of both the late seventeenth- and early eighteenth-century Lower Creeks of middle and eastern Georgia (where the "Ocmulgee Fields" ceramic series was first recognized) and the late eighteenth- and early nineteenth-century Cherokees in northwestern Georgia (where the "Galt" ceramic series was first recognized) are to be found in completely distinct locations, though nonetheless in areas with late prehistoric Lamar occupation (see, for example, Hally 1986; Knight 1994b).

The lower Chattahoochee Valley is now correctly viewed by most archaeologists as the ancestral home of the Lower Creeks, since it was here that the Apalachicola province was situated upon first European contact in the 1630s and 1640s (see, for example, Hann 1988; Schnell 1989). Despite the fact that these documented Apalachicola towns subsequently assimilated a diversity of extralocal groups, many of which arrived as refugees from early European slaving and frontier wars, it seems abundantly clear that the core constituency of the polity that later became known as the Lower Creek Indians was already residing along the lower Chattahoochee River by approximately A.D. 1650. Because the Chattahoochee River Lower Creek towns of a century later (circa A.D. 1750) largely represented an amalgam of local and extralocal groups under the overall political leadership of the same principal Apalachicola towns (though apparently operating under considerably different political systems), my own discussion of Lower Creek origins will begin with the Apalachicola province of about A.D. 1650 and its direct antecedents. While this largely overlooks the prehistoric origins of several immigrant groups who attached themselves to these original Apalachicola towns during the late seventeenth and early eighteenth centuries (Westo, Yuchi, et cetera), from an archaeological perspective there is good reason to argue that late eighteenth-century Lower Creek material culture (especially ceramics) represents a more-or-less direct stylistic evolution from the Abercrombie/Blackmon phases of about 1650. All other extralocal influences that may have been introduced by immigrants after that date appear to have been largely subsumed within the local ceramic sequence as it evolved from that point (each perhaps contributing individually to that stylistic evolution).

The archaeological chronology of indigenous occupation on the lower Chattahoochee River has been considerably refined in recent years. Given that Apalachicola/Lower Creek material culture of the historic period can ultimately be seen as a derivative of the broader late prehistoric Lamar culture (Hally 1994b; Williams and Shapiro 1990), it is from this point that my discussion will depart. The local variant of the Lamar culture first emerged on the lower Chattahoochee Valley during the Singer phase between A.D. 1300 and 1400 (Schnell and Wright 1993:15, 20–21), as occurred simultaneously across much of Georgia and surrounding states about

A.D. 1350 (see, for example, Hally 1994b:47; Hally and Rudolph 1986:63; Williams and Shapiro 1990:4). During this phase Lamar ceramic types first appeared alongside Fort Walton types, showing influences from the Florida panhandle region (and consistent with previous phases). The Singer phase was succeeded by the Bull Creek phase (A.D. 1400–75), and subsequently by the Stewart phase (A.D. 1475–1550), both of which represent the localized stylistic evolution of a typical late prehistoric Lamar assemblage with continuing influences from the Fort Walton culture to the south (Knight 1994a: 380–81, 1994b:188; Knight and Mistovich 1984:224–25; Mistovich and Knight 1986; Schnell 1990; Schnell and Wright 1993:15, 21–22, 30).

The Stewart phase is of particular interest here, since it straddles first European contact in 1540, thus forming a benchmark against which later, postcontact developments can be compared. By the time of the Hernando de Soto expedition during the Stewart phase (the Spanish army, however, completely bypassed the entire Chattahoochee Valley), indigenous lower Chattahoochee River populations were distributed in numerous farmsteads and mound sites stretching along the river for a distance of some 160 kilometers (Knight 1994a:380–81). Stewart phase occupations were characterized by what might be described as a typical southern Lamar ceramic assemblage, including the standard range of Middle Lamar decorative styles—complicated stamped (predominantly curvilinear motifs), incised, and check-stamped treatments as well as folded rims—along with incised and punctated decorations of the Fort Walton culture to the south. Significantly, Stewart phase ceramics were almost entirely grit-tempered, in stark contrast to later phases.

A crucial period of interest for the origins of the Apalachicola province of mid-seventeenth-century Spanish records, and thus also for the emergence of the Lower Creeks, is the succeeding Abercrombie phase (A.D. 1550–1650), which apparently witnessed dramatic transformations in both material culture and settlement patterns (Knight 1994a:383, 1994b:188; Knight and Mistovich 1984:225; Schnell 1990:383). At the few sites known to have been occupied during this phase (see below), a diverse range of new ceramic types appeared, including an entirely new series of shell-tempered types not present in the Stewart phase, but at least reminiscent of contemporaneous Dallas, McKee Island, and Alabama River ceramics from Alabama and eastern Tennessee. These new types included distinctive incised, brushed, black-burnished, and plain shell-tempered wares. Grit-tempered Lamar and Fort Walton types (incised and complicated and check-stamped decorations) seem to have continued during the Abercrombie phase but were significantly reduced in relation to the Abercrombie wares.

Of no small import, the material culture assemblage characteristic of the century-long Abercrombie phase appears only at an extremely limited number of sites, including the Abercrombie site (1Ru61) and the Cooper (also known as Woolfolks) site (9Me3), both of which originally contained mounds (Hurt 1975:17; Knight 1994a:383, 1994b:189). This contrasts markedly with the comparatively dense distribution of sites bearing the earlier Stewart phase material culture and implies a radical reduction in local population size along the Chattahoochee River corridor during the first century after European contact. As has been noted by many authors, this phenomenon is probably best explained by a dramatic local population collapse in the wake of early European epidemics. The Stewart phase Lamar polity on the lower Chattahoochee collapsed, and in its wake a small number of sites near the Fall Line witnessed the emergence of a new ceramic tradition that would eventually form the roots of Lower Creek material culture (that is, the subsequent Blackmon phase).

The most important question regarding the Abercrombie phase, and thus Lower Creek origins, is whether the massive ceramic transformation noted above resulted from in situ stylistic evolution among local populations (almost certainly with outside influences), or from the direct immigration of extralocal people into the Chattahoochee Valley, or both. While the nuances of this debate are beyond the scope of this essay, a review of the evidence is instructive. In recent years, Vernon J. Knight (1994a, 1994b) greatly clarified the prehistoric origins of broader historic Creek material culture (principally ceramics). He identified three regional subtraditions that eventually formed the basis for later historic Creek ceramics: the Coosa subtradition (ancestral to the Abihka group of Muskogee-speaking towns), the Tallapoosa subtradition (ancestral to the Tallapoosa group of Muskogee-speaking towns), and the Chattahoochee subtradition (ancestral to the Apalachicola group of Hitchiti-speaking towns). In this context, while acknowledging stylistic connections between the shell-tempered Abercrombie phase ceramics along the Chattahoochee and contemporaneous phases in Alabama and Tennessee containing Dallas, McKee Island, and Alabama River stylistic influences, Knight nonetheless concluded that the "hybrid" character of the Chattahoochee sequence probably resulted from external borrowing by resident local populations: "What these external relationships might signify for cultural process is still unclear, yet they are not so pervasive as to cancel out the essential continuity of the sequence as a local sub-tradition" (Knight 1994b:185). The Abercrombie phase mounds, therefore, can be seen as "stable political and population centers" that survived the late sixteenth-century population collapse along the Chattahoochee and that served as the basis for local population growth during the subsequent Black-mon phase (Knight 1994a:384).

Even more recently, Chad Braley (1998:9–11) reexamined the evidence for culture change during the period assigned to the Abercrombie phase, suggesting instead that large-scale population replacement may at least in part explain the observed transformations in the Chattahoochee Valley and elsewhere. In this context, the material culture that has been defined as the Abercrombie phase might be better conceived as a result of the mixing of terminal Stewart phase and initial Blackmon phase components at these archaeological sites, reflecting the reoccupation of abandoned sites by im-migrant populations. As has been amply demonstrated by Marvin Smith (1987, 1989), such population movements did occur during this period, and the Chattahoochee Valley is already known to have been an important area of population "coalescence" during subsequent decades (see, for example, Knight 1994a:384). Braley noted that not only did local aboriginal ceramics change radically during the Abercrombie phase (shell tempering rapidly eclipsed grit tempering, complicated stamping ultimately disappeared, wide folded rims plummeted in popularity, brushed decoration and strap handles appeared), but there were also simultaneous changes in other areas of ma-terial culture, including the abrupt appearance of Guntersville type arrow-heads at least as early as the Blackmon phase (in contrast to the almost total absence of Mississippian triangular arrowpoints in Stewart phase contexts). Depending on when mound construction at the Abercrombie site is dated (and this is not clear from existing literature), mound construction, too, may have ceased during the Abercrombie phase (Braley 1998:9; but see also Knight 1994a:383).

Perhaps most important, Braley (1998:10) correctly saw a correspon-dence between the dramatic changes in the Chattahoochee Valley between 1550 and 1650 and simultaneous changes that occurred in the Tallahassee Hills region of northwestern Florida (the Apalachee chiefdom of the early historic era). Just as Stewart phase occupation on the Chattahoochee waned and was ultimately replaced by Blackmon phase material culture with north-ern and western influences during the period denoted as the Abercrombie phase, Lake Jackson/early Velda phase populations in Apalachee were experiencing a similarly radical change in material culture (see, for example, Scarry 1994:170). During the period between 1540 and 1633, the late prehistoric Fort Walton material culture, still predominant at the capital town of Anhaica during its occupation by the army of Hernando de Soto in 1539–40 (see, for example, Ewen 1990:87), was gradually dominated by the Lamar-derived Leon-Jefferson material culture, which possessed the same wide folded pinched rims, curvilinear complicated stamping, and check stamping as previous Stewart phase populations along the Chattahoochee, though with mixed grog and grit tempering (Braley 1998:10). Once again, while John Scarry (1994:170) viewed these changes as in situ transformations among local populations resulting from shifts in external influences (principally from the Georgia Piedmont), Braley also developed a strong case for possible direct migration from the Chattahoochee Valley, which would make the Stewart phase directly ancestral to the Velda phase.

In fact, the two processes described above (in situ culture change and population relocation) may have been operating simultaneously. Importantly, linguistic and folkloric evidence relating to the Lower Creeks strongly implies dual origins, implying both local population continuity and external immigration. Lower Creek towns ultimately incorporated two major linguistic subdivisions: Hitchiti and Muskogee (Swanton 1922; and see Hann 1996:66–67). This division appears to have been present as early as the period 1675–86, since most of the major towns identified with each language group appear on the earliest Spanish lists. While a precise roster of Apalachicola province towns belonging to each linguistic group is somewhat difficult to reconstruct (see the complete list in table 10.1), the Hitchiti towns appear to have included at least Hitchiti, Apalachicola, Sawokli, Ocmulgee, and Oconee, while the Muskogee towns included Coweta, Kasihta, and Kolomi. The town of Tuskegee should probably also be listed alongside the Muskogee towns in 1685, since its inhabitants were later noted to have spoken Koasati, a related dialect that evidently originated in eastern Tennessee, and that derived its name from the Coste chiefdom there (Hudson 1990:109; Swanton 1922:207–11). The close political relationship between Coste, Tasquiqui (Tuskegee), and other Koasati-speaking towns and the nearby Coosa chiefdom, as well as their similarities in late prehistoric material culture, suggests a closer connection with the Muskogee towns than those of the Hitchiti language. The town of Osuchi may have been Hitchiti speaking, if for no other reason than its early location in the southern part of Apalachicola, and in any case was certainly not identical with the Timucua town of Uzachile, as originally suggested by Swanton (1922:26, 165–66; see Hann 1996 and Worth 1998). Other documented early Apalachicola province towns are of uncertain linguistic affiliation and origin, though Chicahuti, Talipasle, Ylapi, and Tacusa might be classified as Hitchiti based solely on their southern geographic location, while Cuchiguale/Chavagale might be placed in the Muskogee division due to its northern location.

Early Spanish documentary evidence from the Soto and Pardo expeditions reveals that at least two of the four Muskogee-related towns listed above (Kasihta and Tuskegee) were indeed originally located far to the north. During the mid-sixteenth century, Casiste (Casista was the subsequent Spanish name for Kasihta) was a town within the Talisi chiefdom along the middle Coosa River in Alabama, but it was relocated to the Chattahoochee River valley several decades before 1675. The town of Tasquiqui was originally situated just south of the town of Tasqui, probably in the upper Conasauga River drainage in southeastern Tennessee (Hudson 1990: 109, 1997:229; Smith 1987:138, 1989:28). This town, which was not present in 1675, may have been part of a larger group of fugitive Koasati who were noted in 1686 by Spanish visitor Marcos Delgado to have fled their northern homeland previously on account of "persecution" by the English-allied Chichimeco (or Westo; see Worth 1995:15–18) and Cherokee, first settling in the Coosa River valley before moving farther south into the Apalachicola province (Boyd 1937:26–27). While some of these Koasati refugees returned to the Coosa in 1686, the Tuskegee remained among the Apalachicola/Lower Creek for several decades.

In contrast to these documented Muskogee-Koasati relocations, however, none of the Hitchiti towns are known to have been immigrant to the Chattahoochee Valley. (A town called Ocute, which appeared very briefly among the Apalachicola in 1685, was at that time a similarly displaced Yamassee community originally from the eastern Georgia Piedmont.) This evidence, in concert with Creek legends explicitly describing the Muskogee speakers as immigrants into the Hitchiti area (see, for example, Gatschet 1969; Hawkins 1980:327; and Swanton 1922:173), would seem to provide strong support for the conclusion that the lower Chattahoochee Valley was indeed originally occupied by indigenous Hitchiti speakers (see Knight 1994a:380–81), to which were probably added an immigrant population of Muskogee speakers after A.D. 1540.

Specifically, Stewart phase populations of the Chattahoochee Valley may be hypothesized to have represented an indigenous Hitchiti chiefdom that

Table 10.1. List of documented towns in north-south order, with hypothesized archaeological site correlations, for the seventeenth-century Apalachicola province, Chattahoochee River, ca. 1630s–1691

Town	Possible site(s)
Cuchiguali	?
Tuskegee	area of 1Ru9
Coweta/Cabeta	*1Ru61* (Abercrombie)
Kolomi	*9Me3* (Cooper)
Kasihta/Casista	area of 9Ce33, alternate 9Me2 (Kyle's Landing)
Hitchiti	area of 9Ce1
Ocmulgee	area of 1Ru45
Osuchi	*1Ru63* (Yuchi Town)
Tacusa	area of 9Sw50
Ylapi	area of 9Sw12
Apalachicola	*1Ru66* (Patterson)
Oconee	area of 1Ru34
Talipasle	area of 1Ru2, 4, 5
Sawokli/Sabacola	*1Br25* (Blackmon)
Chicahuti	?

Source: Town list based on Hann 1996, with standardized spellings for later towns.
Note: Sites in italics have known Blackmon phase components.

was severely impacted by post–de Soto epidemic population decline, in response to which at least some of the population may have migrated downriver (like other contemporaneous groups) toward the Apalachee chiefdom of the Tallahassee Hills region during the late sixteenth century, accounting at least in part for the Velda phase ceramic transformation there. The subsequent appearance of Abercrombie phase material culture assemblage in the northern end of the lower Chattahoochee Valley (certainly prior to 1650) thus may have represented the early immigration of several Muskogee-speaking towns from Alabama into the partially depopulated Chattahoochee Valley, presumably coexisting for at least a time with remaining Stewart phase (that is, Hitchiti) populations. Based on traditional and available historical evidence, the earliest of these Muskogee immigrants was presumably Kasihta (Casista), and other towns in this northern cluster represented subsequent splits or relocations, such as Coweta, Kolomi, and finally Tuskegee after 1675.

Benjamin Hawkins's descriptions of three mounds clustered on both sides of the river about the mouth of present-day Mill Creek (his Chulucintigatoh) might provide possible locations for the first three Muskogee-speaking towns, especially when combined with his comment that Creeks believed this to be the place where the Kasihta first "crossed the river" and "took possession of the country" from "a race of people with flat heads in possession of the mounds in the Cussetuh fields" (Hawkins 1916:54, 63, 1980: 310, 327). The westernmost mound noted by Hawkins (1916:63)—Abercrombie (1Ru61)—was clearly located within the field boundaries below the residential portion of Coweta Tallahassee (1Ru11) and must be considered a strong candidate for the original Coweta town. The Cooper-Woolfolks mound (9Me3, Hawkins's "conic mound") and what is recorded in the Georgia Archaeological Site Files as Kyle's Landing mound (9Me2, presumably Hawkins's "oblong" mound) just upriver might well have been occupied by the original Kasihta town, and perhaps Kolomi, before the former's establishment downriver at Lawson Field (9Ce1). Some Abercrombie phase occupation has been noted (Frank Schnell, personal communication), and even earlier on the terrace overlooking it, according to Hawkins (1980:310). While only one of these eroded mound sites (Cooper-Woolfolks) has been noted to have a possible Abercrombie phase component (Knight 1994b: 188), the probable location of the original Coweta town at the nearby type site for the phase might make these other identifications more likely. Only extensive and focused archaeological work at these and other sites will be able to address these questions.

Given that local Stewart phase material culture was ultimately replaced by the Abercrombie-derived Blackmon phase of the mid-seventeenth century, which subsequently is known to have characterized both Muskogee-*and* Hitchiti-speaking towns, an important question is precisely when and how indigenous Stewart phase (Hitchiti) populations in the southern part of the valley adopted elements of Abercrombie/Blackmon phase (Muskogee) material culture. Is the apparent drop in the number of sites between Stewart and Abercrombie phases totally real, or is it in part an artifact of the brief coexistence of two separate material culture assemblages in the same valley during the period 1550–1650? Were some Stewart phase sites actually occupied well into the Abercrombie phase, only adopting immigrant material culture with the Blackmon phase a century later (and thus "reappearing" in archaeological site distributions)? And as Chad Braley asked, is the Abercrombie phase itself even real, or is it only an artifact of component mixing between Stewart and Blackmon phase occupations separated by many years or decades of site abandonment? These questions are impossible to answer at present, but future work should at least consider these alternatives.

Regardless of its direct origin during the Abercrombie phase, however, the succeeding Blackmon phase (1650–1715) can unequivocally be identified as the Apalachicola province of seventeenth-century Spanish accounts, and that of the Coweta/Kasihta of English accounts at the end of the century. These were the people whom Spanish missionaries courted, and with whom Spanish soldiers in the Apalachee garrison traded. They were also the people who finally accepted Dr. Henry Woodward and other English traders into their midst in 1685, and who in large part fled the Chattahoochee River only a few years after the Spanish built a fort there in 1689. The Blackmon phase is thus equivalent to the direct and lineal ancestors of the Lower Creeks of eighteenth- and nineteenth-century fame.

The ceramic assemblage of the Blackmon phase marks a direct stylistic evolution from the Abercrombie phase, in that it includes a predominance of shell tempering and several "roughened" surface treatments (brushing and cob-marking), and also several persistent grit-tempered Lamar decorations, such as incising, as well as check and possibly some complicated stamping (see Knight 1994b:189; but see also Braley 1998:9 regarding possible component mixing). Cord marking and red filming appear to reflect external connections to the northwest (McKee Island/Woods Island phases) and south (San Luis phase, or missionized Apalachee), respectively.

Archaeological sites of the Blackmon phase are considerably more common along the Chattahoochee River than the preceding Abercrombie phase (see, for example, Knight 1994a:384), and while documentary evidence dating to this period (before 1691) is comparatively scant, it is possible to make some reasoned guesses as to the specific identifications of some towns using contemporaneous and later evidence, even though these locations must be considered hypothetical (table 10.1, fig. 10.1). One town—Apalachicola—seems very likely to have been located at the Patterson site (1Ru66), based on the fact that it appears to be the closest and largest (indeed the only) documented Blackmon phase component immediately adjacent to the unquestionable location of the 1689–92 Spanish Apalachicola fort, which has also produced what is arguably the best single-component Blackmon phase aboriginal ceramic assemblage predating the eastward migration of the Apalachicola towns before 1692 (Kurjack 1975:175–85; Kurjack and Pearson 1975). Another nearby site just downriver (1Ru65) may also be a candidate, since it fits William Bartram's (1955:313–14) description of the early eighteenth-century location of Apalachicola, abandoned by that time.

Using the Patterson site and its nearby fort as a benchmark, we can

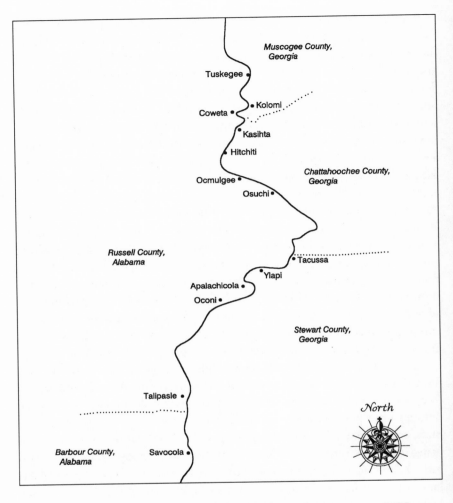

Fig. 10.1. Hypothetical locations for Apalachicola province towns ca. 1685.

extrapolate other Apalachicola town locations. The earliest surviving Spanish list of towns, not based on direct visitation, is the 1675 account of Bishop Gabriel Díaz Vara Calderón, which apparently lists the Apalachicola towns in south-north order along the river (see Wenhold 1936). Later Spanish accounts, which date to the time of the various military expeditions led by the provincial lieutenant of the Spanish garrison in the Apalachee mission province during 1685 and 1686, provide several important additional clues regarding town locations (Hann 1996; Steve Hahn, personal communication 1998). The southernmost town in the province was that of Savacola (Sawokli), abandoned as of that date. (Its inhabitants had twice relocated south to form short-lived Spanish missions near the confluence of the Chattahoochee and Flint Rivers during the 1670s and 1680s [see Hann 1988:47–49, 1996:71–72].) Just north of that town site, at a distance of some 1.5 leagues (just under 4 miles), was the first occupied town in the province, called Talipasle. From there, a trail evidently ran through several towns on the west side of the river (Oconi, Apalachicola, Osuche, and Ocmulque) some 9 leagues up to the important town of Casista (Kasihta) on the eastern side, which was the southernmost of four northern towns (Casista, Colome, Caveta, and Tasquique, in that order). The northernmost, Tasquique (Tuskegee), was located 1.5 leagues south of the falls of the river. The town of Ocmulque (Ocmulgee) was furthermore noted to be located 2 leagues (just over 5 miles) south of Casista.

As a second "benchmark," the type site for the Blackmon phase (1Br25) is known to have been located in the immediate vicinity of the hypothesized eighteenth-century town of Sawokli (1Br30) and is furthermore roughly 9 leagues south of the approximate location of the original eighteenth-century town of Kasihta (Casista) in the vicinity of site 9Ce33. (See below for a full list of eighteenth-century town identifications.) For this reason, I would identify the Blackmon site (1Br25) as the original site of Savacola/Sawokli. Other identifications shown in table 10.1 link relative locations and known archaeological site distributions, although not all sites postulated are yet known to contain Blackmon phase components. As suggested by Chad Braley (1998:110–13), the Apalachicola town of Osuche was possibly identical to the Blackmon phase component of the later Yuchi town (1Ru63). Of the four northern towns, at least two (Coweta and Kasihta) and perhaps three (Kolomi) may correspond to the cluster of mound sites near the Abercrombie site, two of which apparently possess Abercrombie phase occupations, as discussed previously. Tasquique (Tuskegee) may have been located on either side of the river in the vicinity of site 1Ru9 (the late eighteenth-century site of Coweta), since its location was said to be roughly the same distance downriver from the falls (1.5 leagues or 4 miles) as was the later town of Coweta (3 miles). Other towns were also located in the southern portion of the province, but since they may have been located on the eastern side of the river (and would not have been visited during Matheos's 1685 expedition), only the bishop's 1675 list provides clues as to their relative positions with respect to the other towns (see table 10.1). The identification of additional Blackmon phase sites and components must await further research.

Toward this end, based on both documentary and archaeological data, terminal Abercrombie and early Blackmon phase sites (circa 1630s–1685) of the Apalachicola province would be expected to be characterized not just by their characteristic aboriginal ceramic assemblage but also by a distinctive European trade assemblage that is apparently common to contemporaneous sites throughout eastern Alabama and Tennessee (Smith 1987; Waselkov 1989). Specifically, sites predating the Carolina trade along the Chattahoochee would presumably contain only a limited range of European goods, including predominantly glass beads, sheet brass ornaments, brass bells, and iron tools (see, for example, Knight 1985:103–7). Given that beads, bells, and iron tools also occur in later contexts (though different types and styles), the most prominent marker for sites occupied during the heyday of the Apalachicola province (the mid-seventeenth century) would be sheet brass ornaments, including large disk gorgets, collars, arm bands, and animal-effigy pendants. While the precise origin of these items is not certain, their dating and geographic distribution led Gregory Waselkov (1989) to conclude that their source was within the seventeenth-century Spanish mission system, and that they may have been manufactured by mission Indians from Spanish raw material for purposes of trade with the deep interior. Typical sheet brass ornaments of this period have indeed been recovered at the Abercrombie site (1Ru61), with both Abercrombie and Blackmon components (Kurjack 1975:174), but other sites generally show only later items postdating 1685 (with the dawn of the English trade). This is likely a factor of the limited sample size at earlier sites.

Exile and Return, circa 1691–1715

Beginning not long after the 1689 construction of the Spanish Apalachicola fort (site 1Ru101) as a response to early Carolina trade, the constituent towns of the emergent Lower Creeks subsequently entered a period of considerable population mobility, guided in large part by the geopolitics of the broader English/Spanish borderlands struggle in which they found themselves (see, for example, Crane 1981). The primary population movement during this pivotal period in Lower Creek history was the voluntary exile of virtually all major towns in the Apalachicola province of the lower Chattahoochee River by the spring of 1692, when the valley was said by the Spanish garrison commander to have been totally abandoned (Steve Hahn, personal communication 1998), and their reestablishment along the Fall Line zone of the Ocmulgee and Oconee Rivers (neither of which were previously known by those names), and along the lower Savannah River. In their new locations, these immigrant towns (and others that joined them) placed themselves in direct contact with resident Carolina traders operating out of Charles Town.

It should be noted that there is debate as to whether the Chattahoochee was completely or only partially abandoned throughout this period, or whether the eastern immigrants simply represented "daughter" towns attached to inhabited towns on the Chattahoochee River (Frank Schnell, personal communication 1998). Documentary references to 1695 and 1702 raids by Spaniards and Apalachee Indians against the Lower Creeks are somewhat ambiguous with regard to the precise location of the towns targeted, and archaeological evidence is still unclear with respect to occupational continuity during this period (see, for example, Hann 1988:231, note 4).

Nevertheless, my own interpretation of available evidence is that the lower Chattahoochee Valley was indeed abandoned between 1692 and 1715, although I would imagine that the traditional territories of each town would have remained intact during this period, and that hunting and foraging probably continued here from their new residential bases in central and eastern Georgia. I base this interpretation in part on two specific sources: the explicit Spanish reference to the total depopulation of the Apalachicola province by the spring of 1692 (Steve Hahn, personal communication 1998), and the far-reaching 1708 English overview of their trading partners in the interior (Johnson et al. 1708), which makes no reference to any "mother" towns or other isolated occupation along the lower Chattahoochee at that time, instead noting explicitly that the more westerly Muskogee groups in present-day Alabama had decided to establish a completely new town where the trading path crossed the Chattahoochee River. This fact suggests to me that there were no remaining indigenous population centers in that portion of the valley during this period.

In any case, the majority of the eastward immigrants settled in a group of towns along the Ocmulgee River, then known by the English as Ochese Creek (Uchise in Spanish; see below). Ethnohistoric documentation of the precise names of these relocated towns, and particularly their relative order and specific locations with respect to one another, is extremely limited. Carolina records predating the Yamassee War record the existence of either

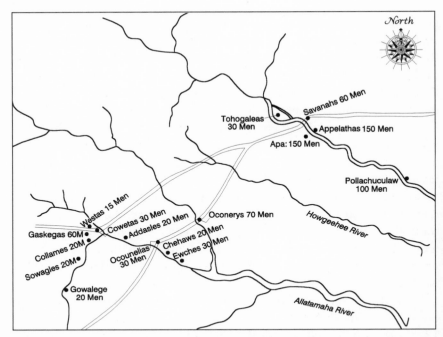

Fig. 10.2. Tracing of anonymous map ca. 1715 showing towns and trails on the Ocmulgee, Oconee, and Savannah rivers.

ten (Nairne et al. 1715) or eleven (Johnson et al. 1708) towns among the Ochese Creek Indians, including total populations said to range between 600 and 731 male warriors ("gun men"). The 1715 census recorded a total population of 2,406 for the ten unnamed towns. Two contemporaneous maps (drawn subsequently, but apparently based at least in part on pre-Yamassee War information) provide the only comprehensive evidence for the identity of the Ocmulgee River towns (Anonymous circa 1715; Herbert and Hunter 1744). One of these, the 1744 Herbert-Hunter map (redrafted by George Hunter from a 1725 map by John Herbert), has been reproduced in several publications (Pluckhahn 1997:354; Smith 1992:41), but the other, anonymous 1715 map (traced in fig. 10.2) has never been published with all original data (see Swanton 1922:plate 3). Subsequent maps either used these earlier maps as a base model or drew their information from later sources. (The 1733 Popple map, for example, includes precisely the same towns as that of the 1725/1744 Herbert-Hunter map.) As can be seen in table 10.2, the combined list forms a total of twelve towns (not including Oconee or Apalachicola), conforming well to contemporaneous estimates.

Table 10.2. List of documented towns, with hypothesized archaeological site correlations, for Uchise Creek towns along the Ocmulgee River, ca. 1691–1715

Town	1715 map[a]	1725 Map	Possible site(s)
Kealedji(?)	Gowalege (20)	—	unidentified (upper Towaliga River)
Sawokli	Sowagles (20)	—	unidentified (upper Towaliga River)
Kolomi	Collames (20)	Colomies	9Mo15, 16, 17, alternate unidentified
Tuskegee	Gaskegas (60)	Taskegees	unidentified, alternate 9Mo1, 2, 4
Westo	Westas (15)	—	9Bs1, 2, 9Ja47, alternate unidentified
Coweta	Cowetas (30)	Cowetas	9Mo1, 2, 4, alternate 9Bs1, 2, 9Ja47
Kasihta	—	Cusitees	unidentified, alternate 9Jo6, 198 (Tarver)
Atasi	Addasles (20)	Attasees	9Jo6, 198 (Tarver), alternate unidentified
Ocmulgee	Ocounelias (30)	—	9Bi1 (Macon Plateau)
Chiaha	Chehaws (20)	—	9Bi16
Hitchiti	—	Echeetes	9Bi7, 8, 9
Yuchi	Ewches (30)	—	9Bi22

Sources: Possible site correlations based on 1715 map, with alternate locations based on 1725 map.
a. Number of men listed in parentheses for 1715 map.

Based on the clearly distinguishable material culture of the Blackmon phase in central Georgia (also commonly known as the Ocmulgee Fields phase), the archaeological sites corresponding to many of these short-lived Apalachicola/Lower Creek towns have been located, although precise identification remains uncertain or extremely tenuous in most cases (the 1715 and 1725/44 maps differ in important ways; see table 10.2). Two clusters of contemporaneous Blackmon sites are currently known along the Ocmulgee River near and upriver from Macon. The northernmost cluster generally centers on the confluence of the Towaliga River with the Ocmulgee, and the southern cluster centers on the confluence of Walnut Creek with the Ocmulgee, in and around present-day Macon, Georgia (see Pluckhahn 1997: 353–60; Smith 1992:39–45). Based on admittedly limited evidence, I would tentatively suggest that four of the northernmost Apalachicola towns listed by Spanish chroniclers for the Chattahoochee River (Hann 1996), including Coweta, Kasihta, Tuskegee, Kolomi (all of which were burned in the winter of 1685–86 by Matheos, and all of which could be broadly grouped as immigrant Muskogee), maintained their relative position on the Ocmulgee River and probably settled to the north of the other towns, forming the northernmost cluster of archaeological sites noted below. Most of the southern towns of the original Apalachicola province (the Hitchiti towns) apparently settled either in the southern cluster of sites along the Ocmulgee River or much farther to the east. The northernmost of these towns, including at least Ocmulgee and Hitchiti, probably settled in the southern Ocmulgee cluster (around Macon). The town of Osuchi, which appeared on Spanish lists for the Chattahoochee River both before and after the eastward migration, does not appear as such in contemporary maps, though the name of a town burned in a 1695 Spanish raid—Uchichi—might be Osuchi instead of Uchise/Ochese (Hann 1988:363). In any case, Osuchi should probably also be included among the Ocmulgee immigrants, especially since this town later was one of three (Ocmulgee, Chiaha, and Osuchi) that became linked as the eighteenth-century "Point Towns" on the Chattahoochee. Two of the central Apalachicola province towns eventually settled in isolated locations to the east, including Oconee on the eastern side of the Oconee River, and Apalachicola along the lower Savannah River. Finally, the southernmost of the Hitchiti towns—Sawokli/Sabacola—also relocated from its more distant mission site and apparently settled in the northern cluster of Ocmulgee sites, probably along the Towaliga River.

During their stay, other immigrants arrived and attached themselves to the Lower Creeks. Two Muskogee towns from the Tallapoosa River—Atasi and Kealedji (Gowalege; see Swanton 1922:271)—appear on early maps, apparently settling in both the northern and southern Ocmulgee site clusters. The immigrant town of Chiaha, originally located high in the Appalachians of western North Carolina, also settled among the Hitchiti towns in the southern cluster (see Smith 1987:137, 1989:29). Furthermore, at least some of the formerly powerful Westo/Chichimeco slavers seem to have eventually formed a town along the Ocmulgee, although they soon vanished as a distinct group following their 1681 destruction by Carolinians. Finally, if the single 1715 map reference of "Ewches" is accurate (the reference might have been a mistranscription of either Hitchiti or perhaps Uchisi, both of which are missing from the map), at least some immigrant Yuchi may have also established a town among the southern Hitchiti towns shortly prior to their return west in 1715.

There is even a possibility that there were already people living on the Ocmulgee River when the Apalachicola towns arrived in the early 1690s. At least one early Spanish account makes note of an Indian group known as the Uchise, who participated with other groups in the 1680 assault on the Guale mission of Santa Catalina (Worth 1995:31; see also Hann 1996:67). Since this reference predates the arrival of the Apalachicola towns along "Ochese

Creek" by a decade (thus predating the "attachment" of the same Ochese/
Uchise name to the immigrant towns previously known exclusively as the
province of Apalachicola, or Coweta/Kasihta), it may instead refer to remnants of the original chiefdom of Ichisi, perhaps still located along the Ocmulgee River some 150 years after Hernando de Soto's visit (the name, after
all, was still in use at that time). The original capital of this chiefdom, located
at the Lamar mounds site (9Bi2), does possess some Blackmon/Ocmulgee
Fields phase occupation, and recent reanalysis of Lamar ceramics by David
Hally at least hints at possible continuity between mid-sixteenth- and late
seventeenth-century occupations (see Smith 1992:32). Only further analysis
or testing at this site will permit this possibility to be explored. Uchisi might
have been identical with the "Uchichi" town said to have been burned during
the 1695 Spanish raid along with Cavetta, Cassista, Ocmulgee, Taisquique,
and Oconi (Hann 1988:363), but in any case the absence of this name on
subsequent Lower Creek town lists suggests that this group, if indeed
present, was largely absorbed into adjacent towns, as apparently was the
fate of the remnant Westo.

Only a few of the known Blackmon/Ocmulgee Fields phase sites along the
Ocmulgee have been subjected to extensive archaeological work, including
the Macon Plateau site (9Bi1) and the Tarver (9Jo6) and Little Tarver (9Jo
198) sites (Mason 1963a; Pluckhahn 1997; Pluckhahn and Braley 1999);
the rest have only witnessed limited testing (that is, Nelson et al. 1974;
Wauchope 1966). Of these two sites, only Macon Plateau can be identified
with any degree of certainty. In contrast with several other interpretations
(for example, Smith 1992; Swanton 1946), I agree with Mason (1963a; see
also Pluckhahn 1997:358) in her identification of the Macon Plateau site
(9Bi1) as the town of Ocmulgee, confirming subsequent Creek and Anglo-
American oral traditions regarding its identity (see, for example, Adair
1986:39; Hawkins 1980:51). This site is consistent with the town's placement along the primary lower trading path in the 1715 map (see fig. 10.2),
and furthermore the discovery of the English stockade at Macon Plateau
(Kelly 1939; Mason 1963a; Waselkov 1994) matches its importance as the
staging ground for Carolina governor James Moore's military operation
against the Apalachee missions in 1704 (Crane 1981:79; Hann 1988:385–
97). The Tarver sites probably represent either Atasi or Kasihta, although the
former seems more likely given the north-south groupings mentioned above,
and the 1715 map placement of this town.

Both sites produced substantial evidence for the burgeoning English trade between 1691 and 1715, including a wide range of firearms-related material, as well as iron tools, brass kettles, tobacco pipes, rum bottles, and diverse items relating to clothing and ornamentation (beads, buttons, buckles, et cetera). At least some of these objects, including Spanish majolica, a Spanish-style Colono-ware vessel, and glass and lapidary beads of Spanish origin, may indeed have been plunder from Creek slave-raids against Apalachee and Timucua missions (Pluckhahn 1997:370; Pluckhahn and Braley 1999).

Beyond the simple assimilation of selected European objects into a predominantly aboriginal material culture, however, the broader context of the Carolina slave and deerskin trade obviously resulted in more fundamental changes in the domestic economy of these Ochese Creek towns. As discussed by Mason (1963a, 1963b) and others, the Carolina trade had the greatest impact on male activities, since men rapidly became the principal procurers of Indian slaves and deerskins for purposes of trade. As slave raiders and deer hunters, Creek males increasingly dedicated the lion's share of their time and labor to such activities, eventually becoming almost wholly dependent on English munitions as the bow and arrow was replaced by the flintlock musket. In this context, it was Creek women who ultimately provided considerable cultural stability through their agricultural and household activities, and through their importance in the traditional matrilineal control of land. As summarized by Mason (1963b:73), "women . . . , and particularly the matrilineage, served as the thread of cultural continuity from generation to generation." This is particularly demonstrated by the archaeological evidence for domestic pottery, which seems to have largely retained its aboriginal character even through the removal period and later.

Another area of cultural transformation documented at Macon Plateau and Tarver is consistent with broader patterns of architectural change witnessed throughout Creek territory. Specifically, by the end of the seventeenth century, the typical late prehistoric Lamar "winter houses," characterized by substantial wattle-and-daub construction and semisubterranean floors, were apparently abandoned in favor of the somewhat less substantial rectangular "summer house" structures. After this period, these rectangular structures formed the basis for small household compounds (see, for example, Waselkov 1994; Waselkov and Smith, this volume). The apparent lack of such "winter houses," and the presence of a number of rectangular domestic structures (roughly 3–4 by 6–7 meters) identified at the short-lived Ocmulgee River sites, some organized into household compounds, seem consistent with this pattern (Mason 1963a:76–91; Pluckhahn 1997:360–67). Considerably larger square and rectangular structures at Macon Plateau may have represented public structures of some sort (Mason 1963a:84–87; Smith 1992:71–72).

In addition to the Ocmulgee towns, other towns were established to the east along the Oconee and Savannah Rivers at about the same time. Oconee Town has been identified at the Fall Line zone of the Oconee River (9BL16), along with the site of the relocated town of Apalachicola (Palachacola Town) along the lower Savannah River at Stokes Landing in Hampton County, South Carolina. Based on limited excavations at both sites, aboriginal ceramic assemblages and European trade goods at both sites generally conform to those from Macon Plateau and Tarver (Caldwell 1948; Fairbanks 1940; Smith 1992:45; Mark Williams, personal communication 1998).

Additional contemporaneous towns were established in general proximity to the Lower Creeks but will only be mentioned here in passing. These include the town of Chattahoochee (rendered variously as "Chochtaruchy" and "Chattahuces"), which was "settled for conveyniency of carrying on trade" directly on the path between the relocated Coweta on the Ocmulgee River and Okfuskee on the Tallapoosa River (Johnson et al. 1708). This new town, located somewhat upriver along the Chattahoochee from the then-abandoned towns of the former Apalachicola province, probably represented a short-lived eastward migration from the Tallapoosa region and thus will not be grouped within the Lower Creek designation.

It was also during this time that the enigmatic group bearing the name Yuchi immigrated from their probable Appalachian homeland into the Savannah River valley, and ultimately among the Lower Creeks. (For the debate on Yuchi and/or Chisca origins, see Hann 1988:75–79, 1996:238–39; Worth 1998:18–21, 34–35, 208 notes 47–48.) Early documentary evidence, including the 1715 map (table 10.1, fig. 10.2), indicates that the Yuchi began their association with the Lower Creeks prior to the Yamassee War. Importantly, while some of the Yuchi and most of the Lower Creek towns relocated west to the Chattahoochee River following the war, a substantial number of Yuchi remained along the Savannah River through the establishment of Georgia in 1733, and only abandoned that valley as late as the 1740s. Archaeological sites identified as early eighteenth-century Yuchi have been investigated along the Savannah, including Mount Pleasant (Elliott 1991) and Stallings Island (Claflin 1931; Smith 1992:47–48), and the site of

Ogeechee Town to the west has also recently been identified and tested (Moore 1998). Material culture at these sites is not inconsistent with that of contemporaneous Lower Creek occupations farther to the west, suggesting fairly rapid assimilation by Yuchi immigrants (confirmed by work at later Yuchi sites).

Stability, Expansion, Retreat, and Removal, circa 1716–1836

In the aftermath of the Yamassee War, the brief eastward movement of the Apalachicola/Lower Creeks was reversed, with most of the surviving towns regrouping once again along the lower Chattahoochee. Some changes in the overall roster of towns had occurred, however (see Boyd 1949, 1952). A splinter group under the Apalachicola town leader known as Cherokee-leechee (meaning "Cherokee killer") established a new town far to the south just above the forks of the Apalachicola River (probably sites 9Se20, 21, and 29), leaving the original Apalachicola town under its old name at or near its original location among the rest of the Lower Creek towns (see below).

In addition, at least one of the original late seventeenth-century Apalachi-cola province towns—Kolomi—did not resettle among the Lower Creeks along the Chattahoochee, but instead along the Tallapoosa River farther to the west. At the same time, while the immigrant Chiaha and Yuchi towns (which had attached themselves to the Lower Creeks during their stay on the Ocmulgee) remained among the rest of the Lower Creek towns throughout the rest of the historic period, other immigrant towns, including Atasi and (probably) Kealedji, similarly resettled farther west along the Tallapoosa (see Swanton 1922). At least one settlement connected to Atasi—Eufala— may have nevertheless remained or returned subsequently to Lower Creek territory (it did not appear on lists dating to 1716–25), since the "governor" of Eufala along the lower Chattahoochee was listed in 1738 as "Atasi mico" (Márquez del Toro 1738).

The return west also marked the beginning of the Lawson Field archaeo-logical phase. By this time Blackmon phase material culture had evolved into a predominantly grit-tempered assemblage characterized predominantly by Chattahoochee Brushed, Ocmulgee Fields Incised, and Kasihta Red Filmed decorative types (Knight 1994b:189; Willey and Sears 1952), all of which have been incorporated into a newer type-variety scheme developed for east Alabama phases (Knight 1985:185–91). This assemblage would ultimately characterize the rest of Lower Creek occupation prior to the removal period.

During their subsequent stay of more than a century along the Chattahoo-chee River, the Lower Creek towns witnessed a multiplicity of changes, both internal and external. One of the most important changes seems to have been an overall demographic rebound, leading in part to an increasing number of out-settlements, including both new towns and (presumably) dispersed sat-ellite farmsteads. Simultaneously, many of these towns experienced one or more short-distance relocations along the Chattahoochee River, combined with some very long-distance moves in response to a variety of factors.

As a result, the overall portrait of Lower Creek town locations during the middle and late eighteenth century is considerably more complex than that for previous periods. For the primary Chattahoochee Valley corridor, John Swanton (1922:plate 2) did an admirable job of reducing the masses of data into a simple list of successive town locations, and Harold Huscher (1958, 1959) subsequently used this map to compile a list of provisional site iden-tifications, included here (table 10.3). Even twenty-five years later, Hu-scher's (1959) final list was characterized as "the most extensive, and still the best general effort," despite the simultaneous recommendation that "all of them demand reconsideration in light of primary source materials and im-proved knowledge of Lawson Field phase site distributions" (Knight and Mistovich 1984:227).

As noted at that time by Huscher, however, the lengthy Swanton list was actually underlain by a basic roster of just a few primary Lower Creek towns: "Allowing for overlaping or synonymous terms, 13 main towns are usually listed in the Spanish and English census lists or on early maps, and usually in a fairly definite sequence" (Huscher 1959:31). These towns were, in order: Kawita, Kasihta, Yuchi, Osotchi, Chiaha/Chiahutci, Ocmulgee, Hit-chiti, Apalachicola, Oconee, Sawokli/Little Sawokli, Kawaigi, Tamatli, and Eufala. Most of them (including some "old" and "new" towns) were in-cluded in Benjamin Hawkins's (1980:285–327) "A Sketch of the Creek Country in the Years 1798 and 1799," which is without question the single most important source of information on Creek town locations at the turn of the nineteenth century. Various reconstructions of this detailed descriptive account (for example, Brannon 1930; Hurt 1975) point to very specific locations for individual towns at the turn of the nineteenth century. While a comprehensive review of Huscher's provisional site list is far beyond the scope of this chapter, a few revisions and comments are prudent (see asterisks in table 10.3).

Based on what is clearly an error in Swanton's (1922) map placement of

Table 10.3. Huscher's archaeological site correlations for Lower Creek towns along the Chattahoochee River

Sites(s) (Huscher 1958)	Provisional identification (Swanton 1922)
1Ru9	Kawita (3)
not identified	Tlikatcka (2)
1Ru60	Claycatskee
1Ru61 (1Ru10, 11, 12)	Kawita (2)
9Ce5, 33*	Kasihta (7)
9Ce1*	Kasihta (6) and Chickasaw (3b)
1Ru63, 57	Yuchi (3b)
1Ru52	Osochi (4)
not identified	Tlikatcka (1)
1Ru54	Chiaha (5a)
1Ru55, 56	Okmulgee (2)
1Ru70	Chiahutci or Hitchiti (4)*; latter "may be in Georgia"
1Ru68	Westo (Yuchi 4b) or Chiahutci or Apalachicola "new town"
1Ru18, 66 *	Apalachicola "new town"
1Ru27	Apalachicola (4), "old town" abandoned 1757
1Ru65	alternate Apalachicola (4) "old town"
9Sw12, 29, 30	possibly "Apalachicola field villages"; Palachocota of Purcell map
1Ru34, 35, 36, 37	Kolomi, Atasi, Tuskegee
9Sw5, 6, 7	Oconee (2a) or Apalachicola field villages
9Sw3, 4, 57	Oconee (2a)
1Ru20, 21, 28	Kasihta (5)
1Ru3	Ocmulgee (1)
9Sw25, 27	Sawoklutci or Oconee
9Sw21, 22	Tamahita
1Br30 *	Sawokli
1Br22, 23	Chiaha (4a) or Sawokli (3) or Okawaigi
1Br21, 44	Okawaigi
1Br17	Hogologee (Yuchi 3b)
1Br35	Tamatli
1Br56, 60	alternate Tamatli "field houses"
9Qu22, 23, 24, 25	Eufala Hopai
9Qu10, 11, 12, 13, 14	alternate Eufala Hopai, or Okitiyakni
1Br2	Okitiyakni
9Cl35, 36, 37	Okitiyakni (alternate)
9Cl38, 39, 40	Eto-Husse-Wakkes/Itahasiwaki
not identified	Hitchiti (3)
mouth of Omusee Cr.?	Yamassee (4b, 6b)

Sources: Huscher 1959:32–35; Swanton 1922.
Notes: Site numbers shown in italics were noted to be "major sites" by Huscher (1959:110), possibl representing "large, heavily populated prosperous 'Square Ground' towns." Sites and towns marked with asterisks have revisions or additional information in the text of this chapter.

the successive locations of Kasihta town (Swanton's #6 and #7), Huscher's list almost certainly confounds the corresponding site locations. Close reading of Hawkins's (1916, 1980) descriptions of his journey from Coweta to Kasihta make it abundantly clear that the earlier Kasihta location (also subsequently a Chickasaw village) was atop the high ground just *north* of the 1797–99 location (not south as shown in his map), making site 9Ce1 (the Lawson Field site) identical with the subsequent Kasihta of Hawkins's day, and sites 9Ce33 and perhaps 9Ce5 or another, undiscovered site connected with the earlier Kasihta.

Farther south, Huscher was correct in his suggestion that Hitchiti was located in Georgia; 1961 excavations at site 9Sw50, called the Hitchitee site (Kelly et al. n.d.), confirmed the Lawson Field phase component at the site. In addition, excavations at two sites, the Patterson site (1Ru66) and the Blackmon site (1Br25), revealed the presence of earlier components dating to the recently defined Blackmon phase (Kurjack 1975; Mistovich and Knight 1986).

For this reason, the Patterson site seems a good candidate for the original late seventeenth-century town of Apalachicola. While Huscher's identification of 1Ru18 and 1Ru66 as Apalachicola "new town" is probably accurate (both sites have Lawson Field components; see Hurt 1975:21), his identification of site 1Ru27 downriver as the Apalachicola "old town," abandoned several decades prior to William Bartram's (1955:313) visit there, may be too close; site 1Ru65 may be a better candidate for this low-lying site. Despite these identifications, however, based on present information the Patterson site clearly predates all these sites and thus likely constitutes the earliest Apalachicola town adjacent to the Spanish fort.

Farther downriver, the Blackmon site (9Br25) is also the most likely candidate for the late seventeenth-century town of Sawokli/Sabacola; Huscher's identification of site 9Br30 just upriver as the eighteenth-century town of Sawokli may thus be true (perhaps linked with contemporaneous Lawson Field phase occupation at Blackmon), but the probable original location of Sawokli at 9Br25 is not indicated on Huscher's list since he was unable to survey this area (Frank Schnell, personal communication 1998), and thus deserves mention here.

Excavations were conducted at a number of notable Lawson Field phase sites along the primary Chattahoochee River corridor, including several on Huscher's (1959) list. These include the Lawson Field site (9Ce1, or Kasihta town), the Yuchi Town site (1Ru63), the Hitchitee site (9Sw50), and the

Jackson site (1Br35, or Tamatli), among several others without firm identifications (Braley 1991, 1998; Chase 1960; Kelly et al. n.d.; Kurjack 1975;
Willey and Sears 1952). Survey and testing were also carried out at a multiplicity of other Chattahoochee Valley sites with Lawson Field phase components, and particularly within the area of Fort Benning below Columbus.
These projects included not only riverbank towns, hamlets, and farmsteads,
but also more isolated outlying settlements such as Upatoi Town, established
in the uplands along an eastern tributary to the Chattahoochee at the end of
the nineteenth century (see, for example, Briner et al. 1997; DeJarnette
1975; Elliott et al. 1995, 1996, 1998; Elliott and Wood 1997; Espenshade
and Roberts 1992; Hargrave et al. 1998; Holland 1974; Knight and Mistovich 1984; Ledbetter and Braley 1989; Mistovich and Knight 1986).

Beyond the Chattahoochee sites, one subject that has generally received
little attention is the late eighteenth-century expansion of Lower Creek
settlement eastward into the Flint River drainage, where by the turn of the
century there were a number of "daughter" towns attached to the Chattahoochee communities of Kasihta, Yuchi, Hitchiti, and Chiaha (Worth
1997). Only limited surface collections had previously been undertaken on
a few sites dating to this period, including the evidently dispersed Kasihta
town of Salenojuh (including sites 9Tr7, 10, 41, 42, and 54) and the Yuchi
town of Padgeeligau (9Tr18 and 23), but several of the Salenojuh farmsteads
were recently subjected to more extensive testing and mechanical stripping
in recent years, resulting in far more substantial data (Gordy 1966; Ledbetter 1998; Worth 1988:136, 1997).

Although a comprehensive review of the results of recent testing and data
recovery at a number of late Lawson Field sites along the Chattahoochee and
Flint Rivers will not be attempted here, it seems likely that once final reports
are generated for recent and ongoing projects, archaeologists may actually
know more about Lower Creek farmsteads and "daughter" towns than they
do about the primary "core" communities so prominent in the historic
record. What seems evident from the archaeological record is that during the
eighteenth and early nineteenth centuries, Lower Creek culture was undergoing the same kinds of transformations experienced by many other southeastern Indian groups at the same time (for a recent overview, see Ethridge
1997). These changes pervaded many elements of Creek life, including material culture, foodways, architecture, and settlement distribution. European goods and foodstuffs found increasingly important roles in Creek

life (especially as cattle raising and plow agriculture took root among the Creeks); domestic architecture seems to have eventually shifted from aboriginal to Euro-American patterns (log cabins began to replace traditional Creek rectangular domestic residences with prehistoric "summer house" roots); and settlements appear to have become more and more dispersed in concert with ongoing transformations in the domestic economy.

While these statements seem obvious, one additional observation is worth noting here: although the forces that shaped the world in which the Lower Creeks found themselves were indeed largely external (that is, Euro-American political and economic trends on a global scale), many of the most significant changes that can be observed in Lower Creek culture were substantially internal. As other authors have noted, the Creeks and other Native American groups were not simply passive recipients of Euro-American culture in a simple acculturative transfer; their culture changed and adapted *internally* to reflect new external circumstances. In this sense, many observed changes were in fact very conscious adaptations to the expanding colonial system surrounding early Spanish, English, French, and American settlement. By the same token, just as some traditional elements of Lower Creek culture did change in response to external forces, other elements continually resisted transformation, even as the Creeks were forcibly removed west in the 1830s.

Surviving Lower Creek communities in Oklahoma of the later nineteenth and twentieth centuries thus formed a curious blend of old and new, representing the outcome of nearly three centuries of adaptation in the east, in which the sixteenth-century Stewart phase chiefdom of the Lower Chattahoochee River metamorphosed into the seventeenth-century Apalachicola province, and finally into the eighteenth-century Lower Creek tribe. Internal cultural innovation during that period was fueled not only by European traders and settlers but also by Native American immigrants and refugees who aggregated to the original core Hitchiti chiefdom during the following centuries. While modern oral traditions and preserved ethnohistoric documents form crucial sources of evidence, archaeological work has been and will undoubtedly continue to be an important component in reconstructing that journey.

Bibliography

Adair, James
1986 [1775]   *The History of the American Indians*. Reprint of 1930 ed., edited by
S. C. Williams. New York: Promontory Press.
Anonymous
ca. 1715 Map of North and South Carolina and Florida. Crown Collection of Maps,
Series 3, Maps 13–16. Photographic copy in the Hargrett Rare Book and
Manuscript Library, University of Georgia, Athens.
Bartram, William
1955   *Travels of William Bartram*. Reprint edited by Mark Van Doren. New York:
Dover.
Boyd, Mark F.
1937   The Expedition of Marcos Delgado from Apalache to the Upper Creek Coun-
try in 1686. *Florida Historical Quarterly* 16:2–32.
1949   Diego Peña's Expedition to Apalachee and Apalachicolo in 1716. *Florida
Historical Quarterly* 28:1–27.
1952   Documents Describing the Second and Third Expeditions of Lieutenant Diego
Peña to Apalachicolo in 1717 and 1718. *Florida Historical Quarterly* 31:109–
39.
Braley, Chad O.
1991   *Archaeological Data Recovery at Yuchi Town, 1Ru63, Fort Benning, Alabama*. Report submitted to U.S. Army Corps of Engineers, Savannah District,
Savannah, Ga., by Gulf Engineers and Consultants, Baton Rouge, La., and
Southeastern Archeological Services, Athens, Ga.
1995   *Historic Indian Period Archaeology of the Georgia Coastal Plain*. Georgia
Archaeological Research Design Paper no. 10. Athens.
1998   *Yuchi Town (1Ru63) Revisited: Analysis of the 1958–1962 Excavations*. Report submitted to Environmental Management Division, Directorate of Public
Works, U.S. Army Infantry Center, Fort Benning, Ga., by Southeastern Ar-
cheological Services, Athens, Ga.
Brannon, Peter A.
1930   Coweta and the Lower Creeks. *Arrow Points* 17(4):37–47.
Briner, Frederick L., Janet E. Simms, and Lawson M. Smith
1997   *Site Mapping, Geophysical Investigation, and Geomorphic Reconnaissance
at Site 9ME395 Upatoi Town, Fort Benning, Georgia*. Miscellaneous Paper
EL–97–3. Waterways Experiment Station, U.S. Army Corps of Engineers,
Vicksburg, Miss.
Caldwell, Joseph R.
1948   Palachacolas Town, Hampton County, South Carolina. *Journal of the Wash-
ington Academy of Science* 38:321–24.
Chase, David W.
1960   *An Historic Indian Town Site in Russell County, Alabama*. Coweta Memorial
Association Papers no. 2. Transcribed in *Yuchi Town (1Ru63) Revisited:
Analysis of the 1958–1962 Excavations*, by Chad O. Braley, C5-C14. Report
submitted to the Environmental Management Division, U.S. Army Infantry
Center, Fort Benning, Ga., by Southeastern Archeological Services, Athens.

Claflin, William H., Jr.
1931   *The Stallings Island Mound, Columbia County, Georgia.* Papers of the
        Peabody Museum of American Archaeology and Ethnology, Harvard Univer-
        sity, vol. 14, no. 1. Cambridge, Mass.
Crane, Verner W.
1981   *The Southern Frontier, 1670–1732.* Originally published 1929. New York: W.
        W. Norton.
DeJarnette, David L.
1975   *Archaeological Salvage in the Walter F. George Basin of the Chattahoochee
        River in Alabama.* Tuscaloosa: University of Alabama Press.
Elliott, Daniel T.
1991   Ye Pleasant Mount: 1989 and 1990 Excavations. LAMAR Institute, Wat-
        kinsville, Georgia.
Elliott, Daniel T., Rita F. Elliott, W. Dean Wood, Russell M. Weisman, and Debra J.
        Wells
1998   Archaeological Testing of Nine Sites on Fort Benning in Muscogee County,
        Georgia. Legacy Resource Management Program Report. Draft. Prepared for
        Environmental Management Division, Directorate of Public Works, U.S.
        Army Infantry Center, Fort Benning, Ga., by Southern Research, Ellerslie, Ga.
Elliott, Daniel T., J. L. Holland, P. Thomason, M. Emrick, and R. Stoops, Jr.
1995   *Historic Preservation Plan for the Cultural Resources on U.S. Army Installa-
        tions at Fort Benning Military Reservation, Chattahoochee and Muscogee
        Counties, Georgia, and Russell County, Alabama.* Vol. 2, *Technical Synthesis.*
        Report submitted to National Park Service, Atlanta, by Garrow and Associ-
        ates, Atlanta.
Elliott, Daniel T., Karen G. Wood, Rita Folse Elliott, and W. Dean Wood
1996   *Up on the Upatoi: Cultural Resources Survey and Testing of Compartments
        K-6 and K-7, Fort Benning Military Reservation, Georgia.* Report submitted
        to Environmental Management Division, Directorate of Public Works, U.S.
        Army Infantry Center, Fort Benning, Ga., by Southern Research, Ellerslie, Ga.
Elliott, Daniel T., and W. D. Wood
1997   Settling Out at Upatoi, A Creek Farming Community in Muscogee County,
        Georgia. Paper presented at Annual Meeting of the Society for American
        Archaeology, Nashville.
Espenshade, Christopher T., and Marion Roberts
1992   *Archaeological Assessment of 1RU135, a Nineteenth-Century Creek Site,
        Uchee Creek Recreation Area, Fort Benning, Alabama.* Report submitted to
        N.A.F. Procurement Office, Fort Benning, Ga., by Brockington and Associ-
        ates, Atlanta.
Ethridge, Robbie F.
1997   A Contest for Land: The Creek Indians on the Southern Frontier, 1796–1816.
        Ph.D. diss., University Microfilms, Ann Arbor, Mich.
Ewen, Charles R.
1990   Soldier of Fortune: Hernando de Soto in the Territory of the Apalachee, 1539–
        1540. In *Columbian Consequences,* vol. 2, *Archaeological and Historical
        Perspectives on the Spanish Borderlands East,* edited by D. H. Thomas, 83–
        91. Washington, D.C.: Smithsonian Institution Press.

Fairbanks, Charles H.
1940   Archaeological Site Report on the Ennis Site. Manuscript on file, Southeast Archaeological Center, National Park Service, Accession no. 239. Tallahassee, Fla.
1952   Creek and Pre-Creek. *In Archeology of Eastern United States*, edited by J. B. Griffin, 285–300. Chicago: University of Chicago Press.
1958   Some Problems of the Origin of Creek Pottery. *Florida Anthropologist* 11-(2):53–63.

Gatschet, Albert S.
1969   *A Migration Legend of the Creek Indians*. New York: Kraus Reprint.

Gordy, Don
1966   Site Reconnaissance: Sprewell Bluff, Lazer Creek, and Lower Auchumpkee Creek Dams. Georgia Archaeological Site Files, manuscript no. 18. Report submitted to the U.S. Corps of Engineers, Athens, Ga., by the University of Georgia, Athens.

Hally, David J.
1971   The Archaeology of European-Indian Contact in the Southeast. In *Red, White, and Black: Symposium on Indians in the Old South*, edited by Charles Hudson. Southern Anthropological Society Proceedings no. 5. Athens, Ga.
1986   The Cherokee Archaeology of Georgia. In *The Conference on Cherokee Prehistory*, edited by D. G. Moore, 95–121. Swannanoa, N.C.: Warren Wilson College.
1994a   *Ocmulgee Archaeology, 1936–1986*. Athens: University of Georgia Press.
1994b   An Overview of Lamar Culture. In *Ocmulgee Archaeology, 1936–1986*, edited by D. J. Hally, 144–74. Athens: University of Georgia Press.

Hally, David J., and James L. Rudolph
1986   *Mississippi Period Archaeology of the Georgia Piedmont*. Georgia Archaeological Research Design Paper no. 2. Athens.

Hann, John H.
1988   *Apalachee: The Land between the Rivers*. Gainesville: University Presses of Florida.
1996   Late Seventeenth-Century Forebears of the Lower Creeks and Seminoles. *Southeastern Archaeology* 15(1):66–80.

Hargrave, Michael L., C. R. McGimsey, M. J. Wagner, L. A. Newsom, L. Ruggiero, E. Brietburg, and L. Norr
1998   *The Yuchi Town Site (1Ru63), Russell County, Alabama: An Assessment of the Impacts of Looting*. USACERL Special Report 98/48. Cultural Resources Research Center, U.S. Army Construction Engineering Research Laboratories, Champaign, Ill.

Hawkins, Benjamin
1916   *Letters of Benjamin Hawkins, 1796–1806*. Collections of the Georgia Historical Society, vol. 9. Savannah.
1980   *Letters, Journals, and Writings of Benjamin Hawkins*. Edited by C. L. Grant. Savannah: Beehive Press.

Herbert, John, and George Hunter
1744   A New Mapp of His Majesty's Flourishing Province of South Carolina (from 1725 original by Herbert). Hargrett Rare Book and Manuscript Library, University of Georgia, Athens.

Holland, C. G.
1974   A Mid-Eighteenth Century Indian Village on the Chattahoochee River. *Florida Anthropologist* 27(1):31–43.
Hudson, Charles
1990   *The Juan Pardo Expeditions: Exploration of the Carolinas and Tennessee, 1566–1568.* Washington, D.C.: Smithsonian Institution Press.
1997   *Knights of Spain, Warriors of the Sun: Hernando de Soto and the South's Ancient Chiefdoms.* Athens: University of Georgia Press.
Hurt, Wesley R.
1975   The Preliminary Archaeological Survey of the Chattahoochee Valley Area of Alabama. In *Archaeological Salvage in the Walter F. George Basin of the Chattahoochee River in Alabama,* edited by D. L. DeJarnette, 5–24. University: University of Alabama Press.
Huscher, Harold
1958   Historic Lower Creek Sites. Georgia Archaeological Site Files, manuscript no. 182. Athens.
1959   Appraisal of the Archaeological Resources of the Walter F. George Reservoir Area, Chattahoochee River, Alabama and Georgia. Report prepared as part of the River Basin Surveys, Smithsonian Institution. Georgia Archaeological Site Files, manuscript no. 257. Athens.
Johnson, Nathaniel, Thomas Broughton, Robert Gibbs, George Smith, and Richard Beresford
1708   Letter to the Lords Proprietors, September 17, 1708. British Public Records Office, Records Pertaining to South Carolina, 5:203–10.
Kelly, A. R.
1939   The Macon Trading Post, An Historical Foundling. *American Antiquity* 4: 328–33.
Kelly, A. R., Clemens de Baillou, Frank T. Schell, Margaret V. Clayton, Francis J. Clune, and Ann L. Schlosser
n.d.   Excavations in Stewart County, Georgia, Summer and Fall, 1961. Georgia Archaeological Site Files, manuscript no. 37. Athens.
Knight, Vernon James, Jr.
1985   *Tukabatchee: Archaeological Investigations at an Historic Creek Town, Elmore County, Alabama, 1984.* Office of Archaeological Research, Report of Investigations 45. Alabama State Museum of Natural History, Tuscaloosa.
1994a   The Formation of the Creeks. In *The Forgotten Centuries: Indians and Europeans in the American South, 1521–1704,* edited by C. Hudson and C. Tesser, 373–92. Athens: University of Georgia Press.
1994b   Ocmulgee Fields Culture and the Historical Development of Creek Ceramics. In *Ocmulgee Archaeology, 1936–1986,* edited by D. J. Hally, 181–89. Athens: University of Georgia Press.
Knight, Vernon James, Jr., and Tim S. Mistovich
1984   *Walter F. George Lake: Archaeological Survey of Fee Owned Lands, Alabama and Georgia.* Office of Archaeological Research, Report of Investigations no. 42. Alabama State Museum of Natural History, Tuscaloosa.
Kurjack, Edward B.
1975   Archaeological Investigation in the Walter F. George Basin. In *Archaeological*

Salvage in the Walter F. George Basin of the Chattahoochee River in Alabama, edited by D. L. DeJarnette, 87–198. University: University of Alabama Press.

Kurjack Edward B., and Fred Lamar Pearson, Jr.
1975   Special Investigations of 1Ru101, The Spanish Fort Site. In *Archaeological Salvage in the Walter F. George Basin of the Chattahoochee River in Alabama,* edited by D. L. DeJarnette, 200–222. Tuscaloosa: University of Alabama Press.

Ledbetter, R. Jerald
1998   *Archaeological Investigations of a Portion of a Creek Farmstead, Taylor County, Georgia.* Report submitted to the Georgia Department of Transportation, Atlanta, by Southeastern Archeological Services, Athens, Ga.

Ledbetter, R. Jerald, and Chad O. Braley
1989   *Archeological and Historical Investigations at Florence Marina State Park, Walter F. George Reservoir, Stewart County, Georgia.* 2 vols. Report submitted to Georgia Department of Natural Resources, Atlanta, by Southeastern Archeological Services, Athens, Ga.

Márquez del Toro, Alonso
1738   Account of Gifts Distributed to the Caciques of Uchizes and Cabetas, April 16, 1738. Archivo General de Indias, Santo Domingo 2593.

Mason, Carol I.
1963a   The Archaeology of Ocmulgee Old Fields, Macon, Georgia. Ph.D. diss., University Microfilms, Ann Arbor, Mich.
1963b   Eighteenth Century Culture Change among the Lower Creeks. *Florida Anthropologist* 16:65–80.

Mistovich, Tim S., and Vernon James Knight, Jr.
1986   *Excavations at Four Sites on Walter F. George Lake, Alabama and Georgia.* Office of Archaeological Research, Report of Investigations no. 51. Alabama State Museum of Natural History, Tuscaloosa.

Moore, Sue Mullins
1998   Excavations at Galphin's Trading Post: Preliminary Results 1997 Season. Paper presented at the Thirty-first Annual Conference of the Society for Historical Archaeology, Atlanta.

Nairne, Thomas, John Wright, Price Hughes, and John Barnwell
1715   An Exact Account of Ye Number and Strength of All the Indian Nations That Were Subject to the Government of South Carolina and Solely Traded with Them in Ye Beginning of Ye Year 1715. British Public Records Office, Records Pertaining to South Carolina, vol. 7.

Nelson, Ben A., David Swindell III, and Mark Williams
1974   Analysis of Ocmulgee Bottoms Materials at the Southeast Archaeological Center. Georgia Archaeological Site File, manuscript no. 505. Report submitted to the National Park Service, Athens, Ga., by Florida State University, Tallahassee.

Pluckhahn, Thomas J.
1997   *Archeological Investigation of the Tarver (9Jo6) and Little Tarver (9Jo198) Sites, Jones County, Georgia.* Report submitted to the Federal Emergency Management Agency, Region IV, Atlanta, by Southeastern Archeological Services, Athens, Ga.

Pluckhahn, Thomas J., and Chad O. Braley
1999   Connections across the Southern Frontier: Spanish Artifacts from Creek Contexts at the Tarver Sites (9Jo6 and 9Jo198). *Florida Anthropologist* 52 (4): 241–53.

Powell, Mary Lucas
1994   Human Skeletal Remains from Ocmulgee National Monument. In *Ocmulgee Archaeology, 1936–1986,* edited by D. J. Hally, 116–29. Athens: University of Georgia Press.

Russell, Margaret Clayton
1975   Lamar and the Creeks: An Old Controversy Revisited. *Early Georgia* 3(1):53–67.

Scarry, John F.
1994   The Apalachee Chiefdom: A Mississippian Society on the Fringe of the Mississippian World. In *The Forgotten Centuries: Indians and Europeans in the American South, 1521–1704,* edited by C. Hudson and C. Tesser, 156–78. Athens: University of Georgia Press.

Schnell, Frank T.
1989   The Beginnings of the Creeks: Where Did They First "Sit Down"? *Early Georgia* 17:24–29.
1990   Phase Characteristics of the Middle Chattahoochee River. In *Lamar Archaeology: Mississippian Chiefdoms in the Deep South,* edited by M. Williams and G. Shapiro, 67–69. Tuscaloosa: University of Alabama Press.

Schnell, Frank T., and Newell O. Wright, Jr.
1993   *Mississippi Period Archaeology of the Georgia Coastal Plain.* Georgia Archaeological Research Design Paper no. 3. Athens.

Sears, William H.
1955   Creek and Cherokee Culture in the Eighteenth Century. *American Antiquity* 21:143–49.

Smith, Marvin T.
1987   *Archaeology of Aboriginal Culture Change in the Interior Southeast: Depopulation during the Early Historic Period.* Ripley P. Bullen Monograph. Gainesville: University Press of Florida.
1989   Aboriginal Population Movements in the Early Historic Period Southeast. In *Powhatan's Mantle: Indians in the Colonial Southeast,* edited by P. H. Wood, G. Waselkov, and M. T. Hatley, 21–34. Lincoln: University of Nebraska Press.
1992   *Historic Period Indian Archaeology of Northern Georgia.* Georgia Archaeological Research Design Paper no. 7. Athens.

Swanton, John R.
1922   *Early History of the Creek Indians and Their Neighbors.* Smithsonian Institution, Bureau of American Ethnology Bulletin 73. Washington, D.C.
1946   *Indians of the Southeastern United States.* Smithsonian Institution, Bureau of American Ethnology Bulletin 137. Washington, D.C.

Waselkov, Gregory A.
1989   Seventeenth-Century Trade in the Colonial Southeast. *Southeastern Archaeology* 8(2):117–33.
1994   The Macon Trading House and Early European-Indian Contact in the Colonial Southeast. In *Ocmulgee Archaeology, 1936–1986,* edited by D. J. Hally, 190–96. Athens: University of Georgia Press.

Wauchope, Robert
1966   *An Archaeological Survey of Northern Georgia.* Society for American Archaeology Memoir 11. Menasha, Wisc.

Wenhold, Lucy L.
1936   A 17th-Century Letter of Gabriel Díaz Vara Calderón, Bishop of Cuba, Describing the Indians and Indian Missions of Florida. *Smithsonian Miscellaneous Collections,* 95(16). Washington, D.C.

Willey, Gordon R., and William H. Sears
1952   The Kasita Site. *Southern Indian Studies* 4:3–18.

Williams, Mark, and Gary Shapiro (editors)
1990   *Lamar Archaeology: Mississippian Chiefdoms in the Deep South.* Tuscaloosa: University of Alabama Press.

Worth, John E.
1988   Mississippian Occupation on the Middle Flint River. Master's thesis, Department of Anthropology, University of Georgia, Athens.

1995   *The Struggle for the Georgia Coast: An Eighteenth-Century Spanish Retrospective on Guale and Mocama.* Anthropological Papers of the American Museum of Natural History no. 75. New York.

1997   The Eastern Creek Frontier: History and Archaeology of the Flint River Towns, ca. 1750–1826. Paper presented in the symposium "Recent Advances in Lower Creek Archaeology" at the Annual Conference of the Society for American Archaeology, Nashville.

1998   *The Timucuan Chiefdoms of Spanish Florida.* Vol. 1, *Assimilation.* Vol. 2, *Resistance and Destruction.* Gainesville: University Press of Florida.

11

Archaeological Perspectives
on Florida Seminole Ethnogenesis

Brent R. Weisman

For archaeology to be even minimally relevant to an understanding of contemporary Florida Seminole society, it must contribute to a resolution of the fundamental and most perplexing question in Seminole Indian studies: why do the Seminoles exist? Because the continued and persistent existence of the Seminoles is in part due to their continued and successful self-identification, and because at least some of the self-identity process involves intentional relationships with material culture, archaeology is well positioned to play a role in the study of Seminole ethnogenesis. But because the relationship between ethnic (or cultural) identity and its reinforcing material symbols is often intentionally hidden from outside observation, the archaeology of ethnogenesis can only proceed after a detailed study of ethnographic and documentary sources.

By what means do the Seminoles identify themselves? How far back in time can this identity be traced? What were the processes responsible for creating a Seminole identity, and how has this identity changed through time? Is, in fact, Seminole identity one-dimensional? Are political and cultural identities completely congruent? If not, how can archaeology help discern relevant cultural processes? To respond to these questions, two general archaeological research orientations can be employed. The first of these puts archaeology to use in answering the central question of Seminole culture history: how did the Seminoles become Seminole? The second approach uses the archaeological record itself to discover those processes of ethnogenesis obscured or unrecognized in documentary sources. The first is concerned with providing archaeological "in the ground" evidence for the time depth and geographical range of known core practices, such as the Green

Corn Dance, while the second seeks to discover forces or processes that may no longer exist, and for which we lack direct evidence from oral history or written documentary sources. An example of the latter, presented below, would be archaeological evidence of a nativistic movement resulting from a historically documented period of stress. Both approaches share a concern with joining all lines of evidence into a synthetic understanding of Seminole ethnogenesis that might be of interest and relevance to the Seminoles themselves. One of the benefits of such a pursuit, if successful, is the opportunity to demonstrate the value of archaeology to people for whom archaeology has traditionally had little utility or has even been considered antithetical to their worldview (Cypress 1997).

Before we move forward with the central concern of this essay, the archaeological study of Seminole ethnogenesis, a summary of the basic archaeological sequence is in order. The Florida Seminoles today are divided into two federally recognized tribes. The Seminole Tribe of Florida, with a population of approximately 2,500, controls reservations at Hollywood (location of the tribal office), Brighton, Big Cypress, Immokalee, Tampa, and Fort Pierce (fig. 11.1). Tribal revenues, overseen by a separate corporate arm of the tribe, are derived from gaming, cigarette sales, citrus farming, ranching, and various other investments. The Seminole Tribe is strongly interested in state politics, and its members are visible players on issues relating to tribal sovereignty such as land and water rights (Kersey 1996). The Seminoles at Brighton speak the Muskogee language and thus are probably descended from Muskogee-speaking bands among the nineteenth-century Seminoles. Most of the other Seminoles and members of the Miccosukee Tribe speak the Mikasuki language.

The Miccosukee Tribe of Indians has its main reservation on the Tamiami Trail, U.S. Highway 41, about 40 miles west of Miami. Its members, numbering about 600, regard themselves as more traditional than the Seminoles, an attitude that contributed to the split between the two tribes during the process of formal federal recognition in the 1950s. A third group living on the fringes of the Big Cypress, the Independents, have continued to resist federal recognition and have limited involvement with the outside world. For the purposes of this essay, these three groups will be referred to collectively as the Florida Seminoles except in those cases where cultural historical distinctions are warranted.

The south Florida location of the contemporary Seminoles underscores one of the basic facts of their history. Beginning with U.S. control of Florida

Fig. 11.1. Locations of reservations and sites discussed in the text.

in 1821, federal Indian policy required consolidation of the widely dispersed
Seminoles on a central Florida reservation, from which their deportation to
Indian Territory (present-day Oklahoma) could be efficiently accomplished
(Mahon 1967:54–68). Even before this, when Florida was still under Spanish rule, Andrew Jackson's covert campaign against the Florida Seminoles
(known to history as the First Seminole War) sought to push them farther
south in the peninsula, if not to eliminate them outright. This southward

movement was given further impetus during the Second Seminole War (1835–42) when those Seminoles resisting deportation moved away from the advancing military into the nearly impenetrable wilderness of the Big Cypress and Everglades regions (Mahon 1967; Sprague 1848). A third, smaller outbreak of hostilities in 1857–58, the Third Seminole War, resulted in the near total isolation of the remaining Seminoles from the outside world (Covington 1993:128–44).

By 1860, approximately 200 Seminoles remained in Florida, dramatically reduced from an estimated 1821 level of 5,000 (Sturtevant 1971:111). Those few Indians that survived in Florida after 1858 are directly ancestral to the contemporary Seminole and Miccosukee peoples. From a strictly anthropological perspective, this drastic population decrease provides an opportunity to study the cultural implications of the founder's effect, among other things, and indeed this is one area of anthropological fascination with the Seminoles of the ethnographic present. Those deported during the war era, numbering at least 4,000, were the founding population for the federally recognized Seminole Tribe of Oklahoma. Ethnographic and ethnological collections indicate strong continuities between Florida Seminole and early Oklahoma Seminole ceremonialism and material culture (Hadley 1935; Howard 1984), but specific archaeological studies are needed.

Seminole occupation of Florida began during the first period of Spanish control as individual towns of Creeks and related groups migrated to the largely vacant Florida peninsula upon Spanish invitation (Fairbanks 1974, 1978). Brushed pottery found in single component sites or in surface deposits of multicomponent sites has been interpreted as archaeological evidence of Creek migration into Florida (Fairbanks 1978:163, 176), a movement stimulated by escalating tensions between the Creeks and Yamassees of Georgia and the British colony of Carolina. When the Creeks, led by Emperor Brim, failed to smash the Carolina colony in the Yamassee War of 1715, Spanish Florida was appealing to the Creeks of the lower Chattahoochee drainage as a safe haven from British retaliation. In fact, Spain had failed to protect the Florida hinterland from British aggression earlier in the century when Franciscan missions among the Timucua and Apalachee in north Florida had been overrun and destroyed by combined British and Creek forces in 1704.

Clearly, north Florida was not unknown territory to the Creeks, who began to settle there in the years after the Yamassee War. Nor were the cultures of the Timucuans and Apalachees entirely foreign to the Creeks.

Both Brim and his son Secoffee, who became a central figure in early Seminole politics, were married to Apalachee women (Fairbanks 1978:164). The archaeology of Florida's Spanish missions (see, for example, McEwan 1993) reveals that considerable interaction between the mission Timucua and Apalachee and the Creek towns of lower Georgia was taking place in the seventeenth century. When revolts, raids from the north, and disease ultimately combined to bring down the mission system, remaining Apalachees dispersed to points south and west while Timucua populations regrouped around St. Augustine. The degree to which these groups absorbed remnants of surviving Florida Indians remains open for study and is a subject to which archaeology can contribute. The Suwannee River corridor would be one likely place to begin such a study, particularly because this region was occupied during the late mission period and was a focus of early Seminole settlement, and material remains, particularly pottery, are relatively plentiful.

Documentary mentions of the Seminoles during this era are few; archaeological evidence is at best uncertain. The earliest material evidence of the Seminole presence in the peninsula—axes, mirrors, flintlocks, knives, and spontoon tomahawks from burial contexts along the St. Johns River (Goggin 1952:62–63; Rouse 1951:84, 257, plate 12, 1953), on the Gulf coast near Charlotte Harbor (Goggin 1953; Luer 1989), and from a refuse site underwater in the Suwannee River (Gluckman and Peebles 1974)—could be of Spanish origin or from the subsequent British period (1763–83). In either case the objects may represent diplomatic gifts from colonial authorities rather than trade goods.

Brushed pottery, in jar or bowl forms, and open "casuela" bowls found in the big bend area of the middle Suwannee River indicate the Seminole connection to their ancestral Creek roots. Rim styles are variable and may indicate clan affiliation (Sears 1959:29; Weisman 1989:45) (fig. 11.2). Pottery, either aboriginal or European, has never been found in a Seminole burial context, early or late.

Glass beads are not common at the presumed earliest sites but are very numerous on sites dating to the nineteenth century. The abundance of glass beads and other trade items, such as European ceramics, iron kettles and hardware, and glass containers, is a hallmark of the British and Second Spanish (1763–1821) periods, when economic interactions between Seminoles and colonists were most intense (Weisman 1989:59–81). For their part, the Seminoles provided livestock, including cattle and pigs, agricultural

Fig. 11.2. Rim styles of late eighteenth-century Seminole pottery: *A–D*, Oven Hill site on the Suwannee River, ca. 1760s–70s; *E*, A-296 near Paynes Prairie; *F*, Spalding's Lower Store, St. Johns River.

crops such as corn and rice, and hides, pelts, and honey from the forest (Bartram 1955:205). The increased visibility of Seminole archaeological sites from these periods reflects both the increased acquisition of goods by the Seminoles and a proliferation in number of sites.

Several trading houses were located and excavated, and they provided abundant material for study (Goggin 1961; Lewis 1969; Mykel 1962).

Stroud cloth, a coarsely woven cotton fabric, and calico became important mediums of exchange but are, of course, rarely represented in the archaeological record. Appliqué techniques of clothing decoration using strips of cloth or beaded strips eventually gave way to a patchwork style with the adoption of the sewing machine early in the twentieth century (Downs 1995:86); today colorful Seminole patchwork is one of the most visible markers of Seminole cultural identity and has been elevated to an art form by many contemporary Seminole women.

When Spain yielded Florida to the United States in 1821, the era of Seminole prosperity came to a close. Already driven from their initial villages in the region of Lake Miccosukee east of present-day Tallahassee and from the Suwannee-Alachua savanna heartland by Jackson's Tennesseeans and a separate force of Georgia volunteers even before Florida changed hands, the Seminoles were deeply suspicious of U.S. motives and were slow to comply with the federal policy of containment. Despite offers of annuities and land in Indian Territory, many Seminoles could not be enticed to leave Florida voluntarily, particularly because they were required to relinquish control of their black slaves, the so-called Black Seminoles (Porter 1996:30–33), who lived apart from the Seminoles in their own villages but were nonetheless considered to be property.

By 1835 it was clear to the U.S. government that force would be required to remove the Seminoles from Florida. The resulting seven-year Second Seminole War, although mostly fought as an infrequent series of guerilla actions rather than pitched battles, took heavy tolls on both sides and failed to result in a conclusive victory for the United States. In my view, the Second Seminole War was the crucial period for the ethnogenesis of the contemporary Seminoles and Miccosukees and will be the focus of more detailed discussion later in this essay.

The archaeological record of the war era is scanty but distinctive. Several battle locations are known in which both Seminole and military positions have been revealed archaeologically, thus allowing inferences about the strategies and tactics of both sides (Carr et al. 1989; Ellis et al. 1997). Village sites were discovered in one region, the "Cove of the Withlacoochee," which was the heart of the early resistance movement. These sites show the dispersed settlement pattern that would characterize later Seminole settlement of the South Florida wetlands, and they contain traditional brushed pottery. Burials of warriors may typically have been in shallow graves, sometimes intrusive in earlier prehistoric middens, but a range of burial practices including scaffold style and placement in trees are reported in military documents and local legends.

The richest source of archaeological information from the war period comes from the Fort Brooke cemetery, where captured Seminoles who died awaiting deportation were buried (Piper and Piper 1982). Beneath the city streets of modern downtown Tampa, this site yielded as many as thirty-seven probable Seminole burials. As will be argued below, the pattern of artifact distribution in the graves, particularly those of children, reflects behaviors meant to reinforce and strengthen clan ties.

The archaeological record of the latter half of the nineteenth century documents the isolation experienced by the remaining Seminoles. The earliest of these sites are poorly known but appear to be low-density, surface artifact scatters overlaying prehistoric black dirt middens on the tree islands or hammock margins of the Big Cypress and Everglades regions (Ehrenhard et al. 1978). Seminole pottery, brushed or otherwise, is absent from interior South Florida south of Lake Okeechobee. Glass wine bottles and demijohns are found, associated with iron tools and hardware, fragmentary gun parts, and small quantities of glass beads (Ehrenhard et al. 1978:79–81).

Site numbers and artifact densities increase toward the end of the century, and several site types are recognized, including Green Corn Dance grounds (Ehrenhard et al. 1980), small villages, and outlying slash-and-burn agricultural fields in various stages of preparation. Canoe landings and the occasional remnants of wooden docks or piers indicate the importance of water travel in this settlement system. The open-air, thatched "chickee" architectural style is evidenced by burned support posts found in the ground at some sites (Ehrenhard et al. 1978:67, 71; Ehrenhard et al. 1980:47), which adds to the ample documentary record indicating that this was the prevalent housing style after midcentury. Parts of sugarcane grinding mills, lantern glass from kerosene lamps, and new types of glass beads are some of the artifacts found at turn-of-the-century sites that reflect limited Seminole reinvolvement with white society, mostly by contact at trading posts or stores around Miami or on the lower southwest Florida coast. Pelts, plumes, and hides went to the traders, in exchange for cloth, beads, canned foods, iron pots and skillets, bullets, and other supplies (fig. 11.2). Burials from this period are solitary and appear to be strictly aboveground in log crypts or biers erected at some distance from the camps or villages. Grave goods or personal possessions continued to be placed with the deceased and have made ready targets for present-day artifact hunters.

By the 1930s shifts in settlement patterns associated with loosely organized bands set the stage for the development of the modern South Florida
reservations. Families that moved from the Everglades or eastern Big Cypress to the vicinity of the Tamiami Trail highway, which opened in 1928,
were the direct founding population of today's Miccosukee Tribe. The archaeological record discovered thus far has proved insufficient to differen-
tiate the Miccosukees and Seminoles in cultural historical terms, but genealogy combined with a direct historic approach offers some potential in this
regard. The three oldest Seminole reservations—Big Cypress, Brighton (on
the northeast rim of Lake Okeechobee), and Hollywood (west of Fort Lau-
derdale)—reflect connections to those areas spanning several generations.
The newest reservations—in Tampa (established on the basis of the Fort
Brooke burials), Immokalee, and Fort Pierce—were granted reservation status on cultural or historical grounds rather than by continuous occupation.

In recent years the Seminole Tribe has supported efforts to preserve significant cultural or historical sites, and has contributed either cash or political clout in support of such projects as the public purchase of Pine Island
Ridge and Snake Warriors Island in South Florida and the Izard battlefield
survey in the Withlacoochee Cove region (Weisman 1999). The tribe has also
funded a statewide heritage study and archaeological surveys of its reservations for planning purposes (Carr and Steele 1993; Cypress 1997). We can
hope that this new recognition of the value of archaeology will lead to future
cooperative efforts between the Seminoles and archaeologists, particularly
in research combining ethnoarchaeology, oral history, and genealogy.

Having considered this cursory overview of the Seminole archaeological
record as a prelude, let us now consider the issue of Seminole ethnogenesis
from an archaeological perspective.

How the Seminoles Became Seminole: Archaeological Approaches

The question can be presented in two ways: when did the Seminoles stop
thinking of themselves as Creeks, and when did they begin thinking of
themselves as Seminoles? The answer to the first can be teased from historic
documents and phrased in political terms and may have no directly discernible archaeological correlates. It can be argued that the Seminoles stopped
thinking of themselves as politically bound to the Creek Confederacy some
seventy years before their cultural identity became defined in its own unique
way. This is the period from Cowkeeper's diplomatic refusal to participate

in the Treaty of Picolata in 1765 (between the British colonial government and representatives of the Creek Confederacy) to the outbreak of the Second Seminole War in 1835, which dramatically showed the Seminoles' rejection of the Treaty of Moultrie Creek, which had called for their removal. During this period of enterprise, stable trading relations contributed to prosperity among the Seminoles, particularly on the family level. There were few events or processes that outwardly stimulated the development of group identity, especially an ethnic identity created in response to external stress.

All of this would change drastically when the United States took control of Florida, and especially with the onset of the Second Seminole War. Thereafter, there was no shortage of stress on Seminole society. I argue here for a model that considers the formulation of Seminole ethnic or cultural identity as a direct response to various external stresses brought about by the circumstances of the Second Seminole War. A crucial aspect of this new identity is its opposition to the "other," in this case dominant American society as personified by the military. Put simply, in my view the Indians of Florida did not consider themselves Seminole until they met and resisted an invading force that was not Seminole.

Three processes propelled this transition: first, an attempt to symbolically equalize power relations; second, the desire to reject the values of the dominant culture; and, third, the need to revitalize traditional social and religious behaviors. To the extent that evidence of these processes is recoverable archaeologically, archaeology can contribute to a subject of broader anthropological interest.

Equalizing Power Relations: Military Buttons and Their Archaeological Contexts

Military buttons found in Seminole burial and domestic contexts dating to the Second Seminole War can be interpreted to indicate that Seminoles were wearing military clothing during this period and that this clothing had achieved a certain level of value for them. The archaeological contexts are the village sites of Zellner Grove (8CI215) and Newman's Garden (8CI206) in the Withlacoochee Cove (Weisman 1989:112–21) (fig. 11.3), the Fort Brooke cemetery (8HI998) (Hardin in Piper and Piper 1982:255–59), and the Hialeah burial on the eastern edge of the Everglades (Laxson 1954).

The buttons themselves are of the brass General Service type (so-called greatcoat buttons) found at Zellner and Fort Brooke, plain brass types found

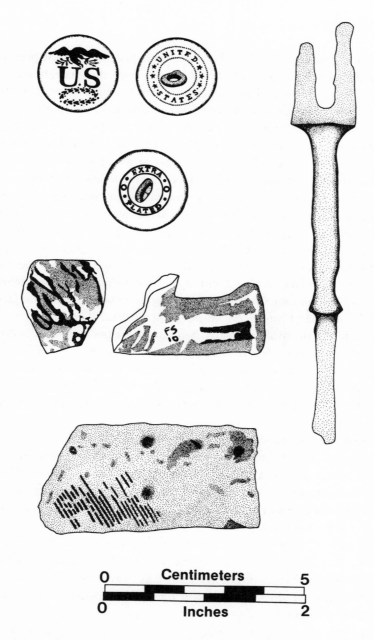

Fig. 11.3. Second Seminole War artifacts from village sites at Newman's Garden and Zellner Grove, ca. 1836. *Top left*, dragoon "great coat" brass button from Zellner Grove and plain brass button from Newman's Garden; *top right*, iron fork from Newman's Garden; *center*, green-glazed kaolin pipe bowl from Zellner Grove; *bottom*, iron flat file from Newman's Garden.

at Newman and Fort Brooke, white metal from Fort Brooke, and plain brass buttons attributable to state militia uniforms from the Hialeah burial. Although the buttons may have originated as trade goods (Olsen 1963:552), their specific historic and archaeological contexts make this explanation less than satisfactory. The twenty-five identifiable military buttons in the Fort Brooke cemetery were found only with adult burials, despite a much broader distribution of trade goods among other age groups, particularly subadults. The fact that at least one of the burials containing military buttons was that of an adult female suggests that military jackets or coats were not strictly limited to the male domain. The specific archaeological provenience of the Hialeah buttons (Laxson 1954: 114–16), in association with the remains of a Kentucky rifle, soapstone bullet mold, and other personal items, suggests that the buttons belonged to an article of clothing and were not themselves trade objects. In fact, firsthand military accounts from the Second Seminole War describe Seminoles in combat wearing army coats, caps, and jackets, possibly obtained from dead soldiers (Prince 1998:20).

If we accept the probability that Seminole warriors occasionally dressed in U.S. Army blues to face the enemy, we must then seek an explanation that derives from broader cultural or historical contexts. These contexts suggest that this behavior was intentional, a deliberate attempt to achieve some desired result, and that such behavior had value and meaning to the Seminoles.

Partial support for this premise comes from the self-portrait drawn by Hillis Haya, the prophet Francis, leader of a nativistic movement among the Creeks during the Creek War of 1814 and resident of a village on Florida's Wakulla River south of Tallahassee. While in London seeking formal British support for the Creek cause, Francis apparently sketched a picture of himself completely garbed in a British uniform (Wright 1986:194–97). Inasmuch as the rejection of the white man's culture (particularly American culture) was central to Francis's nativism, the intentionality of his dressing in uniform is nearly certain. Whether or not his desire was to symbolically align himself with his potential allies or to present himself in a manner that would be immediately comprehensible to the British cannot at present be determined. But in either case he used clothing to get others to see him differently.

The process of transforming self-image by manipulating perception is one feature of an unequal power relationship and is a strategy by which the less powerful strengthen their ability to negotiate their identity. Within the specific cultural context of the historic native Southeast, the practice of wearing military clothing may be one expression of the warrior trophy complex, in which trophy scalps, heads, or other body parts or possessions of the enemy were displayed. In this connection it is worth mentioning that the practice of scalping persisted at least through the years of the Second Seminole War, with scalp poles, complete with freshly obtained scalps, several times discovered by advancing U.S. troops.

Combined archaeological, historical, and cultural evidence suggests that military buttons found in Second Seminole War–period burial and domestic sites were part of uniform coats or jackets worn by Seminoles both to convey a message to their enemy and as a symbol of power.

Archaeological Evidence of a Nativistic Movement

The second process in Seminole ethnogenesis involved the rejection of the dominant culture in favor of the traditional ways of doing things. This process does not seem to have been a spontaneous response of the masses to circumstances of conflict but instead reflects the individual actions of the prophets, each of whom defined and interpreted the old ways in similar but idiosyncratic ways. The influence of Tecumseh and Tenkswatawa (the Shawnee prophet) are well described in the literature, particularly their effects on the Creek Red Stick element, who later formed the core of support for Osceola's early war efforts (Drake 1856:143–44; Nuñez 1958; Wright 1986:152–53, 168–69).

Direct historic evidence of prophets among the Seminoles is largely restricted to the activities of Otulke-thloco, a former Creek who exerted great power over the South Florida Seminoles after migrating to the region in 1836 (Sprague 1848: 270–71). Archaeological evidence, however, suggests the existence of an undocumented nativistic movement in the first years of the Second Seminole War. Systematic archaeological surveys of village sites in the Cove of the Withlacoochee, the Seminole stronghold targeted by early military offensives, have yielded no European or American ceramics, although brushed pottery, dark green bottle glass, iron hardware, lead shot, and military buttons were found with some frequency in surface survey and limited excavations of one burned structure (Weisman 1989:113–19). These villages, one of which was called Powell's Town, Osceola's wartime encampment, were occupied by several different individuals or distinct bands according to the documents, and apparently reflect different prewar origins. The absence of Euro-American ceramics is striking, given their abundance at numerous Seminole sites predating 1835 (Weisman 1989:69–73), such as the associated site of Pilaklikaha (Herron 1994), the town that Black Seminole Abraham established after 1812 and occupied through 1838 (Sprague 1848:143, 146, 180, 250).

The most compelling explanation for the lack of these ceramics is their conscious rejection by the Seminoles. It is certainly conceivable (and likely) that access to Euro-American ceramics was limited during the war years, but, even so, this is insufficient to account for their total absence at the Withlacoochee sites. By the last third of the eighteenth century throughout the Southeast, European ceramics had become prestige items to the Indians (Knight 1985:180–81) and were signs not only of wealth but of access to the dominant culture. As such, in my view, these ceramics became symbols of American society itself. Thus the rejection of the ceramics meant both the rejection of the dominant American society and the strengthening of native identity.

Revitalizing Traditional Social and Ritual Behaviors

I would further argue that two core features of Seminole society of the ethnographic present—the clan system and the Green Corn Dance ceremony—were directly stimulated as a stress response to the circumstances of war. The importance of the medicine bundles in the Green Corn ceremony of the twentieth century seems to date back to the Second Seminole War era (Sturtevant 1971:94–95) and is one significant difference between the Seminole ceremony and similar busk ceremonies practiced by other southeastern Indians. One important goal of the Seminole ceremony is to ensure that the "power-in-war" and other war-related medicines are intact (Sturtevant 1954:35–36, 1955:378–82). Beyond this direct relationship, it is likely that other elements of the Green Corn Dance reflect composite influences from a number of different bands, each with its own distinct cultural traditions and some arriving in Florida from Creek country as late as the 1830s. At the moment, this line of research lies largely within the realm of documentary or ethnological investigation and thus will not be further explored here.

The reinforcement of clan bonds has been archaeologically investigated, however, with interesting and provocative results. At Fort Brooke, now beneath the city of Tampa, a number of Seminoles died during the Second Seminole War while awaiting deportation to Indian Territory and were buried in an unmarked cemetery. Upon excavation of the cemetery in 1980, prior to the construction of a municipal parking garage, archaeologists observed that the subadult burials contained quantities and types of grave goods absent in the adult burials (Piper and Piper 1982; Piper et al. 1982: 132). Of the thirty-seven burials of probable Seminole cultural affiliation, nineteen were children under the age of seven. Additional analysis suggests that twenty-one of the total thirty-seven burials can be divided into at least five contemporaneous burial groups, which consist entirely or mostly of the burials of children (fifteen of the total twenty-one) (Weisman 1989:86–92). Children under the age of seven, in three of the five groups, were buried with perforated coins (four burials with a total of six coins). Additional perforated coins were found with child burials that could not be placed in groups, but no perforated coins were buried with individuals over the age of seven. Iron cups, iron knives and spoons, metal bodice pieces (ornaments designed to be sewn on clothes), and metal crescent gorgets are among the other items that occur exclusively with child burials (except for one bodice piece included with an adult male burial).

The site archaeologists interpreted this burial pattern to indicate ceremonial exchange (Piper et al. 1982:132) and further suggested that the exchange was initiated by lineages in an attempt to promote social cohesion under conditions of stress. Given the later amply documented importance of the clan in Seminole society (see, for example, MacCauley 1887:507; Spoehr 1941:14–16), it is reasonable to suggest that the ceremonial exchange is exemplified by the Fort Brooke cemetery data and involved members of different clans, at least five of which are represented by the identified burial groups. Such behavior would reinforce reciprocal relationships between clan groups, the preeminent units of social interaction in Seminole society, and would also encourage the bonding necessary to sustain the annual Green Corn Dance ceremony, which, at least in later times, depended on a gathering of clans. Thus the archaeological evidence from the Fort Brooke cemetery can be interpreted to indicate the process of clan bonding under way during the Second Seminole War, a process fundamental in shaping contemporary Seminole society.

Conclusion

Archaeology can be relevant to the broader field of Seminole studies if it addresses the main questions of interest to scholars, to the general public, and to the Seminoles themselves. How the Seminoles came to be and why they have persisted and thrived in the face of nearly insurmountable odds are certainly central questions. Archaeology can contribute to these issues in a unique way and can provide information not obtainable by any other means. The Seminole archaeological record is indeed variable across space and through time—just what is required for any cultural reconstruction based on archaeology. But it is also clear that the archaeologist hoping to make a contribution to Seminole studies must first become totally immersed in the historic and anthropological sources. Meaningful archaeology cannot exist apart from these sources, because they provide the appropriate context for the interpretation of archaeological findings. This is not to say that archaeologists are constrained to interpret their findings merely to confirm what is already known from other sources. This limits archaeology to a subordinate role, which is unacceptable because its evidence is primary and of the same order as the evidence of history and ethnography. After more than fifty years of practice (Fairbanks 1978; Goggin 1964; Goggin et al. 1949), Seminole archaeology is ready to take its place as a full partner in the study of the Seminole people.

Bibliography

Bartram, William
1955   The Travels of William Bartram. Edited by M. van Doren. New York: Dover.
Carr, Robert, and W. S. Steele
1993   Seminole Heritage Survey. Archaeological and Historical Conservancy Technical Report no. 74. Miami.
Carr, Robert S., Marilyn Masson, and Willard Steele
1989   Archaeological Investigations at the Okeechobee Battlefield. Florida Anthropologist 42:205–36.
Covington, James W.
1993   The Seminoles of Florida. Gainesville: University Press of Florida.
Cypress, Billy L.
1997   The Role of Archaeology in the Seminole Tribe of Florida. In Native Americans and Archaeologists, edited by N. Swidler, K. E. Dongoske, R. Anyon, and A. S. Downer, 156–60. Walnut Creek, Calif.: Altamira Press.
Downs, Dorothy
1995   Art of the Florida Seminole and Miccosukee Indians. Gainesville: University Press of Florida.
Drake, Benjamin
1856   Life of Tecumseh and of His Brother the Prophet. Cincinnati: Queen City Publishing House.
Ehrenhard, John E., Robert S. Carr, and Robert C. Taylor
1978   The Archeological Survey of Big Cypress National Preserve: Phase I. Southeast Archeological Center, National Park Service, Tallahassee, Fla.
Ehrenhard, John E., Robert Taylor, and Gregory Komara

1980   *Big Cypress National Preserve Cultural Resource Inventory Season 4.* Southeast Archeological Center, National Park Service, Tallahassee, Fla.

Ellis, Gary, Robin L. Denson, Russell A. Dorsey, James R. Jones III, and Jeanne E. Ellis
1997   *The Archaeological Study of the Camp Izard Tract, Marion County, Florida.* Gulf Archaeological Research Institute, Inverness.

Fairbanks, Charles H.
1974   *Ethnohistorical Report on the Florida Indians.* New York: Garland Publishing. (Identical to the 1957 presentation before the Indian Claims Commission, Dockets 73, 151.)
1978   The Ethno-Archaeology of the Florida Seminole. In *Tacachale: Essays on the Indians of Florida and Southeast Georgia during the Historic Period,* edited by J. T. Milanich and S. Proctor, 163–93. Gainesville: University Presses of Florida.

Gluckman, Stephen J., and Christopher Peebles
1974   Oven Hill (Di-15), a Refuse Site in the Suwannee River. *Florida Anthropologist* 27:21–31.

Goggin, John M.
1952   *Space and Time Perspective in Northern St. Johns Archaeology, Florida.* Yale University Publications in Anthropology 47. New Haven.
1953   Seminole Archaeology in East Florida. *Southeastern Archaeological Conference Newsletter* 3(3):16, 19.
1961   Can Brass Trade Kettles Be Identified? Paper presented at the Second Annual Conference on Historic Site Archaeology, Ocmulgee National Monument. Manuscript on file, Special Collections, George A. Smathers Library, P. K. Yonge Library of Florida History, University of Florida, Gainesville.
1964   Seminole Pottery. In *Indian and Spanish Selected Writings,* 180–213. Coral Gables: University of Miami Press.

Goggin, John M., Mary E. Godwin, Earl Hester, David Prange, and Robert Spangenberg
1949   A Historic Indian Burial, Alachua County, Florida. *Florida Anthropologist* 2:10–24.

Hadley, J. N.
1935   Notes on the Socio-Economic Status of the Oklahoma Seminoles. In *The Physical Anthropology of the Seminole Indians of Oklahoma,* by W. M. Krogman. Reprinted in William C. Sturtevant 1987, *A Seminole Sourcebook.* New York: Garland Publishers.

Herron, Jordan Thomas
1994   The Black Seminole Settlement Pattern. Master's thesis, Department of Anthropology, University of South Carolina, Columbia.

Howard, James H.
1984   *Oklahoma Seminoles: Medicines, Magic, and Religion.* Norman: University of Oklahoma Press.

Kersey, Harry A., Jr.
1996   *An Assumption of Sovereignty.* Lincoln: University of Nebraska Press.

Knight, Vernon J., Jr.
1985   *Tukabatchee: Archaeological Investigations at an Historic Creek Town,*

Elmore County, Alabama, 1984. Office of Archaeological Research, Report of Investigations 45. Alabama State Museum of Natural History, Tuscaloosa.

Laxson, D. D.
1954   An Historic Seminole Buried in a Hialeah Midden. *Florida Anthropologist* 7:111–18.

Lewis, Kenneth E., Jr.
1969   History and Archaeology of Spalding's Lower Store (Pu-23), Putnam County, Florida. Master's thesis, Department of Anthropology, University of Florida, Gainesville.

Luer, George M.
1989   A Seminole Burial on Indian Field (8LL39), Lee County, Southwestern Florida. *Florida Anthropologist* 42:237–40.

MacCauley, Clay
1887   The Seminole Indians of Florida. In *Fifth Annual Report of the Bureau of Ethnology*, 469–531. Washington, D.C.

Mahon, John K.
1967   *History of the Second Seminole War*. Gainesville: University of Florida Press.

McEwan, Bonnie G. (editor)
1993   *The Spanish Missions of La Florida*. Gainesville: University Press of Florida.

Mykel, Nancy
1962   Seminole Sites in Alachua County. Manuscript on file, Department of Anthropology, Florida State Museum, Gainesville.

Nuñez, Theron A., Jr.
1958   Creek Nativism and the Creek War of 1813–1814. *Ethnohistory* 5(1):1–47, (2):131–75, (3):292–301.

Olsen, Stanley
1963   Dating Early Plain Buttons by Their Form. *American Antiquity* 28:551–54.

Piper, Harry M., and Jacquelyn G. Piper
1982   *Archaeological Excavations at the Quad Block Site, 8Hi998*. Piper Archaeological Research, St. Petersburg, Fla.

Piper, Harry M., Kenneth W. Hardin, and Jacquelyn G. Piper
1982   Cultural Responses to Stress: Patterns Observed in American Indian Burials of the Second Seminole War. *Southeastern Archaeology* 1:122–37.

Porter, Kenneth W.
1996   *The Black Seminoles: History of a Freedom Seeking People*. Gainesville: University Press of Florida.

Prince, Henry
1998   *Amidst a Storm of Bullets: The Diary of Lt. Henry Prince in Florida*, edited by Frank Laumer. Tampa: University of Tampa Press.

Rouse, Irving
1951   *A Survey of Indian River Archeology, Florida*. Yale University Publications in Anthropology 44. New Haven.

Sears, William
1959   A-296, a Seminole Site in Alachua County. *Florida Anthropologist* 7:25–30.

Spoehr, Alexander
1941   Camp, Clan, and Kin among the Cow Creek Seminole of Florida. *Field Museum of Natural History Anthropological Series* 22(1):1–27.

Sprague, John T.
1848   *The Origin, Progress, and Conclusion of the Florida War.* New York: Appleton.
Sturtevant, William C.
1954   The Medicine Bundles and Busks of the Florida Seminoles. *Florida Anthropologist* 7:31–70.
1955   The Mikasuki Seminole: Medical Beliefs and Practices. Ph.D. diss., Yale University, New Haven.
1971   Creek into Seminole. In *North American Indians in Historical Perspective,* edited by E. B. Leacock and N. O. Lurie, 92–128. New York: Random House.
Weisman, Brent R.
1989   *Like Beads on a String: A Culture History of the Seminole Indians in North Peninsular Florida.* Tuscaloosa: University of Alabama Press.
1999   *Unconquered People: Florida's Seminole and Miccosukee Indians.* Gainesville: University Press of Florida.
Wright, J. Leitch, Jr.
1986   *Creeks and Seminoles.* Lincoln: University of Nebraska Press.

CONTRIBUTORS

Ann M. Early is the state archeologist of Arkansas and associate professor of anthropology at the University of Arkansas.

Jay K. Johnson is professor of anthropology at the University of Mississippi.

Karl G. Lorenz is associate professor of anthropology at Shippensburg University.

Bonnie G. McEwan is director of archaeology at Mission San Luis, Florida Bureau of Archaeological Research.

Jerald T. Milanich is curator in archaeology at the Florida Museum of Natural History, University of Florida.

George Sabo III is an archeologist with the Arkansas Archeological Survey and professor of anthropology at the University of Arkansas.

Rebecca Saunders is assistant curator of anthropology at the Museum of Natural Science, Louisiana State University.

Gerald F. Schroedl is associate professor of anthropology at the University of Tennessee.

Marvin T. Smith is professor of anthropology at Valdosta State University.

Gregory A. Waselkov is professor of anthropology at the University of South Alabama.

Brent R. Weisman is associate professor of anthropology at the University of South Florida.

John E. Worth is director of programs at the Coosawattee Foundation in Calhoun, Georgia.

INDEX

Note: Page numbers in italics indicate figures, maps, and tables.